WealthWise

WealthWise

A Study of Socioeconomic Conflict
in Hebrew Wisdom

Michael S. Moore

PICKWICK *Publications* • Eugene, Oregon

WEALTHWISE
A Study of Socioeconomic Conflict in Hebrew Wisdom

Pickwick Publications
An Imprint of Wipf and Stock Publishers
199 W. 8th Ave., Suite 3
Eugene, OR 97401

www.wipfandstock.com

PAPERBACK ISBN: 978-1-7252-8964-2
HARDCOVER ISBN: 978-1-7252-8965-9
EBOOK ISBN: 978-1-7252-8966-6

Cataloguing-in-Publication data:

Names: Moore, Michael S., author.

Title: WealthWise : a study of socioeconomic conflict in Hebrew wisdom / by Michael S. Moore.

Description: Eugene, OR: Pickwick Publications, 2021 | Includes bibliographical references and index.

Identifiers: ISBN 978-1-7252-8964-2 (paperback) | ISBN 978-1-7252-8965-9 (hardcover) | ISBN 978-1-7252-8966-6 (ebook)

Subjects: LCSH: Wisdom literature—Criticism, interpretation, etc. | Economics in the Bible | Social justice—Religious aspects | Middle East—History—Sources

Classification: BS1455 M66 2021 (print) | BS1455 (ebook)

07/19/21

Contents

Abbreviations | vii

1. Introduction | 1

2. Socioeconomic Motifs in Ancient Near Eastern Wisdom Texts | 6
   Mesopotamian Wisdom 7
      Didactic Wisdom 7
      Pessimistic Wisdom 22
   Anatolian Instructions 46
   Aramaic Wisdom 54
   Summary 58

3. Socioeconomic Motifs in Biblical Hebrew Wisdom | 59
   Proverbs of Solomon 60
      Parental Advice (Prov 1–9) 62
      Sentence Sayings (Prov 10–31) 72
   Wisdom Psalms 92
   Qohelet 98
   Job 110
   Summary 128

4. Socioeconomic Motifs in Early Jewish Wisdom | 129
   4QInstruction 130
   Wisdom of Ben Sira 141
   Wisdom of Solomon 160
   Summary 164

5. Socioeconomic Motifs in New Testament Wisdom | 165
Luke's Sermon on the Plain 166
Letter of James 176
Summary 187

6. Summary and Conclusions | 188
Textual Observations 188
Socioeconomic Motif Trajectories 192
Final Remarks 197

Bibliography | 199
Subject Index | 237
Author Index | 245

Abbreviations

1 En.	1 Enoch
1QapGen	*The Genesis Apocryphon* from Qumran Cave 1
1QH	*The Hodayot Scroll* from Qumran Cave 1
1QM	*The War Scroll* from Qumran Cave 1
1QS	*The Scroll of the Rule* from Qumran Cave 1
2mp	2nd person masculine plural
4QI	4QInstruction
4QMMT	*The Halaka Letter* from Qumran Cave 4
A	Codex Alexandrinus
AASF	Annales Academiae Scientarium Fennicae
ÄAT	Ägypten und Altes Testament
AAWG.PH	Abhandlungen der Akademie der Wissenschaften in Göttingen. Philologische-Historische Klasse
AB	Anchor Bible
ABD	*Anchor Bible Dictionary.* Edited by David Noel Freedman. 6 vols. New York: Doubleday, 1992.
ABoT	*Ankara Arkeoloji Muzesinde Bulunan Boğazköy Tableteri*
ABR	*Australian Biblical Review*
ABS	Archaeology and Biblical Studies
AcBib	Academia Biblica

AcSum	*Acta Sumerologica*
act.	active
ad loc.	"to the (appropriate) place"
AE	Anthropology and Ethnography
AEL	*Ancient Egyptian Literature.* Miriam Lichtheim. 3 vols. Berkeley: University of California Press, 1973.
Aen.	Aeneid
Aes.	Aeschylus
AfO	*Archiv für Orientforschung*
AG	Analecta Gorgiana
AGH	*Die akkadische Gebetsserie "Handerhebung."* Erich Ebeling. Berlin: Akademie-Verlag, 1953
Aḥq	*The Words of Aḥiqar*
AHw	*Akkadisches Handwörterbuch* . Wolfram von Soden. 3 vols. Wiesbaden: Harrassowitz, 1965–81
AIL	Ancient Israel and Its Literature
AJ	*Antiquities of the Jews.* Flavius Josephus. Translated by William Whiston. London: Bell & Sons, 1889
AJEC	Ancient Judaism and Early Christianity
AJES	*American Journal of Economics and Sociology*
AJSL	*American Journal of Semitic Languages and Literatures*
AJT	*Anglican Journal of Theology*
AKG	Arbeiten zur Kirchengeschichte
ALGHJ	Arbeiten zur Literatur und Geschichte des hellenistischen Judentums
AnBib	Analecta Biblica
AND	*Archiv des Nur-šamaš und anderen Darlehensurkunden aus der altbabylonische Zeit.* Fauzi Reschid. PhD diss., University of Heidelberg, 1965
ANE	Ancient Near Eastern
ANEM	Ancient Near East Monographs

ANESSup	Ancient Near Eastern Supplement Series
ANET	*Ancient Near Eastern Texts Relating to the Old Testament*. Edited by James B. Pritchard. 3rd ed. Princeton: Princeton University Press, 1969
AOAT	Alter Orient und Altes Testament
aor.	aorist
AOS	American Oriental Series
AOTC	Abingdon Old Testament Commentaries
APA	*The Aramaic Proverbs of Aḥiqar*. James M. Lindenberger. Baltimore: Johns Hopkins University Press, 1983
APR	annual percentage rate
Ar.	Aristophanes
AR	Assyrian Recension
ARC	*ARC: The Journal of the Faculty of Relgious Studies, McGill University*
Arm	Armenian
ARM	Archives royales de Mari
ARTU	*An Anthology of Religious Texts from Ugarit*. Johannes C. de Moor. Leiden: Brill, 1987
AS	*Aramaic Studies / Assyriological Studies*
ASNU	Acta Seminarii Neotestamentici Upsaliensis
ASOR	American Schools of Oriental Research
ASV	American Standard Version
AT	Anatolian Texts
ATD	Alte Testament Deutsch
Atr	*Atraḫasis*
AUS	American University Studies
AYB	Anchor Yale Bible
AYBRL	Anchor Yale Bible Reference Library
B	Codex Vaticanus

BabTh	*Babylonian Theodicy*. In *BWL* 63–91
BAGD	*Greek-English Lexicon of the New Testament and Early Christian Literature*. Edited by W. Bauer, W. F. Arndt, F. W. Gingrich, and F. W. Danker. Chicago: University of Chicago Press, 1979
BAM	*Die babylonische-assyrische Medizin in Texten und Untersuchungen*. Franz Köcher. Berlin: de Gruyter, 1963
Barn.	Epistle of Barnabas
BASOR	*Bulletin of the American Schools of Oriental Research*
BBB	Bonner Biblische Beiträge zum Vorderer Orient
BBR	*Bulletin of Biblical Research*
BBRel	*Beiträge der Babylonischen Religion. Ritualtafeln*. Heinrich Zimmern. Leipzig: Hinrichs'sche Buchhandlung, 1899
BBSt	*Babylonian Boundary-Stones and Memorial-Tablets in the British Museum*. Edited by Lawrence William King. London: Longmans, 1912
BBVO	Berliner Beiträge
BCE	"before the common era"
BCH	*Bulletin de Correspondance Hellénique*
BDB	Brown, Francis, S. R. Driver, & Charles Briggs. *A Hebrew and English Lexicon of the Old Testament*
BE	Biblical Encyclopedia
BECNT	Baker Exegetical Commentary on the New Testament
BETL	Bibliotheca Ephemeridum Theologicarum Lovaniensium
BHS	*Biblia Hebraica Stuttgartensia*
BI	*Biblical Interpretation*
Bib	*Biblica*
BibEnc	Biblical Encyclopedia
BibInt	Biblical Interpretation Series
BibOr	Biblica et Orientalia
BibSem	Biblical Seminar

BIN	*Babylonian Inscriptions in the Collection of J. B. Nies*
BIS	Biblical Interpretation Series
BJ	*Bellum Judaicum*. Flavius Josephus. Translated by William Whiston. London: Bell & Sons, 1889
BJS	Brown Judaic Studies
BJSoc	*British Journal of Sociology*
BKAT	Biblischer Kommentar, Altes Testament
BKBC	*The Bible Knowledge Background Commentary: Matthew-Luke*. Edited by Craig Evans. Colorado Springs: Victor, 2003
BLS	Bible and Literature Series
BM	British Museum
BO	*Bibliotheca Orientalis*
BRLA	Brill Reference Library of Ancient Judaism
BSOAS	*Bulletin of the School of Oriental and African Studies*
BT	Babylonian Theodicy
BTB	*Biblical Theology Bulletin*
BTCB	Brazos Theological Commentary on the Bible
BThS	Biblische-Theologische Studien
BVB	Beiträge zum Verstehen der Bibel
BWAT	Beiträge zur Wissenschaft vom Alten Testament
BWL	*Babylonian Wisdom Literature*. Wilfrid G. Lambert. Oxford: Clarendon, 1960
BZ	*Biblische Zeitschrift*
BZABR	Beihefte zur Zeitschrift fur Altorientalische und Biblische Rechtsgeschichte
BZAW	Beihefte zur Zeitschrift fur die alttestamentliche Wissenschaft
BZNW	Beihefte zur Zeitschrift fur die neutestamentliche Wissenschaft
c.	*circa* ("approximately")

CAD	*Chicago Assyrian Dictionary*
CAH	*Cambridge Ancient History*
CANE	*Civilizations of the Ancient Near East.* Edited by Jack M Sasson. 4 vols. New York, 1995. Repr. in 2 vols. Peabody: Hendrickson, 2006
CAP	*Aramaic Papyri of the 5th Century B.C.* Arthur E. Cowley. Oxford: Clarendon, 1923
C. Ap.	*Contra Apionem.* Flavius Josephus. Translated by William Whiston. London: Bell & Sons, 1889
CB	Coniectanea Biblica
CBC	Cornerstone Biblical Commentary
CBET	Contributions to Biblical Exegesis and Theology
CBQ	*Catholic Biblical Quarterly*
CBQMS	Catholic Biblical Quarterly Monograph Series
CBS	Tablets in the collections of the University Museum, the University of Pennsylvania in Philadelphia, Pennsylvania
CC	Continental Commentaries
CCT	*Cuneiform Texts from Cappadocian Tablets in the British Museum.* Edited by Paul Garelli & Dominique Collon. 1921. Reprint. London: Trustees of the British Museum, 1975
CD	The Damascus Document
CDA	*A Concise Dictionary of Akkadian.* Edited by Jeremy Black et al. Wiesbaden: Harrasowitz, 2000
CDOG	Colloquien der Deutschen Orient-Gesellschaft
CE	"common era"
CEJL	Commentaries on Early Jewish Literature
Cf.	"compare/see"
CH	*Codex Hammurabi*
CHANE	Culture and History of the Ancient Near East

CHD	*Chicago Hittite Dictionary.* Edited by Hans. G. Güterbock et al., Chicago: The Oriental Institute of the University of Chicago, 1980-
CM	Cuneiform Monographs
CMHE	*Canaanite Myth and Hebrew Epic.* Frank Moore Cross. Cambridge: Harvard University Press, 1973
CML	*Canaanite Myths and Legends.* Edited by J. C. L. Gibson. Edinburgh: T&T Clark, 1978
COS	*Context of Scripture, 3 Vols.* Edited by William W. Hallo & K. Lawson Younger. Leiden: Brill, 2003
CovQ	*Covenant Quarterly*
CPNIV	College Press NIV Commentary
CPSA	Cambridge Papers in Social Anthropology
CRINT	Compendia Rerum Iudaicarum ad Novum Testamentum
CSICL	Cambridge Studies in International and Comparative Law
CSAWC	Contributions to the Study of Ancient World Cultures
CT	*Cuneiform texts from Babylonian Tablets in the British Museum*
CTH	*Catalogue des textes hittites.* Emmanuel Laroche. Paris: Editions Klincksieck, 1971
CTR	*Criswell Theological Review*
D	the intensive form
DA	*Deir `Allā Texts*
DANE	*Dictionary of the Ancient Near East.* Edited by Piotr Bienkowski & Alan Millard. Philadelphia: University of Pennsylvania Press, 2000
DBGGKL	Dresdner Beiträge Geschlechterforschung in Geschichte, Kultur, und Literatur
DCLS	Deuterocanonical and Cognate Literature Studies
DDD	*Dictionary of Deities and Demons in the Bible.* Edited by Karel van der Toorn et al. Leiden: Brill, 1999
DH	The Deuteronomistic History

DI	*Descent of Ishtar*
Did.	*Didache*
DJD	Discoveries in the Judean Desert
DJG	*Dictionary of Jesus and the Gospels*. Edited by Joel B. Green. Downers Grove: InterVarsity, 1992
DMOA	Documenta et Monumenta Orientis Antiqui
DMWA	*A Dictionary of Modern Written Arabic*. Edited by Hans Wehr & J. Milton Cowan. Ithaca: Cornell University Press, 1966
DN	divine name
DOTHB	*Dictionary of the Old Testament Historical Books*. Edited by Bill Arnold & Hugh G. M. Williamson. Downers Grove: InterVarsity, 2005
DOTPr	*Dictionary of the Old Testament Prophets*. Edited by Mark Boda & J. Gordon McConville. Downers Grove: InterVarsity, 2012
DP	Dialogue of Pessimism
DR	*Dictionnaire des religions*. Edited by Mircea Eliade & Ioan Peter Couliano. Paris: Presses Universitaires, 1983
DSB	Daily Study Bible
DSD	*Dead Sea Discoveries*
DSSSE	*The Dead Sea Scrolls Study Edition*. Edited by Florentino García Martínez & Eigbert J. C. Tigchelaar. 2 vols. Leiden: Brill, 1997–98
DT	*Disappearance of Telipinu*
DTTM	*Dictionary of Targumim, Talmud and Midrashic Literature*. Marcus Jastrow. London: Luzac & Co., 1903
DULAT	*Dictionary of the Ugaritic Language in the Alphabetic Tradition*. Edited by Gregorio del Olmo Lete & Joaquin Sanmartín. Leiden: Brill, 2003
EA	*Die El Amarna Tafeln*. Edited by Johannes A. Knudtzon. 2 vols. 1915. Reprint, Aalen: Zeller, 1964
EBC	Expositor's Bible Commentary

EBD	*The Egyptian Book of the Dead*. Edited by Peter Le Page Renouf & Edouard Naville. London: Society of Biblical Archaeology, 1904
ECC	Eerdmans Critical Commentary
ECS	Epworth Commentary Series.
EDSS	*Encyclopedia of the Dead Sea Scrolls*. Edited by Lawrence H. Schiffman & James VanderKam. 2 vols. New York: Oxford University Press, 2000
Ee	*Enūma eliš*
Eg	Egyptian
EHJ	*Encyclopedia of the Historical Jesus*. Edited by Craig A. Evans. London: Routledge, 2008
EIC	*Encyclopedia of Intelligence and Counterintelligence*. Edited by Rodney P. Carlisle. London: Routledge, 2015
EJ	*Encyclopedia Judaica*
En.	*Enoch*
Eng	English
Ep Jer	Epistle of Jeremiah
ER	*Encyclopedia of Religion*. Edited by Lindsay Jones. 2nd ed. 15 vols. Detroit: MacMillan Reference, 2005
ErIsr	*Eretz-Israel*
Erra	*L'Epopea di Erra*. Luigi Cagni. Roma: Istituto di Studi del Vicino Oriente, 1969
ESV	English Standard Version
esp.	"especially"
ET	English translation
et al.	"and others"
ETCSL	Electronic Text Corpus of Sumerian Literature
Eth	Ethiopic
ETSMS	Evangelical Theological Society Monograph Series
EVO	*Egitto e Vicino Oriente*

ExAud	*Ex Auditu*
f.	feminine
FAT	Forschungen zum Alten Testament
FB	Forschung zur Bibel
FBBS	Facet Books Biblical Series
FCB	Feminist Companion to the Bible
FH	Folio Histoire
FLQ	*Family Law Quarterly*
FoSub	Fontes et Subsidia ad Bibliam pertinentes
FOTL	Forms of the Old Testament Literature
fr.	from
FRC	Family, Religion and Culture
FRLANT	Forschungen zur Religion und Literatur des Alten und Neuen Testaments
FS	*Festschrift*
fut.	future
G	the simple form
GAG	*Grundriss der akkadischen Grammatik*. Wolfram von Soden. 2nd ed. Rome: Pontifical Biblical Institure, 1969
GAP	Guides to Apocrypha and Pseudepigrapha
GBH	*A Grammar of Biblical Hebrew*. Paul Joüon. Translated and revised by T. Muraoka. 2 vols. Rome: Pontifical Biblical Institute, 1991
GDNES	Gorgias Dissertations Near Eastern Studies
GE	*Gilgamesh Epic*
GKC	*Gesenius' Hebrew Grammar*. Edited by Emil Kautzsch. Translated by Arthur E. Cowley. 2nd ed. Oxford: Clarendon, 1910
GLH	*Glossaire de la langue hourrite*. Emmanuel Laroche. Paris: Editions Kliencksieck, 1980
GMTR	Guides to the Mesopotamian Textual Record

GN	geographical name
GNT	Greek New Testament
Gos. Thom.	Gospel of Thomas
GRBS	*Greek, Roman, and Byzantine Studies*
Greg	*Gregorianum*
GTR	Gender, Theory and Religion
Guide	Maimonides (d. 1204 CE), *Guide for the Perplexed (Abridged)*, 1952. Translated by Chaim Rabin. Indianapolis: Hackett, 1995
HAL	*Hebräische und aramäische Lexicon zum alten Testament.* Ludwig Koehler *et al.* Translated and edited by Mervyn E. J. Richardson. 4 vols. Leiden: Brill, 1994–99
hapax legomenon	"occurring only once"
HAR	*Hebrew Annual Review*
HAT	Handbuch zum Alten Testament
HBM	Hebrew Bible Monographs
HC	*Hittite Code*
HCOT	Historical Commentary on the Old Testament
HCSB	Holman Christian Standard Bible
HdA	Handbuch der Archäologie
HdO	Handbuch der Orientalistik
HE	*Historia Ecclesiae*
Heb	Hebrew
HED	*Hittite Etymological Dictionary.* Jaan Puhvel. Berlin: de Gruyter, 1984–
HEWS	*Historical Encyclopedia of World Slavery.* Junius P. Rodriguez. Santa Barbara: ABC-CLIO, 1997
HKAT	Handkommentar zum Alten Testament
HL	*The Laws of the Hittites: A Critical Edition.* Harry A. Hoffner. DMOA 23. Leiden: Brill, 1997

HPQ	*History of Philosophy Quarterly*
HRel	Historia Religionum
HS	*Hebrew Studies*
HSK	Handbücher zur Sprach- und Kommunikationswissenschaft
HSM	Harvard Semitic Monographs
HSS	Harvard Semitic Studies
HThKAT	Herders Theologischer Kommentar zum Alten Testament
HTR	*Harvard Theological Review*
HTS	Harvard Theological Studies
HUCA	*Hebrew Union College Annual*
Hur	Hurrian
HW	*Hethitische Wörterbuch*. Johannes Friedrich. Heidelberg: Winter, 1952
IBT	Interpreting Biblical Texts
ICC	International Critical Commentary
ID	*Inanna's Descent*
idem	"the same" (author just cited)
IEJ	*Israel Exploration Journal*
inf.	infinitive
in se	"in itself"
Int	*Interpretation*
ipf.	imperfect
IPT	*Iscrizione puniche della Tripolitania*. Giorgo Levi della Vida Giorgio & Maria Giula Amadasi Guzzo. Roma: "L'Erma" di Bretschneider, 1987
ipv.	imperative
IŠ	Instructions of Šurrupak
ITC	International Theological Commentary
IVP	InterVarsity Press

JAAPOS	*Journal of the American Association of Pediatric Ophthalmology and Strabismus*
JANER	*Journal of Ancient Near Eastern Religions*
JANES	*Journal of the Ancient Near Eastern Society of Columbia University*
JAOS	*Journal of the American Oriental Society*
JB	*Jerusalem Bible*
JBE	*Journal of Business Ethics*
JBL	*Journal of Biblical Literature*
JBLMS	Journal of Biblical Literature Monograph Series
JCS	*Journal of Cuneiform Studies*
JEA	*Journal of Egyptian Archaeology*
JEH	*Journal of Economic History*
JESHO	*Journal of the Economic and Social History of the Orient*
JFSR	*Journal of Feminist Studies in Religion*
JHS	*Journal of Hebrew Scriptures*
JISMOR	*Journal of the Interdisciplinary Study of Monotheistic Religions*
JL	Jeremiah's laments
JNES	*Journal of Near Eastern Studies*
JNSL	*Journal of Northwest Semitic Languages*
JNTS	*Journal of New Testament Studies*
JOAI	*Jahreshefte des Österreichischen Archäologischen Instituts*
JP	Journal of Politics
JPSBC	Jewish Publication Society Bible Commentary
JRAS	Journal of the Royal Asiatic Society
JRE	*Journal of Religious Ethics*
JSJ	*Journal for the Study of Judaism in the Persian, Hellenistic and Roman Period*
JSJSup	Supplements to the Journal for the Study of Judaism

JSNT	*Journal for the Study of the New Testament*
JSNTSup	Journal for the Study of the New Testament Supplement Series
JSOT	*Journal for the Study of the Old Testament*
JSOTSup	Journal for the Study of the Old Testament Supplement Series
JSSI	*Journal of Sport and Social Issues*
JTS	*Journal of Theological Studies*
K.	tablets in the Kouyunjik collection of the British Museum
KAI	*Kanaanäische und aramäische Inschriften.* Edited by Herbert Donner and Wolfgang Röllig. Wiesbaden: Harrassowitz, 1969
KAR	*Keilschrifttexte aus Assur religiösen Inhalts.* Edited by E. Ebeling. Leipzig, 1923
KAT	Kommentar zum Alten Testament
KBANT	Kommentare und Beiträge zum Alte und Neuen Testament
KBo	*Keilschrifttexte aus Boğazköy*
KEK	Kritisch-exegetischer Kommentar über das Neue Testament
KEL	Kregel Exegetical Library
ketiv	"that which is written"
Ketuvim	The Writings (Psalms, Megillot, Proverbs, Job, Qohelet, Daniel, Ezra, Nehemiah, and Chronicles)
KHC	Kurzer Hand-Commentar zum Alten Testament
KJV	King James Version
KTAH	Key Themes in Ancient History
KUB	*Keilschrifturkunden aus Boğazköy*
L	Lucianic recension of OG
Lane	*An Arabic-English Lexicon.* Edited by Edward William Lane. 8 Vols. London: Williams & Norgate, 1863.
LAS	Leipziger Altorientalische Studien

LCBI	Literary Currents in Biblical Interpretation
LD	Lectio Divina
LEC	Library of Early Christianity
Leitwort	“keyword”
LHBOTS	Library of Hebrew Bible/Old Testament Studies
lit.	“literally”
LKU	*Literarische Keilschrifttexte aus Uruk*. Adam Falkenstein. Berlin: Staatliche Museen, 1931
LL	*Law and Literature*
LNTS	Library of New Testament Studies
LSJ	*A Greek-English Lexicon*. Edited by Henry George Liddell, Robert Scott, and Henry Stuart Jones. 9th ed. with revised supplement. Oxford: Clarendon, 1996
LSTS	Library of Second Temple Studies
Lud	*Ludlul bēl nēmeqi*
LW	*Luther's Works*, edited by H. T. Lehmann et al. 55 vols. St. Louis: Concordia; Philadelphia: Fortress, 1955–76
LXX	Septuagint
Lys.	*Lysistratus*
m.	masculine
Maq	*Maqlû*
MARI	*Mari Annales de Recherches Interdisciplinaires*
MBCBSup	Mnemosyne: Bibliotheca Classica Batava Supplements
MBS	Message of Biblical Spirituality
MC	Mesopotamian Civilizations
MIO	*Mitteilungen des Instituts für Orientforschung*
MPAT	*A Manual of Palestinian Aramaic Texts*. Joseph A. Fitzmyer & Daniel J. Harrington. BibOr 34. Rome: Biblical Institute, 1978
ms	manuscript
MSK	Tell Meskene

MSL	*Materialen zum sumerischen Lexicon*. B. Landsberger, M. Civil, *et al*. Roma: Pontificium Institutum Biblicum, 1937-
MT	Masoretic Text
MVAG	*Mitteilungen der Vorderasiatischen Gesellschaft*
n.	neuter
N	simple passive form (*nip'al*)
NA	Neo-Assyrian
NAB	New American Bible
NASB	New American Standard Bible
N.B.	"note well"
NBC	New Bible Commentary
NEA	*Near Eastern Archaeology*
NCB	New Century Bible
NDA	New Directions in Archaeology
NEB	New English Bible
NEchtB	Neue Echter Bibel
Neot	*Neotestamentica*
NET	New English Translation
Nevi'im	The Prophets (Joshua, Judges, Samuel, Kings, Isaiah, Jeremiah, Ezekiel, and the Twelve)
NHC	Nag Hammadi Codices
NICOT	New International Commentary on the Old Testament
NIGTC	New International Greek Testament Commentary
NIV	New International Version
NIVAC	New International Version Application Commentary
NJPS	New Jewish Publication Society
NKJV	New King James Version
NLH	*New Literary History*
NLT	New Living Translation

NovTSup	Supplements to Novum Testamentum
NRSV	New Revised Standard Version
NSBT	New Studies in Biblical Theology
NSKAT	Neuer Stuttgarter Kommentar Altes Testament
NT	New Testament
NTL	New Testament Library
NTOA	Novum Testamentum et Orbis Antiquus
NTR	New Testament Readings
NTS	*New Testament Studies*
NTSup	Supplements to Novum Testamentum
OA	Old Assyrian
OAN	Oracles Against the Nations
OArm	Old Aramaic
OB	Old Babylonian
OBO	Orbis Biblicus et Orientalis
OBT	Overtures to Biblical Theology
OCM	Oxford Classical Monographs
OED	Oxford English Dictionary
OG	Old Greek
OH	Old Hittite
OIP	Oriental Institute Publications
OL	Old Latin
OLA	Orientalia Lovaniensia Analecta
OTL	Old Testament Library
Or	*Orientalia*
ORA	Orientalische Religionen in der Antike
OrAnt	*Oriens Antiquus*
OTM	Old Testament Message

OTP	*Old Testament Pseudepigrapha*. Edited by James H. Charlesworth. 2 vols. Garden City: Doubleday, 1983–85
OtSt	Oudtestamentische Studiën
pace	"with all due respect"
Pal	*Paléorient*
pass.	passive
passim	"throughout, frequently"
PBS	Publications of the Babylonian Section, University Museum, University of Pennsylvania
PEQ	*Palestine Exploration Quarterly*
pf.	perfect
PiNTC	Pillar New Testament Commentaries
PJT	*Pacific Journal of Theology*
pl.	plural
PL	*Patrologia Latina*. Edited by Jacques Paul Migne. http://patristica.net/latina/
PN	proper name
POS	Pretoria Oriental Series
Pres	*Presbyterion*
pret.	preterite
Prom.	*Promotheus*
PRU	*Palais royale d'Ugarit*
PSB	*Princeton Seminary Bulletin*
PSD	*A Compendious Syriac Dictionary*. Robert Payne Smith. Oxford: Clarendon, 1903
Ps.-J.	*Pseudo-Jonathan*
ptc.	participle
Q	Qur'an
QE	*The Qur'an: An Encyclopedia*. Edited by Oliver Leaman. London: Routledge, 2006

qere	"that which is read"
QJS	*Quarterly Journal of Speech*
RA	*Revue d'Assyriologie et d'archéologie orientale*
Rab.	*Rabbah (e.g., Gen. Rab.= Genesis Rabbah)*
RAnt	*Res Antique*
RB	Revue biblique
RBL	*Review of Biblical Literature*
RE	regarding, with reference to
refl.	reflexive form
ResQ	*Restoration Quarterly*
RevExp	*Review and Expositor*
RevQ	*Revue de Qumran*
RGRW	Religions in the Graeco-Roman World
RHA	*Revue hittite et asianique*
RHR	*Revue de l'histoire de religions*
RIDA	*Revue internationale de droits de l'antiquité*
RN	royal name
RPT	Religion in Philosophy and Theology
RST	Regensburger Studien zur Theologie
RSV	Revised Standard Version
RT	*Rural Theology*
RTP	*Revue de théologie et de philosophie*
RTS	Rostocker Theologische Studien
RTU	*Religious Texts from Ugarit*. Nicolas Wyatt. Sheffield: Sheffield Academic Prss, 2002
S	Codex Sinaiticus
Š	the causative form
SAA	State Archives of Assyria
SAAB	*State Archives of Assyria Bulletin*

SAACT	State Archives of Assyria Cuneiform Texts
SAALT	State Archives of Assyria Literary Texts
SAAS	State Archives of Assyria Studies
Sam	Samaritan Pentateuch
SB	Standard Babylonian
SBL	Society of Biblical Literature
SBLAB	Society of Biblical Literature Academia Biblica
SBLANEM	Society of Biblical Literature Ancient Near East Monographs
SBLDS	Society of Biblical Literature Dissertation Series
SBLEJL	Society of Biblical Literature Early Judaism and Its Literature
SBLMS	Society of Biblical Literature Monograph Series
SBLSP	Society of Biblical Literature Seminar Papers
SBLSymS	Society of Biblical Literature Symposium Studies
SBLStBL	Society of Biblical Literature Studies in Biblical Literature
SBS	Stuttgarter Bibelstudien
SBT	Studien zu den Boğazköy-Texte
SCE	*Studies in Christian Ethics*
ScEs	*Science et Esprit*
SCL	Sather Classical Lectures
SCS	Septuagint and Cognate Studies
SDIOAP	Studia et Documenta ad Iura Orientis Antiqui Pertinentia
SDSS	Studies in the Dead Sea Scrolls and Related Literature
SEÅ	*Svensk exegetisk årsbok*
SEAJT	*Southeast Asia Journal of Theology*
SEL	*Studi epigrafici et linguistici*
SemeiaSt	Semeia Studies
sg.	singular

ŠH	Šamaš Hymn
SHANE	Studies in the History and Culture of the Ancient Near East
SHCT	Studies in the History of Christian Traditions
SHR	Studies in the History of Religions
SJC	Studies in Jewish Civilization
SJLA	Studies in Judaism in Late Antiquity
SJOT	*Scandinavian Journal of the Old Testament*
SJud	Studies in Judaism
SMEA	*Studi Micenei ed Egeo-Analotici*
SMS	*Syro-Mesopotamian Studies*
SNTSMS	Society for New Testament Studies Monograph Series
SOR	Studies in Oriental Religions
SOTSMS	Society for Old Testament Studies Monograph Series
SP	Sacra Pagina
SPHS	Scholars Press Homage Series
SPOT	Studies on Personalities of the Old Testament
SSI	*Textbook of Syrian Semitic Inscriptions.* J. C. L. Gibson. 3 vols. Oxford: Clarendon, 1971–82
SSN	Studia Semitica Neerlandica
ST	*Studia Theologica*
STDJ	Studies on the Texts of the Desert of Judah
StPohl	Studia Pohl
STW	Suhrkamp Taschenbuch Wissenschaft
subj.	subjunctive
Sum	Sumerian
SUNT	Studien zur Umwelt des Neuen Testaments
Šur	*Šurpu: A Collection of Sumerian and Akkadian Incantations.* E. Reiner. 1958. Reprint, Osnabrück: Biblio Verlag, 1970
s.v.	*sub verbo* ("under the word")

SVC	Supplements to Vigiliae Christianae
SWBA	Social World of Biblical Antiquity
Syb. Or.	*Sybilline Oracles*
Sym	Symmachus
SymS	Symposium Series
Syr	Syriac (Peshitta)
t.	*Tosefta*
TADE	*Textbook of Aramaic Documents from Ancient Egypt.* Edited by Bezalel Porten & Ada Yardeni. 5 vols. Winona Lake: Eisenbrauns, 1986–99
Tanak	Hebrew Bible/Old Testament
Tanḥ	Tanḥuma
TBSAW	Topoi. Berlin Studies of the Ancient World
TCL	*Textes cunéiformes du Louvre*
TCSPS	*Transactions of the Charles S. Peirce Society*
TD	Didactic texts in Tanak
TDNT	*Theological Dictionary of the New Testament.* Edited by Gerhard Kittel *et al.* 1949-. Translated and edited by G. Bromiley & G. Friedrich. Grand Rapids: Eerdmans, 1964–76
TDOT	*Theological Dictionary of the Old Testament.* Edited by G. Johannes Botterwick & Helmer Ringgren. Grand Rapids: Eerdmans, 1974–2016
Tg	Targum
Tg.-J.	*Targum Jonathan*
Tg. Onk.	*Targum Onkelos*
Theo	Theodotian
ThF	Theologie und Frieden
ThT	Theologisch Tijdschrift
ThTo	Theology Today
T. Job	Testament of Job

TLOT	*Theological Lexicon of the Old Testament*. Edited by Ernst Jenni & Claus Westermann. 2 vols. Translated by Mark Biddle. Peabody: Hendrickson, 1997
Tn	*Die Inschriften Tukulti-Ninurtas I und seiner Nachfolger*. Translated by Ernst Weidner. AfO 12. Graz: Weidner, 1959
TNTC	Tyndale New Testament Commentaries
TO	*Textes ougaritiques: Mythes et légendes*. Edited by AndréCaquot et al., Paris: Éditions du Cerf, 1974
Torah	The Pentateuch (Genesis, Exodus, Leviticus, Numbers, and Deuteronomy)
TOTC	Tyndale Old Testament Commentaries
TP	Pessimistic texts in Tanak
Transeu	*Transeuphratène*
TRu	*Theologische Rundschau*
TSAJ	Texte und Studien zum Antiken Judentum
TT	*Theology Today*
TUGAL	Texte und Untersuchungen zur Geschichte der altchristlichen Literatur
TynBul	*Tyndale Bulletin*
UBCS	Understanding the Bible Commentary Series
UET	Ur Excavations Texts
UF	*Ugarit Forschungen*
Ug	Ugaritic
UNP	*Ugaritic Narrative Poetry*. WAW 9. Edited by Simon B. Parker. Atlanta: Society of Biblical Literature, 1997
USQR	*Union Seminary Quarterly Review*
UT	*Ugaritic Textbook*. 3 vols. Cyrus Gordon. Rome: Pontificium Institutum Biblicum, 1965
UTB	Uni-Taschenbücher
Vg	Latin Vulgate

VS	*Vorderasiatische Schriftdenkmäler der Königlichen Museen zu Berlin*
Vss	Versions
VT	*Vetus Testamentum*
VTE	*Vassal Treaties of Esarhaddon.* Donald J. Wiseman. London: British School of Archaeology in Iraq, 1958
VTSup	*Supplements to Vetus Testamentum*
WAW	Writings from the Ancient World
WBC	Word Biblical Commentary
WBiC	Westminster Bible Companions
WBS	Wisdom of Ben Sira (Sirach)
WF	*Western Folklore*
WGW	Wissenschaftliche und Gesellschaftlicher Wandel
WI	Worlds of Islam
WLAW	Wisdom Literature of the Ancient World
WMANT	Wissenschaftliche Monographien zum Alten und Neuen Testament
WO	*Die Welt des Orients*
WS	Wisdom of Solomon
WUNT	Wissenschaftliche Untersuchungen zum Neuen Testament
WW	*Word and World*
y.	Talmud Yerushalmi (Jerusalem Talmud)
YOS	Yale Oriental Series, Babylonian Texts. New Haven: Yale University Press, 1915–
ZA	*Zeitschrift für Assyrologie*
ZAW	*Zeitschrift für die alttestamentliche Wissenschaft*
ZBK	Zürcher Bibelkommentare
ZNW	*Zeitschrift für die neutestamentliche Wissenschaft*
ZTK	*Zeitschrift für Theologie und Kirche*

1

Introduction

The wicked draw their swords and bend their bows to bring down the poor and needy.[1]

THE PREVIOUS TWO VOLUMES of this "wealth" trilogy survey a number of socioeconomic motifs in Torah[2] and Nevi'im[3] against the backdrops of relevant ANE texts. The task of investigating Ketuvim, however, poses a challenge requiring a bit more methodological clarity. To facilitate this clarity the pages below do not try to engage every Hebrew synonym for "poverty" or "wealth" in Ketuvim, only the socioeconomically relevant material in the so-called "wisdom texts."[4] Use of the phrase "wisdom texts," however, immediately raises objections with some readers because they tend to find this descriptor terribly outdated, even inappropriate.[5] Some are quite vocal about this, even when the objections they submit

1. Ps 37:14.

2. Moore, *Wealth Watch*.

3. Moore, *Wealth Warn*.

4. The discussion below will address a few "wisdom psalms" in the Psalter, but nothing in Megillot except Qohelet.

5. Kynes (*Obituary*, 2), e.g., sees "wisdom" as "an unwieldy scholarly category developed in mid-nineteenth-century Germany to meet the ideological demands of that time and place," and further, that the time is now ripe for the "intertextual reintegration of Wisdom Literature back into the canon." Sympathetic to Kynes' arguments, Fox ("Theses," 75), nevertheless rejects them, insisting that they do not justify abandoning (a) the concept of wisdom literature, or (b) the recognition of wisdom literature as a genre. Sneed ("Grasping," 39) thinks that "genres exist, but that the important question is, 'Where do they exist?' The reality is that genres do not exist in texts themselves, but only in the minds of authors and readers." So, following Frow (*Genre*, 63–67), Sneed ("Methods," 30) prefers to use the word "mode" instead of "genre." Weeks (*Introduction*, 1) dubs this taxonomical debate "an untidy business."

rest on unexamined presumptions, narrowly-restrictive sources,[6] and questionable research methods.[7]

Unable to ignore this debate, Assyrologist Wilfred Lambert rather offhandedly labels "wisdom" a "misnomer" when "applied to Babylonian literature" because this descriptor, in his opinion, mainly describes "what has been called philosophy since Greek times."[8] Manfred Oeming, however, promptly rejects this shot-in-the-dark opinion with the claim that "wisdom" is best defined by what it *is*, not by what it *is not*; viz., an "international phenomenon with its own formal language" expressed through "stories, philosophical treatises of different length, poems, prayers and individual sayings."[9] Michael Legaspi sociologically extends this definition to include "a program of human flourishing that is ordered to a holistic, authoritative account of reality in its metaphysical, cosmic, political and ethical dimensions."[10] More to the point here, Paul-Alain Beaulieu adds that whatever "the general tenor of wisdom texts," their ultimate *raison d'être* is to "teach the art of leading a successful life."[11] Richard Clifford acknowledges the persistence of this debate, suggesting that the published anthologies of ANE "wisdom texts" *in themselves* define for many readers what "wisdom" is,[12] a suggestion which provokes Bendt Alster to complain

6. Barré ("Wisdom," 41–43), e.g., believes that whatever its literary-historical features, early "wisdom" must be religious in nature, yet most agree with McKane (*Prophets*, 54) that religious piety cannot be "a constituent part of the עצה ('counsel') regulating the approach of the חכמים ('wise men') to statecraft." Cf. Moore (*Babbler*, 58–80); Weeks (*Israelite*, 57–73); and Van Dijk (*Sagesse*, 1–18).

7. Firth ("*Obituary*") argues that to "claim . . . the death of wisdom literature as a category means that it takes other things with it to its grave—most notably the idea of an ancient Israelite movement and a host of publishing conventions that mark these books as separate texts" when the truth is that "sages can exist in any culture and be recognized as such." One of the main purposes of the present volume is (a) to recover the work of several ANE sages, and (b) allow them to speak.

8. *BWL* 1. Vanstiphout ("Genre," 1–11) goes so far as to censure the phrase "wisdom literature" altogether.

9. Oeming, "Wisdom," 154. Lindenberger ("Aḥiqar," 486) warns that "if it is important in dealing with any question of literary comparison to distinguish between parallels and influence, it is doubly important when treating material from the realm of wisdom."

10. Legaspi, *Wisdom*, 11. Van der Toorn ("Wisdom," 21) argues that "'wisdom'—*nēmequ* is the word the Babylonians use—is originally a human virtue that expresses itself in the form of legal verdicts, intelligent counsel, and pithy sayings. In the course of time, however, 'wisdom' becomes a virtue solely of the gods. Experience as the soil of wisdom gives way to revelation as its ultimate source."

11. Beaulieu, "Wisdom," 3.

12. Clifford, "Introduction," xi–xiii. Cf. the collections in *BWL*; *ANET* xiii–xiv ("Didactic and Wisdom Literature"); *COS* 1.215–30.

that such anthologies often look like "fossilized relics from the early days of oriental scholarship."[13]

So wide a definitional canyon underscores the prudence of inquiring, at least nominally, into what a "genre" is.[14] Recognizing that "texts are of 'different types' (*Textsorten*)," Chaim Rabin argues that this diversity "largely corresponds to social conventions dictating different varieties of one and the same language in circumscribed social situations."[15] Alistair Fowler recognizes that "genres are often said to provide a means of classification,"[16] but this term—"classification"—alludes to a process to which many literary critics find themselves deathly allergic, their objection being, according to Michael Sinding, that too many definitions of "genre" still bank on the presumption that texts can somehow achieve "generic purity" in diversified literary environments where such purity does not (and indeed, cannot) exist.[17] Keenly aware of this debate,[18] Carolyn Miller suggests that "a rhetorically sound definition of 'genre' centers not on the substance or the form of discourse, but on the action it is used to accomplish,"[19] a definition Jeannine Brown supports when she identifies "genre" as a "formal container holding

13. Alster, *Sumer*, 25. As a general rule religious studies faculties in state-funded universities tend to chafe at literary-historical taxonomies based upon the study of actual texts, not least because these taxonomies tend, in Jones' opinion (*Wisdom*), to rely on a "circular method" which "identifies what wisdom is by selecting certain features and excluding others," so that "texts which line up well with those features are considered to be wisdom, while texts which line up less well are thought to be either peripherally sapiential or nonsapiential."

14. Kynes (*Obituary*, 107–46) argues, in the words of Coleman (*Obituary*, 114), that "genres surface when readers perceive similar features inherent in texts," a postmodern definition more reader-oriented than author-oriented.

15. Rabin, "Discourse," 173.

16. Fowler, *Genres*, 37–40. Fowler prefers to define "genre" not in terms of "boundaries," but in terms of "family resemblance," a notion first proposed by Wittgenstein (*Investigations*, 32).

17. Sinding ("Genre," 185) traces the roots of such binary thinking to Aristotle's *Organon* (cf. Patterson, *Logic*, 11–14), and Newsom (*Contest*, 172) level-headedly contends that "genres are not tight classificatory systems." Of course, to pursue the meaning of a text in the mind of the author (*exegesis*) instead of the reader (*eisegesis*) does not automatically make one guilty of "binary thinking."

18. In Jameson's words (*Postmodernism*, 23), postmodern reading strategies are designed to "short-circuit older types of social-historical interpretation" (on this concern cf. Moore, "*Testimony*," 212–15). Talisse and Aikin ("Pluralists," 101) argue that "although certain varieties of pluralism are logically *consistent* with pragmatism, no pluralism is *compatible* with pragmatism."

19. Miller, "Genre," 151–52.

the content or meaning of a work"; i.e., as something more perceptible as a dynamic "constellation" than a static "inventory."[20]

In light of this debate it is no secret that literary-historical "boundaries" (to use a descriptor some postmoderns now consider quaint) tend to be more porous in sapiential texts than in prophetic, ritual, lyrical, legal, epistolary, and/or historical texts.[21] Yet Mark Sneed still defines a "genre" as "a template formed in the minds of people that enables them to recognize types or kinds of literature that share what can be called a family resemblance."[22] Jumping on the "rhetoric is history" bandwagon,[23] Amar Annus and Alan Lenzi think that "'wisdom' does not *objectively* exist," but that "like other categories used to organize cultural data (e.g., 'religion,' 'art,' and 'kinship')" it *can* serve as a "'rubric' to associate and classify various items in a culture."[24] Struggling to summarize this debate for a dictionary article, Roland Murphy concludes that whether or not "wisdom" can be said to possess its own "genre," two definitional features seem very clear: (a) "wisdom" is "a term which can be used to indicate certain books which deal particularly with (biblical) wisdom," and (b) "wisdom" is "a movement in the ancient world associated with 'teachers' or sages" since the third millennium.[25]

This is an important discussion, to be sure, but at the risk of stating the obvious it should not be overlooked (a) that the cataloguing *process*, however valuable and necessary, is of far less importance than the *texts* being catalogued; and (b) that to focus on *process* at the expense of *product* too often leads to a shallow substitute for holistic research.[26] Thus the methodology guiding the present volume is the same as that guiding the first two volumes; viz., that *texts are always to be prioritized over theories, taxonomical or otherwise*.[27] That being said, the following chapters identify a number of

20. Brown, "Genre," 120. Cf. Jodock (*Bible*, 71–88); Moore (*Bible*, 236–38).

21. Cheung, *Wisdom*, 17.

22. Sneed, *Sages*, 183.

23. Brueggemann (*Astonishment*, 57) puts it bluntly: "History is essentially an act of rhetoric."

24. Annus and Lenzi, *Ludlul*, xxxiv–xxxv. This definition of *genre* closely resonates with those of Miller ("Genre," 151–67) and Kynes (*Wisdom*, 107).

25. Murphy ("Wisdom," *ABD* 6.920); cf. Blenkinsopp (*Sage*, 9–65).

26. Cf. Moore ("*Astonishment*," 740–41). Cohen (*Wisdom*, 7–19) chronicles the history of this debate in considerably more detail. Wilson (*Postmodern*, 61) observes that even though postmodern analysis helps biblical scholars develop a "wide ranging appreciation of textuality (and) an openness and attunement to the demands of alterity," its "creative, if at times chaotic potential" should not be ignored.

27. Cf. Morley (*Theories*, 1–5). Armitage (*Poverty*, 3–7) observes how researchers divide their time looking at poverty "behind the texts" or "in the texts." The pages below follow the latter approach.

socioeconomically relevant texts affiliated at one level or another with ANE wisdom (however defined), including the Instructions of Šuruppak, the Codex Hammurabi, the Poem of the Righteous Sufferer (Ludlul bēl nēmeqi), the Babylonian Theodicy, the Šamaš Hymn, the Dialogue of Pessimism, selected Hittite instructions (*išḫiul*) and laws, the Proverbs of Aḥiqar, the "wisdom psalms" 73, 49, and 112, the Book of Qohelet (Ecclesiastes), the Book of Job, 4QInstruction, the Wisdom of Ben Sira (Sirach), the Wisdom of Solomon, Luke's Sermon on the Plain, and the Letter of James.[28]

28. *Stylistic note:* This book (a) avoids passive voice whenever possible; (b) conforms secondary citations to one tense where possible (usually present); (c) changes singular to plural whenever necessary to maintain gender-inclusive discourse; (d) follows the versification of MT; and (e) conforms to the abbreviations listed in the *SBL Handbook of Style*.

2

Socioeconomic Motifs in Ancient Near Eastern Wisdom Texts

I will incline my ear to a proverb; I will solve my riddle to the sound of a harp.[1]

STUDENTS OF THE ANCIENT Near East spend a good deal of time investigating its wisdom traditions, both didactic and pessimistic.[2] Drawing from Egyptian and Mesopotamian sources, for example, Bernd Schipper compiles a succinct history of research, plausibly concluding (a) that "educative wisdom and cosmotheistic knowledge are closely connected in ANE wisdom literature" and (b) that "both are part of a comprehensive sapiential education."[3] Postmodern critics continue to question this assessment, of course, especially the degree to which wisdom's *raison d'être* might indeed be "educational,"[4] but Yoram Cohen responds to this criticism by insisting that "wisdom literature" is no "empty generic category." Instead, it is a type of literature "specifically cultivated for curricular, intellectual, and academic purposes."[5]

1. Ps 49:1.

2. Lichtheim (*Wisdom*, 4–5) and Weeks (*Wisdom*, 185) thoroughly discuss these subcategories (cf. below).

3. Schipper, *Proverbs*, 12.

4. Schneider ("Knowledge," 45–46), e.g., argues that even for Egypt the terms "teaching" and "instruction" are more appropriate monikers than "wisdom."

5. Cohen, "Cuneiform," 41. Taggar-Cohen ("Didactic," 47) adds that "wisdom literature" is distinguished by a "distinct worldview, specific language, and . . . a didactic voice marked by persuasive rhetoric."

Mesopotamian Wisdom

Tell Nuffar, the contemporary site of ancient Nippur in what today is the nation of Iraq, has so far yielded over fifty thousand cuneiform tablets, an enormous cache preserving approximately eighty percent of all known Sumerian "literary texts."[6] Buried within this cache are dozens of school exercise tablets copied by students evidently sitting under the tutelage of this or that UMMIA.[7] Ada Taggar-Cohen recognizes that much of the material on these tablets eventually makes its way "to other parts of the ancient Near East, where it is adopted into local cultures with innovations introduced by local people, such as in Ḫattuša, where the contents are melded together with historical events," ultimately evolving into "traditional texts from which later . . . kings . . . learn."[8]

Didactic Wisdom

Most of the instructions on these tablets are didactic sayings designed to highlight the motifs of *wealth, prosperity,* and *success.*[9] Readers disagree over whether their taproot is to be found in oral or written tradition,[10] but whatever the case, these sayings ponder the socioeconomic responsibilities expected of shepherds, gardeners, household managers, foremen, slaves, hired laborers, fishermen, fowlers, merchants, sailors, weavers, potters, manicurists, singers, temple personnel, and other "professions."[11]

6. Franke ("Nippur," 1119); Hallo (*Belles-Lettres*, 495–633). Reiner ("Akkadische," 151–210) and Groneberg ("Definition," 59–84) helpfully outline the features of what makes up a "literary text."

7. ETCSL 6.1.02.74–77 (cf. Cole, *Nippur*, 1–23; Frahm, "Proverbs," 155–56). The Sum UMMIA is the non-priestly "teacher/expert" attached to the EDUBBA ("non-cultic school"). Cf. Volk ("Rätsel," 1–30); Kramer (*Sumerians*, 169); Beaulieu ("Intellectual," 4); Roche-Hawley and Hawley (*Scribes*). Black (*Literature*, 117) recognizes the Enlil temple in Nippur (the É-KUR) to be "the holiest shrine in Sumer."

8. Taggar-Cohen, "Didactic," 58–59. Kramer ("Sage," 37) depicts EDUBBA graduates as elitists "imbued with the competitive, aggressive drive for preeminence and prestige . . . nurtured by the teachers of the EDUBBA who write often in ridicule and scorn of the poor, failing student and in lavish praise of the promising student."

9. Cf. Alster (*Proverbs*, 1–14); Veldhuis ("Proverbs," 383–99); Gordon (*Proverbs*, 24, 152); Hallo (*Literature*, 661). Weeks (*Instruction*, 4, 24) subdivides this material into "advice literature," "sentence literature," and "instructions," but Alster and Oshima ("Geneva," 31) subdivide it into "curricular" and "paremiological" literature.

10. Cf. Alster (*Proverbs*) and Volk ("Edubba'a," 1–8), *contra* Veldhuis ("Proverbs," 383–99) and Taylor ("Proverb," 13–15).

11. Veldhuis ("Proverbs," 385–87) tracks the tendency in later Mesopotamian texts to replicate and retread the "stock similes" structuring these old collections (e.g., the *Curse of Agade*; cf. Cooper, *Agade*).

Compared to, say, the mythopoeic epics,[12] the language in which they appear is much less venturesome. In fact, as Niek Veldhuis observes, most of it correlates to the language found in routine legal and administrative documents.[13] Parties to the sale of a house, for example, tend to use a standardized "business contract" shaped by language much like that found on these tablets.[14] For example:

E$_{2}$ AMAR-ABZU DUMU	The house of Amarabzu, son of
LUGAL-EZEN	Lugalezen,
KI AMAR-ABZU-TA	From Amarabzu
^{D}DA-NU-ME-A-KE$_{4}$	Danumea
IN-ŠI-IN-SA$_{10}$	Purchased
SAM$_{2}$ TI-LA-BI-ŠE$_{3}$	Its full price,
⅔ MA-NA KUG-BAB-BAR IN-NA-AN-LA$_{2}$	Paying him ⅔ mina of silver.

Anticipating the prospect of "seller's remorse," the contract goes on to stipulate that

UD KUR$_{2}$-ŠE$_{3}$ AMAR-ABZU	In the future Amarabzu
U$_{3}$ IBILA-A-NI A-NA ME-A-BI	And his heirs,[15] however many there are,
E$_{2}$-BI-ŠE$_{3}$ GU$_{3}$ NU-GA$_{2}$-GA$_{2}$-A	May not register a claim on this house.

Then it is duly "notarized":

12. Dalley (*Myths*, xvi–xvii); Izre'el (*Adapa*, 72–106); Talon (*Enūma Eliš*, ix–x; cf. Moore, *Creation*, 800–2).

13. Cf. Cohen (*Wisdom*, 55–79). With Alter (*Narrative*, 95), a "motif" is "a concrete image, sensory quality, action, or object recurring through a particular narrative."

14. The typical "model business contract" includes a description of the size and location of the property being sold, its price, the names of the buyer(s) and seller(s), plus "official" validation by a responsible third-party (cf. Veldhuis, "Proverbs," 386).

15. Sum IBILI ("heir"). In one collection the text reads LU$_{2}$ DINGIR-RA-A-NI / NU\-MU-UN-KAL-LA /EDIN\-NA MU-UN-ŠUB AD$_{3}$-BI NU-ĜA$_{2}$-ĜA$_{2}$ IBILA-A-NI ALAL-AM$_{3}$ /GIDIM\-MA-A-NI A NU-NAĜ, "A man who does not value his god will be thrown out in the desert, his body left unburied, and his heir will not provide his ghost with drinking water through a libation pipe" (ETCSL 6.2.2.299.1–3). Pope, *Song*, 210–29 documents the responsibility of survivors to slake the thirst of the dead via libation pipes funneled into their tombs.

MU LU-GAL BI IN-PAD$_3$	Thus he swore in the name of the king.[16]

Of greatest relevance to the present study is the fact that some of these cuneiform texts preserve the didactic sayings of an "eloquent sage"[17] (Šuruppak) advising his "son" (Ziusudra) on how to become "successful,"[18] engaging five basic areas of socioeconomic concern:

- ***Agrarian management***—Do not plow a field or dig a well near a busy road, but work hard to maximize good harvests; do not purchase a constantly braying donkey or leave open the "fence-door" (DA-GA) built to keep out pests and thieves.[19]
- ***Food management***—Food production is vitally important, so do not break into someone's house to steal food or siphon away village provisions for strangers/foreigners.[20]
- ***Money management***—Do not recklessly co-sign loans,[21] or harass debtors, or illicitly lay claim to the village "money-chest";[22] do not avoid the acquisition of land, except when such behavior endangers the family inheritance.[23]

16. CBS 6098+, with restorations from CBS 4617, CBS 6527, CBS 13934, N 4074 and N 5334 (cited in Veldhuis, "Proverbs," 386).

17. ĜEŠTUG$_2$ TUKU INIM GALAM INIM ZU-A (lit., "one who knows how to put eloquent words in the ear," ETCSL 5.6.1.4).

18. Sum ZI-UD-SU$_3$-RA$_2$ (ETCSL 5.6.1.8). In *GE* 10.208 Ziusudra is called Utnapishtim, a character some associate with the biblical Noah (Gen 6–9; cf. sources cited in Longman and Walton, *Flood*, 53–60). Whether this "son" is biological or not is not immediately obvious (cf. the student-addressee בני, "my son," in Prov 1:10 and *passim*).

19. ETCSL 5.6.1.15–18, 131–33, 14, 48, 58. Much more detail appears in "The Farmer's Instructions" (ETCSL 5.6.3.65–66) on how to use various plows and eradicate various pests, esp. "small animals" (^{D}NIN-KILIM-KE$_4$) and "locusts" (BIR$_5^{MUŠEN-RA}$).

20. ETCSL 5.6.1.178–80, 39, 28, 29, 60. In the Sum poem "The Debate Between Grain and Sheep" (ETCSL 5.3.2) the gods give grain and sheep to pre-humanoid beings who "do not yet know about eating bread . . . or wearing clothes . . . who like sheep eat grass with their mouths and drink water from the ditches" (cf. Alster and Vanstiphout, "Debate," 1–43; Foster, "Agriculture," 109–28; Foster, "Wool," 115–23).

21. Sum ŠU DU$_8$-A NU-E-TUM$_3$ LU$_2$-BI ŠA-BA-E-DAB$_5$-BE$_2$ (lit. "shake a person's hand," ETCSL 5.6.1.19). This motif has an exceptionally long shelf-life; cf. אל תהי בתקעי כף (lit., "do not be a shaker of the hand," Prov 22:26; cf. Sir 8:13; 4Q416.2.2.4–6).

22. Qur'an stipulates that when a loan is extended, the intention of the creditor cannot simply be to generate profit through the charging of ربا ("interest/usury," Q 30.39).

23. ETCSL 5.6.1.53, 29, 101–2, 262–63, 128–29 (AN SU$_3$-UD-DAM KI KAL-KAL-LA-AM$_3$ AN-DA NIJ$_2$ IM-DA-LU-LU-UN, "heaven is far away and land is precious, but it is in heaven that goods become abundant"). Cf. Matt 19:17–22 and Moore, *WealthWarn*, 172–74.

- ***Labor management***—Good workers are valuable, so do not abuse them; do not procure prostitutes or homebred slaves,[24] and do not take advantage of young slave girls; remember that most successful households are run by sensible women[25] too discreet to "parade themselves" in public.[26]
- ***Poverty-vs.-wealth***—The rich tend to struggle over how, exactly, to deal with the poor,[27] so successful princes[28] should distinguish themselves not by serving things, but by having things serve them.[29]

These are not the only motifs animating the Instructions of Šurrupak, nor is it coincidental that these five categories help shape the sapiential curriculum for centuries to come.[30] The significance of these instructions is twofold in that (a) they help to illuminate the sapiential world of ancient Sumer, and (b) they help identify socioeconomic concerns to which later sages repeatedly respond.[31]

24. Cf. Qoh 2:7. Not to be forgotten is the fact that some slaves are simply "thieves who get caught" (ETCSL 5.6.1.30).

25. Cf. Prov 31:10–31 (cf. Ben Zvi, "Wife," 27–49). Female "irresponsibility" in Qur'an is to be punished (in order of severity) by (a) "admonishment" (فعظوهن); (b) sexual avoidance (المضاجع فى اهجروهن, lit., "forsake them in their bed"); and (c) "spanking" (اضربوهن, Q 4.34).

26. ETCSL 5.6.1.119–23, 153, 154–64, 49, 215, 220, 208–12. Sum ŠAG$_4$-GA HUJ-JA$_2$-AM$_3$ BAR-RA HUJ-JA$_2$-AM$_3$ (ETCSL 5.6.1.209, lit., "both her heart and her body are for hire").

27. Cf. discussion below (esp. on the book of Job). Qur'an addresses the wealth-poverty polarity via a play on the term for "possess(ion)": "God shows his 'favor' (الله فخل, lit., "Allah bestows") more to some than to others (with regard to) "possessions' (الرزق, lit., 'the livelihood'), but those having more are not obliged to hand over their possessions to their 'slaves'" (على ما ملكت ايمانهم, lit., "to those whose right hands they 'possess,'" Q 16.71).

28. Sum ME NAM-NU-NA (lit., "a man possessing the ME of princeliness," ETCSL 5.6.1.204). On the significance of Sum ME, cf. discussion in Moore (*WealthWarn*, 9–12).

29. ETCSL 5.6.1.183–84, 204, 242–44. Cf. the proverb *ri-ṣu-ka ul maš-[ru-u] i-lu-um-[ma]*, "Wealth is not your support; your god is" (*BWL* 227.42–43), and ما غنى غنى ماليه, "wealth has not 'enriched' me" (lit., "given me spoils/booty," Q 69.28).

30. Cf. Lambert (*BWL* 92–138); Crenshaw ("Life," 2445–57); Schipper (*Proverbs*, 11–24).

31. Cf. Civil ("Instructions," 281–98); Foxvog (*Instructions*, 371–74); Hallo ("Instructions," 269–73); Biggs ("Instructions," 594–96); and below.

Lawcodes: Codex Hammurabi

The boundaries between *wisdom* and *law*, while discernible, are often quite porous.[32] As Raymond Westbrook observes, "the rich storehouse of myth, legend, and wisdom from the literatures of the ancient Near Eastern civilizations also contains a good deal of legal material."[33] Agreeing with this observation, Guy Couturier defines wisdom (particularly familial wisdom) as nothing less than a "primary source of law,"[34] even as John Collins contends that "the collections of laws in the ancient Near East, including Israel, do not function as positive law, but are rather akin to wisdom instruction" designed "to form character and sensibility."[35] Harmonizing with this chorus, the pages below attempt to identify some of the more important socioeconomic motifs embedded in one of the best-known (and arguably most influential) of all ANE lawcodes—the Code of Hammurabi.[36]

Echoing the style and substance of "Marduk's Fifty Names" in *Enūma eliš*,[37] the prologue to *CH* promotes Hammurabi's leadership via several socioeconomic titles strategically designed to promote his monarchy, titles like "the one who makes Ur prosper,"[38] "the one who brings prosperity to Egišnugal,"[39] "the one who secures plentiful supplies of water for Uruk's people,"[40] "the one who heaps up produce for Anu and Ištar,"[41] "the one who pours out riches into the temple of Egalmaḫ,"[42] "the one who

32. Using a metaphor popularized by Steck ("Streams," 183–214), Blenkinsopp (*Wisdom*, 151) depicts wisdom and law as "two great rivers which eventually flow together."

33. Westbrook, "Character," 1.12.

34. Couturier, "Loi," 179. Cf. Gerstenberger (*Wesen*, 146–47); Audet ("Origines" 357); Blenkinsopp (*Wisdom*, 151).

35. Collins, "Wisdom," 60.

36. *CH* is not the only Mesopotamian lawcode, of course, but it is widely perceived to be the most influential (cf. Sallaberger, "Prolog," 7–33). *Note:* Though a bit outdated (*pace* Roth, *Law*, 74–76) the citations below follow Harper's numbering system (*Code*).

37. Cf. *Ee* 6.124; 7.1, 7–8, 20–22, 57–59, 65.

38. *CH* 2.16–17, *munaḫḫiš* ALUŠIŠ.AB.KI. Roth (*Law*, 77) reads "enricher of the city of Ur."

39. *CH* 2.19–21, *bābil ḫegallim ana* Ê.NUR.NU.GAL (Egišnugal is Sin's temple in Ur).

40. *CH* 2.39–41, *šākiin mê nuḫšim ana nišišu*. Cf. 4.4–6 *mušešqi nuḫšim ana* ŠID.LAM, "who enables Meslam to drink abundantly" (Meslam is Erra's temple in Kutû).

41. *CH* 2.44–47, *mukammer hiṣbim ana* DANU *u* DNANA.

42. *CH* 2.52–54, *muṭaḫḫid nuḫšim bît* Ê.GAL.MAḪ (Egalmaḫ is Ninurta's temple in Isin).

cultivates arable land in Dilbat,"[43] "the one who fills up the granaries of mighty Uraš,"[44] "the one who makes sacral food abundant for Nintu,"[45] "the one who provides pasture and water supplies for Lagaš and Girsu,"[46] and "the one who procures rich grain-offerings for Eninnu."[47] Following this prologue, the laws themselves target a rather wide variety of socio-economic concerns, including *land, trade, property, debt, labor, slavery, betrothal, marriage, divorce*, and *inheritance*.[48]

Land

As the previous volume of this series tries to show, land is by far the most precious economic commodity of the ancient world.[49] Nothing else comes close, so it is no surprise that *CH* has something to say about it. For example:

eqlum kirûm u bītum ša rēdîm	The field, orchard, or house
bā'irim u nāši biltim	of an officer,[50] constable,[51] or tax-collector[52]

43. *CH* 3.18–20, *mušaddil mêreštim ša* DIL.BAT.KI. Roth (*Law*, 78) reads "the one who enlarges the cultivated area of the city of Dilbat" (Dilbat is a small town southeast of Babylon).

44. *CH* 3.21–24, *mugarrin karê ana* ᴰ*Uraš gašrim* (Uraš is an epithet of Ninurta at Dilbat).

45. *CH* 3.33–35, *mudešši* (lit., "cause to sprout") *mākalī ellutim ana* ᴰNIN.TU (Nintu is an epithet of the fertility deity Mama).

46. *CH* 3.38–42, *šā'im mirītim u mašqītim ana* ŠIR.PUR.LA.KI *u* GIR-SU-KI (Lagaš and Girsu—home of the temple of Ningursa—are neighboring towns in the city-state of Larsa).

47. *CH* 3.43–46, *mukīl nindabê rabûtim ana Eninnu* (Eninnu is the name of Ninurta's temple, god of farming and hunting).

48. The following examples are bound by two delimitations: (a) each addresses a specific legal problem; and (b) this list is representative, not exhaustive.

49. Cf. Moore (*WealthWarn*, 200). Goetze (*Kleinasiens*, 118) insists that nothing is more valuable to pre-urban, pre-industrial folk than "land and livestock," and, in an important seminal study, Brichto ("Land," 1–54) discusses the aboriginal interface between kin, cult, land, and afterlife.

50. *CH* 12.6 (reading with Harper, *Code*, 23). Meek (*Code*, 167), Roth (*Law*, 88), and Richardson (*Laws*, 55) read "soldier."

51. *CH* 12.6 (reading with Harper, *Code*, 23; cf. *CAD* B.32). Meek (*Code*, 167) reads "commissary"; Roth (*Law*, 88) reads "fisherman"; Richardson (*Laws*, 55) reads "trapper."

52. *CH* 12.7. Akk *biltu* ("rent, tribute") appears several times in *CH* (§ 36, 37, 38, 41, 45, 46, 62, 64, 65, and 264), but the epithet *nāši biltim* (lit., "the one who carries the rent/tax"; cf. Heb נשׂא, "to carry") appears in §§ 36, 37, 38, and 41 (cf. Lat *publicanus*).

ana kaspim ul inaddin	Shall not be exchanged for silver.[53]
šumma awīlum eqlam kirâm u bītam ša rēdîm bā'irim u nāši biltim ištām	If someone purchases the field, orchard, or house of an officer, constable, or tax-collector,
ṭuppašu iḫḫeppe	His sales contract[54] shall be scuttled,
u ina kaspišu itelli	He shall surrender his silver, and
eqlum kirûm u bītum ana bēlišu itâr.	The field, orchard, or house shall return to its owner.[55]

TRADE

Due to the accidence of archaeological discovery, the world of Babylonian commerce is much less understood than that of, say, Assyria.[56] Still, enough *is* known for Marc van de Mieroop to deduce (a) that "the exchange between Mesopotamia and its neighbors is not an even one," and further, (b) that its "technologically advanced society dominates the market of the more primitive societies surrounding it."[57] What *CH* does is fill in some of the gaps in our understanding because, as Jackson Spielvogel notes, "the number of laws in Hammurabi's code dedicated to land tenure and commerce reveals the importance of agriculture and trade in the Mesopotamian economy."[58] For example:

Harper (*Code*, 23) reads "tax-gatherer"; Roth (*Law*, 88) reads "state tenant"; Richardson (*Laws*, 55) reads "official tenant"; Meek ("Code," 167) reads "feudatory."

53. Cf. House ("Silver," 29–40); Rapson ("Gold," 61–68).

54. *CH* 12.15 (*ṭuppašu*, lit., "his tablet"). Meek (Code, 167) reads "contract-tablet"; Roth (*Law*, 88) reads "deed."

55. *CH* §36–37 (12.5–21). Cf. *HL* §39–41, 46–56; Westbrook ("Period," 63–92); Zaccagnini ("Nuzi," 223–36).

56. Cf. Goetze (*Kleinasiens*, 67–81); Garelli (*Cappadoce*, 2–11); Veenhof (*Trade*, xxi–xxvii); Orlin (*Colonies*, 45–72); Michel (*Merchants*).

57. Van de Mieroop (*City*, 191); cf. Polyani ("Trading," 12–26). N.B. the cache of old Kassite seals (1595–1157 BCE) found in Greece (Brinkman, "Seals," 73–78; Grayson, "Mesopotamia," 762).

58. Spielvogel (*Civilization*, 10) goes on to note that "laws concerning land use and irrigation are especially strict, an indication of the danger of declining crop yields if the land is used incompetently."

šumma tamkārum kaspam šamallâm iqīpma	If a merchant[59] entrusts silver to an agent,[60]
šamallûm mimma ša tamkārum iddinušum ana tamkārišu uttēr	And the agent repays him everything that he was given,
tamkārum mimma ša šamallûm iddinušum ittakiršu	But the merchant disagrees with him over the amount the agent has given him,
šamallûm šu ina maḫar ilim u šībī tamkārum ukânma	And that agent can prove in the presence of divine and human witnesses that the merchant is wrong,
tamkārum aššum šamallâšu ikkiru mimma ša ilqû	The merchant shall then pay to the agent
adi 6-šu ana šamallîm inaddin	Six times the value of whatever has been exchanged.[61]

PROPERTY

CH laws about "property" break down into two categories, "public" and "private." For "public" property:[62]

šumma awīlum makkūr ilim u ekallim išriq	If a gentleman[63] steals property from a god or a temple,
awīlum šû iddâk	Then that gentleman shall be killed,

59. *CH* 17.68. Reflecting on the use of *tamkārum* in the Šamaš Hymn (see below), Lambert writes (*BWL* 122): "The use of *tamkāru* is a perplexing matter. In the Hymn he is the trader who travels into foreign lands (lines 69 and 139), an MB usage. The present state of knowledge does not allow us to say whether the OB *tamkāru* personally goes on these journeys or merely finances them." *CH* seems to lean toward the second option.

60. *CH* 17.69, reading with Harper (*Code*, 37) and Richardson (*Laws*, 75). Meek ("Code," 170) reads "trader"; Roth (*Law*, 101) reads "trading agent"; von Soden (*AHw* 1153) suggests "Beutelträger" ("bag-carrier").

61. *CH* §107 (17.68—18.14).

62. Cf. the large number of texts using the term *makkūru* ("property, possessions") in *CAD* M.133–36.

63. Chavalas ("Code," 330) points out that like other Mesopotamian texts, *CH* divides society into three categories: (a) *awīlum* (lit., "man")—"gentleman/ aristocrat"; (b) *muškenum*—"workman/palace dependent"; and (c) *wardum*—"slave."

u ša šurqam ina qātišu imḫuru iddâk	And anyone who acquires stolen property from him shall be killed.[64]

For "private" property:

šumma awīlum lu alpam lu immeram lu imēram	If a gentleman steals an ox or a sheep or a donkey
lu šaḫâm u lu eleppam išriq	Or a pig or a boat,
šumma ša elim šumma ša ekallim adi 30-šu inaddin	Then, if it belongs to a god or a temple, he shall pay thirty times its value,
šumma ša muškenim adi 10-šu iriab	Or ten times its value if it belongs to a workman.
šumma šarrāqānum ša nadanim la išu iddak	If the thief does not have the funds to repay, he shall be executed.[65]

Debt

"Debt" also breaks down into two categories: "secured" and "unsecured." For "secured" debt:[66]

šumma awīlum eli awīlim še'am u kaspam la išūma	If a gentleman has not lent another gentleman barley or silver,
nipussu ittepe ana nipûtim ištiat	But has seized a person as a pledge-guarantee
⅓ ma-na kaspam išaqqal	He shall pay ⅓ mina of silver for each person taken in pledge.[67]

64. *CH* §6 (6.31–40).

65. CH §8 (6.54–69).

66. Chirichigno (*Debt-Slavery*) discusses in detail the social (30–54) and legal (55–100) aspects of Mesopotamian debt.

67. *CH* §114 (19.17–25). Van de Mieroop (*Hammurabi*, 10) recognizes that "debt is a widespread problem in Babylonian society" and that "people who are financially squeezed because of taxes or special expenses have to borrow small sums of silver, usually from moneylenders in the cities. Although interest rates are regulated by law to be 20% on silver loans and 33% on those of grain, repayment is difficult (because) the people who borrow are not wealthy, but live on the verge of financial disaster."

For "unsecured" debt:

šumma awīlum eli awīlim še'am u kaspam išūma	If a gentleman lends barley or silver to another gentleman,[68]
ina balum bēl še'im ina našpakim	And without the owner's[69] permission
u lu ina maškanim še'am ilteqe	Takes some grain from a granary or a field-heap,
awīlam šuāti ina balum bēl še'im ina našpakim	They shall then prove that that man
u lu ina maškanim i-na še'im leqêm	Has taken from a granary or a field-heap
ukannūšuma še'am ma-la ilqû utâr	Without the owner's permission, and he shall
u ina mimma šumšu ma-la iddinu ītelli	Return whatever barley he has taken, forfeiting his right to anything he might receive.[70]

Labor

A principal motif in the Atraḫasis myth,[71] "labor" attracts a good deal of attention in *CH*:

šumma awīlam e'iltum iṣbassuma	If poverty seizes a gentleman[72]

68. *CH* 18.75—19.1 (lit., "if a man has barley against a man").

69. CH 19.2 (*bēl še'im*, lit., "lord of the barley").

70. *CH* §113 (18.75—19.16). Charpin (*Hammurabi*, 150) is careful to differentiate that "the maintenance of public order, such as when a borrower is required to pay his creditor according to the terms of their agreement, is covered by *kittum*, whereas *mîšarum* concerns the restoration of balance in society, such as when someone burdened with debt is given a measure of relief."

71. *Atr* 1.1–6. (cf. Moore, *WealthWatch*, 73–81).

72. *CH* 19.54–56. Akk *ṣabātum* often denotes the "seizing" of a person by demons, illness, misfortune, or as a pledge to pay off debt; e.g., *bēl ḫubullīšu aššassu ul iṣabbatu*, "his creditors may not 'seize' his wife" (*CH* 25.41–43).

aššassu mārašu u mārassu ana kaspam uddin	And he sells his wife or his son or his daughter[73] for silver,
u lu ana kiššātim ittandin	Or sells them into debt-service,[74]
šalaš šanāttim bit šāyyimanišunu u kašišišunu ippešū	They shall labor[75] for three years in the house of their purchaser or controller,[76]
ina rebûtim šattim andurāršunu iššakkan	But in the fourth year their freedom must be mandated.[77]

Slavery

As is well known, the laws governing the treatment of *wardū* ("slaves") are different from those governing *muškenū* ("laborers") because, as Annunziata Rositani points out, slaves in Mesopotamia are thought to be "little more than animals, both in monetary value and because of the work they do."[78] For example:

šumma awīlum wardam u lu amtam ana kiššātim ittandin	If a gentleman sells a slave—male or female—into debt-service,[79]

73. The following law (*CH* §118) stipulates a much less equitable exchange-process should the person sold into debt-service be a "slave boy" (*wardum*) or a "slave girl" (*amtum*). Cf. Chavalas, "Code," 330–31.

74. *CH* 19.59. Cf. *ummaša ina bit kišatiša ušteṣiam*, "I had her mother released from her 'house of debt'" (cited in *CAD* K.460; cf. Driver and Miles, *Laws*, 1.216). The Nazarene sage describes the "debt-house" as a φυλακή ("prison") overseen and managed by a βασανιστής ("jailor," Matt 18:30, 34).

75. *CH* 19.64. Akk *epēšu* ("to act, work") often appears in concert with other verbs denoting "labor" (*CAD* E.201–25).

76. *CH* 19.63. N.B. the repetition of the same root (*kašašu*) in 19.59 (*kiššātum*) and 19.63 (*kašišu*). Cf. *CAD* K.459, 289). Van de Mieroop (*Hammurabi*, 95) notes that soldier-farmers called away on military campaigns often have to hire laborers to work the fields in their absence, even though this runs the obvious risk of said laborers cheating them (cf. Matt 24:45–51).

77. *CH* §117 (19.54–67). Wright (*Inventing*, 33) points out that the law in the Covenant Code (Exod 21:2; Deut 15:12) reflects *CH* in that both laws judiciously "limit the length of this enslavement." Cf. *HL* §19–24.

78. Rositani, "Work," 64.

79. Chirichigno (*Debt-Slavery*, 55–100) identifies two types of loans in *CH* §117–18—*kiššitum* and *kaspum*—the first (§117) denoting the type of work done by debtor's dependents to pay off debt to secure their release (after three years); the second (§118) describing (alongside *kiššitum*) an opportunity for merchants and debtors to resolve

tamkārum ušetteq	The merchant may extend (the enslavement beyond three years).[80]
ana kaspim inaddin	He may sell him/her for silver, (but)
ul ibbaqqar	There shall be no reclamation.[81]

BETROTHAL

CH addresses a number of issues having to do with family law, especially betrothal, marriage, and divorce.[82] Unlike the fading custom of "engagement" in the postmodern West,[83] ANE "betrothal" involves a high degree of social, legal, and economic commitment, and *CH* is a primary source of documentation to this effect. For example:

šumma awīlum ana bīt emim biblam ušābil	If a gentleman brings the bridewealth gift to his bride's father's house[84]
terḫatam iddinma abi mārtim	And presents the bridewealth, and the girl's father then declares,
mārti ul anaddikkum iqtabi	"I shall not give you my daughter,"

their issues via *kaspum* ("silver"). Chirichigno argues that even though the two transactions are different the outcome can still lead to the same result. Tsai (*Deuteronomy*, 152–54), however, finds this attempt to distinguish *types* of loans in CH §117–18 "inconsistent."

80. *CH* 19.71. On Akk *etēqu* ("to pass along, extend, expire," *CAD* E.384–95), cf. *awatum ša innepšu wedi itetîq*, "the matter occurring earlier has now 'expired'" (*ARM* 4.59.6). Meek (*Code*, 171) reads "if the merchant foreclosed"; Harper (*Code*, 41) reads "if the merchant transfer or sell such slave"; Richardson (*Laws*, 79) reads "the merchant may pass them on or sell them for silver." The translation here follows Roth (*Law*, 103).

81. *CH* 19.73. Cf. *aḫḫūša ul ipaqqaruši*, "her brothers shall not lay a claim against her" (*CH* 31.41–42). Cf. Tsai (*Deuteronomy*, 113–64), and the sources cited in Moore (*WealthWatch*, 83–89).

82. The definitive study on this is by Westbrook (*Marriage*).

83. Witte (*Family*, 1–17). Bellah (*Habits*, 142) comments on the dramatic changes in American thinking: "We do not argue that Americans should abandon individualism—that would mean for us to abandon our deepest identity. But individualism has come to mean so many things and to contain such contradictions and paradoxes that even to defend it requires that we analyze it critically, that we consider especially those tendencies that would destroy it from within."

84. *CH* 26.49, *biblum* (*CAD* B.220). Meek (*Code*, 173) reads "betrothal gift"; Roth (*Law*, 111) reads "ceremonial marriage prestation"; Harper (*Code*, 57) reads "present"; Richardson (*Laws*, 91) reads "gift."

mimma mala ibbablušum *uštašannāma utâr*	He shall double the size of any gift brought to him as compensation.[85]

MARRIAGE

With regard to marriage several laws lay out various degrees of "marital success"—"success" defined as the production of viable heirs:

šumma awīlum aššatam īḫuz *māri ūlissumma*	If a gentleman takes a wife and she bears him sons
sinništum šî ana šīmtim ittalak	And that woman goes to her fate,[86]
ana šeriktiša abuša ul iraggum	Her father will not lay claim to her dowry.[87]
šeriktaša ša marīšama	Her dowry belongs to her sons.[88]

Another law states:

šumma awīlum aššatam īḫuzma *māri la ušaršišu*	If a gentleman takes a wife and she does not produce sons for him,[89]
sinništum šî ana šīmtim ittalak	And that woman goes to her fate,

85. *CH* §160 (26.47–59; cf. *CH* §159 and §161). Noticeable parallels to these stipulations occur in the Hittite laws (cf. *HL* §26–36). "Compensation" is a major socioeconomic motif in ANE literature (cf. below).

86. *CH* 26.83—27.2. This euphemistic idiom for "death" (*ana šimtu alāku*, "to go to one's fate") occurs several times in *CH* (e.g., §§12, 162, 163, 165, 166, 167, 170, 178, 179, 180, 181, 182, 183, 184).

87. While "the terminology regarding dowry is confusing," Marsman (*Women*, 94) nevertheless argues (a) that "*CH* distinguishes between *nudinnû* and *šeriktu* in view of the devolution of marital property" (citing Westbrook, *Marriage*, 25); (b) that *CH* uses *šeriktu* "as a technical term for that part of the marital property in which ownership does not vest in the husband" (citing Westbrook, *Marriage*, 26); and (c) that dowry often includes "the *terḫatu* which the husband pays, but which at the time of the marriage has lost its function as a surety" (citing Driver and Miles, *Laws*, 1.254–56).

88. *CH* §162 (26.78—27.6).

89. *CH* 27.10, *ušaršišu* (Š-causative of *rašû*, "to obtain, come into the possession of goods," *CAD* R.196–98). Akk *ūlissumma* (from *walādu*, "to give birth"; cf. Heb ילד) in the previous law (*CH* 26.81) can also mean "to produce," but *rašû* lends itself to more of a "production-line" nuance.

šumma terḫatam ša awīlum šu ana bīt emišu ublu	And if his father-in-law returns the bridewealth[90]
emušu uttēršum	which the man brought to his house,
ana šerikti sinništum šuāti mussa ul iraggum	Her husband shall make no claim on that woman's dowry.
šeriktaša ša bīt abišama	For the dowry belongs to her father's house.[91]

Divorce

Like many cultures (ancient and contemporary),[92] *CH* permits divorce as a social/legal/economic failsafe:

šumma awīlum ḫīrtašu ša māri la uldušum izzib	If a gentleman leaves his first wife who bears him no sons
kaspam mala terḫatiša inaddiššim	He shall reimburse to her as much silver as her bridewealth allows, and
u šeriktam ša ištu bīt abuša ublam ušallamšimma izzibši	Before leaving her he shall bring back as much of her dowry as she originally brought over from her father's house.
šumma terḫatum la ibašši 1 mana kaspam	If there is no bridewealth, then he shall provide 1 mina of silver
ana uzubbêm inaddiššim	As a divorce settlement.[93]

90. CH 27.14, *terḫatum* ("bridewealth"). Meek (*Code*, 173) reads "marriage-price"; Roth (*Law*, 112) reads "bridewealth"; Harper (*Code*, 57) reads "marriage settlement"; Richardson (*Laws*, 93) reads "bride-price." Cf. the Ug cognate *tn nkl yrḫ ytrḫ*, "Give Nikkal (that) Yariḫ may 'marry' (*trḫ*)" (*CAT* 1.24.17–18).

91. *CH* §163 (27.7–23). Cf. Harris ("Marriage," 363–69); Roth ("Widow," 1–26); Dalley ("Dowries," 53–74); Lemos (*Marriage*, 1–19); Westbrook (*Marriage*); and Marsman (*Women*, 94).

92. In this same vein Atkin ("Cohabitation," 301–25) examines (a) how unmarried cohabitation and illegitimacy affect the litigation of property disputes, and (b) how one national legislature is changing the law to protect the innocents born into these new realities.

93. *CH* §138–39 (23.14–29). Wunsch (*Urkunden*) and Stol (*Women*) discuss other ANE texts about marriage and divorce, and Howard (*Brides*, 33) documents how the contemporary "jewelry industry portrays marriage as a consumer rite."

Inheritance

Unlike *betrothal*, *CH* laws about *inheritance* continue to exercise great influence.[94] For example:

šumma awīlum ana mārišu nasāḫim panamištakan	If a gentleman decides[95] to disown[96] his son
ana dayāni māri anassaḫ iqtabi	And he states before the judges, "I disown my son,"
dayānū warkassu iparrasūma	The judges shall make a decision about his estate.[97]
šumma mārum arnam qabtam	If the son does not commit an offense serious enough
ša ina aplūtim nasāḫim la ublam	To have the inheritance terminated,[98]
abum mārašu ina aplūtim ul inassaḫ	The father shall not terminate the inheritance of his son.
šumma arnam qabtam ša ina aplūtim nasaḫim ana abišu itbalam	If he commits a serious offense against his father,
ana ištiššu panīšu ubbalū	The first time they shall excuse him, but
šumma arnam qabtam adi šinišu itbalam	If he commits a second serious offense,
abum mārašu ina aplūtim inassaḫ	The father shall disown his son.[99]

94. Beckert (*Wealth*, 1–2). Charpin (*Law*, 55–57) examines several examples of Babylonian inheritance law in action (cf. Moore, *WealthWarn*, 26–27, 37–47, 67–71, 75–76, 83–84, 98–101, 197–98). Weigel ("Inheritance," 279–87) documents how technological advances in health care are changing perceptions from what used to be called the *Jenseitsökonomie* ("afterlife economy") to one in which inheritance funds go not to one's heirs but to the healthcare of one's elderly parents.

95. *CH* 28.12 (*panam ištakan*, lit., "he sets the face").

96. *CH* 28.14 (*nasāḫu*, lit., "to tear out, uproot").

97. *CH* 28.16 (*[w]arkatu*, "estate, legacy, inheritance"; cf. *warkassa ša mārīšama*, "her estate belongs to her sons," 29.4–5).

98. *CH* 28.19 (*aplūtum*, "inheritance"; the *aplu* is the "heir, oldest son"). N.B. that the primary meaning of *bullû* is "to extinguish, (ex)terminate," *CAD* B.72–74).

99. *CH* §168–69 (28.9–37).

Several betrothal laws in *CH* omit any specific reference to "inheritance" (*naḫālu*) yet the motif still lurks in the shadows. For example:

šumma awīlum iššalilma ina bītišu ša akālim la ibašši	If a gentleman is robbed so that no food remains in his house,[100]
ana panīšu aššassu ana bīt šanîm īterubma	And his wife enters another house before his return,
mārī ittalad	And bears sons,
ina warka mussa ittūramma ālšu iktašdam	But her husband later returns to his city,
sinništum šî ana ḫāwiriša itâr	That woman shall return to her first husband
mārū warki abišunu illakū	And the sons shall go with their father.[101]

Many more examples might be cited, of course, but even the most cursory examination of these Babylonian laws shows that *CH* bears strong witness to the socioeconomic bridge spanning the canyon separating ANE *wisdom* from ANE *law*. What the foregoing examples illustrate, in fact, is that the "brick-and-mortar" making up this bridge is comprised of literary motifs specifically designed to address social, legal, and economic questions associated with *land, trade, property, debt, labor, slavery, marriage, divorce, betrothal*, and *inheritance*.[102]

Pessimistic Wisdom

Alongside the "didactic/advice" literature,[103] some sapiential texts address the ever-sensitive problem of (innocent) suffering, each contributing to a trajectory pointedly focused on what Gottfried Wilhelm von Leibniz rather famously calls the "problem of θεοδική."[104] Inspired by the work of Egyptologist

100. CH 22.38. Akk *šalālu* ("to rob, plunder"); cf. Ug ṯ *ll* ("to plunder"); Heb שלל ("to loot, plunder," Hab 2:8); Arab ثلّ ("to tear down, destroy, subvert"; cf. *HAL* 1416–18).

101. *CH* §135 (22.37–56). Roth (*Law*, 107) reads "the children shall inherit from their father." Cf. *HL* §171.

102. Kuran (*Divergence*, 78) notes that "of all the economic rules in Qur'an, the most detailed are those on inheritance."

103. Oshima (*Poems*, 2) prefers the term "didactic"; Weeks (*Wisdom*, 20) prefers the term "advice." Goff (*4QInstruction*, 12) gravitates to the terms "pedagogical" and "eudemonistic."

104. "Theodicy." According to Welz (*Theodicy*, 1) and Larrimore ("Leibniz," 26),

Eberhard Otto,[105] Dorothea Sitzler sets out in her Bonn dissertation to examine this trajectory, selecting eight "theodicy texts" for analysis[106]—four from Egypt (*Coffin Text 1130*,[107] *Instructions of Merikare*,[108] *Admonitions of Ipu-wer*,[109] *Words of Heliopolis*[110]), and four from Mesopotamia (*Sumerian Job*,[111] *Dialogue Between a Man and His God*,[112] *Poem of the Pious Sufferer*,[113] *Babylonian Theodicy*).[114] This leads her to the following conclusions:

- Each text emphasizes restoration and stability over crisis and chaos[115]
- Each text privileges religious loyalty over cosmic renewal[116]
- Each text champions wisdom's stabilizing role vs. the instability created by suffering (especially innocent suffering)[117]
- Each text derives from an era of societal leadership transition[118]
- Each text, however circuitously, privileges hope over despair.[119]

Leibniz (*Théodicée*) coins this term in 1710 by joining together the Greek terms θεος ("God") + δικη ("justice"; cf. Cohen, "Theodicy," 243–70).

105. Cf. Otto, *Vorwurf*. Otto and Wolfgang Helck edit the first volume of the landmark *Lexikon der Ägyptologie* (Wiesbaden: Harrassowitz, 1975).

106. Sitzler, *Vorwurf* (cf. Laato and de Moor, *Theodicy*).

107. *AEL* 1.131–33.

108. *ANET* 414–18.

109. *AEL* 1.149–63; *ANET* 441–44.

110. Osing, "Heliopolis," 347–61. Assmann (*Egypt*, 169–87) discusses these and other theodical texts.

111. *ANET* 589–91.

112. Foster, *Muses*, 148–50.

113. *ANET* 596–600; *BWL* 32–62; Foster, *Muses*, 394–408.

114. *BWL* 70–91; *ANET* 601–4. Crenshaw ("Vorwurf," 327) warns that some of the more traditionalist "understandings of these texts will not hold up well against Sitzler's findings."

115. Sitzler (*Vorwurf*, 114) locates the origins of these texts not in specific historical moments, but in "restorative times often bound together by literary blood."

116. Weeks (*Wisdom*, 2–3) explains: "If one believes that long life and prosperity are a gift from God, then wisdom becomes associated with pleasing God—that is, the skill lies not so much in understanding life itself as in discerning the divine will."

117. Perhaps the clearest examples of this in Tanak are the whirlwind speeches in Job 38–42 (cf. Hartley, *Job*, 6–11).

118. This may be the dissertation's greatest weakness because, as Clifford (*Wisdom*, 158–60) points out, the sociohistorical contexts of wisdom texts are notoriously difficult to pin down.

119. Sitzler (*Vorwurf*, 231–34). Sitzler posits the origin of these theodical texts not in school exercise tablets, but in "literary material used by wisdom-instructors in their preparations" (133), a conclusion Crenshaw (*Vorwurf*, 328) finds too restrictive. Cf. Jiménez, *Poems*, 8–12.

Poem of the Pious Sufferer

One of the best-known pessimistic texts is the so-called "Poem of the Pious Sufferer," a "great text" often identified by its first line: *Ludlul bēl nēmeqi.*[120] Likely written by an *awīlum* ("gentleman") named Šubši-mešre-šakkan,[121] it (a) recounts the "slings and arrows" he holds responsible for his suffering, and (b) imagines their origin in the mysterious will of his divine patron, Marduk.[122] Not all of the motifs in this poem are socioeconomic, of course, yet this dimension of the poem, though often ignored,[123] makes a significant contribution to the ANE wisdom trajectory.[124]

Amar Annus and Alan Lenzi read Ludlul as a chiasm in which "Tablet III's description of physical restoration reverses the misfortunes of Tablet II" and "Tablet IV does the same for the social misfortunes of Tablet I."[125] On the question of *genre*, however, they take careful pause. Like Wilfrid Lambert[126] and Paul-Alain Beaulieu,[127] they resist the contemporary temptation to read the Akkadian term *nēmequ* ("wisdom") through a linguistic prism indebted less to the poem's socioliterary context than to meanings

120. "Let us praise the lord of wisdom" (cf. *BWL* 21–62; Annus and Lenzi, *Ludlul*; Foster, *Muses*, 392–409; Oshima, *Poems*, 3–5). Lambert ("Wisdom," 31) suggests that ^{D}*Ši-du-ri* . . . ^{D}XV *ni-me-qí* ("Šiduri . . . goddess of wisdom") in Š*ur* 2.173 refers to the ale-wife counseling Gilgamesh not to despair over Enkidu's death (*GE* 10.1).

121. This overtly socioeconomic name means "Gather up the wealth, O Šakkan" (Šakkan is the god of domestic livestock, a primary economic resource in agrarian societies; cf. Foster, *Agade*, 154; Nolan and Lenski, *Macrosociology*, 154). Noting its trifold appearance in Ludlul (*Lud* 3.44; 4.111, 119), Lambert ("Wisdom," 34) suggests that this "extremely rare" name refers to "an historical figure under Nazimurattaš, important enough as an official in the fourth year of the king to have a messenger of his fed at state expense."

122. Krüger ("Poems," 184) finds it "more plausible" that the "speaker assumes that he himself has made a mistake out of ignorance than to assume that the gods do not act properly." Leick (*Mesopotamia*, 22) recognizes that "towards the end of the second millennium Marduk assumes many of the functions of Ea/Enki (the old wisdom deity) without replacing him."

123. Exceptions include Gurney (*Economic*, 79–81) and Luukko ("Roles," 246–48). Gerhards (*Gott*, 98–99) mentions Ludlul's incantational and medicinal influences, but nothing about its socioeconomic motifs.

124. *Contra* van der Toorn ("Theodicy," 57–89), Cohen ("Theodicy," 270) argues that theodical texts are not necessarily generated by socioeconomic catastrophe.

125. Annus and Lenzi, *Ludlul*, xix (cf. the similar structure of Jonah in Nevi'im). Lambert (*BWL* 21–24), working with fewer mss, is more cautious about matters of literary structure.

126. Lambert, *BWL* 1.

127. Beaulieu, "Wisdom," 3–19.

determined by "modern categorizational imposition."[128] Yet, agreeing with the proposals of Sara Denning Bolle[129] and Giorgio Buccelatti,[130] they nonetheless conclude that Ludlul can be nothing else except "wisdom literature . . . according to all but the strictest definition."[131]

At any rate, this poem begins with an opening hymn to Marduk depicting Babylon's divine patron as an aloof monarch caught up in the throes of *Sturm und Drang*,[132] a typically capricious deity whose personality, in Hermann Spieckermann's view, "rhythmically" oscillates between "wrath and mercy."[133] Opening hymn completed, the protagonist itemizes several "attacks" mounted against him,[134] including (a) the abandonment of "my prosperity daemon" ([D]ALAD *dum-qí*),[135] (b) the "expulsion from my house"

128. Annus and Lenzi, *Ludlul*, xxxv. Cf. *CAD* N/2.160–63. On the question of "wisdom genre" cf. the assortment of pro-vs.-con essays in Sneed, *Prospects*.

129. Denning Bolle, *Wisdom*, 67.

130. Buccelatti, "Wisdom," 35–47.

131. Annus and Lenzi, *Ludlul*, xxxvi (cf. Alster, *Wisdom*, 18–24; Lambert, *BWL* 1; Lambert, "Wisdom," 30–31). That some continue to call Ludlul the "Babylonian Job" continues to complicate the question of genre because even though some taxonomies catalogue the book of Job as "wisdom literature," it's difficult to disagree with Pope (*Job*, xxxi) that "there is no single classification appropriate to the literary form of the book of Job."

132. *Lud* 1.1–40 ("storm and stress," a phrase first associated with von Klinger's play *Sturm und Drang*, first performed in Hamburg in 1777). Lenzi ("Marduk," 483) thinks that Marduk is hardly "the divine equivalent of the cat that toys with the mouse before devouring it. Rather, he ultimately shows mercy to frail and imperfect humans who anger him. Šubši-mešre-šakkan has experienced this mercy and is intent upon telling others what Marduk has done for him."

133. Spieckermann, "Wrath," 6. Whether Marduk *subordinates* his mercy to his wrath, however, is not as clear as Spieckermann would suggest. N.B. the summary statement *ka-bat-ta-šu muš-ne-šat* ("his temper is benevolent," *Lud* 1.34) alongside the jussive proclamation, *libbaka liṭib ka-bat-ta-ka liḫdu* ("May your heart be content, your temper positive," *BBRel* 31—37.30). For comparison, N.B. that lines 176–85 of the Šamaš Hymn, as Foster recognizes (*Muses*, 627), "consider the alternately harsh and tender qualities" of the sun-god Šamaš (cf. Moran, "Marduk," 255–60; Albertz, "Mardukfrömmigkeit," 25–53; Collins, "Wrath," 67–77).

134. Assyrologists debate whether Ludlul more likely resembles a lament psalm or a thanksgiving psalm, but as Weinfeld ("Parallels," 217–18) points out, both Ludlul and the Sumerian poem "A Man and His God" contain a recounting of the protagonist's troubles *as well as* eventual praise of the divine, so it is more likely, in Oshima's opinion (*Poems*, 32), that "the main intention of these texts is to demonstrate the gratitude of the sufferers for their redemption, not to draw the gods' attention to their sufferings."

135. *Lud* 1.45. Good and evil [D]*šēdū* ("daemons") populate the occult world of the ancient Near East. An Assyrian prayerbook references both side-by-side within the same prayer: [D]*šêdu ḫa-a-a-ṭu al-lu-ḫap-pu ḫab-bi-lu gal-lu-u râbiṣu ilu limnu*, the Šêdu, the 'Lookout,' the 'Snatching Net," the *Gallu*, the *Rabiṣu*, the evil god" (*KAR* 2.58.42) . . . [D]*šêdu na-ṣi-ru ilu mu-šal-li-mu*, "the protecting *šêdu*, the healing god" (*KAR* 2.58.47).

(*uš-te-ṣi ina é-ia*),[136] and (c) the failure to secure the king's "redemption" (*pa-ṭā-ru*).[137] Reacting to what he perceives to be the prosecutorial tactics of Marduk's priestly "attendants" (*nanzazū*),[138] he dramatizes his dilemma by reporting their accusations in the first person:[139]

na-piš-ta-šu u-šat-bak-šu	"I will make him give up his provisions;[140]
ú-šat-bi te-er-tu-šú	I will deduct his commission;[141]
qip-ta-šú a-tam-ma-aḫ	I will confiscate his loan;[142]
er-ru-ub é-uš-šu	I will impound his house."[143]

So ingrained is the notion of a "protecting ^{D}*šêdu*" in Mesopotamia, "pious sufferers" find it vexing when *il-la-ku ú-ru-uḫ dum-qí la muš-te-ʾ-u ì-li*, "those who neglect (their) god 'experience' (lit., 'go the way of') prosperity," *BWL* 75.70). In the Sum "A Man and His God" (*COS* 1.485), the deity restores his devotee with ^{D}UDUG SIG$_5$ KA-E EN-NU-UJ$_3$ MACKIM MU-UN-DA-AN-TAB ^{D}LAMMA, "a protective daemon who stands guard at the mouth as a divine guardian." Eventually the ^{D}LAMMA ("divine guardian") and ^{D}ALAD ("protective daemon") return to support Šubši-mešre-šakkan (*Lud* 4.56).

136. *Lud* 1.50. On the socioeconomic structure and function of the Mediterranean "household," cf. Moore, *WealthWarn*, 166, 181, 193.

137. *Lud* 1.56. Akk *paṭaru* ("to unravel," *CAD* P.286) is cognate to Ug *pẓr*, Heb פשר, Syr ܦܫܪ, and Arab فسر ("to explain, interpret," *DMWA* 713) and serves as a major motif in the Hittite *išḫiul* texts (cf. below). Given the appearance in 4.45 of the phrase *e'-il-ti ip-pa-ṭir* ("my debt is redeemed"; cf. *šumma awīlam e'iltum iṣbassuma*, "If a debt brings about the seizure of a man . . ." *CH* §117), it may be that what the king refuses to "redeem" is an outstanding debt like a pledged field (cf. *CAD* P.294–95; cf. Job 29:25; van der Toorn, "Theodicy," 78).

138. *Lud* 1.57 Oshima (*Poems*, 81) reads "courtiers." Cf. the king's סרכין ("tacticians," Theo τάκτικοι) who try to find in Daniel some sign of שלו ("neglect"; Theo πρόφασις, "pretext," Dan 6:5). On the behavior usually expected of royal assistants N.B. the proverb *na-da-nu šá šarri ṭú-ub-bu šá šá-qi-i na-da-nu šá šarri dum-mu-qu šá a-ba-rak-ku*, "Giving pertains to a king, doing well to a cupbearer. Giving pertains to a king, showing favor to a steward" (*BWL* 259.5–8).

139. Cf. the similar prosecutorial tactics of the גבריא אלך הרגשו ("these troublemaking men") conspiring against Daniel (Dan 6:16; cf. van der Toorn, "Lions," 626–40).

140. *Lud* 1.59. Oshima (*Poems*, 81) reads "I shall make him spill his life." Like Heb נפש, the root meaning of Akk *napištu* is "life," but in some contexts it can mean "livelihood, provisions, sustenance" (*CAD* N/1.302). N.B. the designation *é na-pi-iš-tim* in an OB letter ("house of provisions," *PBS* 7.125.32) and the phrase *é-iš-šu* ("his house") in *Lud* 1.62.

141. *Lud* 1.60. Oshima (*Poems*, 81) reads "I will make him lose his post." Akk *têrtum* means "assignment" (*AHw* 1350), but N.B. that at Mari a *bēl têrtum* ("commissioner," *ARM* 1.61.29) works in a *bīt têrtum* ("house of commissions," *ARM* 2.76.31).

142. *Lud* 1.61. Annus and Lenzi (*Ludlul*, 32) read "I will seize his office," but N.B. the phrase *šūtma la ana qí-ip-tim addiššina*, "I did not give them (the textiles) on loan" (*BIN* 6.26.17; cf. *CAD* Q.261).

143. *Lud* 1.62 (lit., "I will enter his house"; the next logical step after "expulsion,"

Then he shifts back to the third person:

ana ṣi-in-di u bir-ti ú-za-'i-zu mim-ma-a	They (re)distribute my property to commoners and riff-raff;[144]
pi-i ÍD-ia u-man-ṭi-ṭù sa-ki-ka	They silt up the entrances to my canals,[145]
ina qer-bé-ti-ia ú-ša-as-su-ú a-la-la	They drive the work-song from my fields,[146]
par-ṣi-ia u-šal-qu-u ša-nam-ma	They let another take my commission,[147]
ù ina pil-lu-de-e-a a-ḫa uš-ziz-zu	They appoint a stranger to my office.[148]

These are serious charges, yet in spite of the damage he has suffered he still dares to hope that "prosperity" (*da-me-eq-tum*) will someday return,[149]

1.50). The same epithet occurs in the Šamaš Hymn (*a-na bīti-šú ul ir-ru-bu šu-nu aḫḫu*^{MEŠ}*-šu*, "nor will his brothers take over his estate," *BWL* 132.117). Cf. *ina qāt qēberiya marra īkim*, "he took the spade from the hand of the one who wished to bury me" (cited in Cohen, *Wisdom*, 34.168.43′).

144. *Lud* 1.99. Annus and Lenzi (*Ludlul*, 33) read "commoners"; Oshima (*Poems*, 85) reads "the gang and the riff-raff." On the term *mimmu* ("property, possessions") cf. the Amarna statements *ul la ḫalqu mi-im-mi šarri*, "the property of the king is not lost" (*EA* 96.20) and *kali mi-im-mi* PN, "all the property of PN" (105.25).

145. *Lud* 1.100. One of the complaints of the Igigi-gods is that they have to do "canal duty"; i.e. restore commercial water traffic by "digging out the canals" (*i-ḫer-ru-ú nara*, "dredging the river," *Atr* 1.23).

146. *Lud* 1.101. Pecchioli Daddi ("Song," 559–60) examines an antiphonal work-song sung by LÚ$^{\text{MEŠ GIŠ}}$TUKUL-*uš* ("workers"; lit., "men of the tool/weapon") in a Hittite ritual text (*KBo* 37.68; cf. also the princely warning to noblemen to stop oppressing their "workers" in *KBo* 1.22.3′; see below). Gilgamesh laments the death of Enkidu by listing those who will most likely miss him, including the "farmer" (^{LÚ}*ikkaru*) reflecting on his "sweet work-song" (*a-la ṭa-a-bi, GE* 8.23–24). On *qerbetu* ("field") cf. *nam-maš-še-e* ^{D}*šakkan lik-tamme-re . . . ina qir-bé-te*, "let Šakkan's creatures be gathered into the field" (*BWL* 170.19).

147. *Lud* 1.103 (Akk *parṣu*). Reacting to the multiple nuances embedded in Sum ME and GARZA in *ID* 127–63, *DI* 44–62 compresses them all down into the administrative term *parṣu* (cf. *Lud* 4.61).

148. *Lud* 1.104. The word-pair *parṣu//pilludû* ("commission//office") is not uncommon (cf. *Ee* 5.67; *BWL* 78.135).

149. *Lud* 1.119. Akk *dumqu* ("prosperity") appears earlier on the tablet (1.45) in the "prosperity daemon" epithet (^{D}ALAD *dum-qí*; cf. above).

grounding this hope on the simplistic presumption that "prosperity" (*išartu*) always increases[150] whenever "wickedness" (*zapurtu*) decreases.[151]

Accused by the *nanzazū* of neglecting his religious duties,[152] he draws a line in the sand, insisting to his critics that "the day of worship . . . brings delight to my heart."[153] Why? Because it affords him an opportunity to remember "the day of Ištar's procession"[154] as a "day of profit and wealth."[155] His detractors fail to comprehend this, he suggests, because they are little more than fickle adolescents used to "reaching up to their god" (*i-ša-an-na-na* DINGIR-*šin*)[156] during times of "satisfaction" (*i-šib-ba-a-ma*),[157] but fleeing the very prospect of "Netherworld descent" (*a-rad ir-kal-lu*) during seasons of "distress" (*ú-táš-šá-šá-ma*).[158]

150. *Lud* 2.3. Cf. ᴰ*Ea* ᴰ*Šamaš u* ᴰ*Marduk yâši ruṣannima ina annikunu i-šá-ru-tam lullik*, "Help me, O Ea, Šamaš and Marduk, and give me your blessing so I may enjoy prosperity" (*KAR* 267.4′).

151. *Lud* 2.3. This presumption underlies the words of the "friend" in the Babylonian Theodicy when he says, *n[a]-ak-di pa-li-iḫ* ᴰ*ištar u-kam-mar ṭuḫ-[da]*, "the humble person who fears Ištar will accumulate wealth" (*BWL* 71.22; *contra* the "sufferer/sceptic's" words in 75.70–71). Von Rad (*Theology* 1.425) depicts this polarized thinking as "old wisdom," what economists today call "zero-sum" theory (Thurow, *Zero-Sum*, 3–25; Hornborg, *Exchange*, 6–26; Rachman, *Zero-Sum*, 261–78), the socioeconomic cousin to what theologians call "health-and-wealth" religion (cf. Fee, *Disease*; Bowler, *Blessed*).

152. *Lud* 2.12–24. Caring for the humanoid statues of the gods is an expensive enterprise prone to all sorts of corruption (cf. *EpJer* 10–11; Walker and Dick, *Induction*, 3–31; Moore, *WealthWarn*, 140–42).

153. *Lud* 2.25. Markter (*Ezechiel*, 67) documents how "heart" is a "central notion" (*Zentralbegriff*) in ANE thought.

154. *Lud* 2.26, UD-*mu ri-du-ti* ᴰ*ištar*. In light of *a-rad ir-kal-la* ("descending to the Netherworld," 2.47) a few lines down, it's difficult to avoid wondering how much *ri-du-ti* ᴰ*ištar* resonates (intentionally or otherwise) with the socioeconomic motifs in *ID/DI* (cf. Moore, *WealthWarn*, 4–17).

155. *Lud* 2.26, *ne-me-li ta-at-tur-ru*. Akk *nēmelu* often appears in word-pairs; cf. *ni-me-lu//išdiḫa*, "profit//income" (*BAM* 315.2.7); and *nēmelu//kušīru*, "profit"//"success" (Sidursky, "Prayer," 570.19′–20′). Annus and Lenzi (*Ludlul*, 35) read "wealth and weal" (cf. Moore, *Babbler*, 49–50).

156. *Lud* 2.45 (Akk *šanānu*); cf. *ši-mat-ka la ša-na-an*, "your (Marduk's) destiny is untouchable" (*Ee* 4.4, 6).

157. *Lud* 2.45 (Akk *šebû*); cf. *āšib ali lu rubû ul i-šeb-bi akla*, "the prince who dwells in the city is never satisfied with food" (*Erra* 1.52); cf. Heb שׂבע (Exod 16:3; Ruth 2:18).

158. *Lud* 2.47. Cf. *la ta-šu-uš u4-me-šam-ma*, "You (Šamaš) are not distressed during the day" (*BWL* 129.41). Acknowledging Marduk's success in sparing him from the "pit/grave" (*ḫaštu*, 4.4–5), Šubši-mešre-šakkan is grateful to have this option removed from consideration (4.29). In fact, an Akkadian prototype of Ludlul at Ugarit shows him praising Marduk for *ultu erṣēti ušēlânni*, "raising me from the Netherworld" (cited in Cohen, *Wisdom* 168.41). Qur'an also recognizes this all-too-human tendency, noting

Eventually securing Marduk's "redemption" (*paṭāru*),[159] Šubši-mešre-šakkan begins the arduous task of orchestrating what Alan Lenzi appropriately calls his "reintegration into society."[160] Ascertaining what this means is difficult, of course,[161] yet it hardly seems coincidental that the ritualization of his *paṭāru* involves (a) passing through several "gates," one named "Productivity" (*ḫé-gál-la*),[162] another "Gifts" (*šul-ma-na*),[163] and (b) donating several of his own "gifts" to a now-placated Marduk, including

that when "the Lord is generous" (ربه فاكرمه), this triggers the belief that "he is honoring me" (اكرمن), but when he "tests by restricting provisions" (ابتلاه فقدر عليه رزقه), this leads to the fear that "the Lord 'is disgracing me'" (اهنن, Q 89.15–16).

159. How this occurs is not stated.

160. Lenzi, "Gates," 734. Spieckermann (*Liebe*, 106) prefers to decribe this reintegration as "kultische." From Ludlul and other texts (particularly BM 35046 and 38602) George (*Topographical*, 83–98) describes each of the Esagila gates in *Lud* 4.38–50.

161. When attempting to locate the sociohistorical context of this or any other wisdom text it is critical that readers learn to accept, in Beaulieu's words ("Wisdom," 6), that "the sapiential tradition of ancient Mesopotamia" is simply designed "to tell us something important about the purpose of wisdom teachings . . . foundational to civilized life."

162. Lud 4.39. Akk *ḫé-gál-lu* (from Sum ḪÉ.GÁL) occurs in one of Hammurabi's titles: *bābil* ḪÉ.GÁL *ana* É.GIŠ.NU_x.GAL, "the one who makes the temple (of Sin named) Egišnugal productive" (*CH* 2.20). This term can signify abundance, productivity, or fertility. Cf. ^{D}IM *šārik* ḪÉ.GÁL *ana mati*, "Adad, who gives fertility to the land" (OIP 2.112.7.87, cited in *CAD* Ḫ.168). George (*Topographical*, 87–89) identifies this gate as the western portal into Esagila (Marduk's temple in Babylon), a location he describes as "fitting" because "it would then give access to the left bank of the Araḫtu-Euphrates, itself the 'river of abundance' (*nar ḫengalli*)." Further, the gate called KÁ.NUN.ḪÉ.GÁL, "Gate of the Prince of Abundance" stands in *E-temen-anki* (the ziggurrat-tower above Esagila).

163. *Lud* 4.41, 49. Cf. *šul-ma-ni babbanu ana Bēl inandin*, "he (the king) should give an exceptional gift to Bel" (*ABL* 1431.8′). One of the "Prescriptions of Queen Ašmunikkal to the Guardians of the Musoleum" reads "a dog barks, but when he arrives he is silent" (*KUB* 13.8.7), a proverb Collins ("Animals," 242) attributes to "zealous bureaucrats who 'bark' for payment of an obligation they cannot collect from exempted (dead) persons, and so fall silent." Lenzi ("Gates," 748) suggests that the "gates" sequence in *Lud* 5.42–53 "uses the same hermeneutical and philological methods that ancient Mesopotamian scribes employ extensively in commentaries and explanatory texts." Mythopoeically speaking, however, "gates" signify not only physical portals, but the personified guardians designed to protect such portals (e.g., שערי צדק, "gates of justice," Ps 118:19; and שערי מות, gates of death," Job 38:17). Cf. Hundley (*Dwellings*, 207–84).

irbu,[164] *ṭa'tu*,[165] and *igisû*[166] comprised of "fatted bulls" (*le-e ma-re-e*) and "prized sheep" (*šap-ṭi*).[167] Sociologically, the primary purpose of this ritual is to create a publicly recognizable vehicle for this "pious sufferer" to recommit himself to the supersessionist agenda of the Marduk cult.[168] Why is this necessary? Because, as Jack Barbalet argues, "both the micro- and the macro-power structures in any given society are inevitably accompanied by some level of resistance."[169]

Unlike, say, the Mesopotamian "Dialogue of a Man with His God"[170] or the Egyptian "Complaints of Khahkheperre-sonb,"[171] Ludlul bēl nēmeqi manipulates several well-known socioeconomic motifs having to do with *work*, *productivity*, and *wealth*, molding it into a compelling work of art designed to spotlight how difficult it is to experience authentic success.[172]

164. *Lud* 4.53. Akk *irbu*/*erbu* is the nominal form of the verb *erēbu* ("to come in, enter"). Thus *erbu* can mean "that which comes in," or "income." Cf. *šumma la išqulu ana bīt* PN *e-re-bu*, "If he does not pay up he will enter into the house of PN" (i.e., "debtor's house," *TCL* 6.68.14; cf. Matt 18:30).

165. *Lud* 4.53. In some lexical lists Sum KADRA is equivalent not only to Akk *ṭa-a-tum* ("purpose gift"), but also to *kadrû* ("bribery") and *šulmānu* ("recompense, reward"; *MSL* 13.113.12; 116.42; *AHw* 1382).

166. *Lud* 4.53 (IGI.SÁ). Cf. IGI.SÁ-*e šul-ma-ni u-šá-bi-lu šu-nu ana sá-a-šu*, "they (the gods) bring him (Marduk) gifts and presents" (*Ee* 4.134).

167. *Lud* 4.54. Olyan (*Ritual*, 8) insists that even "though we have no access to historically-situated ritual practice, we do have literary representations of texts" in which the "literary representations of rites must also have had some relationship to contemporary practice in order to resonate with their intended audiences."

168. Cf. Sommerfeld (*Aufstieg*, 185–212). Al-Rawi and George ("Sippar," 135–36) publish a NB epistle addressed to Hammurabi's son Šamšu-iluna condemning any priesthood daring to hoist itself higher than the priesthood of Marduk. Finn (*Marduk*, 37–41) summarizes the many times Marduk's statue is violently removed from Esagila, and the impact this has on Babylonian culture.

169. Barbalet ("Power," 531–48), cited in Finn (*Marduk*, 1).

170. Cf. Foster (*Muses*, 148–50); Sitzler (*Vorwurf*, 61–71).

171. *AEL* 1.145–49.

172. This is not the only way to read Ludlul, of course. Focusing on Šubši-mešre-šakkan's desire to praise Marduk and the community's desire to "welcome him back," Oshima (*Poems*, 28–34) explains the poem's *raison d'être* in predominantly cultic terms.

Babylonian Theodicy

Another pessimistic piece is the Babylonian Theodicy,[173] a text which in some ways resembles the Hebrew scrolls of Qohelet[174] and Job.[175] Here another "pious sufferer"[176] (Saggil-kīnam-ubbib)[177] converses with a "friend" who appears to listen empathetically before woodenly (and sometimes comically) responding.[178] Socioeconomic components of the poem surface when the "sufferer/sceptic," lamenting the built-in perils associated with being an *aḫurrû* ("younger child"),[179] complains about how *šimtum* ("destiny, fate")[180] has taken away the family *zārû* ("seedgiver, progenitor");[181] i.e., when his parents abandon him for the *erṣet là târi* ("land of no return").[182]

To this the "friend" replies (a) that sooner or later everyone (including parents) must someday "cross the river Ḫubur";[183] and (b) that not every

173. Sitzler (*Vorwurf*, 99–109). Lambert (*BWL* 301) points out that the first word of this text, *ašiš*, is likely a ptc. of *ašāšu*, meaning (a) "to lay foundations"; (b) "to experience distress" (cf. *Lud* 2.47); (c) "to rage" (e.g., a storm); and/or (d) "to gather, collect." Focusing on the last of these four options, Lambert imagines the author of the Babylonian Theodicy to be a "collector of knowledge" (Newsom, *Job*, 92, calls the author a "sage"). Evidently the first to call this text the Babylonian Theodicy is the pioneer Assyriologist Bruno Landsberger ("Theodizee," 32).

174. Dating the Babylonian Theodicy to c. 1000 BCE, Sneed (*Politics*, 45) calls it the "Babylonian Ecclesiastes."

175. N.B. Job's interaction with רעי איוב (the "friends of Job," Job 2:11); cf. Lambert (*BWL* 63); Oshima (*Theodicy*, xiii–xv); and Moore (*Babbler*, 216–23). Salters ("Acrostics," 426) reads the Babylonian Theodicy as "the earliest example of the acrostics phenomenon in Babylonian literature," a phenomenon Murphy ("Wisdom," 160) identifies as a predominant characteristic of "wisdom."

176. Oshima (*Poems*, 115) prefers the term "sceptic."

177. Read in sequence, the signs in this twenty-seven-stanza acrostic text spell out *a-na-ku sa-a-gi-il-ki-[i-na-am-u]b-bi-ib ma-aš-ma-šu ka-ri-bu ša i-li ú šar-ri*, "I am Saggil-kīnam-ubbib the incantation priest, a devotee of god and king." This PN means "May Esagila (Marduk's temple) declare the righteous pure," but whether it refers to the "sufferer/ sceptic" or the recording scribe is not readily determinable.

178. On the similar dynamic between Eliphaz and Job, cf. Moore (*Babbler*, 175, 216–23).

179. *BWL* 70.9 *a-ḫu-ra-[k]u-ma*. The antithetical parallel with *bukru* ("firstborn") in 70.19 repeats again in *LKU* 43.13, 15.

180. *BWL* 70.9. This is perhaps the most significant *Leitwort* in *Enūma Eliš*; cf. *ši-mat-ka la ša-na-an*, "your 'destiny,' (O Marduk), is unequaled" (*Ee* 4.4). In fact, Bottéro (*Mésopotamie*, 189) sees it as "le terme le plus fort et le plus riche et significatif."

181. *BWL* 70.9 (cf. Heb זרע).

182. *BWL* 70.10; cf. *DI* 1 (*qaqarri l[ā târi]*); Job 16:22; *DT* §27).

183. *BWL* 70.17. "While originally the subterranean river of fertility, Ḫubur later becomes known as the river of death" (Albright, "Rivers," 171; cf. Job 33:18).

bukru ("firstborn son")[184] automatically grows up to be a "prosperous . . . wealthy lord" (*ešērū*[185] . . . *bēl mešrū*).[186] Indeed, he insists, only the *nakdu* ("vigilant man")[187] possesses the skill-set necessary to achieve *ṭuḫdum* ("prosperity").[188] This prompts the "sufferer/sceptic" to cry out:

ku-ši-ri še-te-qu e-et-ti-iq mu-tu-t[i]	My success vanishes,[189] my "half-portion" relocates;[190]

184. *BWL* 70.19. The editors of *CAD* insist that even though the cognates בכר, ܒܟܪ, بكر, and Ug *bkr* (*CAT* 1.14.6.25) all signify "first-born," there is "no indication that such is the nuance in Akkadian" (*CAD* B.310). Yet since the editors of *HAL* disagree (*HAL* 125), it seems more than likely that *bukru* in line 19 counterbalances *aḫurrû* in line 9.

185. *BWL* 70.19. One of Marduk's "Fifty Names" in *Enūma Eliš* is *šá ri-i-ta maš-qí-ta uš-te-eš-še-ru*, "the one who makes pasture and watering holes plentiful" (*Ee* 7.59).

186. *BWL* 70.20. N.B. the prominence of the wealth motif in Torah; e.g., in the Joseph novella (Gen 47:13–19; cf. Sadler, "Genesis," 131). In a prayer to Ištar the supplicant prays that *ša im-nu-uk-ki meš-ra-a lu-uṣ-ṣip dum-qa lu-uk-šu-da ša šu-me-lu-uk-ki*, "From your right (hand) may I receive wealth (and) from your left hand good things" (*AGH* 62.32). Lambert (*BWL* 303, n. 20) reads *namrû* in 70.20 from *marā'u* ("to fatten up"; cf. מריא, Isa 1:11), taking it as "a jibe at the plumpness of the wealthy in the same spirit as when Amos calls the opulent Samaritan ladies 'cows of Bashan' (Amos 4:1)." Also the term *lamassu* in the next line (70.21) Lambert reads as "a common expression for being successful" (*BWL* 303, n. 21).

187. *BWL* 70.22, defining this term from the root *naqādu* ("to be alert, anxious") instead of *nakādu* ("to palpitate, worry"). As a general rule the slothful do not *produce* anything. Cf. גם מתרפה במלאכתו אח הוא לבעל משחית, "the slacker in his 'work' is akin to a vandal" (Prov 18:9, lit., "is brother to a lord of destruction"; cf. below).

188. *BWL* 70.22. Von Soden (*AHw* 1393) translates *ṭuḫdum* as "*überreichliche Fülle*" ("overwhelming fullness"). N.B. that one of Marduk's "Fifty Names" is *mu-ṭaḫ-ḫi-du ú-ri-sin*, "the one who makes their stables prosper abundantly" (*Ee* 6.124; cf. Seri, "Names," 507–19).

189. *BWL* 72.28. Lambert (*BWL* 72.28) reads *ši-ti-qa*, but Oshima (*Theodicy*, 30) reads *še-te-qu* (with the commentary), taking it as a G stative form of *šêtu*, "to escape, vanish." That which "escapes" is *kušīru*, the final element in the traditional expression *ina še-e-ri du-un-qi ina mu-uṣ-la-li ni-me-li ina šum-še-e ku-ši-ru* ("in the morning prosperity, at noon profit, at sunset success") habitually concluding prayers to Sin, Ninurta, and Marduk (cited from Sidursky, "Prayers," 570.18′–20′).

190. *BWL* 72.28. Oshima (*Theodicy*, 30, n. 193) plausibly suggests that *e-te-ti-iq* is the result of a scribe's insertion (distracted by the previous word *ši-ti-qa*) of a *ti* sign between *te* and *iq*, obscuring the "fact" that the root is *etēqu*, "to transfer, relocate" (cf. *CAD* E.384–95). Should *mu-tu-t[i]* (Oshima) be preferred over *mu-tu-r[i]* (Lambert), then what likely "relocates" (*etēqu*) is "half" of the "sufferer/sceptic's" estate.

ku-bu-uk-ku i-te-niš	(My) power dwindles,[191]
ba-ṭi-il iš-di-ḫu	(my) income fades.[192]

Baffled and irritated, he asks:

ak-kat-ti bēl pa-an ša	Does the landlord[193] building
uṣ-ṣu-bu-šú na-ḫa-šú	his fortune[194]
[aq-r]a-a ṣa-ri-ri i-ḫi-ṭa	Weigh out rare-and-valuable
a-na ^{D}*ma-mi*	gold for Mami?[195]

Before the "friend" can reply, however, the "sufferer/sceptic" blurts out that "regular sacrifices to the goddess"[196] are part of his religious routine, solemnly insisting (with characters like the "pious sufferer" in Ludlul and the namesake of Tobit)[197] that whatever his flaws, religious infidelity is not one of them.[198]

Responding to this testimony, the "friend" then issues a warning:

gi-šim-ma-ru iṣ [ma]š-re-e	O date-palm, tree of wealth,[199]
a-ḫi aqr[u]	esteemed brother . . .

191. *BWL* 72.29. Erra argues that even though a few city-dwellers are *puggulat ku-bu-ku-uš* ("mighty in power"), they hardly compare to the rugged, self-sustaining power of field-dwellers (*Erra* 1.55; Moore, *WealthWatch*, 91–94). N.B. the *enēšu*// *lapānu* ("to be poor") word-pair in *BWL* 74.71.

192. *BWL* 72.29. A business which is *išdiḫu* ("income-producing, profitable") is by definition proactively engaged in *šadāḫu* ("moving forward").

193. *BWL* 74.52. If *bēl pa-ni* is equivalent to *bēl makkūri* (NÍG-GA), as Lambert suggests (*BWL* 74), then "lord of property/landlord" is preferable to "*nouveau riche*" (*BWL* 75.52) or "rich man" (Oshima, *Theodicy*, 19).

194. *BWL* 74.52. One of Marduk's "Fifty Names" includes the epithet *mu-na-ḫiš da-ád-me*, "the one who enriches humanity" (*Ee* 7.66).

195. *BWL* 74.53. On *ḫâṭu* cf. *kaspa ša ina pāniya ana PN kî a-ḫi-ṭu la taddissu*, "you did not give PN the silver at my disposal after I had it 'weighed out'" (*BIN* 1.94.37). Elsewhere this deity is called *tab-sú-ut ili*^{MEŠ} *e-ri-iš-tam* ^{D}*ma-mi . . . ba-ni-a-at a-wi-lu-ti*, "Wise ^{D}Mami, midwife of the gods . . . humanity's creator" (*Atr* 1.193).

196. *BWL* 74.55 (*[ak-]ru-ub sat[tu]k-kēe il-tim-ma*). Most of these offerings are agrarian in nature. Cf. *suluppē . . . ana* SÁ.DUG$_4$ *ša Šamaš ana Ebabbar bēlu liddin*, "May the lord give dates as an 'offering' for Šamaš at (his temple in) Ebabbar" (YOS 3.102.9).

197. Tob 1:6–8 (cf. Moore, *WealthWarn*, 142–55).

198. *[ak-]la-ma-a nin-da-ba-a*, "[D]o I hold back offerings?" (*BWL* 74.54). Contrast this with the satirical comment of a "slave" to his "master" on how to "worship" one's deity: *ila tu-lam-mad-su-ma ki-i kalbi arki-ka it-ta-na-lak*, "Can you teach your god to run after you like a dog?" (*BWL* 148.60).

199. *BWL* 74.56. Citing Borger ("Weihe," 171, 176), Jiménez (*Poems*, 193) contends

gi-riš ina u_4*-um la ši-ma-ti i-qa-am-me-šu ma-al-ku*	The king tends to burn at the stake[200]
gi-is maš-re-e bel pa-ni ša qur-ru-nu ma-ak-ku-ru	Any landlord who rashly stockpiles his own wealth.[201]
gi-ir-ri an-nu-tu-ú i-ku-šu a-la-ka taḫ-ši-iḫ	Do you wish the same fate?
gi-mil du-um-qí ša ili da-ra-a ši-te-ʾ-e	Compensate the eternal ones![202]

Finally the "sufferer/sceptic" (like Job)[203] scolds his "friend" for succumbing to a worldview so naïve:

il-lu nu-us-su-ku mi-lik-ka d[am-qu]	Dear friend, you do share profitable advice,[204]
il-te-en zik-ra mut-ta-ka lut-t[i-ir]	But let me remind you that sometimes even

that "according to Mesopotamian tradition, the palm is the king of the trees," and that its symbolism is strong enough to provide Sennacherib the title, "date palm of Aššur," not to mention its association with Ištar who in one NA hymn is called "palm tree, daughter of Nineveh, stag of the lands" (Livingstone, *Poetry*, text #7). In the annals of Sargon II the ^{GIŠ}*immaru* is called *balti nagišunu*, "the wealth of their region" (cf. Lie, *Sargon*, 335; Porter, *Trees*, 18), and Giovino (*Tree*, 135) finds it significant that *BWL* 74.63 "links the Akkadian words *mašrû/mešrû* ('wealth/prosperity') with the palm tree."

200. *BWL* 74.64. The "friend" compares this punishment to that doled out to wild donkeys trampling village crops and/or carnivorous lions devouring village livestock (lines 59–62). Citing a line from the Instructions of Šuruppak (NI-ZUḪ PIRIĜ NA-NAM UL-DAB$_5$ SAĜ NA-NAM, "the thief is a lion, and when caught, the thief is actually a slave"), Oshima (*Theodicy*, 34) proposes that the "lion"-saying here "refers to the fact that when livestock is stolen," the ancients "view the big cats not only in terms of their strength, but also in terms of their thieving acts" (cf. Alster, *Wisdom*, 62).

201. *BWL* 74.63. The noun *makkūru* derives from *makāru* ("to do business, buy"; a *bīt makkūri* is a "house of business/treasury"). Some of the Hittite *išḫiul* texts illustrate this "taxation" mentality more directly. Should the "royal granary" (LUGAL-*wa-aš* ARÀḪ-*an*) be burglarized, e.g., it is the "men of the city" (LÚ^{MEŠ} URU-*LÌ*) who must "compensate" (*šar-ni-in-kán-zi*) the king for his loss (*KUB* 13.9+40.62.3–10; cf. below).

202. *BWL* 74.66. On Akk *dārû* as "eternal" cf. Ug *dr* (*DULAT* 279–80), Heb דור (*HAL* 209), Syr ܕܪ, Arab دور (*DMWA* 299). On *gimillu* as "compensation," cf. *[aš]šum gi-mil dumqi epē [ša] tīda*, "for you know what it means to receive compensation" (*KAR* 297.8 + 256.9).

203. E.g., Job 21:17, 20.

204. That is, the "sufferer/sceptic" rarely allows his setbacks to push him beyond the point where he no longer recognizes that which is "profitable" (*dumqu*). Socioeconomic notions rooted in and correlating with Akk *dumqu* permeate the Babylonian Theodicy (*CAD* D.180–83).

il-la-ku ú-ru-uḫ dum-qí la muš-te-'-u ì-l[i]	Those who are prosperous neglect the god,[205]
il-tap-ni i-te-en-šú muš-te-mi-qu šá ì[l-ti]	While those petitioning the goddess remain poor and homeless.[206]

Acknowledging his "naïveté,"[207] the "sufferer/sceptic" nevertheless begins to wonder (a) whether the life assigned to him "yokes (him) to state service as a slave,"[208] and (b) whether his indentured servitude somehow correlates with the "deity's decision to impose poverty instead of wealth."[209] To this the "friend" replies that even though he usually finds him to be "rational" (*kina ra-áš*), he now wonders whether his suffering has driven him over the edge into some dark realm of "irrational fantasy" (*la mur-qa*),[210] or worse, caused him to reject altogether "the cosmic plans of the gods."[211] Cloaking himself in the mantle of asceticism,[212] the "sufferer/sceptic" then responds by suggesting to his friend that an even more radical response lurks on the horizon:

205. *BWL* 74.70. This complaint occurs often in the speeches of "pious sufferers"; e.g., Jeremiah asks Yhwh, מדוע דרך רשעים צלחה ("Why does the way of the wicked prosper?" Jer 12:1).

206. *BWL* 74.71. Citing several parallels, Lambert (*BWL* 303, n. 19) argues that *ītenšu* in *BWL* 74.71 and *itnušu* in *BWL* 74.275 "are not expressions for physical weakness, but for impecuniosity." The list of compliant birds attacking violent ones (*DA* 1.7–9), and Jeremiah's lament (12:1–7) attest to the probability that expectational inversion is one of the primary factors responsible for challenging the "old wisdom" (cf. Assmann, *Ma'at*, 72; Kruger, "Scenarios," 59–61).

207. *BWL* 76.72 (*ligimû*). This term pops up again in 76.128.

208. *BWL* 76.74 (*il-ku ša la né-me-li a-šá-aṭ ab-šá-nu*). Likely this is another reference to taxation.

209. *BWL* 76.75 (*il-ta-kan* DINGIR *ki-i maš-re-e ka-tu-ta*).

210. *BWL* 76.78 (lit., "nonsensical").

211. *BWL* 76.79 (*ú-ṣur-ti i-li ta-na-ṣu*). Lambert (*BWL* 77) reads "blaspheme against your god's designs." Noting that Akk *uṣurtu* often translates Sum GIŠ.ḪUR, Farber Flügge (*Inanna*, 183) notes that GIŠ.ḪUR closely parallels ME, the Sum *Leitwort* used to represent the fundamental elements of the cosmos Enki presents to Inanna and Inanna tries to smuggle into the Netherworld (*ID* 13–63; cf. Moore, *WealthWarn*, 12).

212. Oshima (*Theodicy*, xlvii) thinks the Babylonian Theodicy "offers a degree of consolation for unrewarded piety," but Lambert's (*BWL* 65) reading focuses on the theological question: "Both 'sufferer' and 'friend' begin by assuming that the gods are responsible for maintaining justice among men. They end by admitting that these very same gods make men prone to injustice. In a sense the real problem is shelved."

bi-i-ta lu-ud-di	I will abandon my home;
bi-šá-a a-a aḫ-ši-iḫ	I will no longer crave possessions.[213]

He ponders whether he should

bé-e-ra lu-up-ti a-ga-a lu-maš-šèr	Open the mountain passes and release the water,[214]
bi-it-bi-ti-iš lu-ter-ru-ba lu-ni-'i bu-bu-ti	Drive hunger away from every home,[215]
bi-r-iš lu-u-te-e'-lu-me su-le-e lu-ṣa-a-[a-ad]	And though famished, patrol the streets.[216]

Like the distraught king Gilgamesh,[217] he begins to imagine a future in which he might

bi-ir-ta lu-ul-lik né-sa-a-ti lu-ḫu-uz	Take to the road and travel great distances,[218]
be-e-ra ki-di šar-ra-qiš [lu-u]r-tap-pu-ud	Roaming[219] the countryside like a bandit.[220]

213. *BWL* 76.133–34. The *bītu/bīšu* ("house/possessions") word-pair occurs elsewhere; e.g., in the apodosis *ana bītim šuāti še'am kaspam u bīšam inaddin*, "let him pay for the house with grain, silver, or personal possessions" (*CH* L67+a; Richardson, *Laws*, 66).

214. *BWL* 78.138. Like *ašîš* in 70.1, *bēru* is another polyphonic root, meaning (a) "choice, select"; (b) "remote, distant"; and/or (c) "mile/measure of distance" (*CAD* B.207–11). Cf. *ḫuršāni be-ru-ti ša GN kīma qê lusellit̩*, "I made a cut through the distant mountains (like) a taut string" (*Tn* 30.17.31).

215. Cf. the proverb *bi-ru-ú-um bit a-gur-ri i-pal-la-aš*, "A starving man will break into a solid brick house" (*BWL* 235.19–20).

216. *BWL* 78.140. Guillaume (*Finance*, 99) contends (*a là* Albertz, "Theodizee," 349–72) that this text "uses the *topos* of the hunger of the poor and attributes it to the rise of a new rich class."

217. George, *Gilgamesh*, 91–137.

218. *BWL* 78.137 (cf. *GE* 9.1–4; Moore, *WealthWatch*, 71).

219. *BWL* 78.139. Near the end of *GE* the protagonist (Gilgamesh) reverts to an Enkidu-like role as a "roamer (*rapādu*) of the wilderness (*ṣēru*)"—the so-called "Robin Hood option" (Hilton, "Origins," 197–210). This phrase, repeated ten times on tablet 10, reprises Šamḫat's (the prostitute) words to Enkidu on tablet 1 (*GE* 1:208).

220. Cf. the similar fatalistic tone in the proverb *lu-uš-kun ik-ki-mu lu-ut-tir-ma man-nu i-nam-din*, "If I put things in storage, I shall be robbed. If I squander, who will give to me?" (*BWL* 241.45–47).

Victor Hurowitz wonders whether the "friend's" final response to all this betrays a curious hint of cautious agreement.[221] Maintaining that the "law of rich and poor" beneficently guides the cosmos "since ancient times,"[222] the "friend" nevertheless wonders whether the gods Enlil,[223] Enki,[224] and Mami[225] might in some way be responsible for endowing humankind with "twisted speech" (*itguru dabābu*)[226] in order to "flatter the fortunes of the wealthy" (*ša šarî idabbubū dumqišu*) while "humiliating the poor like thieves" (*šarraqiš ulammanū dunnumâ amēlu*).[227] Whether an explanation like this satisfies this "sufferer/sceptic," however, is as difficult to ascertain as whether or not Yhwh's whirlwind speeches satisfy Job.[228]

Takayoshi Oshima, on the other hand, suggests that the message of the "friend" boils down to three points: (a) human beings do not (indeed, cannot) understand the gods' plans;[229] (b) every creature must nonetheless seek divine blessing through prayer, ritual, and sacrificial offering because (c) wealth achieved via godlessness never lasts.[230] On this last point the words of this "sufferer/sceptic" seem to resonate with those of another "sufferer":

הכי אמרת יהבו לי	Have I ever said, "Give me something?"
ומכחכם שחדו בעדי	Or, "From your wealth offer me a bribe?"[231]

221. Hurowitz, "Theodicy," 778. Krüger ("Poems," 186) thinks not so much of "agreement" as "concession."

222. *BWL* 80.198. Lambert (*BWL* 81) offers no translation, but von Soden ("Weisheitstexte," 153, followed by Oshima, *Theodicy*, 37) reads "ein Gesetz seit jeher sind Reichtum ebenso wie Armut" ("a law in which wealth means just as much as poverty").

223. *BWL* 88.276. According to the ancient commentary to the Babylonian Theodicy, ^{D}Narru is equivalent to ^{D}Enlil (cited in Hurowitz, "Theodicy," 777).

224. *BWL* 88.277. According to the god-list found on *CT* 25.33.16 (published by Civil, "Chariot," 9) ^{D}KA^{ZU}-LUM-GAR^{MAR} = ^{D}É-*a*.

225. *BWL* 88.278 (cf. *Atr* 1.193).

226. *BWL* 88.279.

227. *BWL* 88.281, 283. Lambert (*BWL* 89.283) reads "they harm a poor man like a thief"; Oshima (*Theodicy* 25.283) reads "they treat the *pitiable (man)* badly like a thief." Cf. James' similar approach to the poverty-wealth polarity (Jas 2:1–9; cf. below).

228. Job 38:1—41:34. Schifferdecker (*Whirlwind*, 2) argues that Yhwh's whirlwind speeches "provide an answer to Job's situation," just not the answer he wants to hear.

229. Cf. the proverb *ṭe*$_4$*-im ili ul il-lam-mad . . . mim-mu ili a-na a-* . . . , "The will of a god cannot be understood; the way of a god cannot be known" (*BWL* 265.7–8).

230. Oshima, *Theodicy*, xxii–xxv. On the problem of "wicked wealth," cf. Prov 13:22; Sir 4:27—5:8; 1 En 94.8–10; Luke 6:43–45; Jas 5:1–5 (discussion below).

231. Job 6:22.

אם אשמח כי רב חילי	If I were to rejoice because of my great wealth,
הוא עון	Would that be wrong?[232]

In short, the Babylonian Theodicy engages the "poverty-wealth" continuum in stages. At first the "sufferer/sceptic" passively laments the poverty he sees resulting from the loss of his "progenitor" (*zārû*).[233] This then escalates into active lamentation over his loss of "power," "half-portion," "income," and "success."[234] Next he targets what he perceives to be the vulnerable chinks in the armor of his traditionalist "friend," particularly his inability (or unwillingness) to admit that poverty can occur randomly without regard for religious affiliation or involvement-level.[235] Finally, after the "friend's" Eliphaz-like accusations,[236] the "sufferer/sceptic" abandons organized society altogether, much like the Babylonian king Nebuchadnezzar[237] and the Saxon "gentleman"-turned-outlaw Robin Hood.[238]

Šamaš Hymn

This first millennium poem praises the sun-deity for many things, but not least his role as *chef d'entreprise*.[239] As the primary god of justice in the Babylonian pantheon,[240] Šamaš is not only the *savior* of the cheated; he is their *avenger*:[241]

232. Job 31:25, 28 (cf. below).

233. *BWL* 70.9.

234. *BWL* 72.28–29.

235. *BWL* 74.70–71.

236. Cf. Job 15:1–4; Moore (*Babbler*, 216–23) and below.

237. Dan 4:30–34. Most agree that this biblical portrayal more accurately depicts the experience of King Nabonidus (cf. Sack, "Nabonidus," 973).

238. *BWL* 78.137–39. On *šarrāqiš* ("benevolent bandit"), von Soden (*AHw* 1187) translates "Dieb" ("thief"). Grünewald (*Bandits*, 59–61) lists Eunous, Cleon, and Comanus as Mediterranean examples of the "benevolent bandit."

239. "Supervisor of business transactions" (Foster, *Muses*, 627). As Reiner ("Literature," 307) observes, the Šamaš Hymn appears alongside several other first millennium hymns, each approximately two hundred lines long (e.g., the Ištar Hymn, the Nabu Hymn, the Hymn to the Queen of Nippur, and the Gula Hymn).

240. Charpin ("Solar," 66–82) argues that Šamaš shares his concern for justice with Sîn, Ištar, and to a lesser extent Hadad (cf. Roberts, *Pantheon*, 13–14, 18–19, 31–34, 48, 51–52).

241. Resnick and Curtis (*Justice*, 18–19). Jastrow (*Civilization*, 198) recognizes that "the sun-gods are always associated in the religious literature of Babylonia with justice," and von Soden (*Orient*, 180) notes that Šamaš "comes to be much more widely

na-din kas-pa a-na šid-di ḫab-bi-lu mi-na-a ut-tar	What does the financier[242] gain who invests in corrupt trading ventures?[243]
uš-ta-ka-zab a-na né-me-li-ma ú-ḫal-laq kīsa	His profits vanish and his capital dries up.[244]
na-din kas-pa a-na šid-di rūqūti mu-ter ištēn šiqla	The financier who invests abroad, yet occasionally gives back a shekel,[245]
ṭa-a-bi eli ^{D}*Šamaš balāṭa ut-[tar]*	Is pleasing to Šamaš, the "profits provider."[246]
ṣa-bit ^{GIŠ}*zi-ba[ni-ti e-piš ṣ]i-lip-ti*	The merchant who handles the scales fraudulently,[247]
muš-te-nu-u [a-b]a-an ki-i-si u-[ú]-šap-pal	Who rigs the scales by tampering with the weights,[248]

venerated throughout the land in the OB period than the Sumerian UTU."

242. *BWL* 132.103 (lit., "one who provides silver").

243. *BWL* 132.103 (lit., "who gives money to that which borders on criminality").

244. *BWL* 132.104 (repeated verbatim in 132.109). Lambert (*BWL* 123) thinks the components of this line come originally from the incantation literature, but N.B. that in *Lud* 2.26 the word-pair here, *nēmelu//kīsu*, parallels the word-pair *nēmelu//tatturu* ("profit//wealth"), thereby supporting Polanyi's assessment ("Trading," 16) that ancient Babylon is "a capitalistically-minded business community in which king and god alike engage in profiteering, making the best of their chances in lending money at usury and imbuing a whole civilization with the spirit of money-making."

245. *BWL* 132.105 (i.e., "a sales tax"). The Hittite *Song of Release* shows a devotee giving the storm-god 1 GÍN KÙ.BABBAR, "one shekel of silver" (*KBo* 32.15.2.4′). Queen Ašmunikkal exempts several groups from the *šaḫḫan* ("property tax") and *luzzi* ("utilities tax") as long as they contribute something to the É.NA_4 ("royal mausoleum," *KUB* 13.8.1–6). Aphergis (*Empire*, 176–77) documents the prevalence of such taxes in first millennium Uruk, and Fried ("Exploitation," 161) argues that Neh 5:5 refers to the selling of children to pay the rent (the *ilku*; *CAD* I-J.73); i.e., that the מדת המלך in Neh 5:4 refers to the "king's tax" typically required on land loaned out to subjects by landlords indebted to the king.

246. *BWL* 132.106. *CAD* B.52 defines *balāṭu* as "profit" only in OA texts, but this OB text obviously challenges this. N.B. that in Q 2.276 Alla يمحق الزتا ويزبى الصدقت, "destroys usury, but blesses almsgiving."

247. *BWL* 132.107 (*ṣa-bit* ^{GIŠ}*zi-ba-ni-ti*, lit., "the manipulator of the balances," *CAD* Ṣ.5). Akk *ṣiliptu* derives from *ṣalāpu* ("to cut across, dissect"); cf. the phrase *ša libbi-ša ṣa-al-pu*, "the one whose heart is dissected," i.e., "the one who is vacuously hollow" (i.e., "evil," *MSL* 12.185.8).

248. *BWL* 132.108. Foster (*Muses*, 631) sees this referring to merchants who "buy

uš-ta-ka-zab a-na né-me-li-ma *ú-ḫal-laq kīsa*	Will watch his profits wash away and his capital dry up.[249]

Honest merchants, however, can look forward to a different type of future:

ša ki-ni ṣa-bit ^{GIŠ}*zi-ba-ni-ti* *ma-ʾ-da*	But the merchant who handles the balances honestly[250]
mim-ma šum-šu ma-ʾ-di *qí-ša-aš-šu*	Will accumulate all kinds of abundance.[251]

Finally, the hymn closes with a "blessing-curse" formula similar to that found in treaties:[252]

ṣa-bit sūti e-piš ṣi-l[íp-ti]	The merchant who fraudulently manipulates the scales,
na-din ši-qa-a-ti a-na bi-ri-i *mu-šad-din at-ra*	Who extends loans at one rate, then demands payment at another,[253]
ina la u_4*-me-šu ar-rat niši*^{MEŠ} *i-kaš-šad-su*	Will eventually be ensnared by the people's curse.[254]
ina la a-dan-ni-šú i-šá-al *i-raš-ši bil-ta*	If he demands payment prematurely he will be held accountable,[255]

with a heavy standard and pay back with a light one, taking advantage of varying local standards of weight."

249. *BWL* 132.109 (repeated verbatim in 132.104).

250. *BWL* 132.110. Resnick and Curtis (*Justice*, 19) publish a third millennium image of merchants using scales/balances.

251. Snell ("Umma," 45–50; *Ledgers*, 115–207) painstakingly illuminates the sociohistorical and socioeconomic context of this hymn.

252. Most blessing-curse formulae appear at the conclusion of treaties (e.g., *KAI* 224.1–27; Deut 27–28; cf. Karavites, *Treaty*, 4–7), but one Hittite *išḫiul* text (*KBo* 16.24+16.25.1.1–6) *begins* with a curse (cf. below).

253. Garfinkle ("Lending," 2) notes that "few topics are as richly documented in the cuneiform record as the practice of borrowing and lending." Cf. the fifth century Aramaic contract dictating the terms of a "loan" (זפת) extended to Yehûḥan (daughter of Mešullak) at the standard (!) rate of sixty percent (*CAP* 10.2–3).

254. *BWL* 132.114 (lit., "in not his day"). Cf. *šarram ú-ka-aš-ša-du-šu-ú*, "they will ensnare the king" (*YOS* 10.31.8.16).

255. Similar socioeconomic stipulations appear in *CH* §§112–26.

makkur-šú ul i-be-el IBILA-*šú*	His heir will assume no control over his property,[256]
a-na bīti-šú ul ir-ru-bu šu-nu aḫḫu^{MEŠ}-*šú*	And his brothers will not inherit his estate.[257]

On the other hand,

um-ma-ni ki-nu na-din še-em i-na [kab-ri]m pān u-šat-tar dum-qu	The honest entrepreneur who increases his wealth by extending loans at fair rates[258]
ṭa-a-bi eli ^{D}*Šamaš balāṭa ut-[tar]*	Is pleasing to Šamaš, the "profits provider."[259]
ú-rap-pa-áš kim-ta meš-ra-a i-ra-aš-š [i]	Extends (his) family, compounds (his) wealth
ki-ma mê^{MEŠ} *naq-bi da-ri-i zēr-šu da-[ri]*	And causes his seed to spurt like water from an eternal spring.[260]

256. *BWL* 132.116. Sum IBILA ("heir") accurs near the end of the "Praise Poem of Iddi-Dagan": "O Iddi-Dagan, mighty king, king of Isin, Sumer and Akkad . . . You are the mighty 'IBILA'" (ETCSL 2.5.3.2.78). N.B. that *bīt makkūri* means "storehouse" (*CAD* M/1.137).

257. *BWL* 132.117 (lit., "enter his house," the same idiom in *Lud* 1.62). Cf. במותכה יפרח לעולם זכרכה ואחריתכה תנחל שמחה, "When you die your memory will blossom forever, and your successor will inherit joy" (4Q16.2.7–8).

258. *BWL* 132.118. N.B. that charging interest is not the problem, only charging too much and/or lying about it. Oppenheim (*Mesopotamia*, 88) thinks that "an appreciation for Mesopotamian economics" involves recognizing that the charging of "interest" is a "trait peculiar to Mesopotamia, a characteristic feature that is rejected in regions west of Mesopotamia just as much as, e.g., the practice of drinking beer instead of wine, or using sesame instead of olive oil."

259. *BWL* 132.119 (cf. the same epithet above in 106). Hurowitz ("Allusion," 34) translates " . . . the honest merchant/creditor who weighs out (loans of) corn by the maximum standard, thus multiplying kindness; it is pleasing to Šamaš, and he will add to his life."

260. *BWL* 132.121. In his third משל-oracle (Num 24:3–9) Balaam depicts Israel as a place where יזל מים מדליו וזרעו במים רבים, "water flows from its (Israel's) buckets, its seed (blessed) with abundant water" (24:7). Cf. the Akk proverb *a-di ša-ra[ḫi-ka] ina du-uq-qú ša i-l[i-ka] ana a-ḫi i-d[i-in] . . . du-um-qi šú-ú e-l[i] e-ša-am-ma ul i[l-lak-mi]*, "So long as you thrive give to your brother what you receive from your god" so that "this prosperity might stay with you and not go elsewhere" (*BWL* 271.8–15).

Although beautifully worded, these stipulations break little new ground. Frequently they appear in treaties, lawcodes, and related documents.[261] To cite just one example, the legislators responsible for compiling *CH* (dedicated to Šamaš!) plow quite similar terrain.[262] Commenting on *tamkāru* ("trader/merchant") in the Šamaš Hymn, Wilfrid Lambert suggests that the stipulations listed between lines 69 and 139 apply to the "trader who travels into foreign lands,"[263] but William Hallo disagrees, arguing that the sun-deity's directive is broadly designed "to catch out the dishonest merchant" *wherever* he may be, "whether at home or on the road far from home."[264]

Dialogue of Pessimism

The Babylonian Dialogue of Pessimism consists of several conversations between a "gentleman" (*awīlu*) and his "slave" (*wardu*) in which he (a) declares his desire to do something (to which the slave responds by listing the advantages of doing so), then (b) completely reverses himself (to which the slave dutifully responds by listing the advantages of *not* doing so).[265] It's a strange text, quite unlike any other from the ancient Near East.[266] Some read

261. In addition to CH, the main lawcodes are Codex Ur-Nammu, Codex Lipit-Ištar, Codex Eshnunna, the Middle Assyrian Laws, and the Hittite Laws (cf. Westbrook, "Codes," 201–22; "Edict," 641). Sallaberger ("Lipit-Ištar," 7) traces the literary-historical development within the lawcodes of Ur-Nammu, Lipit-Ištar, and Hammurabi (cf. Roth, *Law*).

262. Cf. above, esp. the laws governing merchandise and trade (*CH* §66–115). Similar socioeconomic stipulations speckle the lawcodes of Lipit-Ištar and Ešnunna (*ANET* 159–63), and N.B. that in Qur'an Allah واحل البيع وحزم الزبا, "permits trade, but forbids usury" (Q 2.275).

263. *BWL* 121. Von Soden (*AHw* 1314–15) reads "Kaufmann, Händler, Finanzier." Lambert cites Oppenheim ("Merchants," 6–17) to delimit these stipulations to seafaring trade, but Foster (*Muses*, 627), citing Nakata ("Merchants," 90–100), is not nearly so restrictive. Potts ("Trade," 1451–63) surveys possible sociohistorical contexts.

264. Hallo (*Origins*, 74). Hallo (75) summarily finds this text "invoking Šamaš as both the protector and the critical observer of the 'entrepreneur' (*ummānu*), the 'traveling merchant' (*tamkāru*) and his 'apprentice' (*šamallû*)."

265. *BWL* 144–48. Nemet-Nejat ("Literature," 78) and Hartley ("Job," 353) call this text "The Obliging Slave." Each of its ten dialogues begins with the phrase *arad mitangurrani* ("Slave, listen to me!"), after which the slave responds by "obsequiously agreeing with him" (Nemet-Nejat, "Literature," 78). Thus thrown back-and-forth, readers soon find themselves tempted to ponder what Pleins (*Introduction*, 485) calls "the inevitable futility of existence" (cf. Bottéro, "Dialogue," 4–24; Loretz, *Qohelet*, 108–10).

266. For Zuckerman (*Job*, 245) "the tenor of this text is quite different from that of Job or, for that matter, any other text within the wisdom tradition."

it as more-or-less serious "philosophy," comparing it to Ludlul bēl nēmeqi, the Babylonian Theodicy, and/or Qohelet.[267] Others view it as clever social satire freckled with comedic "punch-lines."[268] Whatever the possibilities, the socioeconomic motifs animating these dialogues make a significant contribution to the ANE wisdom trajectory.[269]

Dialogue #7, for example,[270] explores the connection, however subtle, between religion and economics by identifying some of the more obvious similarities between "sacrifice" (*nīqu*) and "loan" (*qīptu*):

Gentleman: *arad mi-tan-gur-an-ni*	Slave, listen to me![271]
Slave: *an-nu-u be-lí an-nu-ú*	Here I am, my lord, here I am!
Gentleman: *ši-šìr di-kan-ni-ma mê*^{MEŠ} *ana qātē-ia*	Quickly, bring me water for my hands.[272]
bi-nam-ma niqâ ana ili-ia lu-pu-uš	Give it to me so that I may sacrifice to my god.[273]
Slave: *e-pu-uš be-lí e-pu-uš*	Sacrifice, my lord, sacrifice![274]

267. Ebeling ("Religion," 50); Pfeiffer ("Dialogue, 437–38); Ungnad ("Lebensphilosophie," 75). Langdon (*Wisdom*, 195) is evidently the first to call it The Babylonian Dialogue of Pessimism.

268. Böhl ("Religion," 493–94) calls it a "caricature." Speiser ("Servant," 104–5) calls it "satire" and Hurowitz ("Allusion," 33) calls it "a work of social satire." Nemet-Nejat ("Literature," 78, 79) calls it "contest literature" (like the texts in *BWL* 150–212). Regardless of genre, Foster (*Muses*, 923) sees in it something quite "original," while Lambert (*BWL* 139) simply calls it "an effective piece."

269. *BWL* 148.62–78. The adjective "pessimistic" well describes this text because unlike Ludlul and the Theodicy, its final dialogue (*BWL* 148.79–86) ends on a decidedly negative note (murder/suicide).

270. *BWL* 147.53–61. The dialogues in this text address a wide variety of topics: chariot-driving, dining, hunting, homemaking, revolution (*um-ma sa-ar-tu*, "the day of rebellion"), romance, public service (*um-ma* ú-*sa-tam*, "the day of assistance"), religious sacrifice, and wealth management.

271. *BWL* 146.53. Ungnad ("Lebensphilosophie," 74–75) notes that *magāru* often parallels *šēmu* ("to hear, obey"), a parallel Lambert utilizes (*BWL* 149) to translate "Servant, listen to me." Speiser, curiously, first reads "Slave, oblige me" ("Servant," 99) then later reads "Servant, obey me" (*ANET* 438).

272. *BWL* 146.54 (the same phrase repeats in 144.11). Unger (*Babylon*, 259) discusses the function of a minor deity at Esagila named Nādin-mê-qāti ("Bring water for my hands") whose function is to facilitate various hand-washing rituals.

273. *BWL* 146.55. Akk *niqû* ("sacrifice") appears in a list of activities alongside *lipit qāti ḫiniq immeri ni-iq ni-qi nēpešti bārûte*, "the ritual act, the killing of sheep, the offering of sacrifice, (and) the extispicy procedure" (*Maq* 7.125).

274. *BWL* 146.55. Lit., "Do it, my lord, do it."

amēlu ša niqâ ana ili-šú ip-pu-uš libba-šu ṭāb-šú	Anyone who sacrifices to his god enters into a good transaction,[275]
qip-tu eli qip-tu ip-pu-uš	Loan after loan.[276]
Gentleman: *e arad a-na-ku* ^{UDU}*niqâ ana ili-ia-a-ma ul ep-pu-uš*	No, slave, I will not offer sacrifice to my god.
Slave: *la te-pu-uš be-lí la te-pu-uš*	Do not sacrifice, my lord, do not sacrifice.
ila tu-lam-mad-su-ma li-i kalbi arki-ka it-ta-na-lak	Can you teach a deity to follow you like a puppy-dog?[277]
šum$_4$*-ma par-ṣi šum*$_4$*-ma ila la ta-šal šum*$_4$*-ma mim-ma šá-nam-ma ir-riš-ka*	Will he not still demand rituals from you or say, "Stop inquiring (of me)," or perhaps something else?[278]

Dialogue #8, though, plunges headlong into the world of financial management:

Gentleman: *arad mit-tan-gur-an-ni*	Slave, listen to me!
Slave: *an-nu-u be-lí an-nu-u*	Here I am, my lord, here I am!

275. *BWL* 146.56. Lit. "makes his heart good" (a common semitic idiom; cf. וייטב לבו, "his heart became good," Ruth 3:7). Foster (*Muses*, 925) reads "satisfying transaction"; Lambert (*BWL* 147.56) reads "is satisfied with the bargain"; Hartley ("Job," 353) reads "will be content."

276. *BWL* 146.57 (cf. the similar construction מועד במועד, "appointed time after appointed time," in 4Q416.1.3). "Office" is doubtless the best translation for *qīptu* in *Lud* 32.61, but the occurrence of *ḫubullu* ("debt, interest-bearing loan, interest," *CAD* Ḫ.216–18) in the immediate context (*BWL* 146.64) suggests the translation "loan" (*CAD* Q.262). Speiser ("Servant," 99) reads "investment upon investment." N.B. that *bēl qīpti* means "owner of merchandise" and *bīt qīpti* means "toll-booth" (*CAD* Q.263).

277. *BWL* 148.60. Lambert (*BWL* 326) finds this line to be the reverse of the sentiment found in an ingratiating prayer to Marduk: "I hang on to you like a small child to your belt; like a 'puppy' (*mūrānu*) I run after you" (*AGH* 92.9–12). Speiser ("Servant," 103) suggests that the "overall sense is, 'Be careful not to get your personal god into bad habits,' or in other words, 'One cannot teach an old god new tricks.'" Following Hartley ("Job," 353) the translation here reads this line as a question.

278. *BWL* 148.61. This satire on religious sacrifice practically borders on the asinine because, as Ristvet (*Ritual*, 27) points out, "religion may be realized through ritual, but it tends only to be meaningful to the extent that it is implicated in wider social processes, becoming the basis of a commonsense understanding of reality," esp. when it impacts "social and/or economic practices."

Gentleman: *um-ma-na lud-din*	I will extend loans as an investor.[279]
Slave: *ki-mi i-din be-lí [i-din]*	So invest, my lord, [invest]![280]
a-me-lu ša um-ma-na inamdinu-[n]u uṭṭat-su uṭṭat-su-ma ḫu-bul-lu-šu at-r[i]	For the investor who extends loans keeps his own grain intact while his investment turns a profit.[281]
Gentleman: *e arad a-na-ku u[m-m]a-nam-ma ul a-nam-d[in]*	No, slave, I will not extend loans as an investor.
Slave: *la ta-nam-din b[e-l]í la ta-nam-din*	Do not invest, my lord, do not invest!
na-da-nu ki-ma ra-a-m[e sin-niš-t]i	For extending a loan is like dating a woman,[282]
u tur-ru ki-ma a-la-di ma-ru	And reclaiming it is like giving birth to a child.[283]
uṭṭat-ka ik-k[a-lu u a-n]a ka-a-šá it-tam-na-za-[ru-ka]	It consumes your grain, eats into your profits,[284]

279. *BWL* 148.63. Lenzi (*Secrecy*, 378) recognizes that one of the primary functions of the *ummânu* in the service of a king is to "undergird royal authority" by textualizing the diviner's "*ad hoc* pronouncements from the divine realm" into a corpus of "secret knowledge," but N.B. that the *ummânu* also handles *qīptam bābtam* ("commercial loans," *AND* 124.9).

280. *BWL* 148.63 (lit., "so give, my lord, give").

281. *BWL* 148.64. Alongside "interest" *ḫubullu* can also mean "debt" or "interest-bearing loan," depending on context (*CAD* Ḫ.216–18). On *(w)atru* ("profit"), N.B. the derivative verb *(w)atāru* ("to increase") in the common economic epithet *kaspum i-té-er*, "(his) silver increased" (cited in *AHw* 1489). Cf. Ug *ytr*; Heb יתר; Aram יתר; Syr ܝܬܪ; Arab وتر—all meaning "to have left over, profit."

282. N.B. that "love" and "wealth" come together in Prov 5:7–12 (reading כח as "wealth" in 5:10). Doubtless it is no coincidence that Akk *râmu*, "to love," can also mean "to endow" (*CAD* R.133–47). Cf. the different moneylending rationale in the Instructions of Šuruppak: UR$_5$ TUKU NA-AN-BAD-E LU$_2$-BI CA-BA-E . . . KUR$_2$ ("You should not drive away a debtor; this will make him hostile toward you," ETCSL 5.6.1).

283. In other words, the time needed to collect an outstanding loan needs to be measured in months, not weeks.

284. *BWL* 148.68. Akk *kašû* can mean "increase" or "profit" (*CAD* K.294). Whether this particular group of "profit-eaters" refers to debtors, sons, or daughters is unclear, perhaps by intention.

ù ḫ [u-b]u-li uṭṭat-ka u-ḫal-la-qu-nik-[ka]	And downgrades the profit on your grain to a loss.[285]

Victor Hurowitz contends that the Šamaš Hymn and the Dialogue of Pessimism each "describe the actions as well as the rewards of two types of people: the honest merchant vs. the dishonest merchant."[286] The fact that so many structural, stylistic, and substantive parallels connect these texts together indicates to him that "the satirical text (Dialogue of Pessimism) is dependent upon and alludes to the liturgical work (Šamaš Hymn)."[287] Whether or not such dependence exists, each of these texts utilizes similar socioeconomic motifs for similar reasons.[288]

Anatolian Instructions

As in Mesopotamia, the contours of "wisdom" (Hit *ḫattatar*) in Anatolia can be difficult to trace,[289] even though, as Harry Hoffner emphasizes, it is "an essential part of the ideology of Hittite kingship."[290] Careful examination of the *išḫiul*-texts unearthed at Boğazköy (ancient Ḫattuša) in what is today the nation of Turkey, however, reveals a number of socioeconomic motifs unambiguously designed to address socioeconomic problems and concerns.[291]

285. *BWL* 148.69. Lambert reads "deprives you of the interest"; Foster (*Muses*, 929) reads "swindles you out of the interest." Given that *ḫalāqu* in the D form means "to cause a loss" (*CAD* Ḫ.38–39) the translation here incorporates this nuance.

286. Hurowitz, "Allusion," 34.

287. Hurowitz, "Allusion," 35.

288. Bottéro (*Mesopotamia*, 266) suggests that the Dialogue of Pessimism "does not get involved in blasphemy or mockery of the gods and their cults" because its intention is rather "to criticize the traditional religiosity of the milieu represented by its principal character, if not the 'pressure groups' hidden behind the representations of the gods."

289. Singer (*Prayers*, 17) speaks of "the conspicuous scarcity of Hittite wisdom literature," but Beckman ("Literature," 250–52) discusses Hittite proverbs, anecdotes and the Hurrian-Hittite "Song of Release" under the rubric "Wisdom Literature."

290. Hoffner, "Speech," 38. Cf. Taggar-Cohen ("Didactic," 45–64).

291. *Contra* Miller (*Instructions*, 12), Taggar-Cohen ("Hittite," 461–88) argues that "the *išḫiul* genre includes both the treaty texts and the instruction texts," but peremptorily excludes the *išḫiul* texts from the "wisdom" genre. Weinfeld ("Apodictic," 64–65) does something similar, designating these instructions a "literary type" associated not so much with "wisdom" as "apodictic law." Cf. Alaura ("Proverbs," 1–15).

Royal Reprimand

In one *išḫiul*-"instruction," for example, a young Hittite prince valiantly attempts to uphold the "word of my father" (i.e., the king)[292] by admonishing several of his father's friends to stop oppressing their employees:

šu-me-eš $^{\text{LÚ.MEŠ GIŠ}}$TUKUL *ta-me-eš-kat-te-ni a-pe-e-ia ka-ta-a[n . . .]*	You continually oppress your workers,[293] (to the point that) they start oppressing (others) . . . .[294]
ma-a-an A-BI tu-li-ia-aš ḫal-za-i nu-uš-ma-aš gu-la-ak-ku-wa-an ša-aḫ-zi na-at-ta	When my father convenes the assembly, will he not investigate your corruptions?[295]
$^{\text{LÚ.MEŠ}}$NA-ŠI ṢÍ-DI-TI$_4$-KU-NU-U *ka-a-ša-at-ta-wa*	Do you not see your servants,[296]
$^{\text{LÚ.MEŠ}}$NA-ŠI ṢÍ-DI-TI$_4$-KU-NU-U *da-me-eš-kat-te-ni*	Whom you habitually oppress,[297]
ta LUGAL-*i kar-di-mi-ia-at-tu-uš pe-eš$_{15}$-kat-te-ni*	And do you not see how your behavior enrages the king?[298]

292. *A-WA-A-AT A-BI-IA* (*KBo* 22.1.4′, 6′, 31′). Hoffner ("Anatolia," 561) and Beckman ("Assembly," 440) attribute this phrase to a "reigning king," but Miller (*Instructions*, 73) to a "prince."

293. *KBo* 22.1.3′, LÚ$^{\text{MEŠ GIŠ}}$TUKUL (lit. "men of the wooden tool"; cf. *HW* 283, "Arbeiter, Handwerker"). Beal ("Ḫatti," 304) reads "land tenants," arguing that these Sumerograms refer to "men who work for the government . . . and receive their pay in the form of land whose produce supports them" (so also Miller, *Instructions*, 75). Archi ("Hittites," 45) sees here the "population libre, indépendante de l'organisation du palais."

294. *KBo* 22.1.3′. In Babylonia, texts like Atraḫasis mythologize the master-servant // employer-employee polarity (*Atr* 1.1–6). In Anatolia, the Ḫattuša government expects to commandeer fifty percent of the workers in a given private household (*KBo* 16.54+*ABoT* 1.53.3.5′–15′).

295. *KBo* 22.1.16′–17′. Miller (*Instructions*, 75) translates *gullakuwant* as "corruption" (cf. *HED* K.236–37); Friedrich (*HW* 115) reads "verunreinigt" ("impurity"); Beckman ("Assembly," 441) reads "displeasing activity."

296. *KBo* 22.1.18′. Hoffner ("Grammar," 90) reads "provision carriers." Following Archi ("Hittites," 47), Miller (*Instructions*, 75) reads "pack-bearers." Following Marazzi ("Note," 127), Dardano ("Expressions," 372) reads "*contribuables*" ("taxpayers").

297. *KBo* 22.1.19′ (cf. the same root *damaš* in 22.1.3′).

298. *KBo* 22.1.20′. Hit *kartimmiwa* ("to become angry," *HW* 103).

Particularly infuriating to this young prince are the shady disguises these "gentlemen" hide behind to camouflage their corruption under a facade of "civic responsibility":

zi-ik-ka-wa ^{GIŠ}TUKUL *a-pa-aš-ša* ^{GIŠ}TUKUL *ma-a-an-ša-ma-aš*	You (gentlemen) are workers just as much as they are . . . .[299]
A-BI na-at-ta-ša-ma-aš LÚ^{MEŠ} DUGUD-*aš tup-pí* *ḫa-az-zi-an ḫar-zi*	Has not my father written a letter to you "gentlemen,"[300] (saying),
ka-a-ša-at-ta-wa ut-ni-ia *pa-it-te-ni*	"You traipse through your territory,
nu ŠA ^{LÚ}MAŠDA *e-eš-ḫar-še-et* *na-at-ta ša-an-ḫi-iš-kat-te-ni*	But do you ever seek to 'redeem the blood' of the poor?[301]
$^{\text{LÚ.MEŠ}}$NA-ŠI ṢÍ-DI-TI$_{4}$-ŠU *na-a-ta pu-nu-es-te-ni*	Do you ever try to engage your servants?
^{LÚ}*ḫa-ap-pí-na-an-da-aš* *i-iš-te-e-ni*	Or do you just do the rich man's bidding?[302]
pár-na-aš-ša pa-i-ši e-ez-ši *e-uk-ši pí-ia-na-az-zi-at-ta*	You go to his house, eat, drink, accept his gifts,[303]
^{LÚ}*a-ši-wa-an-da-na ši-e-et* *da-a-at-ti,*	But the plight of the poor you ignore,[304]

299. *KBo* 22.1.21′; i.e., "they may serve you, but you serve the king."

300. *KBo* 22.1.23′. Noting the appearance of $^{\text{LÚ.MEŠ}}$ DUGUD ("nobles/dignitaries") in *HC* §173 (*ANET* 195), Hoffner ("Anatolia," 561) applies this umbrella term to "judges" and "magistrates" conducting business on "the judicial level immediately below the king."

301. *KBo* 22.1.24′–25′. Hoffner ("Anatolia," 561) reads "investigate the murder"; Miller (*Instructions*, 75) reads "avenge the blood." The translation here (a) recognizes the payment of "compensation" (*šarnikziliya*) for the shedding of "blood" (*ešḫanant*) to bring about "redemption" (*waš-*) in other *išḫiul* texts (e.g., *KBo* 27.16.3–5), and (b) compares the socioeconomic roles enacted by the גאל-"redeemer" in Tanak, particularly the acquisition of property (Jer 32:6–8), the reacquisition of property (Lev 25:25), and the redemption of enslaved kinfolk (Lev 25:47–52).

302. *KBo* 22.1.26′–27′.

303. *KBo* 22.1.28′. Other *išḫiul* texts speak openly of "bribery" (Hit *maškan*, *KUB* 29.39+*KBo* 50.284.4.10–11; *KUB* 13.9+*KUB* 40.62.3.14′; cf. *HW* 138). Cf. Sum KADRA; Akk *katrû*; Dardano ("L'etimo," 3–12); Wilcke (*Law*, 37–41).

304. *KBo* 22.1.29′. Miller (*Instructions*, 331–32) lists several possibilities for *šiyet*, but Hoffner's translation seems the least problematic ("Anatolia," 561).

DI-IN-ŠU na-at-ta pu-nu-uš-ši nu ki-iš-ša-am	Never asking about *their* situation."[305]

Royal Reforms

Other *išḫiul* texts preserve royal edicts from indignant leaders addressing similar concerns. In one of these edicts King Tudḫaliya[306] returns from a season of military campaigning to find the residents in one of his cities victimized by "evil men" (*i-da-la-u-i-eš* UKU^{MEŠ}-*ši-iš*)[307] opportunistically invading his territory, pilfering his "feudal holdings" (*ú-pa-ti*$^{ḪI.A}$)[308] and enslaving his "laborers" ($^{LÚ.MEŠ}$*ša-ri-ku-wa-aš*).[309] Reacting to this banditry, he lays out several principles and procedures to help (re)establish some semblance of social, economic and political equilibrium.[310] In cases involving capital crimes, for example, the king stipulates:

ma-a-an e-eš-ḫa-na-aš-ša ku-iš-ki šar-ni-ik-zi-il	If someone pays compensation for blood[311]
pí-ia-an ḫar-zi nu-za-ta SAG.DU-*ZU wa-aš-ta*	And redeems himself from you,[312]

305. *KBo* 22.1.30′. Gazing into the future, the Sybilline Oracle imagines a pie-in-the-sky utopia in which people "do not carry out night robberies one against another, nor do they drive off herds of oxen and sheep and goats, nor does a neighbor remove his neighbor's landmarks, nor does a man of great wealth vex his lesser brother, nor does anyone afflict widows but rather assists them, ever ready to supply them with corn and wine and oil, and always the wealthy man among the people sends a portion of his harvest to those who have nothing" (*Sib. Or.* 3.238–45).

306. Miller (*Instructions*, 134–35) reads Tudḫaliya I (d. 1401 BCE); Westbrook and Woodard ("Edict," 641–42) read Tudḫaliya IV (d. 1209 BCE).

307. *KUB* 13.9+40.62.1.9. Cf. Westbrook and Woodard ("Edict," 642); Miller (*Instructions*, 136).

308. *KUB* 13.9+40.62.1.11.

309. *KUB* 13.9+40.62.1.11 (*HW* 235, 185). The same basic scenario recurs in Matt 24:45–51.

310. Bryce (*Kings*, 28–29) discusses the most likely historical context, but the tablet's broken condition complicates interpretation.

311. Cf. the idiomatic phrase *e-eš-ḫar-še-et ša-an-ḫi-iš-kat-te-ni* ("redeem the blood") in *KBo* 22.1.25′ (discussed above).

312. *KUB* 13.9+40.62.2.3. Von Schuler ("Königserlässe," 452) reads *wa-aš-ta* as a pret. 3 sg of *wašta* ("to transgress"), but the present translation reads a pret. 3 sg of *waš* ("to redeem") with Westbrook and Woodard ("Edict," 644–45), Marazzi and Gzella ("Bemerkungen," 71–78), and Miller (*Instructions*, 137, 348).

na-aš-šu A.ŠÀ.*LA*$_{12}$ *na-aš-ma* LÚ.ULÙ$_{19}$.LU	Whether it be a field or a person,[313]
na-aš-ta pa-ra-a Ú-UL ku-iš-ki tar-na-i	Let no one release it.[314]
ma-a-na-aš-za QA-DU DAM^{MEŠ}-ŠU DUMU^{MEŠ}-ŠU *da-a-an ḫar-zi*	If he (the recipient of the compensation) accepts these things along with (the murderer's) wives and children,
na-an-ši-iš-ta pa-ra-a tar-na-i	Then let it be given to him.[315]

Alongside murder, he also addresses the crime of larceny:

ma-a-an ta-i-zi-zi-la-aš-ša ku-iš-ki šar-ni-ik-ze-el pí-ia-an ḫar-zi	If someone pays compensation in response to a theft,
nu ma-a-an A.ŠÀ *na-aš-ta pa-ra-a* Ú-*UL tar-na-an-zi*	If it be a field, let them release it.[316]

Like the Mesopotamians, the Hittites distinguish between "gentlemen" and "slaves":[317]

ma-a-an ÌR-*ma da-ya-at na-an ta-i-az-zi-la-an-ni ḫar-zi*	If the thief is a slave and the bursar detains him,
na-aš ma-a-an ta-šu-wa-aḫ-ḫa-an-za	If the slave has been blinded
na-an-ši-iš-ta pa-ra-a Ù-*UL tar-na-an-zi*	Let them not release him (to his former master).

313. *KUB* 13.9+40.62.2.4.

314. *KUB* 13.9+40.62.2.5 (i.e., the "compensation"). Miller (*Instructions*, 136–37) argues that *parā tarnai*, the phrase repeatedly utilized in this *išḫiul* text, applies only to the "release" of one person to another, but Westbrook and Woodard ("Edict," 642) see here "new light on the mechanics of general debt release."

315. Cf. the similar stipulations in *HL* §7–18, 42–44.

316. Cf. *HL* §57–97, and N.B. that like Babylonian land (*CH* §36–37, see above), Anatolian land is too valuable to be treated like any other asset.

317. Qur'an goes a step further by distinguishing between believing and unbelieving slaves: "Whoever kills a believer 'by mistake' (خطا) should hand over a believing slave and pay 'blood-money' (ديه, cf. Tsafrir, *Liability*, 1–16). If the deceased is a believer from a hostile tribe, then it is appropriate to hand over a believing slave, but if the deceased is from a tribe with whom you are in 'covenant' (ميثاق), then you must hand over the blood-money and the believing slave" (Q 4.92).

ma-a-na-aš Ù-UL ta-šu-wa-aḫ-ḫa-an-za	But if he has not been blinded
na-an-ši-iš-ta pa-ra-a tar-na-an-zi	Let him be released to him.[318]
tak-ku EL-LAM-ma ku-iš-ki da-i-ia-zi	However, if a gentleman steals,
nu da-i-ia-zi-la-aš šar-ni-ik-ze-el	But (provides) compensation for the theft,
U-UL ta-šu-wa-aḫ-ḫa-an-zi . . .	He is not to be blinded.[319]

Another issue comes to light when the king informs the "men of the city" (LÚ.MEŠ URU-*LÌ*) that they are to "compensate" (*šar-ni-in-kán-zi*) the crown if or when the "royal granary" (LUGAL-*wa-aš* ARÀḪ-*an*) is plundered.[320] Should anyone try to sidetrack this compensation with a "bribe" (*ma-aš-ka-an*),[321] his courtiers are to "track down" (*šakuwāi*) the culprits involved,[322] both bribe-*givers* as well as bribe-*takers*,[323] and punish them accordingly.

Another *išḫiul* text shifts attention away from murder and larceny onto the shadowy practice of "skimming."[324] For example, if the

318. *KUB* 13.9+40.62.2.15.

319. *KUB* 13.9+40.62.2.16–19. In *KUB* 13.7.1.13 the "compensation" is *É-ŠU*, "his (the thief's) house."

320. *KUB* 13.9+40.62.3–10. A "thief" is defined as anyone (farmer, steward, doorkeeper) who opens the granary door "without his (the king's) permission" (*PA-NI* ZI-*ŠU*, *KUB* 13.9+40.62.3.7). Cf. the similar instructions for safeguarding the military granary (*KBo* 16.24+16.25.1.41–45), and N.B. the Aramaic papyrus which records how difficult it is to clear one's name of the charge of "thievery" (*CAP* 7.1–10).

321. Recognizing the persistence of this temptation, one *išḫiul* text warns military leaders (*KUB* 13.20.1.32–35) not to let the needs and desires of their families corrupt the decision-making process, while another warns priests and temple personnel not to reroute public temple "provisions" (*ša-ra-a ti-ia-an-da*) into their private homes (*KUB* 13.4.50′–59′), and still another contrasts "accepting a bribe" (*ma-aš-ga-an-na-za*) with doing what is "right" (*ḫa-an-da-an*, *KUB* 13.2+31.84+40.60.3.26–28; cf. Miller, *Instructions*, 150, 228, 250).

322. Westbrook and Woodard, "Edict," 646–53.

323. *KUB* 13.9+40.62.3.14′. Güterbock ("Formel," 78–80) follows Friedrich (*HW* 177) in translating "look at," but Westbrook and Woodard ("Edict," 646–53) translate *šakuwāi* as "pursue"; Miller (*Instructions*, 139) refrains from translating the term at all. D'Andrade ("Bribery," 242) defines bribery not as a two-party, but a three-party transaction: (a) the bribe-payer; (b) the bribe-taker; and (c) the employer from whom bribe-taking employees withdraw their loyalty.

324. *KUB* 13.4.1.39′–49′ (cf. Miller, *Instructions*, 250–51; Bales, *Slavery*, 227–28; D'Amato, *Law*, 364; Gutmann, "Economy," 11). In the Middle East "skimming" falls

personnel responsible for supplying cattle, sheep, bread, beer, wine and other "provisions"[325] to the "festivals" ($EZEN_4$[MEŠ])[326] "take payment for themselves" (*ḫa-ap-pár da-as-ket₉-te-ni*),[327] then this creates two problems: (a) the deities "living" in these temples go hungry,[328] and (b) the economy at large founders.[329] Moreover, should such "provisions" be consumed by spouses, children, servants, relatives, and/or houseguests, then this becomes a "capital crime" (*ag-ga-tar*) punishable by "death" (*a-ku*).[330] If temple personnel confiscate gold, silver, bronze and/or clothing from a divine image,[331] then this too must be punished, even as officials struggle to distinguish "legitimate" gifts from "illegitimate." Whereas the former is a capital crime, the latter is not—but only if the gift-giving process conforms to strict governmental controls. Royal gifts can be exchanged for money, but not in private and not without the king's express permission.[332] Further, those delegated to monitor the transaction, the EN[MEŠ URU]*ḪA.AT.TI* ("lords of Ḫattuša"), must record all transactional details on a GIŠ.ḪUR ("wooden writing board").[333] Whoever discovers a violation of these restrictions and fails to report it, or conceals the identity of the perpetrator(s), is likewise guilty of a capital offense.[334] Stated repeatedly throughout the edict, the principle governing these stipulations is clear: All property belongs to the gods, seeing as it is

---

under the financial umbrella of باقشيش ("*baksheesh*"). As Hendon (*Negotiations*, 121–30) points out, *baksheesh* (like "haggling") is simply the "price of doing business."

325. *KUB* 13.4.1.47′, 50′ (*ša-ra-a ti-ia-an-ta*, lit., "organized things"). Mouton ("Walkui," 92) points out that pigs, usually considered to be an impure food source in the ancient Near East, are thought (at least in Kizzuwatna) "to have the power to bring prosperity."

326. Cf. Cammarosano, *Cults*, 103–38.

327. *KUB* 13.4.1.49′ (changing second-person to third-person). N.B. that the Hittite term *maškan* ("bribe") is conspicuously absent.

328. This type of "thievery" is rather floridly described as "snatching the deity's desired share out of his mouth" (*pa-ra-a ḫu-u-it-ti-at-te-ni*, lit., "cause it to escape out," *KUB* 13.5.2.26). The "crime" is that DINGIR[MEŠ] *me-na-aḫ-ḫa-an-da le-e uš-kan-zi* ("the gods should not be kept waiting for it," *KUB* 13.4.4.38–39). Cf. *HL* §164–70 for other types of cultic crimes.

329. Cammarosano, *Cults*, 139–50.

330. *KUB* 13.5.2.16; 1.59′.

331. The Hittite pantheon is one of the largest (and correspondingly most demanding) of the ancient world (Cammarosano, *Cults*, 51–55).

332. In fifth century Egypt a man named Makkibanit writes a letter to his sister Tashi that he has given מסת כספה ("an amount of money") to a man named Banitsar as a ופד/רת ("ransom?, interest payment?" *TADE* 1.2.2.4–5).

333. *KUB* 13.4.2.41″–42″ (cf. MacGinnis, "Writing," 217–36).

334. *KUB* 13.4.2.49″–50″ ("both of them shall die").

theirs and theirs alone. Through these stipulations the priesthoods serving these deities successfully maintain their grip on power.[335]

Hittite Laws

Careful consideration of *išḫiul*-"instructions" shows Hittite *ḫattatar* ("wisdom") to play a critical role in the Anatolian economy, just as *nēmequ* (Akk "wisdom") does in Mesopotamia and חכמה (Heb "wisdom") in Israel, even though (a) there is much less written evidence from which to draw, and (b) its parameters are considerably less polarized.[336] Alongside these texts many of the Hittite laws focus on socioeconomic concerns quite similar to those addressed in the *išḫuil* texts.[337] For example:

[ták]ku ^LÚ^DAM.GÀR ^URU^*Ḫa-at-ti* *ku-iš-ki ku-en-zi*	If someone kills a Hittite merchant,[338]
1 *ME* MA.[NA].KÙ.BABBAR *pa-a-i*	They shall recompense 100 minas (4000 shekels),
[pár]-na-aš-še-e-a šu-wa-a-ez-zi	Settling the obligation from their household.[339]
ták-ku I-NA KUR ^URU^*Lu-ú-ia-a* *na-aš-ma I-NA* KUR ^URU^*Pa-la-a*	If it occurs in the lands of Luwiya or Pala,[340]
1 *ME* MA.[NA].KÙ.BABBAR *pa-a-i*	They shall recompense 100 minas (4000 shekels),

335. *KUB* 13.4.1.38′; 2.24″, 50″; 4.21–24, 76–77. Cf. Schwemer (*Priesthood*, 99) and Miller (*Instructions*, 254–55).

336. It is difficult to imagine, e.g., any clear distinction between "didactic" and "pessimistic" *ḫattatar* in the Hittite wisdom literature.

337. Bryce (*Hittite*, 56–71) discusses the training of Hittite scribes, but Beckman ("Proverbs," 215) admits that "the sayings and generalized anecdotes by which the Hittites expressed the received wisdom of their civilization are not collected for use in scribal instructions, as is the practice in earlier Mesopotamia." Still, the one example he does cite—a sapiential response to a Hittite law—focuses on "economic compensation."

338. *KBo* 6.3.i (law § 5; cf. Hoffner, *Laws*, 19).

339. *KBo* 6.3.i. Hoffner ("Laws," 238, n. 5) recognizes that "the significance of this phrase (found repeatedly throughout *HL*) is much debated," but "favors the view that the person entitled to make a claim in the case is entitled to recover damages from the estate of the perpetrator."

340. *KBo* 6.3.i. Luwiya and Pala are roughly located in SW-Central and NW Anatolia, respectively.

a-aš-šu-še-et-ta šar-ni-ik-zi ma-a-an	And replace his (stolen) goods as well.
I-NA KUR ^{URU}*Ḫa-at-ti*	If it is in the land of Ḫatti,
[nu]-za ú-na-at-tal-la-an-pát ar-nu-uz-zi	They shall also transport the body of the aforementioned merchant (for burial).[341]

Another law empowers a victim's heir to be compensated for damages:

ták-ku LÚ.U$_{19}$.LU-*aš* LU-*aš na-aš-ma* MUNUS-*za ta-ki-a* URU-*ri a-ki*	If a person, man or woman, is killed in another city
ku-el-la-aš ar-ḫi a-ki 1 *ME* ^{GIŠ}*gi-pé-eš-šar* A.ŠÀ	He (the victim's heir) shall deduct 12,000 square meters (3 acres) from the land of the one on whose property the benefactor was killed
kar-aš-ši-i-e-ez-zi na-an-za da-i	And take it for himself.[342]

In short, the admonitions found in the Hittite *išḫuil* and legal texts show that the Anatolians are just as keen as their neighbors to identify and repair the boundaries broken from socioeconomic conflicts associated with *labor, oppression, corruption, poverty, redemption, bribery, giving, slavery, land, theft, skimming, property,* and *compensation.*

Aramaic Wisdom

Compared to Mesopotamia and Anatolia, Aramaic wisdom is less well-known, doubtless because of the paucity of written evidence. From the evidence at hand, however, it is clear that the Aramaic proverbs resonate deeply with the didactic sayings used to educate students in other ANE cultures.[343]

341. *KBo* 6.3.i (law § 5).

342. *KBo* 6.3.i (law § 6).

343. Kottsieper ("Aramaic," 393–443). Ugaritic wisdom may be a literary genre, but as Rowe points out ("Ugarit," 95–108), the evidence is far too minimal and incomplete to speculate, other than the fact that Ug *ḥkm* (cf. Heb חכם, "wise") applies to El on a few occasions (*CAT* 1.4.4.41–43; 1.4.5.3–4; 1.16.4.3; cf. Perdue, *Stylus*, 37–38; Horwitz, "Scribe," 389–94).

Proverbs of Aḥiqar

Aḥiqar is a celebrated sage whose name,[344] like Solomon and Luqmân,[345] traditionally hovers over a fixed collection of proverbs and instructions[346] associated with the world of international wisdom.[347] Preserved in Aramaic,[348] Syriac,[349] Greek, Arabic, Armenian, Ethiopic, Turkish, and Slavonic,[350] some of these sayings focus on problems prevalent in the world of fiscal management. For example:

[אל תמאס] זי בעדבך ואל תרגג לכביר זי ימנע מנך	[Despise not] that which is your lot, nor covet any great thing withheld from you.[351]

344. An Akkadian text from the Seleucid period reads, "In the time of King Esarhaddon, *a-ba-*ᴰNINNU-*da-ri*, whom the Arameans call *a-ḫu-u-qa-a-ri*, was *ummânu*" (cited in Greenfield, "Aḥiqar," 51). Both *a-ḫu-u-qa-a-ri* and Aram אחיקר mean "my brother is precious."

345. Q 31.12 reads اتينا لقمان الحكمه, "We gave wisdom to Luqmân." Kassis (*Proverbs*, 51) holds Luqmân, for whom a whole Sura in Qur'an is named (Q 31), to be the "Aḥiqar of the Arabs."

346. Cf. Kottsieper ("Aḥiqar," 111–13). Weigl (*Achikar-Sprüche*, 651) thinks these proverbs originate from north-western Syria in the seventh century BCE (cf. Oshima, "Aḥiqar," 141–67).

347. Early exemplars are discussed by Alster ("Proverbs" 1–45), later exemplars by Kassis (*Proverbs*, 51–54). Boccaccini (*Judaism*, 104) points out that "the search for wisdom unites the wise of Israel to the wise of the neighboring nations. Aḥiqar is an Assyrian, Job (and his friends) are from the land of Uz, and *Proverbs* proudly hosts the sayings of Solomon's foreign peers, 'Agur, son of Jakeh the Massaite' and 'King Lemuel' (Prov 30:1–33; 31:1–9)."

348. The oldest known witnesses to the Aḥiqar tradition come from fifth century Aramaic papyri discovered at Elephantine, a small island on the Upper Nile (cf. Sachau, *Elephantine* [Plates #40–50]; *CAP* 212–20; *TADE* C3.7; Lindenberger, *APA* 1–39).

349. Syr *Aḥiqar* is quite helpful for restoring words and phrases missing from the fragmentary Aramaic papyri found at Elephantine. As Evans (*Syriac*, 679) notes, "the Syriac text often does help scholars understand better the Semitic substratum."

350. Conybeare (*Aḥiqar*). Grelot (*Documents*, 427–30) posits a yet-to-be discovered Akkadian version, a possibility entertained by Bodi ("Aḥiqar," 16–18).

351. *Aḥq* 136. Cf. אל תתאו זולת נחלתכה ואל תתבלע בה, "Do not long for anything besides your inheritance, yet do not become swallowed up by it" (4Q16.2.8), and "Do not covet that which God 'apportions' (بضكم) to some and not to others" (Q 4.32).

[אל תרבי] חיל ואל תהשגא לבבא	[Do not amass][352] excessive wealth[353] lest you lose perspective.[354]

Others reflect on poverty's potential to produce bitterness:

טעמת אף זעררתא מררתא ו[אכל]ת חסין	I have tasted bitter medlar[355] and [eaten] endives,[356]
ולא איתי [מ]ריר מן ענות	But nothing is more bitter than poverty.[357]

Some ponder the perils of indebtedness:

נשׂאית חלא וטענת מלח	I have lifted sand and carried salt,
ולא איתי זי יקיר מן [זפ]ת[א]	But nothing is heavier than [debt].[358]

Others weigh its pros and cons:

אנת יה ברי	Listen, my child!

352. *Aḥq* 137 (restoration suggested by Grelot, "Aḥîqar," 521). Lindenberger ("Aḥiqar," 504) restores אל תהשׂגא ("do not heap up") to play on the phrase in the succeeding clause, but this is unlikely because (a) the phrase is too long for the line, and (b) verbatim repetition is extremely rare. Puech (*Aḥiqar*, 591) suggests the antonymous reading תקבל, "Accept (wealth, but . . .)."

353. *Aḥq* 137. Often denoting "strength/honor," חיל can also mean "riches" (Grelot, "Aḥîqar," 521; *DNWSI* 370) or "wealth" (Lindenberger, "Aḥiqar," 504; cf. Deut 8:17; Isa 8:4; Job 5:5).

354. *Aḥq* 137 (lit., "lest you put the heart in a twist"). Cowley (*CAP* 224) reads "and lead not (thy) heart astray." Grelot ("Aḥîqar," 521) reads "et n'égare pas (ton) coeur" ("and let not your heart stray"); Lindenberger ("Aḥiqar," 504): "lest you pervert your heart." Cf. the "friend's" warning to the "sufferer/sceptic" in the Babylonian Theodicy: *gi-riš ina u4-um la ši-ma-ti i-qa-am-me-šu ma-al-ku gi-is maš-re-e bel pa-ni ša qur-ru-nu ma-ak-ku-ru*, "The king habitually burns at the stake any property manager who recklessly stockpiles riches for himself" (*BWL* 74.63–64).

355. Medlar and endives are pungent vegetables often found in Middle Eastern salads and stews (cf. Renfrew, "Diet," 191–202).

356. *Aḥq* 105. Restoring ו[אכל]ת ("I have eaten") to (a) parallel the verb טעמת ("I have tasted"); (b) recognize the format replicated in *Aḥq* 105, 111, and 112; and (c) echo Arm 2.69, "I have eaten endives and I have drunk gall, but neither was more bitter than poverty."

357. *Aḥq* 105. In Qur'an, those doomed to punishment "eat of the most bitter tree" (لاكلون من سجر من زقوم; i.e., the Tree of Zaqqum, Q 56.52).

358. *Aḥq* 111. Restoring זפ]ת[א] ("debt") with Lindenberger (*Aḥiqar*, 98), based on Syr 2.45: "I have carried salt and removed lead, and I have seen nothing heavier than a man having to repay a 'debt' (ܚܘܒܬܐ)." Ginsberg (*ANET* 429) reads "grief" (חמ]ת[א]); Porten and Yardeni (*TADE* 3.47) read "stranger."

זף דגנא וחנטתא	Borrow corn and wheat[359]
זי תאכל ותשבע ותנתן לבניך עמך	So that you may eat well and share with your children.[360]
ז]פתא יקירתא ומן גבר לחה אל תזפ	Do not take out an exorbitant[361] loan from a corrupt man;[362]
אף הן תזף זפתא	But if you do take out a loan,[363]
אל תשים עד זפתא [תש]ל[ם] שלין לנפשך אל תשים	Let not your soul rest until you [repay it].[364]
ז]פתא חליה כ[זי חסי]ר	A loan is sweet[365] in times of need,[366]
ומשלמותה ממלא [ב]י	But (re)payment[367] (can be) a houseful.[368]

A few focus on the inherent value of hard work:[369]

אנת יה ברי	Listen, my child!

359. *Aḥq* 129. N.B. the recognition that "borrowing" (זף, ipv. of יזף) is fully allowable in agrarian economies where famine and drought are common. The predicament to be avoided is not borrowing *per se*, but borrowing *foolishly* (i.e., without a viable plan for repayment).

360. *Aḥq* 129. Cf. בכל עת אהב רע ואח לצרה יולד, "A friend loves at all times, but a brother is born to share adversity" (Prov 17:17).

361. *Aḥq* 130. Aram יקירה also appears in *Aḥq* 111 to describe "heavy" debt (*DNWSI* 466), but "exorbitant" doubtless conveys the intended nuance here.

362. Cf. Cf. מכול איש אשר לוא ידעתה אל תקח הון פן יוסיף על רושכה, "Do not take money from any man you do not know, lest he add to your poverty" (4Q16.2.5–6; cf. below).

363. *Aḥq* 130. N.B. that the text twice uses the verb + cognate accusative (*GKC* 117p–q) to emphasize the gravity of indebtedness.

364. *Aḥq* 131, restoring [ש]ל[ם] with Cowley ("compensation/(re)payment" *CAP* 224; cf. 4Q416.2.2.4) to preserve the semantic play with שלין ("peace"). Cf. ואם שמו ברוא שכה למות הפקידהו ורוחכם אל תחבל בו, "But if he places it at your disposal until death, deposit it, and do not corrupt your soul with it" (4Q16.2.6–7).

365. *Aḥq* 131. Aram חליה recurs in *Aḥq* 188: כפן יהחלה מררותא, "hunger makes the bitter sweet."

366. *Aḥq* 131, restoring כ[זי חסי]ר with Cowley (*CAP* 217) and Grelot ("Aḥîqar," 521), *pace* Lindenberger (*Proverbs*, 124). Cf. Ps 23:1, לא אחסר, "I shall not want."

367. *Aḥq* 131. N.B. that *Aḥq* repeatedly refracts this root (שלם) through an overtly socioeconomic lens.

368. *Aḥq* 131 (N.B. that בי is the common spelling for "house" in Imperial Aramaic; cf. *Aḥq* 125). Lindenberger (*Proverbs*, 124) interprets this line to mean "will cost all which you possess."

369. Powell ("Money," 227; cf. *Labor*, 5–48) emphasizes how much labor "plays a major role in the whole economic system and cheap labor . . . plays a greater role in price stability."

Work every harvest and do every job	הכצר כל כציר ועבד כל עבידה
So that you may eat well and provide for your children.[370]	אדין תאכל ותשבע ותנתן לבניך

Summary

Much more might be said about the socioeconomic motifs animating the sapiential texts surveyed above, but suffice it to say that Mesopotamian, Anatolian, and Aramaic sages posit only two types of socioeconomic behavior: *wise* and *foolish*. This polarity hardly exhausts the depth of their interest in things economic, nor is it surprising that their interests, like those of their neighbors, range over a wide range of property, labor, and investment concerns (*land, trade, property, debt, labor, slavery, marriage, divorce, betrothal, inheritance*), not to mention those issues associated with the macro-polarities of *merchant-client, creditor-borrower, integrity-corruption, profit-loss*, and *economics-religion*.

Question: How do Hebrew sages deal with these concerns?

370. *Aḥq* 127. Cf. תכין בקיץ לחמה אגרה בקציר מאכלה, "it (the ant) prepares its food in summer and gathers its sustenance at harvest" (Prov 6:8; cf. below).

3

Socioeconomic Motifs in Biblical Hebrew Wisdom

Many say, "O that we might see something good! Let the light of your face shine upon us, Yhwh," yet you put more joy in our hearts than when their grain and wine abound.[1]

Wisdom's impact on the Bible is profound,[2] a fact more obvious in some parts of the library than others, due in part to the "traditions of composition . . . long established in the region."[3] In the Proverbs scroll, for example, Hebrew sages rework dozens of *didactic* sayings from data affiliated with, and in some cases originating from Egypt,[4] Mesopotamia,[5] Syria-Palestine,[6] Anatolia,[7] and Persia,[8] producing what Anthony Ceresko

1. Ps 4:7–8. N.B. that this couplet begins and ends with the word רב ("to be great, be many, multiply, abound").

2. Cf. von Rad (*Wisdom*); Crenshaw (*Wisdom*); Clines (*Weisheit*); Sneed (*Wisdom*). For wisdom's influence on the Prophets, cf. Boda (*Riddles*); for the Psalter, cf. Cheung (*Wisdom*, 1–21). *Contra* Mowinckel ("Psalms," 206), Lindblom ("Wisdom," 195–96) posits "classes of the intelligentsia" operating in pre-exilic Jerusalem (cf. Moore, *Babbler*, 58–80).

3. Weeks, *Introduction*, 3.

4. Cf., e.g., the parallel between Prov 22:17—24:22 and the text commonly known as the *Instruction of Amen-em-opet* (*AEL* 2.146–63; cf. N. Shupak, "Egyptian," 265–304; Crenshaw, "Proverbs," 516; Washington, *Wealth*, 7–9).

5. Cf. *BWL* 213–82.

6. Cf. Nougayrol ("Souffrant," 265–73); Foster ("Salvation," 1.486); Khanjian ("Wisdom," 139–208).

7. Cf. Alaura ("Proverbs," 1–15); Beckman ("Anatolia," 48–57).

8. Cf. McLaughlin (*Wisdom*, 16–19); Gerstenberger (*Persian*, 252–69); Paper ("Proverbs," 2–47). With regard to the socioeconomic motifs in Arabic wisdom, cf. the prayer in Q 26.83, رب هب لى حكما والحفنى باصالحين, "Lord, give me 'wisdom' (حكما, Heb חכמה) and unite me with the 'prosperous'(صالل, cf. Heb צלח; Kassis, *Proverbs*, 159–215).

calls "a sophisticated analytical tool" more serviceable to Hebrew sages than anything produced by "the wisdom of other lands."[9] With regard to *pessimistic* wisdom, the book of Job exploits socioeconomic motifs much like those embedded in the Babylonian Theodicy, Dialogue of Pessimism, and Ludlul bēl nēmeqi.[10] The Psalter preserves several "wisdom psalms" manipulating now-familiar socioeconomic motifs,[11] and Qohelet (Ecclesiastes) utilizes a literary format much like that responsible for shaping the Babylonian Theodicy and Dialogue of Pessimism.[12] Each of these Hebrew scrolls is comprehensible on its own terms, of course,[13] yet none is *fully* comprehensible apart from some knowledge of and appreciation for the socioliterary milieu in which they originate.[14]

Proverbs of Solomon

The Book of Proverbs is foundational to this survey because even though this "anthology of anthologies"[15] polyphonically vocalizes the commercial interests of different socioeconomic groups,[16] the "proverb," in Mark

9. Ceresko (*Wisdom*, 39); cf. Hallo (*Literature*, 625–33).

10. Cf. Sitzler (*Vorwurf*), Oshima (*Poems*), and above. In the whirlwind speeches (Job 38–42) Schifferdecker (*Whirlwind*, 122) sees the deity "showing Job the beautiful, dangerous, but ordered world of creation and challenges him to live in it with freedom and faith."

11. Cf. Sheppard (*Wisdom*, 136–43); Mays ("Psalter," 3–12); Berges ("Knechte," 153–78); and Cheung (*Wisdom*, 178–82). Botha ("Wealth," 105–28) contends that "the acrostic wisdom psalms constitute a unified, authoritative voice against secularism, greed, and religious apostasy."

12. Cf. Sneed (*Pessimism*, 45); Lee (*Vitality*, 24); and above. Penchansky (*Wisdom*, 1, 12) attributes Proverbs, Job and Ecclesiastes to a "professional sage class," recognizing that Sirach and Wisdom of Solomon come later as the products of Hellenistic writers who "mistrust outsiders and are defensive against strange ideas."

13. Cf. the still-relevant warnings of the late Samuel Sandmel in his 1961 presidential speech to the Society of Biblical Literature ("Parallelomania," 1–13). On the other hand, Bartholomew and O'Dowd (*Wisdom*, 23) find Crenshaw's approach ("Method," 129–42) problematic because it presumes, in their view, "that wisdom and Wisdom literature can only appear in a very narrow form."

14. Krüger (*Proverbs*) rightly observes that of all its options, Israel's wisdom traditions are most responsible for opening the Hebrews up to "exchange with other cultures." Cf. Mugerauer ("Literature," 407–15); Gottwald (*Introduction*, 320); Roberts ("Environment," 75–121); Perdue ("Scribes," 1–34); Seow ("Ecclesiastes," 179–217); Schmid ("Job," 145–53); Reiterer ("Scribe," 218–43); and Moore ("Wisdom," 9–15).

15. Alter (*Proverbs*, 183, 185) argues that Proverbs "is not merely an anthology, but an anthology of anthologies."

16. Whybray (*Wealth*, 113–18) identifies four blocs, including (a) royal court (Prov 31:1–9); (b) educated urban society (22:17—24:22); (c) prosperous farmers (31:10–31);

Sneed's opinion, remains "the most fundamental, primary genre of the wisdom literature."[17] Prefaced by an Egyptian-like preamble logging a list of sapiential *Leitworten*,[18] Proverbs quickly introduces readers to the language of international wisdom[19] before laying down a protracted set of parental "instructions" deftly refracted through a pedagogical lens:[20]

---

and (d) small farmers trying to eke out a living, often under precarious circumstances (10:1—22:16). Loader (*Proverbs*, 10) less specifically speaks of "simple and sophisticated, rural and urban, learned and court associated carriers of the sapiential tradition."

17. Sneed, "Tradition," 65. Fox (*Proverbs*, 11) sees "Proverbs as a slice of tradition that precedes ancient Israel and continues beyond it," while Whybray (*Composition*, 51) sees it "above all as a book of education." Brown (*Character*, 24) and Murphy (*Proverbs*, 275; *Tree*, 15) read it as a *Handbuch* on character formation. Loader (*Proverbs*, 14) thinks "the revelatory deficiency of sapiential literature" still makes "a salutary contribution to the rehabilitation of natural theology," while Longman (*Proverbs*, 15) finds it to be of "profound theological significance."

18. Prov 1:2–6. Cf. Kayatz (*Proverbien*, 11); Waltke (*Proverbs*, 174–80).

19. In both size and scope the משלי שלמה ("Proverbs of Solomon") outshine every other known ANE collection of didactic sayings. Cf. Eissfeldt (*Mashal*, 26); Kim (*Proverbs*, xi–xvi); Kayatz (*Proverbien*, 17–24); Skehan (*Wisdom*, 9–45); Hildebrandt ("Proverbs," 207–24); and Goldingay ("Proverbs," 75–83).

20. Prov 1:1–7. Whybray (*Composition*, 12–15) counts no less than ten "instructions" in Prov 1–9. OG Sir 38:24 teaches that σοφία γραμματέως ἐν εὐκαιρίᾳ σχολῆς, "The scribe's wisdom (depends) on the opportunity of leisure," utilizing a term (σχολή) transliterated by many as "scholar" (cf. Fox, *Proverbs*, 53–77; Sneed, *Sages*, 34–66; Sandoval, *Proverbs*, 4–6, 29–70). In a classic example of rabbinic exegesis, Rabbi Judah ben Samuel floats the lawyerly claim that the sages seek ספר מ שלי . . . לגנוז ("to suppress the Proverbs scroll") because דבריו סותרין זה את זה ("its statements contradict one other"). For example, "Do not answer a fool according to his folly" (Prov 26:4) appears to contradict "Answer a fool according to his folly" in the very next verse (26:5). Responding to this "contradiction," the rabbi suggests that the first text refers to מילי דעלמא ("mundane matters") while the second refers to דברי תורה ("religious matters"; lit., "words of Torah," *b. Shab.* 30b; cf. Longenecker, *Exegesis*, 6–34; Stern, "Exegesis," 1–19; and Moore, *Babbler*, 192–96). Lyu (*Proverbs*, 68) recognizes that "the wisdom tradition values education" even while "conceding that some people are irredeemable," and Collins (*Wisdom*, 9) posits that Proverbs is about "intellectual training with a moral purpose." OG Sir 4:24 describes the relationship between *wisdom* and *education* via similar rabbinic categories: ἐν γὰρ λόγῳ γνωσθήσεται σοφία καὶ παιδεία ἐν ῥήματι γλώσσης, "wisdom is made known by a word (λόγος) and 'education' (παιδεία) by words of the tongue."

Parental Advice (Prov 1–9)[21]

בני אם יפתוך חטאים	My child,[22] if sinners[23] entice you,[24]
אל תבא	Do not acquiesce.[25]
אם יאמרו לכה אתנו	If they say, "Come with us,
נארבה לדם	So that we may lie in wait for blood,[26]
נצפנה לנקי חנם	So that we may aimlessly[27] hide ourselves away[28] to ambush the innocent,[29]

21. Many view Prov 1–9 as a "hermeneutic preamble" to the entire anthology (Dumbrell, *Faith*, 263), some dating it early (Story, "Proverbs," 319), some late (Toy, *Proverbs*, 2–4). Following Strack (*Sprüche*, 313–16), Schipper (*Hermeneutik*, 36, 198–201, 283) treats Prov 2 as a "table of contents" for the instructions in Prov 1–8, a section he sees explaining the complexities of the relationship between תורה ("law") and חכמה ("wisdom"). Miles (*Semiotics*, 2), on the other hand, views Prov 1–9 as "a satire on Solomon."

22. Prov 1:10. "My son" (בני) is a traditional address-formula in the sapiential/educational literature; cf., e.g., ברי, "my son," (*Aḥq* 127, 129), בני, "my son" (Sir 11:10), even DUMU-ĜA$_{10}$ ("my son," *Šur* 9). Balla (*Sexuality*, 35) recognizes that even though בני "may denote both male and female . . . it is probable that those taught in schools like the one mentioned in Sir 51:23 . . . are males." Ansberry (*Proverbs*, 11–35) and Weeks (*Instruction*, 4–32) assess the impact of Egyptian, Sumerian, Babylonian, and Aramaic "instructions" on Proverbs, and Bland (*Character*, 122–41) discusses the general impact of wealth on character formation.

23. Prov 1:10. MT חטאים ("sinners," followed by Vg, Syr and Tg); OG ἄνδρες ἀσεβεῖς ("ungodly men"). N.B. that by the Second Temple period the term "sinners" (Gk ἁμαρτωλοὶ) becomes a synonym for "outsiders" (e.g., Luke 6:32–34; cf. below).

24. Prov 1:10. MT פתה ("to entice") is the word Jeremiah uses to express his wobbly relationship with Yhwh: פתיתני יהוה, "You have enticed me, Yhwh!" (Jer 20:7; cf. Clines and Gunn, "Persuade," 20–27; Moore, *Babbler*, 79).

25. Prov 1:10 (majority of Heb mss תאבא; minority תב(ו)א; cf. *BHS* 1275). Vss follow the majority: OG βουληθῇς ("wish, profess"); Vg *adquiescas* ("acquiesce"); Syr ܠܚܣܐ ("take shelter"); Tg תתפיס ("to acquiesce," if derived from טפס; cf. *DTTM* 548, "to covenant/clasp hands, be bribed"). Discounting the versions, Sandoval (*Wealth*, 71–72) reads the minority תב(ו)א אל ("do not go").

26. Prov 1:11. MT אורב ("to lie in wait, ambush"); OG κοινώνησον αἵματος, "take a share of blood." Ezra is thankful that "the hand of our God" (יד אלהינו) "delivers" (נצל) him from the אורב (lit., "the one lying in wait") on the road to Jerusalem (Ezra 8:31).

27. Prov 1:11. MT חנם (lit., "without compensation," *HAL* 321); N.B. the use of this term in the Prosecutor's question, החנם ירא איוב אלהים, "does Job fear God 'without compensation?'" (Job 1:9; cf. below).

28. Prov 1:11. MT צפן ("to hide, conceal"); OG κρύψωμεν, Syr ܢܛܫܐ, and Vg *abscondamus* all mean "to hide, conceal," but in some contexts צפן has a socioeconomic nuance. Cf., e.g., צפון לצדיק חיל חוטא, "the sinner's wealth is 'hidden away' for the righteous" (Prov 13:22; *HAL* 982).

29. Prov 1:13. In Qur'an the truly "innocent" (مبروون, from برى, "to be free") are worthy of رزق كريم ("bountiful provision," Q 24.26; cf. 24.38).

כל הון יקר נמצא	So that we may seize[30] all their valuable wealth,[31]
נמלא בתינו שׁלל	And fill our houses with plunder.[32]
גורלך תפיל בתוכינו	Throw in your lot with us,
כיס אחד יהיה לכלנו	So that we may all have one moneybag."[33]

Following a few more stipulations, this first "instruction"[34] ends with a warning:

בני אל תלך בדרך אתם	My child, do not walk on this path with them.[35]
כן ארחות כל בצע בצע	For such is the path of everyone corrupted by greed,[36]

30. Prov 1:13. MT מצא normally means "to find," but cf. OG καταλαβώμεθα ("that we might seize," subj. aorist); Syr ܢܐܚܘܕ ("grab onto"); Tg שׁכח ("uncover"). Cf. פן מצא לו ערים, "lest he 'seize' cities for himself" (2 Sam 20:6).

31. Prov 1:13. OG τὴν κτῆσιν αὐτοῦ τὴν πολυτελῆ ("his valuable possessions"); Syr ܩܢܝܢܗ ܘܐܘܬܪܗ ܟܠܗ ("his wealth and possessions, all of it"). Tg עותרא ויקרא כל ("all the wealth and prizes"). Zabán (*Pillar*, 272) views Prov 1:13–14 as the second of twelve "allusions" to "treasure imagery" in Prov 1–9.

32. Prov 1:13 (cf. Wis 2:9–12). MT שׁלל ("spoil, booty, plunder") is followed by OG and Vg. Syr, however (ܙܝܬܐ, followed by Tg זתא) reads "olives"; i.e., "fill our houses with olives" (likely referring to the village granary). "Plundering" is an activity not just for pirates, but also for unscrupulous kings (1 Macc 6:1–17). Doubtless some of these thieves start out as "benevolent bandits" like the *šarrāqiš* in the Babylonian Theodicy (*BWL* 78.137–39).

33. Prov 1:14. On כיס ("bag, purse") cf. Akk *kī-su* in [LÚ]*tamkāru al-la-ka* [LÚ]*šamallû na-áš kīsi*, "the traveling merchant, the agent carrying the moneybag" (*BWL* 134.139). OG βαλλάντιον ("bag") parallels the βαλλάντιον carried by Tobias and Raphael (Tob 8:2), not to mention the "bags" (θυλάκια) of silver retrieved from Tobit's business partner Gabael (9:5). N.B. that OG κτησώμεθα is a subj. aor. inflection of κτάομαι ("to acquire"). Sandoval (*Proverbs*, 75) tries to advance the metaphorical argument that the antagonists in this first instruction are not "real robbers," but "a figure (trope) for all the things that constitute the wrong way and lead to death."

34. Whybray, *Composition*, 12–15.

35. Prov 1:15.

36. Prov 1:19 MT בצע בצע (lit., "who cut off their cut," an idiom originally referring to cloth/carpet-buying, according to Dalman, *Arbeit*, 5.124). OG reads this as τῶν συντελούντων τὰ ἄνομα τῇ γὰρ ἀσεβείᾳ ("those who perpetrate the lawless deeds by the ungodly"). Vg simplifies as *avari animas* ("live greedily"), as does Syr ܟܠ ܕܥܒܕܝܢ ܒܝܫܬܐ ("all those doing evil"), followed by Tg כל דעבדין עילא ("all those who do evil"). Kellerman ("בצע," 207) observes that of its thirty-nine usages in Tanak, בצע refers "almost entirely to . . . (illegal) profit or gain."

את נפש בעליו יקח	Arresting the souls[37] of those bedazzled by it.[38]

Another instruction comes straight from the archive of "old wisdom":[39]

כבד את־יהוה מהונך	Treasure Yhwh more than your money[40]
ומראשית כל תבואתך	Or the first-fruits of your produce,[41]
וימלאו אסמיך שׂבע	And your granaries will be amply supplied,[42]
ותירוש יקביך יפרצו	And new wine will burst forth from your wine-vats.[43]

37. Prov 1:19. OG τὴν ἑαυτῶν ψυχὴν ἀφαιροῦνται ("it amputates their soul"). Comparing the use of נפש in Ezek 13:17–21 and נבש on the funerary stele of Katumuwa (Pardee, "Zincirli," 52–54), Steiner (*Souls*, 128–66) debunks the notion that Hebrews do not believe in the נפשׁ ("soul") as a separate entity from the בשׂר ("flesh").

38. Prov 1:19 (lit., *ba'alized* by it; cf. the similar use of בעל in 3:27). Tg reads דעבדין ("those enslaved by it"). On the relationship between worship and education, Vayntrub ("Proverbs," 113) challenges on literary-poetic grounds whether the Proverbs scroll is a legitimate "primary data set in the recovery of ancient Israelite and Judean educational values and practices." Cf. كونوا ربانيين بما كنتم تعلمون الكتاب وبما كنتم تدرسون, "Worship the Lord by the way you study the Book and teach it" (Q 3.79; cf. Moore, *Babbler*, 156–65).

39. Cf. *Lud* 2.3; *BWL* 71.22. Schmid (*Weisheit*, 199) differentiates between "old" and "new" wisdom, and von Rad (*Wisdom*, 104–5) argues that "later wisdom is differentiated from old wisdom as something profoundly 'theological,' but this distinction is only a relative one, for it concerns, rather, the intensity of the involvement in specific, individual, theological questions. It is not, however, a difference in principle, for even old wisdom is aware that all life is determined by Yhwh."

40. Prov 3:9. OG σῶν δικαίων πόνων, "your righteous deeds"; Syr ܩܢܝܢܟ, "your deeds/trade/business" (cf. ענין, Qoh 2:26 below); Tg ממונך, "your *mammon*." Perhaps the best known parallel to this prioritization occurs in the Sermon on the Mount: ζητεῖτε δὲ πρῶτον τὴν βασιλείαν [τοῦ θεοῦ] καὶ τὴν δικαιοσύνην αὐτοῦ, καὶ ταῦτα πάντα προστεθήσεται ὑμῖν, "Seek first the kingdom [of God] and its justice, and all these things will be afforded you" (Matt 6:33).

41. Prov 3:9. OG καὶ ἀπάρχου αὐτῷ ἀπὸ σῶν καρπῶν δικαιοσύνης ("and sacrifice to him from the fruits of your justice") "spiritualizes" this text, and even though Syr and Vg do not follow, Sandoval (*Wealth*, 26) follows OG by leaning toward a "spiritual" interpretation rooted in "categories of moral and not just economic discourse."

42. Prov 3:10. On Heb אסם, cf. the Ug blessing *tispk yd aqht ġzr tštk bqrbm asm*, "May the hero Aqhat deposit you (i.e., 'the seedling/heir') inside the granary" (*CAT* 1.19.2.18, 25; cf. Wright, *Ritual*, 168–69). Wyatt (*RTU* 299) identifies this Ug phrase as "bucolic language used of the king and his heir," but N.B. that the "pious sufferer" in *Lud* 2.3 makes the same traditionalist presumption; viz., that "good always leads to reward" and "bad always leads to punishment" (cf. above and Letter to James below).

43. Prov 3:10 (cf. Hos 4:11; Hag 1:11; Matt 6:33). Following Whybray (*Wealth*) and von Rad (*Wisdom*), Sandoval (*Wealth*, 31–39) points out the "ambiguity of wealth and poverty" in the Proverbs scroll, particularly that some sayings critique the poor and others the wealthy (Prov 10:1—22:16; 25–29), but whether the former represents the thinking of literate scribes and the latter the thinking of unlettered folk is undeterminable.

Then, in what must surely rank as one of the most inspired teaching strategies of all time,[44] the sages disclose a powerfully effective metaphor:[45]

אשרי אדם מצא חכמה	Happy are those who find Sophia,[46]
כי טוב סחרה מסחר כסף	For trading with her is better than trading with silver[47]
ומחרוץ תבואתה	Or the revenue generated by refined gold.[48]
יקרה היא מפנינים	More precious than gemstones,[49]
וכל חפציך לא ישוו בה	Nothing of desire is comparable to her.[50]

44. Drawn to the possibility that Prov 2 serves as "the hermeneutical key" to Prov 3–9, Schipper (*Proverbs*, 55) argues that "by stressing the antithesis between two female figures—the 'strange woman' and 'Lady Wisdom'—a concept of wisdom is developed which reduces the idea of divine instruction and focuses on the fear of Yhwh and 'discipline' (מוסר)." Torah does something similar by contrasting the prophetic ministry of Moses with the activities of his Canaanite counterparts (Deut 18:10–22).

45. Readers remain divided over the origin, identity and function of Sophia. Many roads lead to her door through mythological, sapiential, apocalyptic, rabbinic, and early Christian channels. No one, however, can deny the power of her "presence" (cf. Schnabel, *Wisdom*, 343–49; Moore, *Babbler*, 256–67).

46. Prov 3:13, reading with OG σοφία. The literature on Sophia is vast (cf. Frymer-Kensky, *Goddesses*, 179–83; Moore, *Babbler*, 256–67), yet assessing how earlier cognate texts personify "wisdom" greatly depends on the interpretation of texts like *Aḥq* 94b–95, an inscription Lindenberger (*Parables*, 68) reads and translates as חכ[מת]ה מן אלהיא ה[י] אף לאלהן יק[י]רת הי, "Wisdom is of the gods. Indeed, she is precious to the gods," but Porten and Yardeni (*TADE* 3.C1.1.189 and C1.79) read ו[ח]כמת[ה] אלהיא ה[] אף לאלהן יק[י]רה הי, translating "[their wi]sdom the gods the . . . Also to the gods it is precious" (cf. Bledsoe, "Wisdom," 119–37; Emerton, *Wisdom*, 127).

47. Prov 3:14. OG κρεῖττον γὰρ αὐτὴν ἐμπορεύεσθαι, "It is better to do business with her"; Syr ܡܛܠ ܕܛܒܐ ܗܝ ܠܐܬܬܓܪܘܬܐ ܡܢ ܠܐܬܬܓܪܘܬܐ ܕܣܐܡܐ, "for trading with her is better than trading with silver." Qur'an warns that while some merchants equate "trade" (البيع) with the pocketing of "usury" (الربا), only the former is permissible (Q 2.275; cf. Exod 22:25).

48. Prov 3:14. Cf. 3:9, 10:16, and N.B. the word-pair סחר//תבואה ("business//produce") elsewhere in Tanak (e.g., Isa 23:3). Cf. Tg מטול דטבא תגרותה מן תגרותא דסמא ומן דהבא סנינא עללתה, "for business with her is preferable to treasure-chests or warehouses of refined gold." Comparing precious metals to Sophia in order to promote her superiority is common for the sages (cf. Job 28:15–16; Wis 7:9).

49. Prov 3:15. Whether the 3 f s pronoun היא refers to חכמה "wisdom" or תבואתה ("revenue") is ambiguous, perhaps by intention. Cf. OG τιμιωτέρα δέ ἐστιν λίθων πολυτελῶν, "for more valuable is she/it than precious stones"; Syr ܝܩܝܪܐ ܗܝ ܛܒ ܡܢ ܟܐܦܐ ܝܩܝܪܬܐ, "for she/it is more valuable than precious stones" (followed by Tg). Cf. Prov 31:10: רחק מפנינים מכרה, "far beyond gemstones is her/its 'trade value'" (מכר; cf. Ben Zvi, "Successful," 17–51; Liverani, "Trade," 65–79).

50. Prov 3:15. MT שוה (lit., "to be equal"); Syr ܦܫܡ ("to be treated as equal"); Tg וכל מדעם לא פחים ליה ("nothing compares to her"); OG οὐκ ἀντιτάξεται αὐτῇ οὐδὲν πονηρόν εὔγνωστός ἐστιν πᾶσιν τοῖς ἐγγίζουσιν αὐτῇ πᾶν δὲ τίμιον οὐκ ἄξιον αὐτῆς

ארך ימים בימינה	Long life is in her right hand,[51]
בשמאולה עשר וכבוד	Affluence and deference in her left hand.[52]

Having issued several warnings against the "loose woman" (Sophia's "estranged sister"),[53] the sage adds one more explicitly socioeconomic:

הרחק מעליה דרכך	Keep your path[54] away from hers
ואל תקרב אל פתח ביתה	And do not wander near the door to her house,[55]
פן תתן לאחרים הודך	Lest she hand over your wealth to others,[56]
ושנותיך לאכזרי	And your years to the ruthless;[57]

ἐστιν, ("No evil can resist her; to all who draw near to her she is well-known; nothing 'precious' is worthy of her"). N.B. the repetition of similar comparisons in 8:10–11.

51. Prov 3:16. Sinnott (*Wisdom*) examines the personification of Wisdom in Proverbs, Job, Sirach, Wisdom of Solomon, and Baruch, and Méndez-Montoya (*Theology*, 89), following Bulgakov (*Economy*), reads Wisdom as the "true expression of the metaphysical, social, and economic life." Cf. Murphy ("Personification," 222–33).

52. Prov 3:16. N.B. (a) that the mention of what to put in each hand echoes the custom of queenly coronation (cf. Pippin, "Wisdom," 293), and (b) that this instruction, like Hos 2:21–22, trumps immaterial wealth over material wealth (Moore, *WealthWarn*, 96). Zabán (*Pillar*, 274–75) views Prov 3:13–16 as the fifth of twelve "allusions to treasure imagery" in Prov 1–9.

53. Prov 2:16; 7:5 (cf. the divine sisters Inanna and Ereškigal in *ID* 165–72). The אשת זרה ("strange woman") is distinguishable, at least semantically, from the אשת כסילות ("foolish woman," 9:13). Perdue (*Proverbs*, 87), Camp (*Strange*, 14), and Yoder (*Wisdom*, 73) fuse Sophia's counterparts into a singularity, but Pemberton (*Proverbs*, 23–39) distinguishes no less than five separate women in Prov 1–9: (a) the young man's mother, (b) the young man's wife, (c) the other woman, (d) the wisdom woman, and (e) the foolish woman.

54. Prov 5:8. Sandoval (*Discourse*, 56) correctly designates the motif of "the path" (ארח, נתיבה, and דרך) as "one of the important images uniting the book."

55. Prov 5:8. Perdue (*Proverbs*, 120) suggests that "the 'house' of the strange woman (see Prov 2:18 and 7:8) may be her physical dwelling, the temple of a fertility goddess, or even the metaphorical world of folly and wickedness where Death dwells."

56. Prov 5:9 (תתן פן, lit., "lest she give"). On MT הוד N.B. that הודאות is listed alongside הלואות ("loans") in *b. Sanh.* 2b; OG ζωήν σου ("your life"); Vg *honorem tuum* ("your honor"); Syr ܫܠܛܟ ("your wealth, honor"); Tg חילך ("your wealth, honor").

57. Prov 5:9. OG ζωήν σου καὶ σὸν βίον ἀνελεήμοσιν ("your life and its merciless existence"); Syr ܫܢܝܟ ܠܐܠܗܐ ܠܐ ܡܪܚܡܢܐ ("your years to unmerciful gods"); Tg לנוכראין ("to foreigners"). Perdue (*Proverbs*, 120) suggests that the sage may here be warning his male students "not to fritter away their resources in payment to a prostitute or in efforts to try to make amends to an outraged husband who could require payment in blood for the adultery of his wife and lover."

פן ישׂבעו זרים כחך	Lest strangers delight themselves with your property,[58]
ועצביך בבית נכרי	And your legacy be relocated to an alien household.[59]

Of particular concern is the temptation to commit fraud:[60]

אל תמנע טוב מבעליו	Do not withhold[61] good from those who are struggling to hold on[62]
בהיות לאל ידך לעשׂות	When it is in your power to do so.[63]
אל תאמר לרעך	Do not say to your neighbor,
לך ושוב ומחר אתן ויש אתך	"Leave, but come back tomorrow and I will pay," when you already have the money in your possession.[64]

58. Prov 5:10. MT כחך ("your property/strength"; *HAL* 447 reads *Vermögen*, "capital"). Cf. OG σῆς ἰσχύος ("your strength"); Syr ܚܝܠܟ ("your wealth"; cf. Syr 5:9); Tg חילך ("your wealth"). Stoner and Irving (*Prenuptial*, 5) argue that contemporary prenuptial agreements are little more than "the material and financial counterpart to wedding vows." Cf. Brake (*Marriage*, 189–206); Dnes and Rowthorn ("Introduction," 1–9).

59. Prov 5:10. Tg (surprisingly) reads simply דאחריני ("to others"). Halliday (*Wealth*, 4), argues that "the impact of inherited wealth," unlike other socioeconomic concerns, is "easy to forget, or hide, or misrepresent." Qur'an teaches that the "reward" (اجر) allotted righteous "laborers" (العاملين) is eternal life in a garden fed by flowing rivers (Q 3.136).

60. Prov 3:28. Sandoval (*Proverbs*, 105) cautiously admits that verses 27–28 "reveal a concern with economic matters, albeit implicitly." Treier (*Proverbs*, 88) insists that "for Proverbs, the fruitfulness of wealth is tied to flourishing in its means of acquisition—only thereby can one flourish with others in its means of enjoyment."

61. Prov 3:27. Pleading his final case, Job asks אמנע מחפץ דלים "Have I withheld the poor from (their) desire?" (Job 31:16).

62. Prov 3:27. OG μὴ ἀπόσχῃ εὖ ποιεῖν ἐνδεῆ, "Do not refrain from doing good for the needy'; Syr ܠܐ ܬܬܟܠܐ ܠܡܥܒܕ ܕܣܢܝܩ, "Do not exempt yourself from doing as many good works as your hands can do." Cf. the similar occurrence of בעל in 1:19 (*ba'al*, "to own, possess").

63. Prov 3:27 (lit., "in the power of your hand"). The use of אל to convey "power" (not just "G/god") disquiets the versions. Cf. OG ἡνίκα ἂν ἔχῃ ἡ χείρ σου βοηθεῖν, "when your hand has (the ability) to help"; Vg *si vales et ipse benefac*, "if you can do it yourself"; Syr ܟܡܐ ܕܡܫܟܚܐ ܐܝܕܝܟ ܠܡܥܒܕ, "as many good works as your hands can do"; Tg כד אית חילא בידך, "when there is strength/wealth in your hand."

64. Prov 3:28. Perdue (*Proverbs*, 108) suggests that even though this saying might well "apply to all kinds of 'good,' the term probably especially embraces special acts of charity to those in need," esp. to "those who are close in proximity and kinship." N.B. that similar stipulations appear in wisdom texts from Qumran (cf. 4Q416.2.2.4–5, cf. below), prodding Murphy (*Wealth*, 169) to argue that "as the writer hopes God will not shut his hand, so too the maven is not to hide his face from the poor man or cause him to stumble by aggravating his shame."

Whether these admonitions refer to "benevolence" or "indebtedness" (or both),[65] the Proverbs of Solomon,[66] like those of Aḥiqar[67] and Sirach,[68] cautiously adopt a holistic approach to moneylending:[69]

בני אם ערבת לרעך	My child, if[70] you guarantee a loan[71] for your neighbor,[72]
תקעת לזר כפיך	If you cut deals with a stranger,[73]
נוקשת באמרי פיך	If the words on your lips ensnare you,[74]

65. Sandoval (*Proverbs*, 105) translates בעליו (lit., "its owners") as "one who deserves it," arguing that the phrase either refers to (a) "one who deserves it because that person is in want" (so the versions), or (b) "one who deserves it because that person is a creditor" (cf. 4Q416.3.2.1–21).

66. This title (משלי שלמה) derives from the superscription in Prov 10:1 (cf. the longer forms in 1:1 and 25:1).

67. *Aḥq*. §42–43 (129–31; cf. above).

68. Cf. Gregory (*Generosity*, 128–70) and below.

69. Thoughtfully pondering the socioeconomic questions, Goetzmann (*Money*, 2) reimagines financial technology as a "time machine" which, while unable to move people through time, can "move their money." Sandoval (*Proverbs*, 108) understates the dark side of moneylending by remarking that "there is a sense in the wisdom literature that standing surety is risky business."

70. Prov 6:1. N.B. that MT אם ("if") begins a protasis which remains operational until the appearance of אפוא ("then") in 6:3.

71. Prov 6:1. MT ערבת (lit., "become a guarantor/sponsor"). Cf. אל תהי בתקעי כף בערבים משאות, "Do not be someone who makes pledges and guarantees loans" (22:26). Using similar language, Q 74.38 warns the wealthy that كل نفس بما كسبت رهينه, "every soul is 'mortgaged/held in pledge' by that which it acquires." Transliterating ערבון, Saul of Tarsus depicts the Holy Spirit as an ἀρραβὼν ("loan guarantee," 2 Cor 5:5; Eph 1:14).

72. Prov 6:1 (cf. 17:18). On the pros and cons of debt-security cf. *CH* §117; *BWL* 148.68; *Lud* 4.45; and *Aḥq* §29 (all discussed above). Frymer-Kensky ("Israel," 251) argues that "Israel has a system of commercial credit to finance trading ventures, and may facilitate borrowing such sums by providing for equitable rates of interest, but the loans mentioned in the Bible are not part of a commercial credit system, (only) subsistence loans to ameliorate dire poverty." Other opinions appear in Chirichigno (*Debt-Slavery*, 344–56) and Sandoval (*Proverbs*, 106–12).

73. Prov 6:1 (lit., "clasp palms/shake hands"). OG παραδώσεις σὴν χεῖρα ἐχθρῷ, "if you give over your hand to an enemy." Debate is lively over the identities of the רע ("neighbor") and the זר ("stranger"). Meinhold (*Sprüche*, 1.110), Boström (*Proverbiastudien*, 100), Plöger (*Sprüche*, 63), McKane (*Proverbs*, 321–22), and Fox (*Proverbs*, 211) all see the רע as the "creditor" and the זר as the "debtor," but Waltke (*Proverbs*, 332) finds the evidence too meager, suggesting instead that רע "perhaps describes the secured in the view of the careless guarantor, and a זר according to the sage's evaluation of him."

74. Prov 6:2 (changing passive voice to active). In 6:5 the root י/נקשׁ reappears, referring to the fowler's "snare." Oral agreement (supported by testimonials and oaths) is the binding legal force in preliterate cultures—powerful enough to "ensnare" unwitting

נלכדת באמרי פיך	Or the words from your mouth entrap you,[75]
עשׂה זות אפות בני והנצל	Then[76] do this, my child, to secure your release:
כי באת בכף רעך	If you slip under your neighbor's control,[77]
לך התרפס ורהב רעיך	Go quickly[78] and plead with your neighbor.[79]
אל תתן שׁנה לעיניך	Give your eyes no sleep,
ותנומה לעפעפיך	Your eyelids no repose.
הנצל כצבי מיד	Save yourself, like a deer from the bowman,[80]
וכצפור מיד יקושׁ	Or a bird from the fowler.[81]

speakers. Cf. Wells ("Law," 194); Mercer (*Oath*, 33–35); Wilson ("Oath," 129–56); and Cartledge (*Vows*, 15–16).

75. Prov 6:2. At first glance the sages' preoccupation with speech may seem odd, if not obsessive (cf., e.g., Jas 3:5–8), but as O'Connor (*Proverbs*, 45) points out, both "public and private business has to be conducted by word of mouth because no other medium of communication is available." Literacy is rare, so "legal proceedings rest heavily on the reliability of the speech of the witnesses."

76. Prov 6:3. The adverb אפות (Vg *ergo*; Syr ܗܟܝܠ) signals the beginning of the apodosis in this conditional "if . . . then" sentence (so Gemser, *Sprüche*, 111; Sandoval, *Proverbs*, 107; and *HAL* 76).

77. Prov 6:3. Chirichigno (*Debt-Slavery*, 142) attributes debt-slavery in monarchical Israel to the following factors: (a) taxation; (b) high interest loans; (c) rent-capitalism; and (d) the economic and political collapse of prominent kinship groups.

78. Prov 6:3. MT רפס (lit., "to press"). OG μὴ ἐκλυόμενος ("faint not," reading רפה?).

79. Prov 6:3 (cf. Matt 18:15). Wilson (*Proverbs*, 106) recognizes that Prov 6:3–5 is a "sustained call to be urgent about getting released from this (actual or possible) financial bind," for while "there is folly in putting up financial security for others, there is further folly in not facing up to the resulting crisis. The goal is to *save yourself* . . . from the financial obligation you have assumed for another."

80. Prov 6:5. This truncated phrase may be due to the possibility that (a) the noun יקוץ ("trapper") in the next line services both uses of יד; or (b) a final ה has been elided from an original ידה ("shooter," Jer 50:14). Of these two possibilities the versions lean to the latter.

81. Prov 6:5. OG ὥσπερ δορκὰς ἐκ βρόχων καὶ ὥσπερ ὄρνεον ἐκ παγίδος and Syr ܐܝܟ ܛܒܝܐ ܡܢ ܢܫܒܐ ܘܐܝܟ ܨܦܪܐ ܡܢ ܦܚܐ read "like a deer from the noose or a bird from the trap." Various Anatolian texts depict augury as a big business in the first millennium (cf. Ünal, "Augures," 27–56).

Enlisting another image from the natural world,[82] the sages endorse the value of hard work:[83]

לך אל נמלה עצל	Consider the ant, slacker![84]
ראה דרכיך וחכם	Study its[85] ways and wise up![86]
אשר אין לה קצין שטר ומשל	For without a chief, boss, or supervisor,[87]
תקין בקיץ לחמה	It prepares its food in summer,
אגרה בקציר מאכלה	Mobilizing provisions for harvest.[88]
עד מתי עצל תשכב	How long will you lie there, slacker?[89]
מתי תקום משנתיך	When will you crawl out of bed?[90]

82. Cf. the role enacted by the NIM.LÀL ("honeybee") in retrieving Telipinu to revive the Anatolian economy (WAW 2.9; Moore, *WealthWarn*, 34–35).

83. Distinguishing between the destitute poor and the poor refusing to work, the sages "commend hard work," according to Whybray (*Wealth*, 32), "as a safeguard against extreme poverty."

84. Prov 6:6 MT עצל ("slacker"; cf. 6:9; 10:26; 13:4; 15:19; 19:24; 20:4; 21:25; 22:13; 24:30; 26:13–16). Syr omits; Tg עטל ("slacker"). N.B. that the אשת חיל ("successful wife") לחם עצלות לא תאכל, "does not eat the bread of 'laziness'" (עצל, Prov 31:27). Ben Zvi ("Wife," 35) posits that "just as Lady Wisdom (in Prov 1–8) is a caring, reliable provider, so also is the אשת חיל (in Prov 31:10–31)."

85. Vss change MT 2 per (דרכיך) to 3 per. Cf. OG τὰς ὁδοὺς αὐτοῦ ("its ways"); Vg *vias eius* ("its ways"); Syr ܐܘܪܚܬܗ ("its ways"); Tg ארחתהון ("their ways").

86. Prov 6:6. OG γενοῦ ἐκείνου σοφώτερος, "be smarter than that one"; Syr ܠܗ ܘܐܠܦ ܠܗ ܚܨܕܐ, "study the way it harvests."

87. Prov 6:7 (cf. the Akk triad *rēdîm bā'irim u nāši biltim*, "officer, constable and tax-collector," *CH* §36). OG adds: ἐκείνῳ γὰρ γεωργίου μὴ ὑπάρχοντος, "for that one maintains no cultivated land." Q 2.30 revisits the heavenly-vs.-earthly ruler debate: "When the Lord said to the angels, 'I will install a *caliph* (خليفه, 'viceroy') on the earth,' they said, 'What? Will you install someone who 'spreads corruption' (يفسد)?"

88. Prov 6:8. OG adds the honeybee alongside the ant: ἢ πορεύθητι πρὸς τὴν μέλισσαν καὶ μάθε ὡς ἐργάτις ἐστὶν τήν τε ἐργασίαν ὡς σεμνὴν ποιεῖται ἧς τοὺς πόνους βασιλεῖς καὶ ἰδιῶται πρὸς ὑγίειαν προσφέρονται, "Or go to the bee, and learn how diligent she is, how hard she works, and how her work supports the health of both kings and commoners." Cf. *Aḥq* 127, הכצר כל כציר ועבד כל עבידה אדין תאכל ותשבע ותנתן לבניך, "Work every harvest and do every job so that you may eat your fill and provide for your children" (discussed above).

89. Prov 6:9. Ortlund (*Proverbs*, 100) observes that עצל ("slacker, sluggard") displays three basic characteristics: (a) inability to make decisions; (b) inability to finish things; (c) inability to face things as they are.

90. Prov 6:9 (lit., "rise up from your sleep"). Waltke (*Proverbs*, 115) insists that "laziness in Proverbs is more than a character flaw; it is a moral issue, for it leads to a loss of freedom (12:24), the perpetual frustration of getting nowhere (24:34), and a loss of life (6:6–11; 10:4; 18:9; 20:13; 21:25–26; 24:30–34; cf. 28:24) . . . . The lazy person has to look on hard workers as fools; otherwise he stands self-condemned."

מעט שנות מעט תנומות	A little sleep, a little repose,
מעט חבק ידים לשכב	A little folding of the hands to rest,
ובא כמהלך ראשיך	And poverty[91] descends upon you like a thief,[92]
ומחסרך כאיש מגן	And deprivation like a bandit.[93]

The final instruction in Proverbs 1–9 ponders some of the more abstract linkages between "wisdom" and "wealth" functioning within Sophia:[94]

עשר וכבוד אתי	Riches and abundance are with me,[95]
הון עתק וצדקה	Long-lasting wealth and tribute.[96]
טוב פריי מחרוץ ומפז	My fruit is better than fine gold,
ותבואתי מכסף נבחר	And my harvest[97] than fine silver;[98]

91. Prov 6:11. As Saebø ("רוש," 424) points out, רוש/ראש is "indigenous primarily to wisdom literature, as it serves to establish a sharp contrast between the 'poor' (רוש) and the 'rich (עש/תר).'"

92. Prov 6:11. MT מהלך (lit., "a walker"); OG κακὸς ὁδοιπόρος ("wicked walker"); Vg *viator* ("traveler").

93. Prov 6:11. Syr ܬܐܬܐ ܥܠܝܟ ܡܣܟܢܘܬܐ ܘܬܕܘܫܟ ܫܢܕܪܘܬܐ ܐܝܟ ܓܒܪܐ ܡܥܢܝܐ, "poverty will come upon you and hardship will clobber you like a strongman"; Tg גברא כשרא ("strongman"). N.B. that this couplet recurs in 24:34 with two alterations: (a) the causative ptc of הלך is replaced by a reflexive ptc (מתהלך); and (b) the sg ptc of חסר is replaced by a pl ptc (מחסריך). The translation here is influenced by Ehrlich ("Sprüche," cited in Cohen, *Hapax*, 138–39), reading מגן homonymously in light of Ug *mgn* ("gift," *CAT* 1.16.1.45; cf. *RTU* 226–27); Syr ܡܓܢ, and Arab مجان ("free of charge," *DMWA* 894).

94. Sandoval (Proverbs, 205–6) believes that "Proverbs' cause and effect rhetoric, which reveals an act-consequence nexus (or in relation to wealth and poverty language, a wisdom-prosperity axiom), . . . is not the kind of language one ought to understand in overly literal fashion."

95. Prov 8:18. On this nuance of כבוד cf. Gen 31:11; Isa 61:6 (and Q 102.1 الهاكم التكاثر, "abundance distracts you").

96. Prov 8:18. MT צדקה usually means "justice/righteousness" (so OG and Vg), but Syr ܙܗܡܘܬܐ comes from a root (ܙܗܡ) which in the appropriate context means "tribute, portion, allowance" (*PSD* 110), and Tg refracts the saying further through an overtly socioeconomic lens: ממונא ומזלא וצדקתא ("mammon, good fortune, and free gifts"). In addition, צדקה comes to mean "almsgiving" in Second Temple texts like Tob 4:7–8 (ἐλεημοσύνη // צדקה). Nevertheless, as Lyu (*Proverbs*, 43) points out, "Proverbs addresses the issue of wealth and poverty in its own right" even when "the relation between wealth and righteousness is anything but clear."

97. Prov 8:19. OG γενήματα ("produce"); Vg *genimina* ("my harvest"; cf. Job 31:12); Syr ܥܠܠܬܝ ("my harvest, yield").

98. Prov 8:19. OG ἀργυρίου ἐκλεκτοῦ ("choice silver"); Vg *argento electo* ("choice silver"); Syr ܣܘܟܐ ܕܟܒܐ ("branch of thorns"); Tg סניא גביא ("cluster of thorns").

בארח צדקה אהלך	I walk the path of prosperity,[99]
בתוך נתיבות משפט	Shadowing the trail of the "fair deal."[100]

Prov 1–9 articulates a number of socioeconomic concerns applicable to a variety of contexts,[101] but, as Bálint Károly Zabán points out, "scholars still debate whether Prov 1–9 is a mere collection of haphazardly placed parental instructions and wisdom poems or . . . a unified composition of instructions spoken by different characters."[102] Unlike late Egyptian wisdom, where Pharaoh practically becomes a mouthpiece for the goddess Ma'at,[103] Israelite wisdom distinguishes itself by its "availability . . . to all who will attend to its call and seek it earnestly."[104] In short, Prov 1–9 contributes to a wisdom trajectory developed not least by its determination to engage seriously the poverty-wealth polarity, thereby leading readers like Richard Clifford to conclude that "the quest for wisdom is a universal quest not limited only to Jews and Christians."[105]

Sentence-Sayings (Prov 10–31)

This largest section of the Proverbs of Solomon preserves dozens of sentence-sayings whose characteristic brevity demands, in Bruce Waltke's tongue-in-cheek opinion, more "wit from the audience" than many are

99. Prov 8:20. Cf. note on צדקה in 8:18.

100. Prov 8:20. Syr ܓܘܢܐ ("custom, manner"); Tg דינא ("equity," cf. *b. B. Meṣ* 30b). Heb משפט often refers to "justice," but not slavishly (cf., e.g., איש כמשפטו, "each according to his fair share," 1 Kgs 5:8). Clifford (*Proverbs*, 95) views Sophia's gifts as reactions to the "gifts" of the אשת זרה ("strange woman," Prov 5:3): "That woman walked on the wrong path (5:5–6); squandered the man's potency and money (5:9–10); took away his honor, and embittered his old age (5:14). What the adulterous woman takes away, Sophia bestows as lasting gifts."

101. Tan ("*Foreignness*," 6–9) lists several possibilities.

102. Zabán (*Pillar*, 344) goes on to note that the latter option is rapidly becoming the majority opinion. Loader ("People," 232–33) cautions against "oversimplifying the process by merely juxtaposing the 'original' composition of oral sayings in the circles of simple folk with the later commitment to writing and redactional work in intellectual institutions of, among others, the royal court."

103. Symbolized by a vertical feather, Ma'at is the Egyptian goddess of truth/wisdom; cf. Assmann (*Mind*, 220–21); Karenga (*Maat*, 237–38).

104. Bartholomew and O'Dowd, *Wisdom*, 270.

105. Clifford, *Proverbs*, 33. This alone helps explain the existence of so many socioeconomic parallels between Tanak and Qur'an, but note also the inclusion of what appears to be Arab wisdom in the דברי אגור בן יקה, "Words of Agur, son of Yakeh" (Prov 30:1–33; cf. Berry, "Agur," 100).

willing to give.[106] It closes with two brief collections: the Words of Agur (Prov 30:1–33) and the Words of King Lemuel (31:1–9).[107] This wide-ranging collection, though occasionally perceived as "inconsistent," "ambiguous," even "contradictory,"[108] actively resonates with the poverty-wealth polarity in several ways.

Wealth: Responsibilities and Expectations

ברכת יהוה היא תעשׁיר	Yhwh's blessing produces a wealth[109]
ולא יוסף עצב עמה	Untainted by anxiety.[110]
אוצר נחמד ושמן בנוה חכם	Valuable treasures decorate the homes of the wise,[111]
וכסיל אדם יבלענו	While the homes of the foolish get swallowed up.[112]
לא יועילו אוצרות רשע	Treasures procured by wickedness produce no profit,[113]

106. Waltke, *Proverbs*, 58 (cf. Polonius' comment to Laertes, "brevity is the soul of wit," *Hamlet* 2.2.90). Weeks (*Introduction*, 4) describes the material in Proverbs 10–29 as "sentence literature."

107. Well-known are the similarities between Prov 22:17—24:22 and the Instruction of Amenemope (*ANET* 421–25; cf. Erman, "Quelle," 86–93; Shupak, "Amenemope," 203–20; and Washington, *Wealth*).

108. Sandoval, *Discourse*, 31. Van Leeuwen ("Proverbs," 25–36) explains this as the by-product of what he calls "systematic contradiction." Whybray (*Wealth*, 113–18) argues that the sentence sayings in 10:1—22:16 express the perspective of small farmers determined to condemn ostentatious wealth and sloth because, "like a disease, poverty is a misfortune to which human beings generally are liable."

109. Prov 10:22. Tg ברכתא דאלהא היא מעתרא, "the blessing of God is better than wealth."

110. Prov 10:22 (lit., "for anxiety does not mix with it"). OG λύπη ἐν καρδίᾳ ("grief in the heart"); Syr ܟܐܒܐ ܢܣܒܐ ܒܓܘܗ ("pain inflicted in it"). Cf. *ri-ṣu-ka ul maš-[ru-u] i-lu-um-[ma]*, "Wealth is not your support; your god is" (*BWL* 227.42–43). Cf. Sirach's association of "greed" with "self-loathing" (14:3–19; cf. below).

111. Prov 21:20. Wealth can be stored in temples (Janssen, "Temple," 509; Robertson, "Temple," 443–54) or private homes (Judg 17:4; Yadin, *Hazor*, 179–80; Hoffner, "Institutions," 565).

112. Prov 21:20. OG ἄφρονες δὲ ἄνδρες καταπίονται αὐτόν ("but foolish men swallow it"); Tg נבלענון ("is swallowed up by it"; cf. the PN בלעם, Balaam, "the people swallower," Num 22:5). Perdue (*Proverbs*, 196) thinks this saying derives from a world where "wisdom represents a conservative social order that is to be perpetuated and not overthrown by activities of revolution or disorder."

113. Prov 10:2. *Contra* Preuss ("יעל," 144) MT יעל ("to profit") can be interpreted both socioeconomically (Isa 30:5) and theologically (Hab 2:18).

וצדקה תציל ממות	While the pursuit of justice[114] rescues from a wrongful death.[115]
הון עשיר קרית עזו	The rich man's wealth is his fortress,[116]
וכחומה נשׂגבה במשׂכיתו	Like an inviolable barricade in his mind's eye.[117]
לא יועיל הון ביום עברה	Wealth profits nothing on the day of distress,[118]
וצדקה תציל ממות	But the pursuit of justice rescues from a wrongful death.[119]
יש מפזר ונוסף עוד	One gives liberally and becomes rich[120]
וחושך מישר אך למחסור	While another withholds what he owes and suffers.[121]

114. Prov 11:4 (cf. צדקות, "almsgiving," Tob 4:7–8). Whereas "justice" and "righteousness" are separate ideas in English, Heb צדקה and Vg *iustitia* incorporate both. That Syr reads ܕܝܢ ("judgment, verdict, justice"), however, indicates a bias toward the former.

115. Prov 10:2. Tg מן מותא ביא ("from a wrongful death"). N.B. that the same phrase appears again in 11:4. Fox (*Proverbs*, 511) thinks that this is to "assert that the wicked will not be able to buy protection or bribe their way out of danger."

116. Prov 18:11 (lit., "the village of his strength"). OG πόλις ὀχυρά ("secure city"); Syr ܡܕܝܢܬܐ ܕܥܘܫܢܗ (lit., "village of his strength"). Tg מזליה דעתירא קריתא דעוניה, "the rich man's fortunes are the village of his strength." Cf. the admonition وتحبون امال حبا جما, "You love wealth to the extreme" (lit., 'with an excessive love,' Q 89.20).

117. Prov 18:11. OG ἡ δὲ δόξα αὐτῆς μέγα ἐπισκιάζει ("whose glory casts a great shadow"); Vg *quasi murus validus circumdans eum* (like a strong wall surrounding him; so Tg). Cf. the storm-god's attempt to bolt the door to his village in order to protect it from his son Telipinu's fury (Hoffner, *Myths* 2.7).

118. Prov 11:4. Whether יום עברה (repeated verbatim in Sir 5:8) is eschatologically intended is possible (cf. Moore, *Babbler*, 45–57), yet Clifford (*Proverbs*, 122) posits this didactic saying to be about "the uselessness of wealth in a life-or-death crisis."

119. Prov 11:4 (verbatim repetition of 10:2). Clements ("Proverbs," 448) holistically recognizes here "the guarded, and sometimes openly hostile, references to wealthier citizens, whose wealth is regarded as endangering their moral and spiritual well-being" vs. "the repeated assurances that the path of wisdom is the way to success and prosperity."

120. Prov 11:24. Clifford (*Proverbs*, 125) finds it "paradoxical . . . that generosity to the poor leads to more wealth," while "stinting on giving makes one poorer." Yet N.B. that Qur'an praises the benefits of giving الفقرء الذين احصروا في سبيل الله لا يسيطيعون ضربا في الارض, "to those in need" if they "are wholly occupied on God's path and cannot travel in the land (to trade)" (Q 2.273).

121. Prov 11:24. Longman (*Proverbs*, 262) reckons that "the contrast of this verse has to do with generosity (or the lack thereof). Contrasting the consequences between philanthropy and miserliness highlights the advantage of generosity. The former gets richer; the latter gets poorer. Thus, the contrast is paradoxical, since common sense

קנה חכמה מה טוב מחרוץ	How much better it is to acquire wisdom than gold,
וקות בינה נבחר מכשׂף	And understanding instead of silver.[122]
בית והון נחלת אבות	House and wealth are an ancestral legacy,
ומיהוה אשה משׂכילת	But a discerning wife is from Yhwh.[123]
אשת היל מי ימצא	A principled woman who can find?[124]
ורחק מפנינים מכרה	For her value is far greater than gemstones.[125]
בטח בה לב בעלה	Since the heart of her husband trusts in her
ושלל לא יחסר	He never misses a business opportunity.[126]

might lead one to believe that holding on to one's possessions is a more certain way to wealth."

122. Prov 16:16. Doubtless it is no coincidence that the primary verb here (קנה, "to acquire, buy") derives from the world of business and commerce rather than, say, the cult or lawcourt, leading Fox (*Proverbs*, 618) to wonder whether the joy of acquiring wisdom comes from "the *effort* of learning, not only its *product*."

123. Prov 19:14. OG παρὰ δὲ θεοῦ ἁρμόζεται γυνὴ ἀνδρί ("but a woman joining to a man is the work of God"). In other words, a spouse is a "gift," not an "acquisition." Clements ("Proverbs," 452) argues that "a special interest of Prov 19 lies in its increased attention to questions of wealth and poverty as issues which especially affect the quality of life for most individual families," and Perdue (*Proverbs*, 185) contends that "the household provides a frequent setting" in that "a stupid child ruins a father, and a quarreling wife is likened to dripping rain (19:13)." Even though "the household and its wealth are inherited, it is Yhwh who provides one a prudent wife" (19:14). A common teaching in Talmud and Midrash is that while wives can marry up to a higher social status, they cannot descend to a lower status should a husband prove to be a failure (*b. Ket.* 48a; 61a; *Gen. Rab.* 20.11). Situating this saying in an Achaemenid context, Ben Zvi ("Wife," 27–49) argues (a) that socioeconomic power brings honor and the strongest endorsement for the pursuit of profit; (b) that the pursuit of profit requires wisdom about how to make a profit; and (c) that wives are often the primary "heroic economic agents" of the culture at large.

124. Prov 31:10. MT חיל can in some contexts refer to "wealth" as well as "honor/strength/capability." Cf. the description of Boaz as a גבור חיל ("wealthy man," Ruth 2:1). Deciding how much of the "wealth" nuance to apply to אשת היל must surely take into account the emphasis on her overtly socioeconomic attributes in the immediately following description of her. Yoder (*Wisdom*, 113) argues a position supported by Ben Zvi ("Wife," 27–49) that "the sage of Prov 1–9 and 31:10–31 uses language and imagery derived from (various) socioeconomic activities of and perceptions about women to personify Woman Wisdom." Frymer-Kensky (*Goddesses*, 180) sees the "principled woman" here as "the very prototype of the wise woman" in Prov 1–8.

125. Prov 31:10. This plural term (פנינים) recurs elsewhere in descriptions of Sophia (Prov 3:15; 8:11; Sir 7:19).

126. Prov 31:11 (lit., "and he does not want"). MT שלל usually refers to "spoil/booty/plunder" (OG σκύλων; Vg *spoliis*). Syr ܐܘܣܢܐ, "provisions"; Tg לא מתבזא ולא חסרה, "he is not exposed (for) he lacks nothing."

היתה כאניות סוחר	Like the merchants with their ships,
ממרחק תביא לחמה	She imports her supplies from great distances.[127]
זממה שדה ותקחהו	She inspects a field and buys it,[128]
מפרי כפיה נטעה כרם	Plants a vineyard on it, and works it with her own hands.[129]
טעמה כי טוב סחרה	Assessing the value of its production,[130]
לא יכבה בלילה נרה	Her lamp does not go out at night.[131]
כפה פרשה לעני	She opens her palms to the needy
וידיה שלחה לאביון	And her hands to the poor.[132]
צופיה הליכות ביתה	She oversees the activities of her house
ולחם עצלות לא תאכל	And does not snack on the crumbs of idleness.[133]

Poverty: Causes and Effects

ריש וקלון פורע מוסר	Poverty and disgrace fall on those who spurn instruction,[134]
ושומר תוכחת יכבד	While those who avoid disgrace become wealthy.[135]

127. Prov 31:14. Cf. Lambert's (*BWL* 121) essay on the work of the *tamkāru* ("trader/merchant") in the Šamaš Hymn (discussed above).

128. Prov 31:16 (lit., "she takes it"). Cf. OG ἐπρίατο ("to buy"); Vg *emit* ("to purchase"); Syr ܙܒܢ ("to buy"); Tg נסבת חלקא ("she takes the field").

129. Prov 31:16 (lit., "from the fruit of her hands").

130. Prov 31:18 (lit., "she tastes her trade"). OG ἐργάζεσθαι ("that which is worked"); Vg. *negotiato* ("the deal"). Syr ܒܚܢ can in some cases mean "to examine." What seems to be "examined" is not only the product *per se*, but the integrity of the process by which it is produced.

131. Prov 31:18. That is, she possesses a strong work ethic.

132. Prov 31:20. Tg reads יד ("hand") and דרע ("arm").

133. Prov 31:27. Ben Zvi ("Wife," 49–51) posits that 31:21, 27 emphasize her work ethic, but the poem as a whole (31:10–31) highlights the socioeconomic motifs of *work, almsgiving, land,* and *trade.*

134. Prov 13:18. OG ἀφαιρεῖται παιδεία ("take away discipline") grasps the intent of MT, but Syr (ܡܣܟܢܘܬܐ ܘܨܥܪܐ ܡܒܛܠܝܢ ܡܪܘܕܘܬܐ, "poverty and disgrace makes rebellion cease") and Tg (מסכנא ומן ליה צערא מרש מדותא, "poverty and what goes with it, disgrace, impoverishes the defiant") reverse it. Reading NJPS, Sandoval (*Discourse*, 175) translates "poverty and humiliation are for the one who spurns instruction."

135. Prov 13:18. OG ὁ δὲ φυλάσσων ἐλέγχους, "but the one who guards his

אל תגזל דל כי דל הוא	Do not rob the poor simply because they are poor,[136]
ואל תדכא עני בשער	And do not crush[137] the needy at the gate.[138]
איש מחסור אהב שמחה	The hedonist is a broken creature,[139]
אהב יין ושמן לא יעשיר	And those addicted to wine and fat do not prosper.[140]
כל ימי עני רעים	For the poor every day is dreadful,
וטוב לב משתה תמיד	But the cheerful heart enjoys a continuous buffet.[141]
בוטח בעשרו הוא יפול	Those who trust in their own fortunes wither,
וכעלה צדיקים יפרחו	While the righteous bloom like thriving plants.[142]

---

convictions." MT כבד can mean "glory, honor," and/or "wealth"; Syr ܝܩܝܪ (ܢܬܝܩܪ in the passive/reflexive) can mean "precious, splendid" (*PSD* 556). Sandoval (*Discourse*, 175) sees this couplet "drawing both on poverty language and the rhetoric of social status."

136. Prov 22:2. Cf. τὴν ζωὴν τοῦ πτωχοῦ μὴ ἀποστερήσῃς, "Do not cheat the poor of their living" (Sir 4:1). Rabbi Samuel ben Naḥmani (*Num. Rab.* 5.2) suggests that this specifically includes (a) the "gleanings" (לקט, Lev 23:22); (b) the "forgotten sheaves" (שכחה, Deut 24:19); (c) the "corner of the field" (פאה, Lev 23:22); and (d) the "poverty tithe" (מעשר עני, Deut 14:28–29).

137. Prov 22:2 (דכא, "to crush"). Cf. מה לכם תדכאו עמי, "What do you mean, crushing my people?" (Isa 3:15).

138. Prov 22:22. Cf. Instruction of Amen-em-opet §2 (*ANET* 422). Sandoval (*Discourse*, 145–46) believes that one of the sages' main goals is to insist that "the virtue of showing kindness to the poor belongs to the way of wisdom" because "one's action toward the poor simultaneously constitutes an action toward God." Qur'an rather famously legislates that all thieves are to have their hands removed (Q 5.38).

139. Prov 21:17 (lit., "the empty/scarce person loves pleasure").

140. Prov 21:17. Cf. Daniel's aversion to eating food מפת־בג המלך, ("from the king's menu," Dan 1:5). On the negative nuancing of אהב as "addiction," cf. Moore (*Babbler*, 56–57).

141. Prov 15:15. Tg מן דטב בלביה, "whoever is good in his heart." *Contra* Clifford (*Proverbs*, 213), Fox (*Proverbs*, 595) rejects the possibility that MT טוב לב might here mean "instructed mind."

142. Prov 11:28. N.B. עלה in the Two Eagles Parable (Ezek 17:8). Waltke (*Proverbs*, 573) argues that "the problem of the poor is not God's creation, but injustice."

The Poverty-Wealth Polarity

Antonymous parallelism structures most of the following sayings:[143]

הון יסיף רעים רבים	Wealth attracts many "friends,"
ודל מרעהו יפרד	While the poor remain friendless.[144]
הון עשׁיר קרית עזו	Wealth is the fortress of the rich,
מחתת דלים רישׁם	While poverty is the slum of the poor.[145]
אל תאהבה שׁנה פן תורשׁ	Do not oversleep lest you become poor;[146]
פיכח עיניך שׂבע לחם	Wake up and be content with what you have.[147]
כפר נפשׁ אישׁ עשׁרו	The rich think of wealth as insurance,[148]
ורשׁ לא שׁמע גערה	But the poor have no need of such.[149]

143. Cf. Watson, *Techniques*, 104–260.

144. Prov 19:4. Sirach says something quite similar: πλούσιος σαλευόμενος στηρίζεται ὑπὸ φίλων ταπεινὸς δὲ πεσὼν προσαπωθεῖται ὑπὸ φίλων, "When a rich person totters, his friends support him, but when a poor man falls, even his friends push him away" (13:21). Clifford (*Proverbs*, 195) recognizes that "rich and poor come into contact in a variety of ways; their relationship to a large extent is determined by considerations of wealth." But perpetual class conflict can be avoided by recognizing that "Yhwh is the creator and sustainer of every human being, a basic relationship coming before all others."

145. Prov 10:15 (cf. 18:11). Toy (*Proverbs*, 208) sees no "ethical thought in this proverb—the sense is that wealth smooths one's path in life . . . a simple recognition of the value of money," and Clifford (*Proverbs*, 199) basically agrees, arguing that "the rich will always do what they want," even when "those who curry favor with them end up the poorer." Yet cf. Rabbi Akiva's curious comment that "poverty is fitting for a Jew" (*Lev. Rab.* 13.4).

146. Prov 20:13 (lit., "Do not love sleep"). Clifford (*Proverbs*, 177) finds it "paradoxical that laziness, not industry, brings deep sleep."

147. Prov 20:13. Cf. Q 2.188, ولا تاكلو اموالكمو بالباطل بينكم, "Do not illicitly consume each other's wealth."

148. Prov 13:8 (lit., "as a ransoming of the soul"). Boadt ("Proverbs," 662) believes that "Wisdom's attitude on the subject of wealth is always ambivalent."

149. Prov 13:8 (lit., "does not hear reproach"). Delkurt (*Einsichten*, 101–2) thinks that Prov 10:15 and 13:8 try to show that "wealth can be advantageous during bad harvests (10:15) or even cancel out a death sentence (13:8)." Perdue (*Proverbs*, 231) recognizes that Proverbs does not engage the poverty-wealth polarity in "black-and-white terms," but that "the subject of wealth and poverty is ambiguous" because "the sages do not give a clear definition of wealth and poverty, nor do they indicate who they consider to belong to the categories of rich and poor." Hausmann (*Menschenbild*, 338) finds no group of sayings in Proverbs so *zwiespältig* ("mottled") as those dealing with the poverty-wealth polarity, but Sandoval (*Discourse*, 190–91) insists that "apparent incongruity does not necessarily suggest that the proverbial discourse of wealth and

טוב רש הולך בתמו	Better to be poor walking straight
מעקש דרכים והוא עשיר	Than to be rich walking a crooked path.[150]
יש מתעשר ואין כל	Some appear to be rich, but have nothing;
מתרושש והון רב	Others appear to be poor, but are actually rich.[151]
תחנונים ידבר רש	The poor resort to begging,
ועשיר יענה עזות	But the rich work hard.[152]
ראש עשה כף רמיה	A slack hand produces poverty,[153]
ויד חרוצים תעשיר	But a diligent hand produces wealth.[154]
אטם אזנו מזעקת דל	Those who close their ear to the cry of the poor[155]
גם הוא יקרא ולא יענה	Will hear no answer when *they* cry for help.[156]

poverty is hopelessly ambiguous," even though עשיר ("the rich") appears to "caricature a 'class' or 'type' of person as one which typically does trust in wealth."

150. Prov 28:6 (cf. 19:1). MT עקש דרכים ("crooked paths"); OG πλουσίου ψευδοῦς ("lying rich man"); Syr ܥܬܝܪܐ ܡܥܩܡ ܐܘܪܚܬܐ ("the rich man crooked of ways"); Vg *dives pravis itineribus* ("rich man of crooked itineraries"). Bar Qappara, in an exposition of Lev 24:2, reveals his take on poverty when he has Yhwh say הרשים שבכם חביבין עלי, "The poorest among you are precious to me" (*Lev. Rab.* 31.4).

151. Prov 13:7. Sandoval (*Discourse*, 199) insightfully calls this an "ironic wealth and poverty saying" like 13:22; 22:16; and 28:8, recognizing how "problematic" it is for those who read Proverbs only as "a wisdom prosperity axiom in a more or less straightforward, literal manner" (i.e., who adhere to a "health-and-wealth" ideology in lieu of a holistic biblical theology). Longman (*Proverbs*, 285) agrees, arguing that "the principle of this verse is to be careful not to allow appearances to deceive."

152. Prov 18:23 (lit., "answer strongly"). Bland (*Proverbs*, 172) thinks that this saying is intended to say that "one's speech betrays one's social class," but this seems a stretch.

153. Prov 10:4. Other proverbs addressing the slacker-vs.-worker polarity are Prov 6:6–11; 10:26; 12:11, 24; and 24:30–34 (cf. Longman, *Proverbs*, 231). Rabbi Tanḥuma posits that showing one's teacher a "slack hand" can result in loss of memory, loss of vitality, and poverty (*Num. Rab.* 15.17).

154. Prov 10:4. Rephrasing the "hand" metaphor, Q 17.29 reads: "Do not be so tight-fisted (ولا تخعل يدك مغلله الى عنقك, lit., 'do not chain your hand to your neck') that you become irresponsible, nor so open-handed (ولا تبسطا كل البسط, lit., 'do not extend your hand too far') that you incur 'loss'" (محسرا; cf. חסר, Prov 21:17; Job 30:3; Ps 23:1).

155. This is precisely what the young Hittite prince warns his father's cronies not to do (*KBo* 22.1.20′–30′; cf. above).

156. Prov 21:13. Longman (*Proverbs*, 505) recognizes that "on the surface of things nothing can be seen to be farther apart than the rich and the poor, and particularly the

עשיר ורש נפגשו	What the rich and the poor have in common
עשה כלם יהוה	Is that Yhwh creates them both.[157]
ראש ועשר אל תתן לי	Give me neither poverty nor wealth;
הטריפני לחם חקי	Just my daily bread,[158]
פן אשבע וכחשתי	Lest I become disillusioned,
ואמרתי מי יהוה	And say, "Who is Yhwh?"
ופן אורש וגנבתי	Or I become poor and steal
ותפשתי שם אלהי	And profane the name of my God.[159]

On Debtors and Creditors

אל תהי בתקעי כף	Do not guarantee loans for just anyone
בערבים משאות	Or too readily take on the burden of debt.[160]
אם אין לך לשלם	Should you not be able to repay,
למה יקח משכבך מתחתיך	Why risk having your bed pulled out from under you?[161]

rich who exploit the poor in order to get rich. The rich live lives of ease and luxury; the poor are dirty and scrape by in life." The truth the sages want to underline, however, is that "both are God's creatures."

157. Prov 22:2. Sirach (10:22) puts it like this: πλούσιος καὶ ἔνδοξος καὶ πτωχός τὸ καύχημα αὐτῶν φόβος κυρίου, "the rich, the eminent, and the poor have one claim in common—the fear of Yhwh." Cf. McKane (*Proverbs*, 321–22); Plöger (*Sprüche*, 63); Boström (*Proverbiastudien*, 100); Meinhold (*Sprüche* 1.110); Fox (*Proverbs*, 211); Murphy (*Proverbs*, 260–64); and Waltke (*Proverbs* 1.331). Westermann (*Roots*, 21) understands that "the proverbs dealing with the poor and the rich make no attempt to articulate the difference in principle between the two or negate their difference. There are poor and there are rich, and one must live with this fact. Hence, the diverse ways in which to react to this reality are left open, and the variety of points of view are not reduced to any common denominator."

158. Prov 30:8. This saying comes from the דברי אגור ("Words of Agur," 30:1). Cf. Syr ܗܒ ܠܝ ܣܘܒܪܐ ܣܘܦܩܝ ("Give me enough to live on"), and GNT Matt 6:11, τὸν ἄρτον ἡμῶν τὸν ἐπιούσιον δὸς ἡμῖν σήμερον, "Give us this day our daily bread."

159. Prov 30:9. In other words, both extremes are problematic. Wilson (*Proverbs*, 308) notes that "while many 'prosperity gospel' teachers think that Proverbs promises that if you are wise or righteous then you will be rich, the book itself explains that there are dangers from both wealth and poverty."

160. Prov 22:26 (cf. *Aḥq* 111, 129–31; Prov 6:3–5, discussed above). Wilson (*Proverbs*, 250) suggests that the point of this saying is not to outlaw moneylending *per se*, but "to count the cost before doing so."

161. Prov 22:27. Perdue (*Proverbs*, 124) explains: "The sages in Proverbs warn strongly against this practice (moneylending), especially when it comes to offering

רע ירוע כי ערב זר	Anyone securing loans for strangers courts trouble,[162]
ושנא תקעים בוטח	But those who avoid it rest secure.[163]
לקח בגדו כי ערב זר	Seize the garment of anyone who secures loans for a stranger,
ובעד נכריה חבלהו	Or who promises pledges on behalf of foreigners.[164]
מלוה ליהוה חונן דל	Whoever is kind to the poor lends to Yhwh,[165]
וגמלו ישלם לו	And receives full compensation.[166]
עשיר ברשים ימשול	The rich dominate the poor,

oneself as surety. This foolish action, whether the offering of oneself or one's possessions, potentially threatens one's well-being by coming under the power of either a neighbor or a stranger. If, however, students one day should find themselves in this predicament, then they should humble themselves before creditors, implore them for additional time and opportunity to make good their promises, and then know no rest until the debts are paid."

162. Prov 11:15. Syr works within the wealth-poverty polarity, but omits any direct reference to the practice of moneylending: ܒܝܫܐ ܡܒܐܫ ܟܕ ܕܐܪܒ ܠܙܕܝܩܐ ܡܛܠ ܕܨܒܐ ܕܡܣܟܢ ܠܦܓܪܐ, "Quite evil is it whenever an adversary fights with a righteous person because he wants to portray himself as poor." OG either (a) attempts to convey the basic underlying meaning of MT or (b) simply bleaches out (with Syr) the socioeconomic element: πονηρὸς κακοποιεῖ ὅταν συμμείξῃ δικαίῳ, "An evil person does evil when he confuses the righteous person." Vg comes closest to MT: *adfligetur malo qui fidem facit pro extraneo qui autem cavet laqueos securus erit*, "Those who put their faith in another by guaranteeing them a loan put themselves in danger by wrapping a noose around their neck."

163. Prov 11:15. Longman (*Proverbs*, 168) reckons that "the problem with loans is that they are often given in contexts where the lender cannot afford to lose the money, and the risk is just too high." Goldingay ("Proverbs," 595) remarks that "the use of wealth requires good sense not to squander it on kind but risky causes such as posting bail or guaranteeing a loan for a stranger."

164. Prov 20:16 (cf. 27:13). Alter (*Wisdom*, 187) sees this saying "grounded not in ethics, but in purely prudential considerations," yet Washington ("Strange," 217–42) posits a setting in which Palestinian Jews are miscegenating with Gentiles.

165. Prov 19:17. In Qur'an the deity rewards those who . . . اقمتم الصلاة . . . واتيتم الزكو . . . اقرضتم الله قرضا, "establish prayer . . . give alms . . . and loan to God a goodly loan" (Q 5.12). Askari (*Economics*, 314) interprets this to mean that "goodly loans . . . provide loans to those in need without expecting a monetary reward." Sirach holds a similar view (Sir 35:12), as does Luke (6:34).

166. Prov 19:17. N.B. that this saying expresses the most basic meaning of שלם (*HAL* 1418–23).

ועבד לוה לאיש מלוה	But the borrower is enslaved to the creditor.[167]

On Labor

כחמץ לשנים וכעשן לעינים	Like vinegar to the teeth or smoke to the eyes
כן העצל לשלחיו	Is the slacker to his employer.[168]
אל תיגע להעשיר	Do not become a workaholic,[169]
מבינתך חדל	But be smart enough to know when to rest.[170]
התעיף עיניך בו ואיננו	If you start searching for wealth it will disappear,[171]
כי עשה יעשה לו כנפים	For suddenly it will sprout wings and take flight
כנשר יעוף השמים	And ascend like an eagle to the heavens.[172]

167. Prov 22:7. Fox (*Proverbs*, 699) posits that "one should keep out of debt, for as surely as the rich subjugate the poor, so does the lender soon subjugate the borrower. The subjugation may be economic (because of the burden of the debt) or legal (if the debtor defaults and is forced into debt slavery."

168. Prov 10:26 (lit., "to those who send him out"). Fox (*Proverbs*, 526) recognizes that since "messengers are indispensable," and so "much depends on their honesty, diligence and accuracy," employers sometimes empower them with the authority "to offer explanations or elaborations or enter into negotiations." *CH* 17.69 addresses some of the more obvious dangers threatening the merchant-trader-agent relationship (cf. Meier, *Messenger*, 545–47, and above).

169. Prov 23:4 (lit., "do not wear yourself out for riches"). OG μὴ παρεκτείνου πένης ὢν πλουσίῳ, do not stretch out the poor as to the rich"; Syr ܠܐ ܬܬܩܪܒ ܠܡܬܥܬܪܐ, "do not draw near (just) to become rich" (so also Tg); Vg *noli laborare ut diteris*, "do not labor (just) to become rich."

170. Prov 23:4. Cf. Instruction of Amen-em-opet §6 (*ANET* 422). Murphy (*Proverbs*, cited in Wilson, *Proverbs*, 251) notes that the sages persistently warn students not to let work become life's "all-consuming purpose." A classic example of this, of course, is the character of Ebenezer Scrooge in Charles Dickens' *A Christmas Carol*.

171. Prov 23:5. OG ἐὰν ἐπιστήσῃς τὸ σὸν ὄμμα πρὸς αὐτόν ("if you fix your eye on it");

172. Prov 23:5. Cf. the similar use of the "flight" metaphor in the Instruction of Amen-em-opet: "If riches come to you by theft / They will not stay the night / When day comes they leave the house / . . . / Making themselves wings like geese / They fly off into the sky" (*AEL* 2.152).

לעג לרש חרף עשׂהו	Those who mock the poor insult their Maker;
שׂמח לעיד לא ינקה	Those who rejoice at disaster are not innocent.[173]
עשק דל חרף עשׂהו	Those who oppress the poor insult their Maker,
ומכבדו חנן אביון	But those who are kind to the poor glorify Him.[174]
תאוה עצל תמיתנו	The slacker's addictions lead to his demise,
כי מאנו ידיו לעשׂות	Because lazy hands refuse to work.[175]
עצלה תפיל תרדמה	Laziness leads to lethargy,[176]
ונפש רמיה תרעב	And idle souls wind up hungry.[177]
טמן עצל ידו בצלחת	The slacker puts his hand in the dish,
גם אל פיהו לא ישיבנה	But cannot pull it back to his mouth.[178]
חכמות נשים בנתה ביתה	Wise women build their houses up,
ואולת בידיה תהרסנו	But foolish women tear them down.[179]
נפש עמל עמלה לו	The laborer's soul works hard on his behalf,

173. Prov 17:5. Prov 17:5 is practically identical to 14:31, only where one ends negatively, the other does not (cf. 19:17; 22:2; 29:13; Sir 11:4). Toy (*Proverbs*, 337) suggests that "taken by itself" this line "may refer to the punishment of heartlessness through the operation of natural laws."

174. Prov 14:31. Yoder (*Proverbs*, 191) suggests that sayings like this "caution against *Schadenfreude*, the enjoyment of another's troubles—even, perhaps especially, when those troubles are self-inflicted."

175. Prov 21:25. Ogden Bellis (*Proverbs*, 205) gives this section the headings "The Lazy Lust; the Corrupt Covet; the Just are Gracious." Cf. "Go forth, whether lightly or heavily equipped, and 'work hard' (جاهدوا) with 'your wealth' (موالكم) and 'your souls' (انفسكم)" (Q 9.41, 44).

176. Prov 19:15. OG reads δειλία κατέχει ἀνδρογύναιον ("timidity leads to effeminacy"), to which Delitzsch (*Proverbs*, 2.28) suggests that OG intends a word denoting "an effeminate man, a man devoid of manliness, a weakling."

177. Prov 19:15. Fox (*Proverbs*, 996) remarks that "an excess of ambition is overweening and unseemly . . . but laziness too is arrogant" for the slacker imagines that he can "gain his needs without a commensurate investment of effort."

178. Prov 19:24 (cf. 26:14). Toy (*Proverbs*, 380) calls this "a humorous and sarcastic rebuke of laziness."

179. Prov 14:1 (lit., "with their hands"). The contrast between חכמת ("wise women") and אולת ("foolish women," OG ἄφρων; Syr ܣܟܠܬܐ) reflects the overarching Sophia trajectory depicted in Prov 8–9, but *contra* Murphy (*Proverbs*, 103), Longman (*Proverbs*, 296) is doubtless correct to apply it here to actual women.

כי אכף עליו פיהו	Because hunger drives him on.[180]
דרך עצל כמשֻׂכת חדק	The slacker's road is strewn with thorns,[181]
וארח ישרים סללה	But the path of the proficient is a clear highway.[182]
בכל עצב יהיה מותר	In all toil there is profit,
ודבר שׂפתים אך למחסור	But lip-service leads to scarcity.[183]
יד חרוצים תמשול	The hand of the diligent prevails,
ורמיה תהיה למס	While slackers wind up in labor camps.[184]
לא יחרוך רמיה צידו	The negligent do not roast their kill,
והון אדם יקר חרוץ	But the wealth of the diligent steadily grows.[185]
גם מתרפה במלאכתו	Anyone slacking off at work
אח הוא לבעל משחית	Is like a dreadful boss.[186]
מתאוה ואין נפשו עצל	The slacker's soul craves what it does not have,

180. Prov 16:26. Toy (*Proverbs*, 331) captions this saying with the words, "Hunger makes a person industrious." In Qur'an God puts Adam in the garden and says, ان لك ولا تجوع, "Here you shall never go hungry," (Q 20.118).

181. Prov 15:19. OG ὁδοὶ ἀεργῶν ἐστρωμέναι ἀκάνθαις ("the roads of the inert—lit. 'non-working'—are sprinkled with thorns").

182. Prov 15:19. MT ישר ("upright") does not always connote moral uprightness (cf., e.g., 2 Kgs 10:3; *HAL* 429, *tüchtig*, "proficient, capable").

183. Prov 14:23. This antonymous contrast מותר ≠ מחסור ("profit" ≠ "scarcity"; repeated in 21:5) is generally maintained by the versions.

184. Prov 12:24. MT מס always refers to *corvée* ("forced labor," 1 Kgs 9:21). Qur'an legislates similar punishment against those who disparage "almsgiving" (الصدقات; cf. צדקות, lit., "the righteous things," Tob 4:7) and the freewill donation of "labor" (جهد, "*jihad*," Q 9.79).

185. Prov 12:27. The meaning of this proverb is difficult to ascertain, as a comparison of the versions makes clear. Cf. OG οὐκ ἐπιτεύξεται δόλιος θήρας κτῆμα δὲ τίμιον ἀνὴρ καθαρός, "The deceitful person does not succeed in capturing a possession, but an honorable person is pure"; Syr ܢܬܩܒܠ ܨܝܕܐ ܠܓܒܪܐ ܢܟܠܐ ܘܩܢܝܢܐ ܕܝܩܝܪܐ ܠܡܣܟܢܐ ܠܐ, "The hunter is not received by the deceitful person, but his precious fortune is entrusted to the poor"; Vg *non inveniet fraudulentus lucrum et substantia hominis erit auri pretium*, "The deceitful person makes no profit, for a person's substance is the price of pure gold"; Tg לא נסתקבל צידא גברא נכילא ומזליה דבר אנש דהבא יקירא, "The hunter is not received by the deceitful person, and his fortunes of precious gold are a human concern."

186. Prov 18:9. (lit., "is a brother to a *ba`al* of destruction"). Describing characters like Old-Age, Fear, and Hunger in the "courts and entrances to hell," Vergil (*Aeneid* 6.278) lists *tum consanguineus Leti Sopor Leti* ("Sleep, Death's next-of-kin").

ונפש חרוצים תדשן	But the diligent enrich their souls.[187]
הדלת תסוב על צירה	Like a door on its hinges,
ועצל על מטתו	Are slackers who lounge on their beds.[188]
עבד אדמתו ישׂבע לחם	Those who work the land produce ample food,[189]
ומרדף ריקים חסר לב	While fools pursue worthless trivia.[190]

On Slavery

עבד משׂכיל ימשל בבן מביש	A sensible servant[191] managing a trying child
ובתוך אחים יחלק נחלה	Should obtain an inheritance alongside its siblings.[192]
לא נאוה לכסיל תענוג	Luxury is not suitable for a fool,[193]
אף כי לעבד משל לסרים	Nor is a slave governing over princes.[194]

187. Prov 13:4. Cf. "My wealth has not 'enriched' me" (ما غنى غنى ماليه, lit., "delivered plunder," Q 69.28), and "Men and women procure the 'profits from what they earn'" (نصيب مما اكتسبوا, Q 4.32).

188. Prov 26:14 (cf. 12:24, 27). Clifford (*Proverbs*, 76) recognizes that "Proverbs is less harsh on the sluggard than on the fool and the wicked," but that unwillingness to help gather in the harvest is "reprehensible."

189. Prov 12:11. In an ideal world יצא אדם לפעלו ולעבדתו עדי ערב, "a person goes out to his work and his labor until the evening" (Ps 104:23).

190. Prov 12:11 (cf. 28:19). Where the מרדף ריקים ("pursuer of empty things") in 12:11 merely חסר לב ("lacks sense"), the מרדף ריקים in 28:19 is ישׂבע ריש ("poverty-filled").

191. Prov 17:2. The expression עבד משׂכיל ("sensible servant") recurs in Prov 14:35; Sir 7:21; 4Q16.2.2.15.

192. Prov 17:2. Cf. *BWL* 132.117 (Šamaš Hymn) and *CH* §168–69 (discussed above). In Qur'an "the heirs" (الوارثون; on ورث, cf. ירשׁ, "to inherit," Isa 54: 3; Jer 49:1) who "inherit Paradise" (يرتون الفدوس) are those who faithfully "give alms" (الزكاة, Q 23.4, 10–11); i.e., pay the "alms-tax" annually collected at the close of Ramadan (الزكة الفطر, lit., at the "charity breakfast").

193. Prov 19:10. MT תענוג ("pleasure, contentment"); OG τρυφή ("luxury"; cf. PN Τρύφων, 1 Macc 11:39); Syr ܦܘܢܩܐ ("daintiness, pleasure"); Vg *deliciae* ("luxury, dainti-ness"); Tg פנוקא ("tenderness, fragility"). Cf. Arab عنجهيه ("haughtiness, pride").

194. Prov 19:10. Voicing the sages' point of view, Fox (*Proverbs*, 652) explains that "when a fool comes into wealth and can indulge himself, it is an affront to those who achieve such things through the application of intelligence and effort—or who never do acquire them. How much the worse when a slave receives powers that properly belong to the free and well-born." Qohelet (10:7–9) makes a similar reverse comparison.

On Sound Stewardship

מחשבות חרוץ אך למותר	The plans of the diligent lead to abundance
וכל אץ אך למחסור	But reckless behavior leads to scarcity.[195]
כל היום התאוה תאוה	Addicts cravenly hunger every day,[196]
וצדיק יתן ולא יחשׂך	But the righteous freely give without hesitation.[197]
בית צדיק חסן רב	The house of the righteous holds great treasure,[198]
ובתבאת רשע נעכרת	But the "revenue" of the wicked is chaos.[199]
טוב ינחיל בני בנים	The good leave a legacy for their grandchildren,
וצפון לצדיק חיל חוטא	While "wicked wealth" is forwarded to the righteous.[200]
הון מהבל ימעט	Wealth hastily acquired soon disappears,[201]

195. Prov 21:5. On the antonymous contrast between מותר ("abundance") and מחסור ("scarcity"), Perdue (*Proverbs*, 244) argues that "the sages never teach that God predestines certain people to be wealthy and others to embrace poverty. God is the one who rewards and punishes, at times with the conditions of wealth and poverty. Yet God is also the defender of the destitute who rises up as their advocate, and the judge who punishes those who oppress the poor or ignore their plight."

196. Prov 21:26 (lit., "the cravers crave"). OG ἀσεβὴς ἐπιθυμεῖ ("the ungodly desire"); Syr ܪܐܓ ܪܓܐ ("the desirer desires"; so Tg); Vg *concupiscit et desiderat* ("he covets and desires"). Lyu (*Proverbs*, 68) argues that "in Proverbs' mode of thought, human desires are neither neutral nor amoral. There are legitimate desires and illegitimate ones. Living as a righteous person means not only doing the right things, but also desiring the right things."

197. Prov 21:26. On חשׂך ("to withhold, hesitate, inhibit"), cf. חשׂך יואב את העם, "Joab restrained the people" (2 Sam 18:16).

198. Prov 15:6. Syr uses a preposition, ܒܒܝܬܗ ܕܙܕܝܩܐ ("*in* the house of the righteous man").

199. Prov 15:6 MT תבאת (from בוא, lit., "that which comes in"). Bland (*Proverbs*, 144) sees in this saying a continuation of "the character-consequence scenario dominating the theology of chapters 10–15."

200. Prov 13:22 (cf. Sir 5:8). Toy (*Proverbs*, 276–77) thinks from this text that Israel views "the bequeathal of wealth to descendants" as "a crowning test of prosperity." For Longman (*Proverbs*, 290–91), however, this saying shows "how the bad person, whether characterized as fool or wicked, could have *any* material wealth."

201. Prov 13:11. Toy (*Proverbs*, 268) imagines מהבל ("hastily") implying "fraudulent business procedures, extortion, and the like."

While compounded wealth keeps growing over time.[202]	וקבץ על יד ירבה
Those who inflate their wealth with exorbitant interest[203]	מרבה הונו בנשך ותרבית
Simply stow it away for those who help the poor.[204]	לחונן דלים יקבצנו
"Bad deal, bad deal," says the buyer,	רע רע יאמר הקונה
Until afterwards, when he starts bragging about it.[205]	ואזל לו אז יתהלל
Better is a little with the fear of Yhwh	טוב מעט ביראת יהוה
Than great treasure tainted with anxiety.[206]	מאוצר רב ומהומה בו
Better is a humble man with provisions[207]	טוב נקלה ועבד לו
Than a boastful man without bread.[208]	ממתכבד וחסר לחם
Better is a vegetarian meal served with love	טוב ארחת ירק ואהבה שם
Than a luxurious meal served with enmity.[209]	משור אבוס ושנאת בו

202. Prov 13:11. OG uses this proverb to contrast wealth achieved by ἀνομία ("lawlessness") with that achieved by εὐσεβεία ("godliness").

203. Prov 28:8. Cf. the similar sentiment in the Dialogue of Pessimism (*BWL* 148.64) and N.B. that Qur'an واحل البيع وحزم الزبا, "permits trade, but forbids interest/usury" (Q 2.275).

204. Prov 28:8. Noting how Torah explicitly prohibits the taking of interest from the poor (Exod 22:24: Lev 25:36; Deut 15:1–6), Fox (*Proverbs*, 823) argues that while "interest-bearing loans are necessary to provide capital for commerce . . . the law is not concerned with these so much as for usurious loans to the poor." Qur'an staunchly condemns those "rabbis" (لاحبار) and "monks" (الرهبان) who "hoard" (يكنزون) gold and silver in order to devour "the property" (اموال)" of others (Q 9.34; cf. EpJer 35).

205. Prov 20:14. Fox (*Proverbs*, 669) notes that "a prospective buyer denigrates wares to lower the price, only to pride himself afterward on his cleverness. Dissembling is common in the marketplace . . . . One can imagine a merchant quoting this proverb to a balky customer."

206. Prov 15:16 (cf. Ps 37:16). Reading ב(ל)ו ("without it") with OG μετὰ ἀφοβίας ("with fearlessness"); Syr ܡܢ ܡܫܘܚܬܐ ܕܫܓܘܫܬܐ ܕܥܘܠܐ ("than a confusing measure of injustice"). N.B. that the parallel in Prov 16:8 reads בלא משפט ("with no justice").

207. Tur-Sinai (משלי שלמה, 102) emends MT עבד ("slave") to עבור ("provisions," Josh 5:11; adopted by Fox, *Proverbs*, 550).

208. Prov 12:9. Qur'an dips into the "What-can-be-worse?" pool by questioning how "obstacles" (الفبه) to social justice may be overcome, one of the most pertinent being "setting free a slave" (فكرفبه, lit. "unshackle a neck," Q 90.12–13). Isaiah voices a similar sentiment via the phrase אגדות מוטה התר, "loosen the thongs of the yoke" (Isa 58:6).

209. Prov 15:17. These two "better" sayings (v. 16 and v. 17) closely resemble those

On Socioeconomic Justice

People curse the grain-hoarder,[210]	מנע בר יקבהו לאום
But bless the vendor's laurel.[211]	וברכה לראש משביר
The poor oppressing other poor[212]	גבר רש ועשק דלים
Is like a driving rain sweeping away much-needed supplies.[213]	מטר סחף ואין לחם
Bread acquired by deceit is sweet	ערב לאיש לחם שקר
Until the mouth clogs up with silt.[214]	ואחר ימלא פיהו חצץ
Oppressing the poor to enrich oneself	עשק דל להרבות לו
By overindulging the rich leads to loss.[215]	נתן לעשיר אך למחסור

---

found in the Instruction of Amen-em-opet ("Better is poverty in the hand of the deity / Than wealth in the storehouse // Better is bread with a happy heart / Than wealth with vexation," *AEL* 2.152). Murphy (*Proverbs*, 112) sees them exemplifying quintessential "wisdom" because of the way they "point up paradox."

210. Prov 11:26 (lit., "withholder of grain"). Cf. OG ὁ συνέχων σῖτον, "the one who withholds wheat"; Syr ܕܟܠܐ ܥܒܘܪܐ, "the one who withholds grain"; Tg מן דכלא עבורא באולצנא נשבקוניה לבעל, "Whoever withholds grain in a famine is to be abandoned to Ba`al." Clifford (*Proverbs*, 126) justifiably understands this to refer to "holding back grain to drive up prices."

211. Prov 11:26. Farmer (*Good*, 93) understands this saying to be "a comment on what some merchants might think of as 'good business' in hard times."

212. Prov 28:3. MT גבר רש ("poor man"); OG ἀνδρεῖος ἐν ἀσεβείαις ("impious man"; i.e. reading רשע); Syr ܓܒܪܐ ܡܣܟܢܐ ("poor man"); Vg *vir pauper* ("poor man"); KJV ("poor man"); NRSV ("ruler"); NIV ("ruler"). N.B. that James makes a similar argument: "You have dishonored the poor; is it not the rich who oppress you?" (Jas. 2:6; cf. below).

213. Prov 28:3. Even though several translators cannot imagine poor people oppressing other poor people, and that "the rain is ordinarily expected to be a blessing, and the poor would ordinarily expect empathy and support from those who share in their poverty" (Farmer, *Good*, 84), some cannot bring themselves to recognize that the same phenomenon routinely occurs today as a result of what Brainard menacingly calls "the doom spiral" ("Web," 2–5).

214. Prov 20:17. Reacting to what she calls the "deception" motif, Yoder (*Proverbs*, 212) compares this saying to others depicting "deceptive speech as junk food" (Prov 9:17: 18:8; 26:22).

215. Prov 22:16. Cf. the Hittite prince's reprimand: $^{\text{LÚ.MEŠ}}$NA-ŠI ṢÍ-DI-TI$_4$-KU-NU-U *ka-a-ša-at-ta-wa* $^{\text{LÚ.MEŠ}}$NA-ŠI ṢÍ-DI-TI$_4$-KU-NU-U *da-me-eš-kat-te-ni*, "Do you see your servants, whom you habitually oppress?" (*KBo* 22.1.18′–19′; see above). Qur'an reminds Mohammad that ووجدك عايلا فاغنى, "God found you in poverty and enriched you" (Q 93.8)

On Abominable Activities

פלס ומאזני משפט ליהוה	Honest weights and balances are from Yhwh,[216]
מעשׂהו כל אבני כיס	Every stone in the pouch is there because of his doing.[217]
מאזני מרמה תועבת יהוה	A false weight is an abomination to Yhwh,
ואבן שׁלמה רצונו	Yet accurate balances please him.[218]
אבן ואבן איפה ואיפה	Fluctuating weights and balances
תועבת יהוה גם שׁניהם	Are an abomination to Yhwh.[219]
תועבת יהוה אבן ואבן	Variable weights are an abomination to Yhwh,
ומאזני מרמה לא טוב	And false balances are not profitable.[220]
פעל אוצרות בלשׁון שׁקר	Procuring fortune through a lying tongue
הבל נדף מבקשׁי מות	Is a futile enterprise driven by activists with a death wish.[221]

On Bribery

שׁחד מחיק רשׁע יקח	The wicked take secret bribes
להטות ארחות משׁפט	To pervert the paths of justice.[222]

216. Prov 16:11. Cf. *ša ki-ni ṣa-bit* [GIŠ]*zi-ba-ni-ti ma-ʾ-da mim-ma šum-šu ma-ʾ-di qí-ša-aš-šu*, "The merchant who manages the balances honestly accumulates all kinds of abundance" (*BWL* 132.110; see above).

217. Prov 16:11. This and the next three proverbs focus on the importance of using legitimate weights in business dealings according to an overtly theological rationale; i.e., Yhwh's name appears in each of these proverbs.

218. Prov 11:1.

219. Prov 20:10.

220. Prov 20:23. These last three proverbs utilize a strong cultic term (תועבה) to denote the priestly abhorrence of defilement (cf. Lev 18:22, 26, 27, 29, 30; 20:13; Deut 7:26; 13:15; 14:4; 17:4; 22:5; Ezek 16:50; and *passim*).

221. Prov 21:6. Just as several Hebrew proverbs link death with the tongue (Prov 10:8; 11:11; 12:13; 13:13), so also do several Arabic proverbs; e.g., كصوا السنتكم فان مصتل الرجل بين فكيه, "Hold your tongues, for the destroyer of man lies between his jaws" (al-Maydânî 2.313; cf. Jas 3:1–8).

222. Prov 17:23. OG λαμβάνοντος δῶρα ἐν κόλπῳ ἀδίκως οὐ κατευοδοῦνται ὁδοί ἀσεβὴς δὲ ἐκκλίνει ὁδοὺς δικαιοσύνης, "taking gifts into the bosom unjustly, the wicked bring no prosperity, but pervert the ways of justice"; Syr ܡܢ ܕܢܣܒ ܫܘܚܕܐ ܒܥܘܠܐ

אבן חן השחד בעיני בעליו	Bribes are "lucky charms" in their masters' eyes;
אל כל אשר יפנה ישׂכיל	Everywhere they turn they "prosper."[223]
עכר ביתו בוצע בצע	The greedy consumer drags his house into trouble,[224]
ושׂונא מתנת יחיה	But those who refuse to take bribes eventually prevail.[225]
מטן בסתר יכפה אף	A secret gift turns away anger,
ושחד בחק המה עזה	And a clandestine bribe fierce wrath.[226]
רבים יחלו פני נדיב	Many seek the face of the diligent,
וכל הרע לאיש מתן	But the gift-giver is everyone's friend.[227]
מתן אדם ירחיב לו	A gift opens doors,[228]
ולפני גדלים ינחינו	Making larger-than-life individuals accessible.[229]

ܗܘ ܥܘܠܐ ܢܣܒ ܐܘܚܕܢܐ ܕܕܝܢܐ, "It is wicked to accept a bribe, for it is the clutching of judgment"; Vg *munera de sinu impius accipit ut pervertat semitas iudicii*, "he who accepts gifts from wicked people perverts the course of justice"; Tg שוהדא מן עובא יסב רשיעא למצלי ארחא דדינא, "the wicked person treats the bribe in his bosom like prayers on the path to judgment."

223. Prov 17:8. Scott (*Proverbs*, 110) sees great uncertainty here because (a) אבן חן (lit., "stone of favor") may refer to a charm or gemstone; (b) שוחד may refer to a gift or bribe (OG translates παιδεία, "discipline"); and (c) בעליו may refer to bribe-*givers* or bribe-*takers*.

224. Prov 15:27 (cf. בצע בצע in 1:19). Qur'an (4.2) similarly warns against "consuming" funds earmarked for the poor: لا تاكلوا اموالهم ("do not devour their property").

225. Prov 15:27. Kassis (*Proverbs*, 211) argues (a) that "the words שחד ("bribe") and מתן ("gift") are used interchangeably," and (b) that "bribery" in Proverbs has both positive and negative connotations. Commenting on מתן in Prov 18:16, he suggests that whether מתן refers "to a gift and not a bribe is debatable." Boadt (*Proverbs*, 661) also posits that "bribery in Proverbs has two sides," and Farmer (*Proverbs*, 88) states bluntly, "The Solomonic sayings do not condemn bribes *per se*." Without denying that there is a small measure of ambivalence about bribery in Proverbs, this trendy attempt to twist it into something it's not doubtless says more about biblical interpreters than biblical texts.

226. Prov 21:14. This and the next two proverbs depict "bribery" as something of a political necessity, like the bribing of Enlil's vizier in Atraḫasis (*Atr* 1.383).

227. Prov 19:6. Fox (*Proverbs*, 650) thinks this saying is designed to satirize "friendship . . . contaminated by money . . . its didactic value (being) to put people on guard against the bogus friend."

228. Prov 18:16. Scott (*Proverbs*, 113) translates, "A man's gift clears the way for him, and brings him into the presence of the great."

229. Clifford (*Proverbs*, 199) interprets this to mean that "many people try to bribe the wealthy or ingratiate themselves with them," yet (a) "the rich always do what they

בז לרעהו חוטא	Those who despise their neighbors are sinners,
ומחונן ענוים אשריו	But those who extend grace to the needy are happy.[230]
הן צדיק בארץ ישלם	If the righteous receive what they deserve on earth
אף כי רשע וחוטא	How much more so do wicked sinners.[231]
פעלת צדיק לחיים	The work of the righteous leads to life,[232]
תבואת רשע לחטאת	While the "produce" of the wicked leads to sin.[233]
רב אכל ניר ראשים	The field of the poor yields plenty of food,
ויש נספה בלא משפט	That is, until injustice sweeps it away.[234]

This remarkable collection of economically-infused sayings, subdivided here into ten overlapping categories, opens a pedagogical portal into the minds of the teachers using them to teach the Hebrews how to live prosperous and successful lives. Tired attempts to situate their origin in the late Persian period, a time when the satrap of Yehud struggles to pay taxes and tribute to insatiable Achaemenid overlords, are not altogether preposterous,[235] yet it cannot be overemphasized how impossible it is to identify the sociohistorical *Sitze im Leben* of these sayings because, as

want," and (b) "those who curry favor with them end up the poorer." Thus Proverbs "memorably expresses the great gulf between the poor and the rich."

230. Prov 14:21. Waltke (*Proverbs*, 599) argues that this proverb "protects misinterpreting the previous verse ('the poor are disliked even by their neighbors,' 14:20) as a rationalization for shunning a poor neighbor . . . . Such favor is freely given, not forced. When extended to the needy it implies pity, mercy, and generosity; it does not imply preferential treatment." The Letter of James deals with this issue in no uncertain terms.

231. Prov 11:31. Waltke (*Proverbs*, 514–15) sees postmortem judgment indicated by this משל, the righteous undergoing remedial punishment on earth, the evil later on in the afterlife, but Fox (*Proverbs*, 546) rejects this, arguing that both righteous and unrighteous receive the same punishment, just the latter with more certainty. This saying underlines that D forms of שלם are definable negatively *as well as* positively (*HAL* 1420–21).

232. Prov 10:16. MT פעלת צדיק is singular, but OG ἔργα δικαίων, "works of the righteous," is plural.

233. Prov 10:16 (cf. 3:9, 14). OG καρποὶ δὲ ἀσεβῶν, "the fruits of the ungodly."

234. Prov 13:23. In 28:3 the poor oppressing the poor sweeps away food like מטר סחף ("driving rain"), but here לא משפט ("injustice") "sweeps" it away (נספה).

235. *Pace* Blenkinsopp ("Woman," 457–73), Washington ("Woman," 217–42), and Yoder (*Wisdom*, 73–110), it's inappropriate, if not altogether untenable, to situate the provenance and application of these sayings only to Jews living under Achaemenid rule.

Christl Maier underwhelmingly states, the process of "determining the sociohistorical context of poetic texts . . . is a difficult undertaking."[236] Instead it seems more profitable to recognize, with Craig Bartholomew and Ryan O'Dowd, that unlike all other ANE collections, the Proverbs of Solomon begin with instructions to "my *son*," and conclude "with an incarnate embodiment of wisdom" personified in a successful Hebrew *woman*.[237]

Glenn Pemberton summarily imagines Proverbs' approach to the poverty-wealth polarity as a series of brush strokes applied by a master painter:[238]

- *Stroke #1—"We never have enough"*—this is where most proverbs begin; i.e., the essentially materialistic desire for more money, more possessions, and more power
- *Stroke #2—"More valuable than money"*—recognizing materialism to be unfulfilling, the sages repeatedly champion what they know to be more valuable in the long run: wisdom, justice, family, humility, integrity
- *Stroke #3—"Getting wealth by the wrong means"*—here the sages admonish their students to avoid the "shortcuts" of robbery, oppression, deceit, cutting corners, and get-rich-quick schemes
- *Stroke #4—"Acquiring wealth by the right means"*—here they lay out the alternatives to such "shortcuts": wisdom, justice, diligence, almsgiving
- Stroke #5—*"Best use for wealth is to help the poor"*—i.e., recognize the value of *both* wealth *and* poverty, rely on honest business practices, protect the vulnerable, defend human rights
- Stroke #6—*"The problem of self-inflicted poverty"*—i.e., avoid laziness, wickedness, greed, hedonism, and addiction.

Wisdom Psalms

Assessing the criteria for determining what is or is not a "wisdom psalm" can be daunting,[239] a task "somewhat akin," in Norman Whybray's memorable analogy, "to the making of bricks without straw."[240] Appreciative of

236. Maier, *Frau*, 1. Watson (*Diaspora*, 349) simply presumes that "historical circumstances occasioning ahistorical moral sayings of parénesis cannot be determined."

237. Bartholomew and O'Dowd (*Wisdom*, 270). Cf. Camp (*Wisdom*, 1–19).

238. Pemberton, *Proverbs*, 137–57.

239. In her Cambridge dissertation, e.g., Engle ("Delight," 32–71) challenges the widely-held view that Ps 119 is a "wisdom psalm."

240. Whybray ("Wisdom," 152; cf. Glatt-Gilad, "Song," 229–35). Cf. the thorough

the attempts of Hermann Gunkel and his students to situate every psalm in the Psalter within its sociohistorical *Sitz im Leben*,[241] Simon Chi-Chung Cheung nevertheless argues, in light of newer developments in genre theory,[242] that the more defensible way to proceed is to determine whether this or that psalm displays a sapiential "family resemblance"[243] comprised of three "signature wisdom features": (a) ruling wisdom thrust; (b) intellectual tone; and (c) didactic speech intention.[244]

Psalm 37: Colonize the Land

Psalm 37 is an acrostic poem[245] highlighting, in Kenneth Kuntz's opinion, the question of "economic power, a prominent theme in biblical wisdom literature."[246] Other motifs animate this psalm as well, but "land inheritance,"[247] a socioeconomic motif recurring no less than six times, is the literary backbone:

בטח ביהוה ועשה טוב	Trust in Yhwh and do good;
שכן ארץ ורעה אמונה	Colonize[248] land and manage its wealth.[249]
כי מרעים יכרתון	The wicked will be cut off,

history of discussion in Cheung (*Wisdom*, 1–20). The following paragraphs deal only with Pss 37, 49, and 112.

241. "Life-setting"; cf. Gunkel (*Psalmen*); Mowinckel (*Psalmenstudien*); Westermann (*Psalms*); Crüsemann (*Danklied*); Hossfeld and Zenger (*Psalmen*). Hunter (*Wisdom*, 102) thinks that any attempt to locate the "life-setting" of an ancient poem "is all too often a cart pulling a horse rather than a genuine deduction from real evidence."

242. Cf. Fowler (*Literature*); Newsom (*Contest*, 11–15); Miller ("Genre," 151–67); Cheung (*Wisdom*, 16–19).

243. Cf. Fowler, *Literature*, 41–42.

244. Cheung, *Wisdom*, 180. Each of these features needs to be critiqued, of course, but this is not the place for it. Cf. instead Kuntz (*Wisdom*); Stewart (*Wisdom*); and Uusimäki (*Wisdom*).

245. Cf. Botha, "Wealth," 105–28.

246. Kuntz, *Wisdom*, 139. Goldingay (*Psalms*, 514–35) entitles it "The Weak Will Take Possession of the Land"; Cheung (*Wisdom*, 53) entitles it "The ABCs of Living in the Land."

247. Citing ANE parallels in which land is never sold by one person to another unless first sanctioned by the king/overlord, Lohfink ("ירשׁ," 385; followed by Joosten, *Land*, 186–87), argues that Yhwh's giving of land, particularly in Torah, is modelled on the same royal grant system.

248. Ps 37:3. Görg ("שׁכן," 695) senses a semantic distinction between ישׁב and שׁכן, positing the former to signify "permanent dwelling," and the latter to signify "an apparently secure but in reality endangered existence" (i.e., "colonization"; cf. Lohfink, "ירשׁ," 385).

249. Ps 37:3, reading with OG (ἐπὶ τῷ πλούτῳ αὐτῆς) and Vg (*in divitiis eius*). Cf. Syr ܗܝܡܢܘܬܐ, "firmness."

While those who hope in Yhwh will possess land.[250]	וקוי יהוה המה יירשו ארץ
A little while longer and the wicked will be gone;	ועוד מעט ואין רשע
You will stare at their seat, but find it empty.[251]	והתבוננת על מקומו ואיננו
The poor will possess land[252]	וענוים יירשו ארץ
And enjoy its rewards.[253]	והתענגו על רב שלום
The wicked draw the sword and bend the bow	חרב פתחו רשעים ודרכו קשתם
To strike down the poor and the needy,[254]	להפיל עני ואביון
And slaughter those striding the upward path.[255]	לטבוח ישרי דרך
But better is a little with the righteous	טוב מעט לצדיק
Than a lot with the wicked.[256]	מהמון רשעים רבים
The wicked borrow without paying back	לוה רשע ולא ישלם
While the righteous generously give.[257]	וצדיק חונן ונותן
Those blessed by him will possess land,[258]	כי מברכיו יירשו ארץ
But the accursed will be cut off.	ומקלליו יכרתו

250. Ps 37:9. MT קוה ("to hope/wait") appears again in 37:7 and 37:34. Cf. Syr ܡܣܝܒܪܝܢ, "endure"; OG ὑπομένοντες, "endure"; Vg *sustinentes*, "forbear"; Tg ודסברין במימרא דיי, "those who hope in the Word of Yah."

251. Ps 37:10. Cf. Prov 23:5 and 4Q171.2.7 אתבוננה, "I will stare" (1st pers. sg.).

252. Ps 37:11. OG οἱ πραεῖς, "the meek" (cf. Syr ܡܣܟܢܐ, "the poor man" (sg.); 4Q171.2.9 ענוים (same as MT) is defined by the *pesher* as עדת האיבונים, "the congregation of the poor" (4Q171.2.10). Cf. also GNT Matt 5:5.

253. Ps 37:11 (cf. the identical phrase, רב שלום, in 72:7); Syr ܡܬܒܣܡܝܢ ܒܫܠܡܐ ܣܓܝܐܐ evidently takes MT על רב adverbially, reading "enjoying themselves in peace." 4Q171.2.11–12 employs this motif not from a metaphorical, but from a socioeconomic perspective, insisting that no slaveowner/landowner/creditor will ever again force the poor to do their bidding.

254. Ps 37:14. OG πτωχὸν καὶ πένητα, "beggar and day-laborer"; Syr ܡܣܟܢܐ ܘܠܒܝܫܐ, "poor and unfortunate"; Tg למקטול עניי וחשיכי למכוס, "to kill the poor and those 'held hostage' (lit., 'darkened') by the customs-house."

255. Ps 37:14.

256. Ps 37:16 (cf. Prov 15:16). Like Sirach, the sage in 4Q171.2.23 hardens the tradition by identifying the צדיק as "anyone who does Torah."

257. Ps 37:21. 4Q171.3.10–11 applies this text to the "congregation of the poor . . . inheriting the high mountain of Israel."

258. Ps 37:22. Ross (*Psalms*, 803) emphasizes that "one of the key considerations of the study of Psalm 37 is the intriguing emphasis on the blessing of the land."

לעולם נשמרו	The righteous will always be protected,[259]
וזרע רשעים נכרת	But the descendants of the wicked will be cut off.
צדיקים יירשו ארץ	The righteous will possess land,[260]
וישכנו לעד עולם	And colonize it forever.
קוה אל יהוה ושמר דרכו	Hope in Yhwh and stay on his path,
וירממך לרשת ארץ	And he will enable *you* to possess land.[261]

Psalm 49: The Value of a Human Being

Psalm 49 breaks down into two sections,[262] each ending with the refrain,

ואדם ביקר בל יב/לין	Human beings do not understand their value,
נמשל כבהמות נדמו	For they are like fragile beasts.[263]

The primary motif spotlighted by this psalm, in other words, is *value* (יקר).[264] *Question:* Do human beings understand their true value?[265] This question is

259. Ps 37:28. Creach (*Refuge*, 17) argues that "the ideas expressed by חסה/מחסה and a related field of words for 'refuge' represent an editorial interest that may be observed throughout the Psalter."

260. Ps 37:29. Tg למחסן ארעא, "take possession of the land" (cf. Tg 37:34).

261. Ps 37:34 (lit., "he will exalt you to inherit," Vg *exaltabit*).

262. Kraus (*Psalmen*, 362–63). Ignoring the versions, Perdue ("Riddles," 538–39) emends the text to read Ps 49:20 as a posed riddle, followed by its answer in 49:12.

263. Ps 49:14, 21 (with slight differences). Cf. OG καὶ ἄνθρωπος ἐν τιμῇ ὢν οὐ συνῆκεν, "humans do not understand their value"; Syr ܒܪ ܢܫܐ ܒܐܝܩܪܗ ܠܐ ܐܣܬܟܠ, "a son of man does not understand his value"; Vg *homo cum in honore esset non intellexit*, "humans with in (*sic*) honor/value do not understand"; Tg גברא חיבה ביקרא לא יבית עם צדיקיא, "a sinful man does not dwell with the righteous."

264. Dell ("Riddle," 445–58) challenges Mowinckel's ("Psalms," 205–44) view that the late wisdom psalms are completely non-cultic, arguing with Murphy ("Psalms," 166–67) and Perdue (*Wisdom*, 267–68) that the boundary between wisdom and worship is quite porous.

265. Cf. Ps 144:3–4. Fischer ("Dignity," 72) postulates that "the expression 'human being' has a normative semantic component, or, in other words, it is a *nomen dignitatis*. Being human—not in a biological sense, but in the social sense of being a member of the human community—means being a creature to whom acknowledgment and respect as a human are due on the grounds of his or her natural human attributes. The fact that being human is founded in acknowledgment makes humans very vulnerable. Human beings can be deprived of acknowledgment as human beings by treating them as non-humans or sub-human beings."

rhetorical, of course, but the psalmist's desire to examine it leads him into poetic engagement with the socioeconomic motifs of *wealth, abundance*, and *redemption*:

למה אירא בימי רע	Why should I fear when the days are evil,
עון עקבי יסובני	When the wickedness of my oppressors encircles me?[266]
הבטחים על חילם	When those who trust in their wealth,
ברב עשרם יתהללו	Praise themselves for their great fortunes?[267]
אח לא פדה יפדה איש	The truth is that no one can effect redemption;[268]
לא יתן לאלהם כפרו	No one can ransom themselves before God.[269]
ויקר פדיון נפשם	For the redemption of the soul is expensive,[270]
וחדל לעולם	And always will be.[271]
כי יראה חכמים ימותו	For anyone can see that the wise die,
יחד כסיל ובער יאבדו	That both fool and dolt perish together,
ועזבו לאחרים חילם	And abandon their wealth to others.[272]
אך אלהים יפדה נפשי מיד שאול	Yet God will redeem my soul from the power of Sheol[273]

266. Ps 49:6. Cf. Syr ܒܥܠܕܒܒܝ, "my enemies" (derived from ܒܥܠ, *ba`al*); Tg אלהי דחובת סורחני, "gods of the sin of my corruption."

267. Ps 49:7. Most ETs read "boast," but N.B. that וללהתי is reflexive. Cf. Prov 11:28.

268. Ps 49:7. Cf. the "pious sufferer's" lament over being denied Marduk's *paṭāru* ("redemption," *Lud* 1.56).

269. Ps 49:8. OG ἐξίλασμα, "propitiatory offering, ransom"; Syr ܠܐ ܝܗܒ ܠܐܠܗܐ ܦܘܪܩܢܐ, "one cannot ransom to God the ransom" (so Tg).

270. Ps 49:9. Tg ויהי יקיר פורקניה ויפסוק בישותיה, "for its redemption is valuable as he cuts away its wickedness."

271. Ps 49:9 (lit., "never changes"). Tg ופורענותה לעלם, "and he will forever pay it."

272. Ps 49:11. Cf. King Munbaz's critique of "earthly treasure," i.e., how it is "vulnerable to human hands," (b) cannot produce genuine "benefits," (c) has more to do with *mammon* than souls, and (d) benefits only "others" (*t. Pe'ah* 4.18; cf. Moore, *WealthWarn*, 164).

273. Ps 49:16. MT יפדה ("he will redeem"); OG λυτρώσεται ("he will redeem"); Syr ܢܦܪܘܩܗ ("he will ransom/redeem it"); Vg *redimet* ("he will buy back"); Tg יפרוק ("he will tear away, rescue"). Qur'an allows that, in lieu of fasting, those who can afford it can on occasion فديه طعام مسكين, "ransom a poor person by feeding him," Q 2.184). Rosenzweig's *Star of Redemption* is widely perceived to be one of the most significant interpretations of "redemption" in the twentieth century.

When he takes me.[274]	כי יקהני
So do not worry whenever someone becomes rich,[275]	אל תירא כי יעשׁר איש
When the wealth in their house compounds.[276]	כי ירבה כבוד ביתו
For when they die they will take nothing;	כי לא במותו יקחה כל
None of their wealth will descend after them.[277]	לא ירד אחריו כבודו

Psalm 112: Their Charity Stands Forever

Psalms 111 and 112 are back-to-back acrostic psalms, each beginning, like the last five psalms in the Psalter, with the phrase הללו יה.[278] Of these two, however, only Psalm 112 incorporates socioeconomic motifs:

Blessed are those who fear Yhwh	אשרי איש ירא את יהוה
And take great delight in his commandments.[279]	במצותיו חפץ מאד
Wealth and riches flood their houses	הון ועשׁר בביתו
And their charity stands forever.[280]	וצדקתו עמדת לעד
Being good people, they generously lend,	טוב איש חונן ומלוה

274. Ps 49:16 (because לקח recurs below in 49:18, "take" seems the best ET here). Cf. OG ὅταν λαμβάνῃ με, "whenever he takes me"; Vg *acceperit me*, "accepts me"; Tg יפרוק נפשי מן דין גהנם ארום ילפנני אוריתיה לעלמין, "He will sever my soul from the judgment of Gehenna, I will arise, and he will impart to me his teachings forever."

275. Ps 49:17. In James' opinion the acquisition of wealth itself is problematic (Jas 2:6–7; cf. below).

276. Ps 49:17. A similar sentiment occurs in Ps 73:12, הנה אלה רשׁעים ושׁלוי עולם השׂגו חיל, "Look at these wicked people. Always at ease, they increase in wealth."

277. Ps 49:18. N.B. that the verb here is ירד ("descend"), not עלה ("ascend").

278. *Hallelu-jah* (i.e., "Praise Yah"). N.B. that Brodersen (*Psalter*, 270–78) definitively refutes Zenger's thesis ("Komposition," 807–10); i.e., that the Psalter's final five psalms are a single unit designed to provide a "suitable conclusion" to the "book" of Psalms.

279. Ps 112:1. Mays (*Psalms*, 360) contends that "the dependance of Psalm 112 on Psalm 111 is a literary signal that the second is meant to be read, interpreted, and used in relation to the first."

280. Ps 112:3, translating צדקה as "almsgiving/charity," as in 4Q200.2.6–9 (Tob 4:7–8). This understanding of צדקה appears also in Talmud (cf. גבאי צדקה, "alms collectors"; מחלקי צדקה, "alms distributors," *b. Šabb.* 118b).

יכלכל דבריו במשפט	Conducting their affairs with fairness.[281]
פזר נתן לאביונים	Freely they share with the poor,[282]
צדקתו עמדת לעד	Their charity forever active.[283]

Qohelet

Like the Babylonian Theodicy and Dialogue of Pessimism, the book of Qohelet (Ecclesiastes)[284] is something of a cross between pessimistic lament and didactic admonition,[285] but in two or three places it looks a bit like a philosophical diatribe.[286] Whether its outlook is predominantly Eastern or Western is not immediately obvious.[287] Acknowledging the pool of suggested proposals for its literary structure, Choon Leong Seow insists that

281. Ps 112:5.

282. Ps 112:9.

283. Ps 112:9. Pss 111–12 precede the so-called Egyptian Hallel Psalms (Pss 113–18; cf. Hayes, "Hallel," 145–56; Hossfeld, "Akzente," 51–63).

284. The first line reads דברי קהלת, "The words of Qohelet, (OG ἐκκλησιαστής, transliterated by Vg as *Ecclesiastes*), from the verb קהל ("to gather, assemble"). Hengel (*Hellenism*, 126) lists several points in Qohelet's thought in which "contacts with the spirit of early Hellenism might be visible."

285. Peterson (*Hope*, 12) simply categorizes the book as a "teaching document."

286. Perry (*Qohelet*); Kim (*Voices*, 5–17). Drawing from his Yale dissertation, Longman (*Ecclesiastes*, 8) compares the book's genre to "fictional Akkadian autobiography," but Crenshaw ("Ecclesiastes," 275) finds in Qohelet *several* literary genres: diatribe, similitude, dialogue, royal testament, anecdote, autobiographical narrative, parable, antithesis, and proverb. Kreeft (*Philosophies*, 7) lavishes high praise upon it, noting that "books of philosophy can be classified in many ways: ancient vs. modern, Eastern vs. Western, optimistic vs. pessimistic, theistic vs. atheistic, rationalistic vs. irrationalistic, monistic vs. pluralistic, and many others. But the most important distinction of all, says Gabriel Marcel (*Philosophy*, 12), is between 'the full' and 'the empty,' the solid and the shallow, the profound and the trivial. So, when you read all the books in all the libraries in the world . . . you will not find three more profound books than Ecclesiastes, Job, and Song of Songs."

287. Gerstenberger (*Persian*, 254) recognizes that "it remains extremely difficult to classify both branches of the wisdom tradition in a reasonable way in the literary and social history of the biblical traditions." On the one hand, some identify Qohelet as a text deeply influenced by earlier ANE wisdom (Dahood, "Qoheleth," 30–52, 191–221), while on the other hand critics like Haag (*Zeitalter*, 112–18), Hengel (*Hellenism*, 115–30), de Jong ("Qohelet," 85–96), Grabbe ("Jews," 53), and Fox ("Qoheleth," 122–23) identify its intellectual contents and literary structure as something at least nominally shaped by Hellenistic rhetoric. Seow (*Ecclesiastes*, 21–36) and Kugel ("Money," 47–49) marshal arguments positing a context in the Persian period, but again, as Bartholomew (*Ecclesiastes*, 54–59) makes clear, this debate is far from resolved.

it cannot be "merely a loose collection of aphorisms."[288] Plunging into the discussion, James Crenshaw singles out what he thinks are four of the most attractive structural proposals.[289] Either (a) an anonymous sage writes the bulk of Qohelet under Solomon's "authority,"[290] after which it then undergoes several editorial changes (e.g., the appended epilogues in 12:9–14);[291] or (b) the author dialogues with a conversation partner, real or imagined;[292] or (c) the author engages traditional "old" wisdom, but only in order to contest it;[293] or (d) the book reflects the evolution of a single author's views over time.[294] Each theory has its champions, of course, but in light of the ANE wisdom literature surveyed above the middle two options seem the most likely. Why? Because from an intertextual perspective it seems clear that this scroll intentionally reworks several socioeconomic motifs focused on *wealth, profit, labor, business, skill,* and *investment.*[295]

288. Seow (*Ecclesiastes*, 450), *contra* Delitzsch (*Koheleth*, 238), finds it difficult to discern *any* type of recognizable structure.

289. Crenshaw ("Ecclesiastes," 272–73); cf. Wright ("Sphinx," 45–66).

290. Unlike the beginning of Proverbs, the beginning of Qohelet does not mention Solomon by name, even though the fact that he is a son of David living in Jerusalem has led many to conclude as much. Bypassing the sociohistorical question of authorship, Brown (*Ecclesiastes*, 11) posits "the character of Solomon as both Qohelet's guise and foil."

291. Longman (*Ecclesiastes*, 284) calls the author of 12:9–14 the "frame narrator." Christianson (*Ecclesiastes*, 255–58) tries to see the epilogues not as editorial, but as the intentional conclusion to Qohelet's "narrative story." Siegfried (*Prediger*, 2–12) posits no less than three editors, each with his own ideological agenda—one an Epicurean Sadducee, one a חכם ("wise man"), and one a חסיד ("pious man").

292. Cf. the Babylonian Theodicy (*BWL* 70–89; Loader, *Polar*, 132–33). Hertzberg (*Prediger*, 30) imagines a *zwar-aber* ("yes, but") structure, and Whitley (*Koheleth*, 92) sees Hertzberg saying that the speaker's uncertainty about the future leads him to the conclusion that "the most unpromising venture may have an unexpectedly successful outcome."

293. Cf. the Dialogue of Pessimism (*BWL* 139–49 and above). Gordis (*Koheleth*, 95–108) sees the writer citing several sapiential "quotations" in order to challenge them (cf. Whybray, "Quotations," 435–51). Fox (*Qohelet*, 19–28) imagines behind the book a lengthy list of contradictions to which the writer apprehensively reacts.

294. Jastrow (*Cynic*, 189) suggests that Qohelet "is not afraid of the charge of 'inconsistency,' but he would have his answer ready, 'Why not? Life is full of inconsistencies.'"

295. Cf. sources cited in Kugel ("Money," 32–49). Dahood ("Qoheleth," 221) claims no less than twenty-nine "commercial terms" in Qohelet, and Eaton (*Ecclesiastes*, 80) lists the book's "key terms" as "toil, vanity, striving after wind, profitability, and under the sun."

Wealth

One of Qohelet's first socioeconomic pronouncements emerges from his early adolescent obsession with material things.[296] Alongside the acquisition of vineyards, gardens, parks, and pools,[297] for example:

קניתי עבדים ושפחות ובני בית היה לי	I purchased male and female slaves, homebred slaves,[298]
גם מקנה בקר וצון הרבה היה לי	And more property (cattle and sheep)[299]
מכל שהיו לפני בירשלם	Than anyone in Jerusalem before me.[300]
כנסתי לי גם כסף וזהב	I also hoarded silver and gold for myself[301]
וסגלת מלכים והמדינות	And the treasure of kings and countries.[302]

296. Cf. Reines ("Koheleth," 80–84); Pemberton (*Proverbs*, 140–41). Heim (*Ecclesiastes*, 69) defines "materialism" in language anyone can understand: "*Homo lupus homini* ('man is wolf to man'). This famous Latin proverb, which likens human beings who hold power over others to wolves, one of the predators at the top of the food chain in the animal world, encapsulates what Qohelet is saying. Greed is *not* good, and whenever one part of the human population seeks their own advantage at the expense of another, the normal rules of public life no longer apply."

297. Philo (*Spec.* 2.105) celebrates the fact that because of Jubilee, even the poor can prosper from "olive gardens and vineyards remaining open, and all their other 'properties' (κτήσεις), whether they come from crops or trees." Bland ("Ecclesiastes," 210) argues that the verb בקש ("to seek") in 3:6 "refers to the people's pursuing their livelihoods, acquiring wealth, lands, and houses, and acquiring treasures."

298. Qoh 2:7. MT בני בית (lit., "sons of the house"; OG οἰκογενεῖς, "homebred"); Vg *possedi servos et ancillas multamque familiam*, "I acquired the male and female slaves (needed for) a great household." Tg reads מבניהון דהם ושאר עממין נוכראין, "from the children of Ham and other foreign nations" (i.e., Egypt, a well-known source of slaves; cf. Hagar, Gen 16:1).

299. Qoh 2:7. MT מקנה ("property") is the nominal form of the first word in this verse, קנה ("to acquire"). Whether OG and Syr are correct to include within it בקר ("cattle") and צון ("sheep") seems likely, yet Tg dodges the question by (a) avoiding direct agreement with the MT, and (b) verbosely camouflaging its reading behind an embellishment involving "officers placed over the food in my house to provide for me and the people of my house, to provide food for me and the people of my house twelve months of the year, and one to provide for me during the 'leap-year' (עיבורא)."

300. Qoh 2:7. Whether "everyone before me" refers to wealthy *kings* is problematic because only two kings precede Solomon (Saul and David). Another possibility, of course, is that the author is not Solomon, but a much later "son of David" (e.g., Hezekiah; cf. Prov 25:1).

301. OG Sirach warns that ὁ ἀγαπῶν χρυσίον οὐ δικαιωθήσεται, "the lover of gold will never be justified" (Sir 31:5), and that πολλοὶ ἐδόθησαν εἰς πτῶμα χάριν χρυσίου, "many have come to ruin because of gold" (31:6). Thus, μακάριος πλούσιος ὃς εὑρέθη ἄμωμος καὶ ὃς ὀπίσω χρυσίου οὐκ ἐπορεύθη, "Blessed is the rich person who is found blameless and does not go after gold" (31:8). Cf. Luke 6:24–26 and Jas 5:3 (below).

302. Qoh 2:8. Syr reads ܩܢܝܢܐ ("possessions, landed properties). On MT סגלה

Experience eventually convinces him, though, that

אהב כסף לא ישׂבע כסף	The lover of money is never satisfied with it,
ומי אהב בהמון לא תבואה	Nor the lover of wealth with gain.[303]

Then he reflects on the implications of this truth:

יש רעה חולה ראיתי חחת השמש	A terrible evil have I seen under the sun:
עשׁר שמור לבעליו לרעתו	Wealth is kept by its owners to their hurt,[304]
ואבד העשׁר ההוא בענין רע	And they lose that wealth in bad business deals,
והוליד בן ואין בידו מאומה	So that when they become parents there is nothing left in their hands.[305]

This sage depicts "God's gift" as something multidimensionally comprised of עשׁר ("riches"), נסכים ("possessions"), and עמל ("labor"):

כל האדם אשר נתן לו האלהים	Anyone to whom God gives
עשׁר ונסכים והשׁליטו לאכל ממנו	Riches and possessions and the ability to enjoy them[306]
ולשׂאת את חלקו ולשׂמח בעמלו	Should shoulder their share and rejoice in their labor.[307]

("treasure"), cf. Ug *sgl* (*DULAT* 754); Akk *sikiltu* ("personal property," *AHw* 1041); OArm סגיל ("treasure house, temple," *DNWSI* 776–77); Aram סגולא, "cluster" (e.g., of grapes, *DTTM* 953). With regard to מדינות, Kugel ("Money," 37) rejects the meaning most often assigned (cf. the 127 "satrapies" of Persia in Esth 1:1, *HAL* 521; cf. مدينه, "Medina"), suggesting instead that it be read as a nominalization of the root דין ("judgment") here and in 5:7, translating "judgment-seat" or "legal dispute."

303. Qoh 5:10. N.B. the contrast here between "acquiring" money (Qoh 2:7) and "loving" it (5:10; cf. 1 Tim 6:10).

304. Qoh 5:12. Rabbi Abbahu (*Exod. Rab.* 31.3) comments: "Happy is the one who can 'withstand the test' (בנסיונו) . . . He tries the 'rich' (עשיר) to see if their hand is open to the 'poor' (עניים), and the poor to see if they will accept 'trials' (יסורין) without 'anger' (כועס)."

305. Qoh 5:13. Tg adds ההוא עתרא נטיר ליה לאבאשא ליה לעלמא דאתי לסוף יומיא, "and at the end of days these riches are kept for him for his degradation in the world to come." In other words, poor fiscal management leads to bad consequences which extend even into the afterlife.

306. Qoh 5:18 (ET 5:19). MT אכל ("to eat, devour"); OG φαγεῖν ("to eat"); Syr ܠܡܐܟܠ ("to eat"); Tg אשלטיה למיכל מניה בעלמא הדין ולמעבד מניה צדקתא ולקבלא אגר שלים בעלמא דאתי ("And if the Lord gives him the power to eat of it in this world, and do good with it, then he will receive a full reward in the world to come").

307. Qoh 5:18 (ET 5:19). Tg adds ולמבדח בטורחיה עם צדיקיא ("and to rejoice in his work with the righteous").

Not everybody, however, enjoys "shouldering their share," especially when the prospects of "profitability" look dim:

יתן לו האלהים עשר ונכסים וכבוד	God gives them riches, possessions, and wealth
ואיננו חסר לנפשו מכל אשר יתאוה	So that they lack nothing of all they desire
ולא ישליטנו האלהים לאכל ממנו	Yet God does not enable its consumption
כי איש נכרי יאכלנו	Because foreigners devour it.[308]

Profit

One of the most prominent motifs in Qohelet emerges from the term יתרון ("profit"),[309] a motif common to several sapiential texts.[310] One Middle Egyptian text, for example, shows a "suffering sceptic" putting a question to his *ba* ("soul"): "What 'profit' do you gain by complaining about life like

308. Qoh 6:2. As is his wont, Tg delimits this warning to a specific socioeconomic context, in this case one dictated by the tenets of levirate law (Deut 25:5–10): ולא אשלטיה יי על עותריה למטעם מניה אלהין ימות בלא ולד ולא חס על קריביה לא חסנותיה ליה ארום אנתתיה תהא מתנסבא לגבר חילונאי ויחסניניה ("The Lord does not enable him, on account of his sins, to enjoy it; but he dies without issue and his kinsman takes no possession of his inheritance, and his wife is married to a stranger who takes his inheritance away to consume it").

309. Qoh 1:3 and *passim*. Schoors (*Qoheleth*, 423–27) recognizes ten occurrences; Kugel ("Money," 32) sees eighteen. Deriving from the verb יתר (Syr ܡܘܬܪܢܐ; cf. Ug *ytr*, *DULAT* 993; *CAD* A/2.487–92; Arab وتر), this noun often means "advantage" (*HAL* 431–32), but as Kugel points out, Qohelet presumes it "to have a more technical sense of 'profit' or 'net gain.'"

310. Akk *(w)atāru* often appears in economic texts to denote "excessive wealth" (*CAD* A/2.489–91; cf. وتر, "to repeat successfully"). Found three times in the Šamaš Hymn in the chorus *ṭa-a-bi eli* [D]*Šamaš balāṭa ut-tar* ("Šamaš is pleased to make his life profitable," *BWL* 132.100, 106, 119), it describes the sun-deity's approval of those judges who refuse to be bribed even after losing their *nēmelū* ("profits," 104). Cf. the PN יתרו, "Jethro" ("his profit," Exod 18:1). One rabbi explains that "his name is 'Jethro' because he 'increases' (ייתר) Torah by an additional chapter" (*Tanḥ Yithro* 4). Qohelet also uses another term, כשרון, to denote the "profit" motif, e.g., in the phrase ברבות הטובה רבו אוכליה ומה כשרון לבעליה כי אם ראות עיניו, "When goods increase so do those who devour them; so what 'profit' is it to the owners except to feast their eyes?" (Qoh 5:10).

some wealthy person?"[311] Alongside the primary theme of הבל ("futility),[312] Qohelet engages repeatedly the "profit" motif. Three times, for example, he voices the question מה יתרון ("What does it profit?"), each time referring to the challenge of finding "profit" in "labor":

• מה יתרון לאדם בכל עמלו	What does it profit anyone for all their labor . . . ?[313]
• מה יתרון העושׂה באשר הוא עמל	What does it profit workers in what they labor . . . ?[314]
• מה יתרון לו שׁיעמל לרוח	What does it profit anyone to labor for the wind?[315]

In addition to its use of third person, Qohelet, like Ludlul bēl nēmeqi,[316] periodically utilizes first person speech:[317]

ופנתי אני בכל מעשׂי	Then I considered all my doings
שׁעשׂו ידי	Which my hands have done,
ובעמל שׁעמלתי לעשׂות	And the labor which I labor to do.[318]

311. Eg *ptr.km.k.* Lichtheim (*AEL* 1.165) and Allen (*Debate*, 46) translate "gain," but Wilson ("Dispute," 405) reads "goal," and Eaton (*Ecclesiastes*, 39) reads "profit" (cf. Morenz, *Religion*, 157). That ANE complainants often talk to themselves (i.e., to their "hearts") is not unusual. Just as Erra's "heart" (*libbu*) provokes him into desperate action (*Erra* 2C.9), so also does the "heart/inner spirit" (Ug. *ggn*) of Kirta's son Yaṣṣib (*CAT* 1.16:6:26; cf. Luke 12:19).

312. Just as the superlative construct phrase שׁיר השׁירים ("Song of Songs") entitles another biblical scroll, this one might well be entitled הבל הבלים ("Futility of Futilities"; KJV "Vanity of Vanities"; cf. *GKC* §133.3.2), particularly since this superlative construct phrase occurs at the *end* (Qoh 12:8) as well as the *beginning* (1:2).

313. Qoh 1:3.

314. Qoh 3:9. Cowan and Rizzo (*Profits*) edit several essays exploring the (im)morality of twenty-first century profiteering.

315. Qoh 5:15 (ET 5:16). Perry (*Dialogues*, 4) rejects Gordis' ("Quotations," 123–47) understanding of these texts as an "attempt to palliate Qohelet's radical condemnation of creation."

316. *Lud* 1.59–62 (cf. above).

317. Salyer ("Rhetoric," 277) argues that the use of 1st person speech shows "just how important the search for self-understanding, or perhaps more appropriately, world-understanding is for the ancients. When their sacred canopy develops leaks, as it does for Qoheleth, this concern rises to the top of their consciousness."

318. Qoh 2:11. N.B. the appearance of parallel cognate accusatives (*GKC* §117p-r) focusing on עשׂה ("to do") and עמל ("to labor"), here expressed by an intentionally wooden translation. Whitley (*Koheleth*, 23) and Crenshaw (*Ecclesiastes*, 83) suggest the translation "gain" or "wealth" for עמל, but this seems a semantic stretch.

והנה הכל הבל ורעות רוח	Yet all of it is futile, a chasing after wind,[319]
ואין יתרון תחת השמש	Producing nothing "profitable" under the sun.[320]

Labor

Over the course of the book Qohelet's attitude toward "labor" changes,[321] or, to put it more precisely, gradually deepens.[322] Where chapter 8 applauds the

319. Qoh 2:11. This, of course, is the thematic mantra voiced throughout the first half of the book (1:14; 1:17; 2:11; 2:17; 2:26; 4:4; 4:6; 4:16; 6:9; cf. Ps 144:4). For Longman (*Ecclesiastes*, 61) it indicates "Qohelet's ultimate conclusion—everything is completely meaningless." For Peterson (*Hope*, 41), however, it means everything is "unjust."

320. Qoh 2:11. OG οὐκ ἔστιν περισσεία ὑπὸ τὸν ἥλιον ("no 'profit/abundance' under the sun"). Tg consistently reads תחות שמשא בעלמא הדין ("under the sun in this world"; cf. 2:17, 18, 19, 20, 22). Following a suggestion by Seow (*Ecclesiastes*, 104–6), Janzen ("Qohelet," 470) suggests that the phrase תחת השמש ("under the sun") carries "connotations of human existence as lived out under the delegated rule of the sun; and further, given Qohelet's specific circumstances, where Jewish existence under foreign rule is at odds with eschatological expectation, that such delegated rule has the character of oppression." Should this be the case, then "unprofitable" (אין יתרון) may well refer to a specific sociohistorical context, whether Persian (Cross, *CMHE* 346) or Hellenistic (Hengel, *Judaism*, 115–30; Fox, *Ecclesiastes*, xiv). In light of the sun-deity's "title" in the Šamaš Hymn as "profits provider" (*balāṭa ut-tar*, *BWL* 132.106), it seems simply ironic.

321. Gordis (*Koheleth*, 418–20) notes that עמל, found twelve times in the book (and normally translated "labor, toil, work") can sometimes mean "earnings" and/or "possession." Wazana ("Qohelet," 692) suggests that the קנאת איש ("jealousy") in Qoh 4:4 results not from "labor-vs.-laziness," but "labor-produced wealth vs. the reaction of one's neighbors."

322. Reading Qohelet from a perspective influenced by Einsteinian physics, Atkinson ("Work," 395) suggests that "prior to a perceptual transformation in the first of the book's so-called *carpe diem* passages, Qoheleth is dissatisfied with his labor because he construes it, temporally-speaking, within a chronology characterized by competition. Within such a construal, death poses the ultimate obstacle to the enjoyment of labor, because it strips away the promise of an immortal inheritance produced by human hands. What transforms Qoheleth's relationship to labor is a new understanding of time as καιρός (vs. χρόνος), defined as the 'opportune time' in which God unexpectedly intervenes in human work 'under the sun' and does something paradigmatically new. Under this 'kairological' perspective, Qoheleth assumes a posture of receipt, declaring present labor as a gift from God, with internal as well as external goods for the worker. Qoheleth's '*accipe diem* work ethic' draws the eschatological ultimacy of life and peace into present labor, re-orienting eschatological understandings of work that fall prey to competitive-chronological notions of progress."

mysterious resolve of *divine* labor,[323] for example, chapter 2 earlier laments the jaded weariness brought on by *human* labor:

ושׂנאתי אני את כל עמלי	I hated all my labor[324]
שׂאני עמל תחת השמש	Which I labored under the sun.[325]
כי יש אדם שׂעמלו	For sometimes a portion[326] of the fruits of one's labor
בחכמה ובדעת ובכשׂרון	(performed with wisdom, knowledge, and skill)[327]
ולאדם שׂלא עמל בו יתננו חלקו	Is left to someone who has not worked for it.[328]
כי מה הוה לאדם	So what advantage does anyone have[329]
בכל עמלו וברעיון לבו	For all their labor and striving [330]
שׂהוא עמל תחת השמש	With which they labor under the sun?[331]

323. "Then I saw all the work (מעשׂה) of God, and how no one is able to find out what is happening under the sun" (Qoh 8:31; cf. below).

324. Qoh 2:18. Otzen ("עמל," 200) recognizes that for Qohelet, עמל tends to "denote the ceaseless toil that characterizes human existence." In Job, however, the term takes on a more negative connotation, rendering it parallel to terms like און ("wickedness, misery," Job 4:8; 5:6; 15:35) and שׁוא ("emptiness, futility," 7:3).

325. Qoh 2:18 (again, woodenly translated to highlight MT's repetition of עמל). Influenced by Isaksson (*Qoheleth*, 29), Longman (*Ecclesiastes*, 101) less woodenly translates "Then I hated all my toil that I do."

326. Qoh 2:21a. Following Delitzsch (*Ecclesiastes*, 250), Longman (*Ecclesiastes*, 101), translates חלקו as "his reward" (2:21c; on חלק in Nevi'im, cf. Moore, *WealthWarn*, 67).

327. Qoh 2:21. In Tanak, כשׁרון ("skill"), like יתרון ("profit") occurs only in Qohelet. Cf. the Ug cognate *kṯr* ("crafty") in Canaanite names (*UT* 19.1171), including the compound name of Ba`al's chief architect, *kṯr wḫss* (Koṯar-wa-Ḫasis, "crafty and wise," *CAT* 1.6.6.59–60).

328. Qoh 2:21 (cf. Ps 49:11; Sir 14:15). Crenshaw (*Ecclesiastes*, 88) rather abrasively suggests that "the sages' egocentric perspective stands out here, for there is no indication that the donor derives genuine pleasure from bestowing happiness on someone else. The attitude is one of complete self-centeredness; 'I earned the wages, and therefore am entitled to derive satisfaction from them.'"

329. Qoh 2:22 (lit., "for what is it for a man"). Vg adds *proderit* ("profit"); Tg adds הנאה ("enjoyment").

330. Qoh 2:22. MT ברעיון לבו ("with the striving of his heart"); Syr ܒܨܒܝܢܐ ܕܠܒܗ ("with the desire of his heart"); OG προαίρεσις ("purpose, plan, conduct"). MT רעיון means "striving, yearning," but Longman (*Ecclesiastes*, 101) bumps this up to "anxiety."

331. Qoh 2:22. N.B. again the appearance of the cognate accusative underlining the root עמל ("to labor"), here (again) woodenly conveyed.

אין טוב שיוכל ושתה	There is nothing better than to eat and drink,[332]
והראה את נפשו טוב בעמלו	That the soul might find something good in its labor.[333]
כי לאדם שטוב לפניו	To those who please him
נתן חכמה ודעת ושׂמחה	God provides wisdom, knowledge, and joy,
ולחוטא נתן ענין לאסוף ולכנוס	But to sinners he consigns the business[334] of gathering and reaping,
לתת לטוב לפני האלהים	To transfer goods to those who truly please him.[335]

As indicated above, however, Qohelet is not averse to examining "labor" from a divine perspective:

וראיתי את כל מעשׂה האלהים	Then I saw all of God's work,
כי לא יוכל האדם למצוא את המעשׂה	For no human being can detect the work
אשר נעשׂה תחת השמש	Which is done under the sun.[336]
בשׁל אשר יעמל האדם לבקש ולא ימצא	However much one labors to look for it, it cannot be found;
וגם אם יאמר החכם לדעת	Even the wisest, most intelligent person
לא יוכל למצא	Cannot find it.[337]

332. Qoh 2:24. N.B. that Qohelet never refers to the abject poor struggling just to *find* edible food and potable water.

333. Qoh 2:24.

334. Qoh 2:26. MT ענין ("business," cf. below); περισπασμός ("distraction"; lit., "wheeling round"); Syr ܥܢܝܢܐ ("business, toil"); Vg *adflictionem et curam superfluam* ("affliction and needless care"); Tg broadens this considerably: ולגברא חיבא יהב גוון ביש למכנש ממון ולמצבר קנין סגי למהוי מתנסיב מניה ולמהוי מתיהיב לגבר דשפיר קדם יי ("to the wicked he allots every evil means to gather *mammon* and amass much property to be taken away from him and given to those who please the Lord").

335. Qoh 2:26 (lit., "does good before God"). N.B. that טוב ("good") occurs repeatedly in situations where (a) mortals may find something "good" in their work (2:24); (b) wisdom, knowledge and joy may be given to the one who is "good" before God (2:26); and (c) sinners gather and reap only to turn over what they produce to those who are טוב לפני האלהים ("good before God," 2:26).

336. Jensen (*Labor*, 44) warns readers not to "commodify God to an idol of our own making," even while recognizing that "the only way to talk about God is by drawing on our own language and experience of God."

337. Qoh 8:17. Like the wisdom poem in Job 28, with its "you-can-search-all-you-

Business

To develop and deepen the "labor" motif Qohelet utilizes two more terms, ענין[338] and חפץ.[339] Likely derived from the polysemantic root ענה,[340] the first of these terms appears eight times in Qohelet, usually to designate a wasteful or wicked "business." For example:

ונתתי את לבי לדרש ולתור בחכמה	I urged my heart to seek out and wisely examine
על כל אשר נעשׂה תחת השמים	Every activity under the sun.
הוא ענין רע נתן אלהים	*Conclusion:* It is a bad business God assigns
לבני האדם לענות בו	To human beings to busy themselves with.[341]

Reflecting on his own anxieties about "labor," Qohelet notes that, for the average worker,

כי כל ימיו מכאבים	All his days are filled with pain as
וכעס ענינו	Frustration becomes his business.[342]

want-but-you-won't-find-it" theme, the sage here tries to help readers accept the fact that some things are simply out of reach, or, to use the language here, "undetectable" (מצא לא), regardless of how much "labor" (עמל) goes into the "search" (בקשׁ). Aware of this pedagogical intentionality, Brown (*Ecclesiastes*, 88–91) labels this paragraph "The Vanity of Character and the Mystery of God."

338. Based on Aram עינין (*CAP* 26.22) and Syr ܥܢܝܢ ("business, toil," *PSD* 420), Wagner (*Aramäismen*, 222) identifies this term as an Aramaic loanword.

339. Although primarily associated with "desire" and/or "delight," חפץ can more neutrally denote a "matter of business" (cf. Sir 10:26; Aram צבו in Dan 6:18); e.g., לכל זמן ועת לכל חפץ תחת השמים, "there is a time and season for every 'business' under heaven" (Qoh 3:1; cf. 3:17; 8:6; OG πρᾶγμα, "occurrence").

340. Cf. Moore ("Anomalies," 234–38). Delekat ("Wörterbuch," 42) rejects all attempts to assign multiple semantic options to this root, but Gerstenberger ("ענה," 231) summarily rejects the "single-root" theory.

341. Qoh 1:13. N.B. the repetition of the root ענה (noun + infinitive). Commenting on Qoh 3:10, Rabbi Aibu (*Qoh. Rab.* 3.10.1) argues that the ענין ("business") mentioned here has fundamentally to do with the management of ממון (*mammon*), to which Rabbi Joshua of Siknin (in the name of Rabbi Levi) responds, "If a man is 'worthy' (זכה) and uses 'his wealth' (ממונו) in accordance with the 'commandments' (מצוות), his prayers will be 'answered' (ענה).

342. Qoh 2:23. OG θυμοῦ περισπασμὸς αὐτοῦ ("anger becomes his distraction"); Syr ܘܪܘܓܙܐ ܥܢܝܢܗ ("anger becomes his business"); Tg ותקיף רוגיה גוניה ("his anger distracts his business"). Cf. Studs Terkel's opening sentence to his bestseller *Working* (xiii): "This book, being about work, is by its very nature about violence—to the spirit as well as the body."

Sometimes several socioeconomic motifs fuse together, as in the portrayal of the "forlorn workaholic":[343]

יש אחד ואין שני	There is one, but not two;
גם בן ואח אין לו	Neither son nor brother does he have,
ואין קץ לכל עמלו	So there is no end to all his labor,
גם עינו לא תשׂבע עשׁר	Nor is his eye satisfied with riches.[344]

Isolated and secluded, he eventually asks:

ולמי אני עמל ומחסר נפשי מטובה	"For whom am I working, depriving myself of happiness?"[345]

Unable to answer this question, he defaults to the book's mantra:

גמ זה הבל	This, too, is futile,
וענין רע הוא	A bad business.[346]

Skill

Qohelet uses two terms to denote "skill"/"craftsmanship": חכמה and כשרון.[347] The first refers not simply to the technical skills needed to master, say, carpentry, but to the prudence, wisdom, and discipline necessary to become a

343. Cf. Johnston, "Workaholic," 133–48.

344. Qoh 4:8. In other words, work can never take the place of family, or, to cite Heim (*Ecclesiastes*, 166), "true happiness . . . can be achieved only through the traditional Jewish values of family life," which means that "Qohelet's audience will have to abandon their new (Persianized/Hellenized) value system."

345. Recognizing that *karoshi* (death from overwork) is the second largest killer of Japanese men between the ages of forty and fifty-two, Fassel (*Working*, 28–30) sees it masquerading as a "positive trait" elsewhere in the EuroAmerican West.

346. Qoh 4:8. The other five references to ענין occur in 2:26; 3:10; 5:2; 5:13; and 8:16. Brown (*Ecclesiastes*, 51) observes that "the individual whom the sage identifies is one who has renounced all forms of meaningful relationships. Afflicted with an insatiable appetite for wealth, the loner is consumed by work." Weeks (*Scepticism*, 65) suggests (a) that Qohelet believes that "rather than just a failure to gain . . . human activity may constitute an actual loss, and (b) if so, the phrase "bad business" is just another way of describing a "losing deal."

347. One may argue that two more terms appear in Qoh 9:11: לא נבנים עשר, "wealth is not to the proficient"; לא לידים חן, "favor is not to the skillful." Commenting on this text, one rabbi argues that the tribes of Gad and Reuben, the first to go into exile, do so because of their decision to "separate themselves from their brothers" in order to maintain control of "their 'possessions' (קנינם, lit., 'acquisitions,' *Num. Rab.* 22.7)."

good carpenter.[348] The second, deriving from the well-known word transliterated as *kosher* (כשׁר),[349] also melds the ideological with the technical:

I saw that every labor and skill-set[350]	וראיתי אני את כל עמל ואת כל כשׁרון המעשׂה
Results from jealousy[351] between people and their neighbors.	כי היא קנאת איש מרעהו
This too is meaningless, and a chasing after wind.[352]	גם זה הבל ורעות רוח

Investment

James Kugel sees the author of Qohelet "inhabiting a world, or more precisely a *class*, of financial high-rollers in which fortunes are amassed (Qoh 2:8) or lost in bad business deals (5:13)."[353] Money-managers employed by

348. Cf. Exod 28:3; 31:3; 1 Kgs 7:14. N.B. ענין // חכמה in Qoh 8:16 (cf. Müller, "חכם," 373). Reiterer ("Verhaltnis," 133) refers to these two dimensions of חכמה as *Grundlagenweisheit* ("basic wisdom") and *Angewandte Weisheit* ("applied wisdom").

349. *HAL* 479; Kellermann, "כשׁר," 367–70.

350. Qoh 4:4 (lit., "every skill of doing"); OG reads πᾶσαν ἀνδρείαν τοῦ ποιήματος ("every masculine activity"). Syr reads ܟܠ ܟܘܫܪܐ ("every skill"), but Tg moralizes: אנא ית כל טורחא וית כל אוטבות עובדא דעבדין בני אנשא וחזית ("I saw all the trouble and all the good work done by the children of men").

351. Qoh 4:4. MT קנא is usually taken to refer to "jealousy" or "zealotry" (so the Vss and most ETs), but can on occasion be taken to mean "acquisitiveness/covetousness" (cf., e.g., *MPAT* 41.12; cf. *HAL* 1038).

352. Qoh 4:4 (cf. above on 2:21). Syr ܡܛܠ ܕܛܢܢܗ ܕܓܒܪܐ ܡܢ ܚܒܪܐ ("on account of the jealousy of a man against his neighbor"). Vg *rursum contemplatus omnes labores hominum et industrias animadverti patere invidiae proximi* ("I saw that all of a man's labor and achievement are due to envy of his neighbor"); Tg again applies the notion here to a specific socioeconomic problem—*indebtedness*: וחזית אנה ית כל תורחא וית כל אוטבות עובדא דעבדין בני אנשא ארום היא קנאתא דקני גבר דחבריה למעבד כותיה דמקני ליה למעבד טבה כותיה מימרא דשמיא יוטב ליה ודמקני ליה לביש למעבד כבשתיה מימרא דשמא יבאיש ליה ואף דין הבלו לחיבא ותבירות רוחא ("I saw all the labor and all the good work which the children of men do to be nothing but jealousy, one emulating the other. For the one who emulates the good his neighbor does, the word of heaven does good for him. But for the one who emulates his neighbor's evil, the word of heaven does evil to him. These things not only drive the debtor to futility, they break his spirit").

353. Kugel, "Money," 46. Presuming with Seow (*Ecclesiastes*, 31) that the use of money does not become pervasive until the Persian period, Kim (*Voices*, 142–43) argues that "the monetary system benefits the colonizers and the local ruling class by providing them with a convenient means of collecting and maximizing taxes," resulting in "the ordinary population becoming poorer . . . and the powerless more vulnerable to discrimination and oppression."

these financiers either wisely or foolishly manage their clients' portfolios (5:12–13), but it is important to note that Qohelet is conspicuously silent about sharecroppers, slaves, the homeless, and/or the destitute.[354] Unlike Proverbs and Sirach, the debtor-creditor polarity here garners relatively little attention. Why? Because the sage's primary focus is the wealthy and their "needs,"[355] whether it be the family whose disgraced patriarch squanders the family fortune (5:12–17) or the negligent client who mismanages his family's wealth so recklessly he makes them an easy target for pirates and thieves (6:1–5).

Bluntly put, Qohelet is interested in the rich, not the poor. Alongside Proverbs, Sirach, and to some extent Job, this sage appeals to a class of readers shaped by a worldview more conservative than liberal, or, to dust off a well-worn twentieth-century polarity, more bourgeois than proletarian.[356] Much of this one-sidedness is due to the simplistic way he engages Greek thought, or, as Norbert Lohfink puts it, "the book of Qoheleth can only be understood as an attempt to profit as much as possible from the Greek understanding of the world without forcing Israel's wisdom to give up its status."[357]

Job

Identifying the protagonist in Job "not as a poor man who once was rich, but as a rich man who loses his wealth, regains it, and becomes richer than ever," David Clines notes that Job, like Qohelet, (a) displays a complete lack of realism with regard to poverty; that is, simplistically depicts the poor either by wholly appreciating them or wholly depreciating them;[358]

354. That is, Qohelet says nothing about the types of loans Torah specifically warns Israel not to discount or pervert (Deut 23:20–21).

355. Granted, attention at one point falls on the דמעת עשוקים ("tears of the oppressed," Qoh 4:1) and the fate of the איש מסכן חכם ("poor wise man," 9:15), but unlike Proverbs, Qohelet's overall interest in poverty is minimal. As Rudman ("Ecclesiastes," 73) argues, "wisdom is better than strength (4:13; 9:16) or weapons of war (9:18), but poverty nullifies its advantages."

356. Cf. Reines, "Wealth," 80–84. Sunkara (*Manifesto*, 215) contends that "for all its resilience capitalism remains prone to crisis . . . . Its inequalities provoke resistance. Billions resent the unfair choices offered to them."

357. Lohfink (*Qoheleth*, 6). Rudman ("Determinism," 233) argues that "Qohelet is a determinist and his work is a product of the Hellenistic period."

358. This is even more pronounced in *T. Job*, esp. chapters 11–12 (cf. below). This assessment, however, is not as simplistic as that of Rab Naḥman, who imagines poverty as "a wheel (גלגל) encircling the world which, like a bilge-water pump, alternately fills up and empties out" (*Ruth Rab.* 5.9), an interpretation based on his reading of the rare preposition בגלל in Deut 15:10 (cf. a similar understanding of poverty in *Exod. Rab.* 31.14).

and (b) never depicts wealth as in any way "problematic."[359] Pointing out parallels between the laments of Job (3:3–13) and Jeremiah (20:14–18), John Hartley suggests that a possible sociohistorical context for the book might be the eighth–seventh century BCE.[360] Reading Job through a neo-Marxist lens, Kirsten Dawson applies Slavoj Žižek's trifold definition of "violence" (*subjective, systemic, symbolic*)[361] to the character of Job, presuming him to be the innocent victim of *subjective* violence, then arguing that this "distraction" transforms him into the principal victim of *systemic* violence (like that systemically suffered by prisoners and slaves).[362] For Dawson the book of Job is "elitist literature"[363] in which the "distraction" of *subjective* violence (Job's individual suffering) siphons the reader's attention away from the "deeper issues of *systemic* and *symbolic* violence woven throughout and within the fabric of human social existence."[364] Whatever the (de)merits of this sociopolitical analysis,[365] the book's depiction of

359. Clines, *Parties*, 126–28. Sandoval (*Proverbs*, 3) marginalizes the significance of the poverty-wealth polarity in Job altogether, calling it "subsidiary."

360. Hartley (*Job*, 20) senses a resonance with this context because it is a time when "the poor face great hardship under the oppressive acts of the rich (as witnessed by the prophets Amos and Hosea)."

361. Dawson ("Violence," 435–68). According to Žižek (*Violence*, 1–7), "subjective" violence refers to acts of aggression and terror upsetting the status quo; "systemic" violence to the oppressive and destructive workings of economic, social, and political systems; and "symbolic" violence to the language used to enforce specific ways of constructing and interpreting reality.

362. Cf. Patterson (*Slavery*, 105–298); Lemos (*Violence*, 99–131).

363. Hoffman ("Literature," 66) presumes the Bible as a whole to be "elitist literature."

364. Dawson, "Violence," 437. Asencio (*Job*, 11) reads Job as "a song to the dignity of the human being." Boer (*Marxism*, 335) observes that "for one who holds Christianity and Marxism at the end of each arm, Žižek emerges as a proponent of both at the beginning of the new millennium," and whereas Marxist *diagnosis* can be helpful, Marxist *prognosis* can be as problematic as that of, say, (neo)classical capitalists (cf. Wolff and Resnick, *Theories*, 1–50; Harvey, *Madness*, 172–206).

365. Cf. Lemos (*Violence*, 99–131); and Neville ("Radical," 181–200). Sheldon ("Theodicy," 1–2) observes that Job "provides a solution to the problem of divine justice and human suffering in a natural step forward in a long trajectory of its ancient predecessors . . . Ludlul bēl nēmeqi and the Babylonian Theodicy . . . . For Job the solution involves two innovations: an appeal to cosmology and use of the combat myth. In order to accomplish this the poet of the divine speeches utilizes Enūma Elish, Tablets 4 and 5, whose chaos-creation order he reverses in order to show that evil has not been fully conquered by God . . . . Questions about divine justice are hosted by the Satan who serves as an ambiguous figure, not unlike Erra in the Poem of Erra. Unlike the Babylonians who suffer at his hands, Job does not remain a helpless victim, but dares to ask Yhwh to meet him in court. Likewise Job revolts against the Mesopotamian notion of humanity as slaves of the gods (*Atr* 1.1–6) and his role in the book centers around the question, 'Is he Yhwh's honored servant or abject slave?'"

the poverty-wealth polarity still looks more like that found in Ludlul bēl nēmeqi than that in Qohelet or Sirach:[366]

איש היה בארץ עוץ איוב שמו	Once there was a man in the land of Uz whose name was Job,
והיה האיש ההוא תם וישר	A blameless, upright man[367]
וירא אלהים וסר מרע	Who feared God[368] and turned away from evil.
ויולדו לו שבעה בנים ושלוש בנות	He had seven sons, three daughters,
ויהי מקנהו שבעת אלפי צון	And his property[369] included seven thousand sheep,
ושלשת אלפי גמלים	Three thousand camels,
וחמש מאות צמד בקר	Five hundred yoke of oxen,
וחמש מאות אתונות	Five hundred donkeys,
ועבדה רבה מאד	And a sizeable contingent of slaves.[370]
ויהי האיש ההוא גדול מכל בני קדם	This gentleman was greater than anyone in the East.[371]

366. Cf. Sitzler (*Vorwurf*, 111–230); Nadel ("Elites," 413–24); Adams ("Rethinking," 555–83); Goff (*4QInstruction*, 23); and above.

367. Job 1.1. Tg שלים ותריץ ("compensated and established").

368. Job 1:1. Tg reads יי דחל מן קדם ("who feared before Yh").

369. Job 1:3. MT מקנה can mean "property, possessions" (from the verb קנה, "to acquire"; cf. Syr ܩܢܝܢܗ; Vg *possessio*; Tg גיתא), or more narrowly, "livestock" (Gen 47:17; so Job 1:3 OG τὰ κτήνη), a possibility less likely given the appearance of עבדים ("slaves") at the end of this opening list.

370. Job 1:3. OG ὑπηρεσία πολλὴ σφόδρα καὶ ἔργα μεγάλα ("very large group of slaves doing great works"); Syr ܥܒܕܘܬܐ ܣܓܝܐܐ ("many slaves"); Tg פולחנא סגיאה לחדא ("huge contingent of slaves"); Vg *familia multa* ("large household"). Even a cursory glance at the versions challenges the applicability of Dawson's "distraction" thesis ("Violence," 435–68).

371. Job 1:3. OG εὐγενὴς ("well-born") parallels Akk *awīlu* ("gentleman"; e.g., *CH* 6.31). Kronholm ("קדם," 506) observes that "like West Semites in general, so too do the Israelites take their basic orientation from the east. The east is "in front" (קדם), the west "behind" (אחור), the south "to the right" (ימין and תמן) and the north "to the left" (אחרית). N.B. that Job's opening list of "property/possessions" increases significantly after his cyclonic encounter with the deity at the end of the book (42:12–15).

The Wager

Following this prototypical portrayal of the "prosperous gentleman,"[372] the prologue records a "divine wager"[373] between two heavenly beings in which one (the Judge) commends this "gentleman" for his blamelessness while the other (the Prosecutor)[374] identifies what Walter Moberly calls the "critical issue around which the whole story revolves":[375]

החנם ירא איוב אלהים	Does Job fear God "for nothing?"[376]

After this the Prosecutor burrows in:

הלא אתה שׂכת בעדו ובעד ביתו	Have you not erected a barricade[377] around him, his house,

372. OB *awīlum* (*CH* 12.15 and *passim*); cf. Hamilton ("Elite," 69).

373. Adapting "Pascal's wager" (*Pensées* 3 §233), Ticciati (*Job*, 73–74) suggests that "when God makes his wager with the satan, he is not only allowing Job to be put to the test, but is also allowing himself to be put to the test."

374. Prov 1:6 MT השׂטן ("the adversary, prosecutor"); Cf. Syr ܣܛܢܐ ("the adversary, prosecutor"); OG ὁ διάβολος ("the devil"; lit., "divider"). MT, Syr and OG all use a common noun modified by the definite article. Vg is the first version to translate השׂטן with the PN *Satan*. Stokes (*Satan*, 6–10) implausibly suggests the translation "executioner." Day (*Adversary*, 15; cf. Moore, *Adversary*, 508–10) justifiably questions the developmental presumptions camouflaging the few Tanak texts in which שׂטן appears, but Aimers ("Devil," 66) counters that "the Joban *satan* deserves the status of a primary character if we allow for the expansion of his role, in connection to the divine wager and 'the satanic agenda,' to extend throughout the Dialogues."

375. Moberly (*Bible*, 85). Habel (*Job*, 90) observes that in the Prosecutor's first response (Job 1:9) חנם conveys "not only doubts about Job's piety as an individual, but also questions a basic tenet of a wisdom theology which assumes an inevitable nexus between reward and righteousness." Playing the devil's advocate, Lewis (*Glory*, 27) insists that rewards are not in themselves "mercenary," only those which are not "proper" because "the proper rewards are not simply tacked on to the activity for which they are given, but are the activity itself in consummation."

376. Job 1:9 (חנם); OG μὴ δωρεὰν ("no cost"); Syr ܣܪܝܩܐܝܬ ("empty-handedly"); Tg מגן ("undeserved gift"). Waltke (*Theology*, 930) sees this as "the ultimate question that the book of Job seeks to answer," and Aimers ("Devil," 58) agrees, arguing that the Prosecutor "is after all the instigator of the Divine Wager which is the prime plot catalyst." Clines also agrees (*Job*, 25), arguing that "the Satan implicitly assents to the assessment of Job expressed by the narrator (1:1) and God (1:8). He cannot call into question Job's incomparable piety. Nor does he doubt its sincerity, its genuineness. What he must question—and what *must* be questioned (there is nothing 'satanic' about the question)—is what the link between Job's godliness and his prosperity is . . . . In a word, does Job *gratuitously* fear God?" (חנם, "for nothing, for no reward"; cf. Gen 29:15; Isa 52:3; Job 2:3). Hoffman (*Blemished*, 224–53) discusses this question under the overall semantic rubric of "recompense" (i.e., שׁלם).

377. MT שׂ/סכך ("to barricade") appears repeatedly in priestly texts describing how the wings of the cherubim "erect a barrier" over the holiest place on earth, the כפרת

ובעד כל אשר לו מסביב	And everything surrounding him?
מעשׂה ידיו ברכת	You bless the work of his hands
ומקנהו פרץ בארץ	And multiply his possessions on the land,[378]
ואולם שׁלח נא ידך וגע בכל אשר לו	But send forth your hand and touch something of his,[379]
אם לא על פניך יברכך	And see if he does not curse you to your face.[380]

Contextualizing this wager for *his* readers, Peruvian theologian Gustavo Gutiérrez argues that while "it is impossible for the *satan* to deny that Job is a good and devout man, what he questions is rather the disinterestedness of Job's service . . . objecting not to Job's works, but to their motivation."[381] From a structural perspective, of course, the Prosecutor's question overtly sets the stage for the following Dialogues.[382]

Job's Lament

In a lament much like that of the "pious sufferer" in Ludlul bēl nēmeqi, Job seizes on one of the Prosecutor's *Leitworten* (סכך, "to barricade") to express to his three "friends" how it *feels* to be "barricaded."[383] Bewailing his situ-

("mercyseat," lit. "place of covering," Exod 25:20; 37:9; 40:3). The Prosecutor, in other words, uses a strong priestly verb to challenge the integrity of Job's character. Citing the use of סכך/שׂ in Hos 2:8, Seow (*Job*, 257) derives the source of this "barrier" from texts more disposed to retribution than redemption.

378. Job 1:10. Cf. the note above on מקנה ("possessions") in 1:3. With this question the Prosecutor basically accuses the Judge of "organizational nepotism" (cf. the critical essays in Jones, *Nepotism*).

379. Job 1:11. MT נגע sometimes denotes inappropriate "touching." For example, Boaz protects Ruth from anyone who would inappropriately "touch" her (נגע, Ruth 2:9).

380. Job 1:11. Tg אין לא באנפי מרירך ירגזנך, "whether in the face of your words he reacts angrily." MT ברך usually means "bless" (as in 1.10), but in some texts it operates as a contrastive euphemism (i.e., "curse"; cf. 1 Kgs 21:10, 13; Ps 10:3; and five occurrences in the Job Prologue—1:5, 11, 21; 2:5, 9). Cf. S. Paul ("Euphemism," 959).

381. Gutiérrez, *Job*, 4.

382. Cf. Clines, *Job*, 25. Heb חנם appears in Tanak thirty-two times, including Job 1:9; 2:3; 9:17; and 22:6, but prompts no dictionary article in either *TDOT* or *TLOT*, doubtless because its primary meaning is *economic*, not theological.

383. *Lud* 1.45–74. Like the Dialogue of Pessimism, Joban characters often respond to ideas and notions first introduced by other conversation partners. In Job 3:23, e.g., Job reinterprets a word found on the lips of the Prosecutor (סכך, "to erect a fence," 1:10), and in 22:2–3 Eliphaz (mis)quotes what Job has to say about "profitability" (יעל, 21:15; other examples in Moore, *Babbler*, 222–23).

ation, he muses about what might have happened had he not survived the trauma of birth:[384]

למה לא מרחם אמות	Why did I not die at birth . . . ?[385]
כי עתה שכבתי ואשקוט	For then I could have lain down peacefully;
ישנתי אז ינוח לי	I could have slept soundly and found rest
עם מלכים ויעצי ארץ	Amidst the kings and counselors of the netherworld[386]
הבונים חרבות למו	Who "rebuild" withered ruins for themselves,[387]
או עם סרים זהב להם	Or with gold-laden princes
הממלאים בתיהם כסף	Who "fill their houses" with silver.[388]

Reflecting on the sociopolitical temper of the netherworld,[389] Job wonders about the character of its economy. Will it be another slave-based economy? If so, how will it function?[390]

שם רשעים חדלו רגז	There the wicked no longer intrude;
יחד אסירים שאננו	There prisoners' anxieties fall away,

384. Job 3:3–4. Lamenting his birth-"day" continues on into the dialogues (e.g., 10:18). Attending to the ANE context, Jacobsen and Nielsen ("Day," 187–204) note several incantation texts in which a particular "day" is cursed (cf. Jer 20:14–18; Seow, *Job*, 312–89). Cf. Paul ("Imprecations," 401–6).

385. Job 3:11. This is the first of three questions in Job's lament, the second being "Why was I not buried stillborn?" (3:16), and the third "Why is light given to the miserable?" (3:20; cf. Janzen, *Job*, 63–66).

386. Job 3:14. Should ארץ signify "netherworld" instead of "earth" (as in *CAT* 1.4.8.8–9; 1.15.3.3, 14; Ezek 26:20; 32:18, 24; Jon 2:7), then Nebuchadnezzar immediately comes to mind (Isa 14:4–20; cf. Shipp, *Dirges*, 117).

387. Job 3:14. MT חרבה is often used to designate the "dry land" left after Yhwh parts a sea (Exod 14:21) or a river (Josh 3:17; 2 Kgs 2:8; Ezek 30:12).

388. Job 3:15. As Seow (*Job*, 360) points out, these "houses" (בתים) "may refer to the worldly palaces of the wealthy rulers and, at the same time, to their treasure–laden abodes of rest, namely, their tombs." Contrast this view of the afterlife with that envisioned in Isa 14:7–20, where the *land* "rests" (נוח, 14:7), not its rulers.

389. Recognizing the prevalence of death mythologies in Sumero-Akkadian and West Semitic culture, Zuckerman (*Job*, 119) emphasizes that it is not so much Death as manifest in the form of a malevolent deity that is the essential focus in the poem of Job. Rather, the Joban author "depicts death more as a realm, a netherworld to which all individuals must eventually go."

390. The culture of slavery translated into the Annunaki-Igigi relationship in the Atraḫasis myth shows (among other things) that the socioeconomic institution of slavery is so ingrained in Mesopotamian culture, even the gods cannot escape it (*Atr* 1.73–81; cf. Moore, *WealthWatch*, 73–81).

לא שמעו קול נגש	No longer obedient to the voices of their oppressors.[391]
קטן וגדול שם הוא	Both small and great are there,
ועבד חפשי מאדניו	And slaves find liberation from their masters.[392]

Then he addresses a wider concern:

למה יתן לעמל אור	Why is light given to the miserable,
וחיים למרי נפש	And life to those whose souls are embittered,
המחכים למות ואיננו	Who long for death and it does not come,
ויחפרהו ממטמונים	Who dig for it more than for hidden treasure?[393]
לגבר אשר דרכו נסתרה	Why is light given to those whose way is hidden,
ויסך אלוה בעדו	Whom the deity "barricades?"[394]

The Prologue and Lament of Job raise important questions, but none reach the magnitude of the Prosecutor's initial question. Put in first person speech, *"Do I do the right thing only when I get paid for it, or do I do it simply because it's the right thing to do?"* John Walton sees three things in this text: (a) it "asks whether Job serves God for nothing"; (b) it shows "Job's friends encouraging him to take the Mesopotamian path of appeasement (confess

391. Job 3:18. OG ὁμοθυμαδὸν δὲ οἱ αἰώνιοι οὐκ ἤκουσαν φωνὴν φορολόγου ("none of the eternals listen to the voice of the taxman"); Syr ܘܠܐ ܫܡܥܘ ܩܠܐ ܕܡܫܥܒܕܢܐ ("and they do not hear the voice of the oppressor"); Vg *quondam vincti pariter sine molestia non audierunt vocem exactoris* ("where those bound together without burdens do not listen to the taskmaster's voice"); Tg לא שמעו ינקי בית רבא קל אמוראה ("and the infants in the Great House do not hear the voice of the Amoraim"; cf. Halivni, *Midrash*, 66–75). The "Amoraim" (אמוראים, from אמר, "to speak, say") are those Jewish readers of the period c. 500–200 BCE who preserve Torah by regularly "speaking/saying" it before an illiterate populace.

392. Job 3:19. On MT חפשי ("freedom") cf. the Ug epithet *bt ḫpṯt* (*CAT* 1.4.8.7) and Heb בית החפשית (2 Kgs 15:5), each denoting a chthonic "freedom house."

393. Job 3:21. OG ἀνορύσσοντες ὥσπερ θησαυρούς ("digging it up like treasures"); Syr ܒܥܝܢ ܠܗ ܐܝܟ ܕܠܡܛܡܪܬܐ ("seek for it as if from a hidden reservoir"); Tg reads טומעיא ("secret, hidden place"), but many see MT מטמון as a morphological forerunner of ממון ("mammon," *HAL* 543). N.B. that the poem in Job 28 highlights this "digging-for-buried-treasure" motif (Job 28:1, 6, 15–17, 19; cf. Lo, *Rhetoric*, 172–78; Jones, *Rumors*, 40–42, 63).

394. Job 3:23. Where the Prosecutor uses סכך to indicate "protection" (1:10), Job uses it to indicate "prison" (cf. 12:14).

anything to restore favor with the gods)"; and (c) it shows Job "maintaining his integrity" in the face of their pressure.[395]

Job's Critics

Separate analysis of Job's critics' speeches apart from the spirited responses of Job himself runs the risk of unsettling the book's polyphonic balance,[396] somewhat like focusing on the responses of the "friend" in the Babylonian Theodicy apart from the words of the "sufferer/sceptic."[397] Yet the prospect of learning how the socioeconomic motifs in these speeches operate makes it a risk worth taking.[398] So, in response to Job's opening lament,[399] Eliphaz the Temanite[400] takes off on what at first appears to be a complete tangent, censuring the behavior of "fools" and "bullies":[401]

אני ראיתי אויל משריש	When I see fools taking root,[402]
ואקוב נוהו פתאם	I immediately curse their dwelling.[403]

395. Walton, *Ancient*, 119.

396. Newsom (*Contest*, 16) argues that (except for the Elihu speeches) the book of Job is the product of a single author, yet one who "juxtaposes and intercuts certain genres and distinctly stylized voices, providing sufficient interconnection among the different parts to establish the sense of the 'same' story, but leaving the different parts sharply marked and sometimes overtly disjunctive."

397. The speeches of Elihu (Job 32–37) are exempted here because they basically include nothing of socioeconomic significance.

398. Cf. Hawley ("Job," 459–78).

399. Job 3:3–26. Balentine (*Prayer*, 169) views chapters 29–31 as a "return to Job's lament."

400. That Eliphaz is likely Edomite comes from the fact that Jeremiah (49:7) links Edom with Teman.

401. Hoffman (*Blemished*, 139) posits that "the graduated and sophisticated fashioning of the figure of Eliphaz" appears "not merely as background to the figure of Job, but as his antithesis," and Seow (*Job*, 466) argues that "the problem with Eliphaz's approach is that he dwells in moral universalities. He reflects on the plight of humanity in general (4:17; 5:7), but in so doing he ironically dehumanizes the individual and, hence, misses what it means to be in community." Dunham (*Job*, ix) recognizes that "the unresolved tension over how to interpret the friends' purpose results in a wide gamut of reactions. Vilified or lionized, the friends rarely provoke a neutral response."

402. Job 5:3. Syr ܐܢܐ ܚܙܝܬ ܪܫܝܥܐ ܕܡܬܦܠܓܝܢ, "I see the wicked ripped open and destroyed." Dunham (*Job*, 99) dubs Eliphaz the "champion of orthodoxy."

403. Job 5:3. MT פתאם, OG εὐθέως, Syr ܡܚܕܐ, Tg בתכיף, and Vg *statim* all read "immediately." OG reads "I immediately 'consume' (ἐβρώθη) their dwelling." It hardly feels coincidental that Eliphaz's first act in Job is to "curse."

ירחקו בניו מישע וידכאו בשער	Removed from safety, their children are crushed in the gate[404]
ואין מציל	Because there is no one there to deliver them.[405]
אשר קצירו רעב יאכל	The hungry consume the harvest,
ואל מצנים יקחכו	Scavenging even that which grows between the thorns,[406]
ושאף צמים חילם	While the thirsty cling desperately to their money.[407]
מפר מחשבות ערומים	El frustrates the schemes of the cunning[408]
ולא תעשׂינה ידיהם תושיה	So that their hands realize no success.[409]
וישע מחרב מפיהם	He saves the needy from the sword at their mouth
ומיד חזק אביון	And from the hand of bullies,[410]
ותהי לדל תקוה	So that the poor might have hope
ועלתה קפצה פיה	Whenever malice padlocks their mouth.[411]

404. Job 5:4. Amos utilizes a similar turn-of phrase: אביונים בשער הטו, "they push back (lit., 'stretch out') the needy at the gate" (Amos 5:12).

405. Job 5:4. N.B. that Eliphaz's opening speech bizarrely mirrors the "parent's" instructions in Proverbs (1:10–19).

406. Job 5:5. Cf. Marduk's title in *Ee* 7.1, *ša-rik mi-riš-ti ša is-ra-ta u-kin-nu*, "the donor of arable fields who cultivates even the alleyways in between."

407. Job 5:5. MT שאף (lit., "to pant after"). For MT חיל OG translates ἡ ἰσχύς ("strength"), but Syr (ܩܢܝܢܗܘܢ, "possessions"), Vg (*divitias*, "riches") and Tg (נכסיהון, "properties") all take an explicitly economic tack.

408. Job 5:12 (the deity is called אל in 5:8). Cf. Q 3.120, "If you patiently do what is right, 'their cunning' (كيدهم) will do you no harm whatsoever."

409. Job 5:12 (N.B. the repetition of יד, "hand," in 5:15). Cf. Q 2.5, "those who are on a right course from their Lord shall be 'the successful ones' (المفلحون)" vs. 2.16, "Those who deceitfully 'purchase' (اشتروا) the 'right' direction produce a 'business' (تجرةهم) which is not 'profitable' (ربحت)."

410. Job 5:15 (lit., "from the hand of the strong"); Syr ܥܫܝܢܐ ("the strong"); OG δυνάστου ("rulers"); Vg *de manu violenti* ("from the hand of the violent").

411. Job 5:16. Evidently the purpose of vss 15 and 16 is to contrast different uses of the פה ("mouth")—the mouths of the poor vs. the mouths of bullies (cf. Seow, *Job*, 442–43). De Soto (*Capital*, 4–5) argues that the primary reason why 1.5 billion people live on only $1.00/day is not because they lack entrepreneurial spirit or because their IQs are too low to understand modern technology or because they prefer begging to working. No, he argues, it is because they live in countries too corrupt to sanction their legal right to own real estate, thereby making it impossible for them to provide the collateral needed to generate the capital required to grow their own businesses.

Eliphaz's apology for the poor appears, for lack of a better word, "commendable," at least in terms of diagnosis.[412] Plotting a viable socioeconomic prognosis, however, proves to be something alien to the thinking of this Edomite "gentleman." Instead he simply warns the "cunning" (ערומים) that a "day of darkness" is coming.[413] Afterwards,

וישכון ערים נכחדות	They will settle in desolate cities,
בתים לא ישבו למו	In uninhabitable houses
אשר התעתדו לגלים	Destined to become heaps of ruins.[414]
לא יעשר ולא יקום חילו	They will never become rich, nor will their wealth endure,
ולא יטה לארץ מנלם	Nor will their land-holdings be extensive.[415]
אל יאמן בשיו נתעה	They self-delusionally trust in futile pursuits,
כי שוא תהיה תמורתו	And because they do, futility becomes their reward.[416]

412. Peake (*Job*, 77) finds Eliphaz's speech to be "very considerate and tender." Newsom (*Contest*, 103) suggests that "the narrative Eliphaz offers to Job is not just a series of linked events, but a configured event, a trope of transformation," and Dunham (*Job*, 22–23) thinks OG follows a translation strategy designed to make Eliphaz "more accessible (and perhaps more appealing or eloquent) to Greek readers."

413. יום חשך (Job 15:20; cf. ערומים, "cunning," in 5:12). Newsom (*Contest*, 96–97) sees Eliphaz and his friends offering three responses to the רגז ("turmoil") mourned by Job in his opening lament (Job 3:26): (a) they *resist* it by "attempting to construe Job's experience in terms of narrative structures that integrate and ultimately transcend the present turmoil"; (b) they *displace* it by calling Job back to the symbolic forms, words, and bodily gestures of therapeutic prayer; and (c) they *deny* its ontological status via several iconic poems designed to re-lay the foundations of the moral order (the so-called "fate of the evil" poems). Job counters these arguments by arguing (a) that Eliphaz's construal of narrative reliability ("the world makes perfect sense") hardly reflects the "radical non-narratibility of human existence in general and his own in particular"; (b) that his friends' focus on therapeutic prayer blatantly bypasses the reality of innocent suffering; and (c) that the "fate of the evil" is not the truly central question.

414. Job 15:28. Cf. the similar warning in Amos: "Because you trample on the poor and steal from him his grain allotment, you will build stone-masoned houses, but never inhabit them" (Amos 5:11).

415. Job 15:29. OG οὐ μὴ βάλῃ ἐπὶ τὴν γῆν σκιὰν ("they will never pitch a tent upon the land"); Syr ܘܠܐ ܢܣܓܐ ܡܟܠܐ ܥܠ ܐܪܥܐ ("he will not increase wealth upon the land"). MT מנול and Syr ܡܟܠܐ appear to find an Arabic cognate in موال ("property/possession," Q 2.188).

416. Job 15:31. Cf. Syr ܐܘܢܐ ܬܗܘܐ ܡܫܬܠܬܗܘܢ ("the abyss will be their nursery/hothouse"); Tg שקרא תהי פרוגיה ("fraud will be their marketplace"). MT תמורה ("exchange, reward"), a relatively rare term, recurs in Zophar's second speech (20:18). Qur'an denounces the "exchange" (بدلوا) of God's "blessing" (نعمه) for "infidelity" (كفرا), esp. when it leads to the "House of Futility" (دار البوار, Q 14.28; Berjak, "*Hulul*," 276, reads "house of destruction").

כי עדת חנף גלמוד	For the pagan congregation will grow barren,[417]
ואש אכלה אהלי שחד	And fire will consume the tents of bribery.[418]

Wearied by what he perceives to be Job's resistance to constructive analysis, Eliphaz's third speech targets his integrity:[419]

הלא רעתך רבה	Is your wickedness not great?
ואין קץ לעונותיך	Is there no end to your iniquities?[420]
כי תחבל אחיך חנם	For you exact pledges from your family without cause,[421]
ובגדי ערומים תפשיט	And strip them naked of their clothing.[422]
לא מים עיף תשקה	To the weary you give no water to drink

417. Job 15:34. MT חנף ("godless, pagan"); Syr ܚܢܦܐ ("pagan, Gentile"); OG μαρτύριον γὰρ ἀσεβοῦς θάνατος ("for the testimony of the godless is death"); Vg *congregatio enim hypocritae sterilis* ("for the congregation of the hypocrites is sterile"). Evidently all the vss understand infertility to be a horrible curse (cf. Moore, *WealthWarn*, 196–97).

418. Job 15:34. Syr ܡܫܟܢܐ ܕܥܘܠܐ ("tent of evil"); OG μαρτύριον γὰρ ἀσεβοῦς θάνατος ("for the testimony of the ungodly is death"); Vg *congregatio enim hypocritae sterilis et ignis devorabit tabernacula eorum qui munera libenter accipiunt* ("the congregation of hypocrites will be sterile as fire devours their tabernacle—the one which accepts the pouring-out of bribe-gifts." MT אהלי שחד ("tents of bribery") parallels the construct phrase עדת חנף ("congregation of the godless") in the preceding colon, then acquires further definitional focus in the following verse (15:35) via three terms: עמל ("trouble"; cf. 3:10; 4:8); און ("wickedness"; cf. 5:6, 8); and מרמה ("deceit"; cf. Isa 53:9; Vesely, *Friendship*, 122, 135). Note also the association of "consumerism" (اكل) with "bribery" in Q 2.188: ولا تاكلوا مولكم بينكم بالبال وتدلوا بها الى الحكام (lit., "Do not fraudulently consume your possessions, then present the leftovers to your magistrate"). N.B. that the term here translated "magistrate" is حكم, from which comes the term حكمه, "wisdom" (Heb חכמה).

419. The trajectory plotting Eliphaz's anger is too abbreviated for some, too long for others. Dunham (Eliphaz, 232) thinks the "interpretive trajectory a reader of Job is likely to take with Eliphaz . . . depends in large measure on his or her predisposition to Eliphaz's retributional doctrine."

420. Job 22:5.

421. Job 22:6. Two legitimate reasons for "exacting a pledge" are adultery (Prov 27:13) and co-signing loans for foreigners (20:16). Clifford (*Proverbs*, 75) notes that "the legal practice of standing surety is not mentioned in the biblical law codes, but wisdom texts show the practice is common," not to mention the fact that several "nonbiblical lawcodes mention it." Whether Job is guilty of such activity, as Eliphaz claims, is not automatically preposterous, even in the face of Job's denials.

422. Job 22:6. Doubtless this is an allusion to the practice condemned by Amos: "They lay down beside every altar on garments taken in pledge" (Amos 2:8).

ומרעב תמנע לחם	And from the hungry you withhold bread.[423]
ואיש זרוע לו הארץ	Powerful individuals possess the land
ונשׂוא פנים ישב בה	While the privileged forthrightly settle it.[424]
אלמנות שלחת ריקם	You send widows away with nothing
וזרעות יתמים ידכה	And crush the limbs of orphans.[425]

Yet still he holds out hope for his suffering comrade:

אם תשוב עד שׁדי תבנה	If you return to Šadday you will be restored.[426]
תרחיק עולה מאהליך	If you remove evil from your tents,
ושית על עפר בצר	If you lay down your gold in the dust,[427]
ובצור נחלים אופיר	Your Ophir gold like creek pebbles,
והיה שׁדי בצריך	And if Šadday becomes your "gold"[428]
וכסף תועפות לך	And your precious "silver,"
כי אז על שׁדי תתענג	Then you will take delight in Šadday
ותשא אל אלוה פניך	And lift up your face to Eloah.[429]
תעתיר אליו וישמעך	Then you will pray to him and he will hear you,
ונדריך תשלם	So that you may pay your vows.[430]

423. Job 22:7. In his final speech (Job 31:7–34) Job tries to refute these accusations in some detail (cf. *ANET* 36; Habel, *Job*, 428–29).

424. Job 22:8 (lit., "those of lifted face"; i.e., "highborn"); OG ἐθαύμασας δέ τινων πρόσωπον ("but you behold someone's face") clearly does not grasp the semitic idiom.

425. Job 22:9. Like the Canaanite king Daniel, Eliphaz presumes wealthy "gentlemen" are to *ydn dn almnt yṯpṭ ṯpṭ ytm*, "try the case of the widow and judge the cause of the orphan" (*CAT* 1.17.5.7–8; cf. Deut 10:18; Isa 1:17; Sir 4:10; Jas 1:27).

426. Job 2:23. Where Eliphaz imagines Šadday in benevolent terms, Job most assuredly does not (cf. Moore, *Babbler*, 216–19).

427. Job 22:24. Reading with Alter (*Job*, 96).

428. Job 22:24. Habel (*Job*, 342–43) suggests that "gold is not necessarily a reference to wealth," but here denotes "a symbol for the greatest good." Cf. the parallel depiction of Sophia (Prov 3:14; Wis 7:9).

429. Job 22:26. N.B. (a) that Eliphaz never mentions Yhwh (cf. Moore, *Babbler*, 214–25); and (b) that Job never buys into Eliphaz's Šadday-centered theology (217–19).

430. Job 22:27. Apparently Eliphaz presumes that prayer is useless unless preceded by ascetic denial. He does not say, "then you will come to understand why you are suffering," or "then you will experience redemption" (desires of the "pious sufferer" in *Lud* 1.56). Like the critics of the "pious sufferer" in *Ludlul bēl nēmeqi*, Eliphaz presumes that an accusation of religious infidelity will strike Job where it hurts the most (*Lud* 2.12–24; cf. above; N.B. the recurrence of שׁלם, "to compensate").

Zophar, Job's second "friend," addresses the question of what he perceives to be Job's *consumerism* (אכל) mentality.[431] In an effort to wean Job away from his "obstinancy,"[432] he censures "the wicked" (as Eliphaz does),[433] then predicts that the offspring of the wealthy will so completely consume themselves, they will be forced to reimburse the poor from the tattered remnants of their once-lavish estates:

בניו ירצו דלים	Their children will seek the favor of the poor,
וידיו תשבנה אונו	And their offspring will take back their wealth.[434]

To depict the depth of this disgrace he utilizes some rather coarse metaphors:

חיל בלע ויקאנו	They swallow down wealth and vomit it up again,
מבטנו יורשנו אל	El spewing it out of their bellies.[435]
מישיב יגע ולא יבלע	Not swallowing, but regurgitating[436] the proceeds,
כחיל תמורתו ולא יעלס	Never tasting the returns on their business deals.[437]
כי רצץ עזב דלים	For they suppress and abandon the poor,
בית גזל ולא יבנהו	Seizing houses they have not built.[438]

431. Job 20:21, "to consume, eat, devour." As Crenshaw (*Job*, 105) notes, "the image of eating dominates the entire speech."

432. This is Crenshaw's (*Job*, 105) assessment of Zophar's strategy. Maimonides (*Guide* 3.17) likens Zophar's philosophy to that of the Asharites, a predeterminist Muslim sect devoted to the prioritization of the deity's transcendent sovereignty.

433. Job 20:5 (רשעים); cf. 15:20.

434. Job 20:10. Gordis ("*Yad*," 341–44) reads ידיו ("his hands") as a metaphorical parallel to בניו ("his sons") in the previous line, translating "his offspring." Andersen (*Job*, 211) suggests that "the picture of destitution in verse 10 may include the thought of poetic justice: *his children* will have to beg from the poor who had begged in vain from their father."

435. Job 20:15. MT ירש ("tossing, chucking") is a term often used to denote "(dis) inheritance, (dis)possession." Doubtless it's no coincidence that the Canaanite deity El can on occasion be a vomiting drunkard in *CAT* 1.114.15–23.

436. Job 20:18. Heb משיב (lit., "cause to return").

437. Job 20:18. N.B. the crude, but effective connection between בלע ("swallow") and עלס ("taste"). OG elaborates: εἰς κενὰ καὶ μάταια ἐκοπίασεν πλοῦτον ἐξ οὗ οὐ γεύσεται ὥσπερ στρίφνος ἀμάσητος ἀκατάποτος, "in emptiness and futility they labor for wealth they cannot taste because it is grisly, unchewable, and unswallowable."

438. Job 20:19. Reading pl. with OG (οἴκους, "houses"; cf. Mic 2:2). Andersen (*Job*, 212) contends that Zophar's second speech "reflects common Israelite belief " that "neglect of the poor is the worst fault of the rich."

אין סריד לאכלו	Their greedy consumerism leaves no leftovers;
על כן לא יחיל טובו	Their prosperity will not continue.[439]
יהי למלא בטנו ישלח בו חרון אפו	To fill up their bellies he will target them with his fierce wrath,
וימטר עלמו בלחומו	And spray it upon them as their "food,"[440]
כל חשך טמון לצפוניו	Concealing their provisions behind thick darkness.[441]
תאכלהו אש לא נפח	A smoldering fire will consume them,
ירע שׂריד באהלו	So that even the leftovers in their tents will perish.[442]
יגל יבול ביתו	The produce in their houses will be left unprotected,
נגרות ביום אפו	And thrown out on the day of his wrath.[443]

Job's Response

Responding to these speeches, Job makes a good faith effort to address the socioeconomic questions of his "friends." Responding to Eliphaz, he asks,

הכי אמרת יהבו לי	Have I ever said, "Give me something?"
ומכחכם שחדו בעדי	Or, "From your wealth offer me a bribe?"[444]
אף על יתום תפילו	You, who would cast lots for orphans

439. Job 20:21. Commonly translated "good," טוב can in some contexts denote "prosperity" (cf. Ps 106:5; *HAL* 356–57).

440. Job 20:23. As in the depiction of El's *mrzḥ* feast at Ugarit (*CAT* 1.114.15–23; cf. Smith, *Ba`al*, 140–44), Zophar here stretches the gastrointestinal imagery to farcical extremes.

441. Job 20:26 (lit., "the things stored up"). OG πᾶν δὲ σκότος αὐτῷ ὑπομείναι ("and all the darkness will endure with him); Syr ܘܟܠ ܚܫܘܟܐ ܢܬܛܫܐ ܠܫܪܒܬܗ ("and all darkness will be hidden to his generation"); Tg חשוכא טמיעא כל לטשיויא ("all the darkness will be hidden from those hiding from him"). Doubtless Zophar refers to "hidden things" procured through "secret deals" in "smoky backrooms."

442. Job 20:26. Cf. Bailey (*Bedouin*, 69–106).

443. Job 20:28. Cf. יום חשך ("day of darkness") in Eliphaz's second speech (15:20). Habel (*Job*, 320) thinks that Job seems to imply in his response to Zophar that the wicked will be *spared* on the יום איד/עברות ("day of wrath/fury," 21:30).

444. Job 6:22. Vesely (*Friendship*, 121–22) contends that "Job suggests with these words that since he does not ask his friends for financial gifts or deliverance from enemies, his intentions are pure. His motives toward his friends are not based on utility, pleasure, or securing his own advantage."

ותכרו על ריעכם	And cut deals over your friends.[445]
הלא צבא לאנוש על ארץ	Is it not difficult for people on the land
וכימי שׂכיר ימיו	To spend their days as laborers?[446]
כעבד ישאף צל	Like slaves panting in the shadows?[447]
וכשׂכיר יקוה פעליו	Or workers holding out for their wages?[448]

Deflecting Zophar's "consumerism" arguments, Job ponders the "good life" so often enjoyed by the wicked, perplexed and baffled by how easily they seem to succeed at anything they attempt:

שורו עבר ולא יגעל	Their bulls breed without fail,
תפלט פרתו ולא תשׂכל	Their cows calve without miscarrying.[449]
יכלו בטוב ימיהם	Their days pass by in prosperity,[450]
וברגע שאול יחתו	Before they suddenly descend to Sheol.[451]

Like Eliphaz, Job expresses righteous indignation at the crimes perpetrated against the poor:

גבלות ישׂיגו	The wicked realign the landmarks;[452]
עדר גזלו וירעו	They seize flocks and pasture them.[453]

445. Job 6:27. Tg תחשלון, "you would crush/batter." Seow (*Job*, 466), in an inspired turn of phrase, describes this as the "merchandising of companions." On the final day, Qur'an predicts, the sky will resemble murky oil, the mountains wool, and ولايسٔل حميم حميما, "no friend will ask (anything) of a friend" (Q 70.10).

446. Job 7:1 (cf. Prov 16:26; Qoh 2:18). Responding to Eliphaz's take on the human condition, Job does the same. The difference, in Seow's opinion (*Job*, 489), is that "whereas Eliphaz argues for the condition of sin in which people inevitably find themselves, Job focuses on their condition of pain and hopelessness."

447. Job 7:2. This expression may refer either to (a) holding on until nightfall, when work ceases for the day, or (b) holding on until death, the final "shadow" (cf. צלמות, "shadow of death," Ps 23:4).

448. Job 7:2. Torah specifies that workers' wages must be received before sundown (Deut 24:15; cf. Jas 5:4).

449. Job 21:10. Cf. the lament in *DI* 77–78: "the bull does not mount the cow; the ass does not impregnate the jenny."

450. Job 21:13 (lit., "their days are in the good"); OG (συνετέ λεσαν) and Syr (ܡܓܡܪܝܢ) and Tg (יגמרון) support the *qere* reading, Vg (*ducunt*) the *ketiv*.

451. Job 21:13. Commenting on 17:13–14, Mathewson (*Job*, 105) posits that for Job "kinship ties are exclusively with death: Sheol is his household, the Pit is his father, and the worms are mother and sister."

452. Job 24:2 (cf. Deut 19:14; Hos 5:10).

453. Job 24:2.

חמור יתומים ינהגו	They drive away orphans' donkeys;[454]
יחבלו שור אלמנה	They seize the widow's ox in pledge.[455]
יגזלו משד יתום	They steal orphans from the breast,[456]
ועל עני יחבלו	And seize in pledge the infants of the poor.[457]
רעה עקרה לא תלד	They feed on the barrenness of childless women[458]
ואלמנה לא ייטיב	And do nothing decent for widows.[459]
יטו אביונים מדרך	They force the indigent from the road,
יחד חבאו עניי ארץ	And drive the poor of the land into hiding.[460]
בשדה בלילו יקצירו	They harvest the fields of villains,[461]
וכרם רשע ילקשו	And glean the vineyards of the wicked.[462]

454. Job 24:3. Hartley (*Job*, 346) posits a specific application: "Wealthy lords collect what is owed them from a lowly orphan, perhaps a debt incurred by the deceased father, by entering the field where that young debtor is working unannounced and driving off his donkey." Even though "this animal is the orphan's primary asset to keep from starving, that is no concern to these greedy lords in their drive to amass wealth by every means."

455. Job 24:3 (cf. *CH* 241; Deut 24:10–17; Amos 2:8).

456. Job 24:3. Evidently Job takes seriously the responsibility of well-to-do leaders to "judge the cause of the widow and adjudicate the case of the orphan" (*ydn dn almnt yṯ pṭ ṯpṭ ytm*, *CAT* 1.17.5.7–8).

457. Job 24:9 (reading ע[ו]ל, "infant," *HAL* 783). Job's preoccupation with the יתום ("orphan") echoes Ezekiel's concerns about human trafficking (Ezek 27:13; cf. Moore, *WealthWarn*, 85).

458. Job 24:21. On the socioeconomic consequences of infertility cf. Moore (*WealthWarn*, 4–17).

459. Job 24:21 (cf. Maier, "Stereotypes," 89–90). Janzen (*Job*, 214) contends that Job's treatment of the widow and orphan is predicated on "his awareness of God's parental nurture of him."

460. Job 24:4. Hartley (*Job*, 347) observes that "while the poor must move about stealthily in fear for their own safety, the rich revel in luxury at the expense of those they oppress."

461. Job 24:6. OG ἀγρὸν πρὸ ὥρας οὐκ αὐτῶν ὄντα ("a field not theirs for awhile"); Syr ܘܒܚܩܠܐ ܚܫܝܫܐ ("in a hayfield"); Vg *agrum non suum demetunt* ("in a cornfield not theirs"); Tg בחקלא מדלא דלהון ("in a field of property not theirs"). Noting the differences in the versions as well as the parallel term רשע ("wicked") in the second line of the couplet, Pope (*Job*, 176) joins Larcher (*Job* ad. loc.) in emending בלילו to the DN בליעל ("Belial").

462. Job 24:6. Newsom (*Contest*, 124), recognizes that Job's world has specific moral boundaries, so "an anecdote about the success of the wicked cannot explain the reality of this world . . . . Such things may happen, but they are perceived as anomalies."

In his final defense Job recites his résumé,[463] spotlighting as many acts of generosity to the poor as he can remember:

אמלט עני משוע	I rescue the poor when they cry,
ויתום ולא עזר לו	And the orphan who has no helper.[464]
ברכת אבד עלי תבא	The blessing of the destitute comes upon me
ולב אלמנה ארנן	As I reassure the widow's heart to sing for joy.[465]
אב אנכי לאבינים	I am a parent to the needy.[466]

Significantly, Job's last words to his "friends" come laden with socioeconomic motifs framed by a protracted legal metaphor:[467]

אם שמתי זהב כסלי	If I put my confidence in gold,
ולכתם אמרתי מבטחי	Or say fine gold is my trust,[468]
אם אשמח כי רב חילי	If I rejoice because my wealth is great,
וכי כביר מצאה ידי	Or because my hand has found abundance,[469]

463. Pope (*Job*, 227) calls this Job's "final apology," which he sees resting "on a series of oaths of clearance," and Hartley (*Job*, 410, 429), too, sees here a list of oaths. Crenshaw (*Wisdom*, 8) compares Job 29–31 to the Sermon on the Mount (Matt 5–7; cf. below).

464. Job 29:12. As Pope (*Job*, 212) points out, this line "gives the lie to Eliphaz's charge in 22:6–9."

465. Job 29:13. Hartley (*Job*, 390–91) interprets this to mean that "Job's help for the widow inspires her heart to hum joyfully." In short, "whoever hears about Job blesses him, and those who see him commend him. Job is claiming that the high respect he is given is due to his zealot pursuit of 'righteousness'" (צדקה).

466. Job 29:16. Newsom ("Job," 213) believes that "even in the nobility of his words, it becomes evident why true solidarity with the oppressed is an impossibility." Unlike Clines (*Parties*, 126–28), however, who finds the reason for this "impossibility" best explained by the "grace-vs.-compensation" polarity, Newsom argues that the real culprit is the hierarchical paternalism structuring Job's world, a world she finds patently unable to "conceive of the fundamental changes in the organization of society that would prevent the powerlessness and destitution that so often strike the widow and the orphan." *Response:* One can only wonder why anyone would imagine that the social structure inspired by postmodern egalitarianism has actually created—or indeed, *can* create—any such "prevention of powerlessness and destitution." Rather than reading an ideology (however attractive) *into* the text, Clines' explanation arises *from* the text.

467. Dick ("Metaphor," 38) argues that the core of Job 31 is based on "a defendant's official appeal before a third party for a civil hearing at which the judge would compel the plaintiff to formalize his accusations and to present any supporting evidence," and if needed, finally conclude with an "oath of innocence."

468. Job 31:24. OG λίθῳ πολυτελεῖ ἐπεποίθησα, "been persuaded by precious stones."

469. Job 31:25.

גם הוא עון פלילי	Then this would be a sin to be judged
כי כחשתי לאל ממעל	For disenfranchising God above.[470]
אם עלי אדמתי תזעק	If my land cries out against me[471]
ויחד תלמיה יבכיון	Or its furrows together weep,
אם כחה אכלתי בלי כסף	If I consume its yield without paying for it[472]
ונפש בעליה הפחתי	Or belittle the reputations of its managers,[473]
תחת חטה יצא חוח	Then let thorns grow instead of wheat,
ותחת שערה באשה	And weeds instead of barley.[474]

Job incorporates a number of structural features similar to those structuring the Babylonian Theodicy and Dialogue of Pessimism, but the central *premise* of this "great text" resonates most deeply with Ludlul bēl nēmeqi.[475] Listing no less than eight parallels between Job and other ANE texts,[476] Yair Hoffman concludes that the primary motif in Job is "recompense," a conclusion congruent with that reached by David Clines with regard to the Joban link between "piety" and "prosperity."[477] Honing in on the Prosecutor's question,[478] Clines and many others argue that its purpose is to help readers figure out whether Job *gratuitously* fears God, and

470. Job 31:28. Here Job responds, finally, to the accusations levelled at him by Eliphaz, Bildad, and Zophar concerning the nature of עון ("sin"), the point here being that the response he offers is housed in language fundamentally, intentionally, and unapologetically economic.

471. Job 31:38. Cf. Jer 4:28; 12:4; Joel 1:9; Amos 8:8; Zech 12:12. Cf. Hayes' dissertation (*Mourns*, 235) on the "mourning of the land."

472. Job 31:39 (lit., "without silver"). OG ἄνευ τιμῆς ("without payment"); Syr ܐܢ ܐܟܠܬ ܚܝܠܗ ܕܠܐ ܟܣܦ ("If I have eaten of its wealth without silver"); Vg *si fructus eius comedi absque pecunia* ("If I have eaten its fruit without money"). Textual variations aside, one would be hard-pressed to find a more succinct definition of "consumerism."

473. Job 31:39. Pope (*Job*, 225) reads "snuff out the life of its tenants."

474. Job 31:40. Some interpreters slot 31:38–40 after 31:8 (e.g., Pope, *Job*, 230), but this move (a) ignores the socioeconomic importance of *land*, and thus (b) the significance of listing Job's land-oath at the end of this oath-list (cf. Hartley, *Job*, 422; and Moore, *WealthWarn*, 200–1).

475. Cf. Sitzler (*Vorwurf*) and above.

476. Hoffman, *Blemished*, 253–58.

477. Clines, Job, 25. *T. Job* 45.1–3 depicts "Job" on his deathbed telling his children, "Do good to the poor, and do not overlook the helpless." Balentine (*Job*, 30) interprets this to mean that "a major aspect of Job's piety in *T. Job* is the use of his wealth to care for the poor."

478. "Does Job fear God 'for nothing?'" (חנם, Job 1:9).

whether, following the retributional thinking of his inquisitors, he always expects his actions to be *compensated*.[479]

Summary

As the above survey suggests, Ketuvim preserves a rich assortment of sapiential texts engaging a number of socioeconomic problems plaguing first millennium Hebrews prior to the Alexandrian invasion.[480] The books of Proverbs, Qohelet, and Job in particular cover a wide range of concerns linked in one way or another with *wealth, poverty, debt, credit, profit, value, labor, generosity, business, skill, investment, prosperity, stewardship, justice, integrity, consumerism, power, bribery, almsgiving,* and *compensation.*

How do Second Temple sages address such concerns?

479. Clines, *Job*, 25. Cf. Prov 19:17; Sir 35:12; Q 5.12 and *passim*. Van der Toorn ("Theodicy," 61) posits that "the doctrine of retribution is a law of nature, so to speak, that does not require an act of disclosure on the part of the gods" because "it is the common view of ANE wisdom traditions that retribution belongs to the realm of visible facts," not a "secret that needs to be revealed."

480. Cf. Berquist, "Resistance," 41–58.

4

Socioeconomic Motifs in Early Jewish Wisdom

Blessed are those who help the poor succeed;
Yhwh will deliver them on the day of trouble.[1]

CONFLICT BETWEEN JEWS AND Greeks in the aftermath of the Alexandrian invasion produces several "unavoidable compromises,"[2] but for Hebrew wisdom it ushers in an era of major readjustment.[3] Internally, texts like the Wisdom of Ben Sira (Sirach) begin to associate Sophia (the didactic metaphor)[4] more and more with Torah (the sacred text).[5] Externally,

1. Ps 41:2. N.B. that the causative ptc. מַשְׂכִּיל ("to make prosper, succeed" appears in Tanak twenty-six times (e.g., 1 Sam 18:14, 15). Cf. 1QH 17.16.

2. Cf. examples cited in Holland (*Desert*, 277–84); Hengel (*Judaism*, 55–57); Schwartz (*Alexander*, 1–18); and Barclay (*Jews*, 20–34).

3. Cf. Hengel (*Judaism*, 107–254); Frey ("Judaism," 96–118); Collins (*Wisdom*, 1–20); Moore (*WealthWatch*, 168–201; "Maccabees," 1055–63); and Wright ("India," 136–56).

4. Dunn (*Paul*, 272) describes Sophia not as a "goddess," but simply and only as a "metaphor."

5. Cf. ותופש תורה ידריכנה, "whoever keeps Torah will be led by her" (Sir 15:1), the "her" referring to חכמה ("wisdom," 14:20); ταῦτα πάντα βίβλος διαθήκης θεοῦ ὑψίστου νόμον ὃν ἐνετείλατο ἡμῖν Μωυσῆς, "All this is the book of the covenant of the most high God, the law which Moses commanded for us" (24:23, i.e., "all the things" proclaimed by σοφία in 24:1; cf. Wright, "Torah," 157–86). Following Reiterer ("Verhältnis," 97–133) and Fox (*Proverbs*, 630), Rogers ("Sirach," 117) is careful not simply to *equate* Wisdom with Torah in Sirach, but to depict the relationship more holistically: "Law gives expression to Wisdom, and is thus in its entirety characterized by it; but Wisdom exists before and beyond Law, and is not fully exhausted by it." Collins (*Wisdom*, 15–17) traces the *rapprochement* of wisdom with Torah long before Sirach (cf., e.g., חכמה//תורה in Ps 37:30–31 and תורה//בין in 119:34). Cf. also the claim in Baruch (4:1) that αὕτη ἡ βίβλος τῶν προσταγμάτων τοῦ θεοῦ καὶ ὁ νόμος ὁ ὑπάρχων εἰς τὸν αἰῶνα, "She is the book of God's edicts, the law which endures forever."

texts like 4QInstruction take great pains to avoid the form or substance of anything Greek,[6] while the hyper-hellenized Wisdom of Solomon begins to drift, in David Winston's opinion, toward "disillusionment and disappointment"[7] because "in contrast to Pseudo-Aristeas' mild criticisms of heathen cults,[8] Wisdom's wrathful exhibitions of the innumerable crimes and corruptions connected with pagan idolatry" testify to what he sees as the "complete rupture" of "the Jewish community from the native Egyptians and Greeks."[9]

4QInstruction

Of all the Dead Sea scrolls from Qumran the one most relevant to the present study is 4QInstruction,[10] a fragmentary collection of didactic admonitions engaging a basic set of socioeconomic questions.[11] In her Notre Dame dissertation Catherine Murphy divides these admonitions into three groups: (a) those depicting the poverty-wealth polarity from a cosmological/eschatological perspective;[12] (b) those engaging practical agro-business

6. *Contra* Jefferies (*Wisdom*, 59), Goff (*Wisdom*, 21) argues that 4QInstruction "never explicitly shows familiarity with or interest in the contemporary international world," but Hengel (*Judaism*, 108) contends that even though Palestinian Jews "see their task as the repudiation of alien Hellenistic influences . . . new notions find their way into Judaism precisely in the controversy over and repudiation of alien conceptions."

7. Winston, "Solomon," 120.

8. E.g., *Ps.-Aristeas* 134–38; cf. Wright (*Aristeas*, 286–87); Matusova (*Aristeas*, 41–43); and Shutt ("Aristeas," 380–82). Following Volgger ("Adressaten," 153–77), Gilbert ("Sagesse," 39) finds the addressees of Wisdom (οἱ κρίνοντες τὴν γῆν, "the rulers of the earth," Wis 1:1) to be the "masters of the mediterranean world; i.e., the Romans" ("maîtres du monde méditerranéen . . . les Romains précisément").

9. Winston ("Solomon," 120). Wisdom still ascribes the "world's salvation" (σωτηρία κόσμου), however, to the "multitude of the wise" (πλῆθος δὲ σοφῶν, Wis 6:24).

10. Cf. Strugnell (DJD 34.73–141); Harrington ("Texts," 977–78); Elgvin ("Reconstruction," 559–80); Tigchelaar (*4QInstruction*, 3–27); Rey (*Sagesse*, 1–13); Wold (*4QInstruction*, 1–11); and Goff (*4QInstruction*, 62). Murphy (*Wealth*, 164) sees this text as "one of the most heavily attested texts at Qumran."

11. Also known as Sapiential Work A and מוסר למבין (*Musar le-Mevin*, "Instruction for the Interpreter"), this Hebrew text survives in six fragmentary copies—1Q26, 4Q415–418, and 423 (Harrington, "Texts," 977), and, as Tigchelaar points out ("Reconstruction," 99–101), many of the lacunae in this or that fragment can be reconstructed from the more fragmentary parallel texts.

12. This argument rests on the presumption that the oft-used expression רז נהיה ("the mystery which is," 4Q416.2.3.9 *et passim*) refers to the *future* (e.g., Murphy, *Wealth*, 166–74; Rey, *Sagesse*, 228–54; Goff, *4QInstruction*, 93) instead of the *present* (cf., e.g., Tigchelaar, *DSSSE* 851). Stuckenbruck ("4QInstruction," 261; cf. Moore, *Babbler*, 166–79) posits a "cross-fertilization" of wisdom and apocalyptic traditions in this

concerns;[13] and (c) those advising the מבין ("interpreter")[14] on how to navigate the perils and pitfalls of his socioeconomic environment. Proceeding on the premise that 4Q416 preserves the beginning of this text,[15] the following pages focus on this third category of texts.

Theological Preamble

Like Proverbs and Sirach,[16] 4QInstruction begins with a theological preamble pondering what Armin Lange calls the *präexistente Ordnung des Seins*:[17]

שאל טרפכה מא]ל	Ask God for your food,[18]
כי הוא פתח רחמיו	For he has made his compassion[19] accessible
למל]א כל מחסרי אוטו	To clarify[20] anything unclear[21] about his kindness,[22]

era, a development Adams (*Wisdom*, 276) sees as a "challenge to the standard paradigm of instructional literature."

13. Murphy's dissertation (*Wealth*, 166) is the *sine qua non* for understanding the complexities of the poverty-wealth polarity at Qumran. In the Damascus Document, e.g., she observes four distinct types of socioeconomic behavior: (a) commercial transactions between community members (e.g., CD 9.8–16); (b) sacrificial expenditures of community members (e.g., CD 16.13–20); (c) wealth in familial matters (e.g., CD 13.15–18); and (d) transactions between covenanters and outsiders (e.g., CD 12.6–11).

14. Heb מבין (causative m. sg. ptc. of בין, "to make understand, interpret," Ezra 8:16; Neh 8:9; *m. `Abod. Zar.* 3.5; cf. the English term "maven"). This term appears c. twenty times in 4QInstruction.

15. N.B. the large margin on the right-hand side of Column 1 (Harrington, "Wisdom," 977; Murphy, *Wealth*, 164, 167).

16. Prov 1:1–9; Sir 1:1–20 (cf. Schmidt, *Wisdom*, 37–80; Argall, *Sirach*, 165; and Beentjes, "Wisdom," 139–54).

17. "Preexistent order of being" (Lange, *Weisheit*, 62). Murphy (*Wealth*, 166–67) recognizes that the sayings about poverty and wealth in 4QInstruction "are first grounded in the organization of nature and thus on theological claims."

18. 4Q416.2.1.22. Tigchelaar (*DSSSE* 848) reconstructs ל]שאל, but Goff (*4QInstruction*, 57, 62) reconstructs מא]ל שאל, reading 4Q416.2.1.20—2.3 as a self-contained section designed to "present 'God' (אל) as a munificent provider of food."

19. Using a cognate of רחם, Qur'an often refers to the deity as الرحمن, "the Compassionate One" (e.g., Q 19.78).

20. 4Q416.2.2.1 (lit., "to fill up"). The reconstruction is Goff's (*4QInstruction*, 57).

21. 4Q416.2.2.1 (lit., "scarce, lacking").

22. 4Q416.2.2.1. In Tanak אוט means "gentle" (2 Sam 18:5) or "quiet" (Job 15:11). Recognizing that אוט may denote "financial resources," Murphy (*Wealth*, 166, 169) reads כל מח]סרי אוטו, translating "all the deficiencies of his secrets," identifying אוט as a quasi-sectarian term linked to what Goff (*4QInstruction*, 15) calls 4QInstruction's

ולתת טרף לכל חי	And provide food for all living things,[23]
ואין מת מפני הרעבה	So that none may perish from hunger.
ואם יקפוץ ידו	For if he tightens his hand into a fist[24]
ונאספה רוח כל בשר	The breath of all flesh will expire.[25]

Preamble concluded, the sage engages a series of admonitions dealing with *poverty, loan guarantees,* and *debt-slavery.*

Poverty

That 4QInstruction repeatedly describes the מבין as "poor"[26] is, in Matthew Goff's opinion, one of its "most distinctive features."[27] The problem with this assessment, however, is defining exactly what "poor" means, a problem hardly unique to this particular text.[28] Peter Venter argues that 4QInstruction "does not idealize poverty as such" because its depictions of poverty sometimes indicate something other than a "mere physical state" (an opinion

"most important expression," רז נהיה, "the mystery which is coming" (cf. 4Q416.2.1.5; 2.3.9, 14, 18, 21, and *passim*).

23. 4Q416.2.2.1–2. Cf. טרף נתן ליריו, "he gives food to those who revere him" (Ps 111:5; cf. 145:15).

24. 4Q416.2.2.2. Torah uses this idiom in Deut 15:7 (קפץ יד, lit., "close the hand"; NRSV "tight-fisted"), a *miṣvah* one medieval text interprets as follows: אל תשליט עליך מדת הכילות והנבלה אבל הכן לבבך על כל פנים במדת הנדיבות והחמלה, "Do not let the traits of disdain and idiocy rule over you, but aim your mind in every way toward the traits of generosity and compassion" (*Sefer HaḤinuk* 478).

25. 4Q416.2.2.2 (lit. "be gathered up"). Philo's (*Agr.* 1.53) theology is similar: "It is impossible that there should be a deficiency of anything that is necessary where God presides, who is in the habit of bestowing good things in all fulness and completeness on all living beings."

26. Several terms for "poverty" occur in 4QInstruction, including מחסור, רוש, עני, and אביון.

27. Goff, *4QInstruction*, 23. Hoppe (*Poor*, 120) observes that in lieu of focusing on the needs of the wealthy (as Qohelet does) 4QInstruction "concentrates on giving advice to the מבין in avoiding destitution." It is vitally important to remember, however, with Armitage (*Poverty*, 47) that "the slippery nature of all poverty language, rooted in the intrinsic vagueness of the concept, means that it can be readily reassigned to non-material deficits."

28. Cf. Harrington (*Texts*, 45). Philo (*Virt.* 1.6) tries to argue that "no one whatever is really poor if he has the indestructible and inalienable riches of nature for his purveyor," a definition provoking readers like Pleins ("Poor," 413) to observe that sometimes "the use of terms for the poor tends to be rather vague with regard to their specific circumstances, causing us to wonder if the text is more metaphorical in its use of the terms and therefore more spiritualized in its approach." While this represents Pleins' response to the Psalter, the same tendency surfaces in Sandoval's (*Wealth*, 5, 16) approach to Proverbs and Gregory's (*Sirach*, 26) approach to Sirach.

also endorsed by Benjamin Wold).[29] Johannes Ro insightfully suggests that the "poverty terminology" in the Psalter and at Qumran refers to a type of piety inclined to highlighting "its own sinfulness and lowliness," that is, "a consciously assumed humility circumscribed with traditional attributes . . . regarded as the precondition for the pious to overcome eschatological crisis."[30] While these are but a few of the more prevalent opinions, the pages below try to engage the motifs alluding to *economic* poverty without dismissing the actuality of *spiritual* poverty,[31] keeping in mind Leslie Hoppe's caveat that *any* attempt to "synthesize" the "poverty texts" can be "risky."[32]

וזכור כי רוש אתה	Remember that you are poor.[33]
אם חפצ]ים פוקד לכה	If someone entrusts assets to you[34]

29. Venter ("Ideology," 215–16); Wold ("Metaphorical," 140–53). A good example of this occurs in *Sib. Or.* 5.98: "O you rich with the wealth of cities, you will be rich with distress."

30. Ro, *Poverty*, 185–86. Bar Qappara (*Lev. Rab.* 34.14) teaches that sooner or later everyone becomes "poor"—if not the father, then the son; if not the son, then the grandson.

31. This is an old debate. While Hoppe's attempt (*Poverty*, 72, 75, 171) to minimize the distinction between *economic* and *spiritual* poverty is problematic, it remains difficult to ascertain which passages in 4QInstruction refer to which. Yet this task is no less difficult than ascertaining whether the "release" of this or that *deity* in this or that Hittite ritual refers to the "release" of this or that *human* client (Moore, *Balaam*, 24; *Babbler*, 265).

32. Hoppe (*Poverty*, 121). At times Hoppe recognizes that being "poor" does not automatically equate to being "righteous" (e.g., pp. 72, 75, 171; cf. *Lev. Rab.* 34.4), but his book's ideological *Tendenz* makes it difficult to see these identifications as anything other than "exceptions."

33. 4Q416.2.3.2. The expression "you are poor" occurs four times in 4Q416.2.3: line 2 (רוש אתה), line 8 (אביון אתה), line 12 (אביון אתה), and line 19 (רש אתה). So whether the admonition is to exercise caution when safekeeping something valuable for one's employer (lines 3–5), or to beware taking money from someone with whom one is unfamiliar (lines 5–8), or to tending to the needs of one's familial inheritance (lines 8–12), or to refusing to define oneself as a poverty "victim" (lines 12–19), or to raising one's family in a healthy way (4Q416.2.3.19—4.14)—all these activities are as expected of the poor as they are of the rich.

34. 4Q416.2.3.3. Goff (*4QInstruction*, 96) plausibly reads this as a conditional sentence, reading אם before the (now missing) word-ending ים- (cf. the appearance of אם in line 5). Strugnell and Harrington (DJD 34.114) suggest the reconstruction כסף ערב]ים ("pledge money"; lit., "silver of pledges") and Murphy (*Wealth*, 189–90) connects this expression to the discussion about marital finances in lines 20–21, but Elgvin's ("Analysis," 221) reconstruction חפצים (translating "assets"; lit., "desires") seems to have the fewest problems. N.B. that Goff (*4QInstruction*, 285) takes Elgvin's suggestion seriously by noting that חפץ occurs elsewhere in 4QInstruction referring to "items desired in the context of trade" (e.g., 4Q417.2.1.18 and 4Q418.126.2.12).

אל תשלח ידכה בו פן תכוה	Do not lay your hand upon them lest you ignite them
ובאשו תבער גיתכה	And blister your flesh with its fire.[35]
כאשר לקחתו כן השיבהו	So just as you receive these assets, return them
ושׂמחה לכה אם תנקה ממנו	That you may experience joy, assuming you remain blameless.[36]

Like the sages before him, this one advises caution before situations involving monetary exchange:

וגם מכל איש אשר לוא ידעתה אל תקת הון	Do not take money from someone unknown to you
פן יוסיף על רישכה	Lest your poverty increase.[37]
ואם שׂמו בראשׁכה למות	And should the debt be held over you on pain of death,[38]
הפקידהו ורוחכה אל תחבל בו	Take responsibility for it, but not so much that it paralyzes your spirit.[39]

Holistic comprehension of the "institution of debt,"[40] however, can be a difficult thing to grasp:

אביון אתה אל תתאו זולת נחלתכה	Since you are poor, desire nothing but your inheritance;[41]

35. Cf. Sir 3:30 אש לוהטת יכבו מים כן צדקה תכפר חטאת, "As water extinguishes a blazing fire, so 'almsgiving' (OG ἐλεημοσύνη) atones for sin."

36. 4Q416.2.3.5.

37. Murphy (*Wealth*, 188) subtitles this section "Living Within One's Means."

38. 4Q416.2.3.6. Strugnell and Harrington (DJD 34.112) argue that the expression למות means that the מבין has until he dies to repay the loan, but in light of Sir 18:22 it seems more likely that it refers to the debtor being "threatened with death to ensure repayment" (Goff, *4QInstruction*, 98).

39. 4Q416.2.3.6–7. Doubtless it is no accident that חבל ("to seize") recurs frequently in language about moneylending; e.g., תחבל אחיך חנם, "you have seized pledges from your brothers for no reason" (Job 22:6; cf. Prov 20:16; 27:13), which if so, suggests that the admonition here is a paronomasiacal pun.

40. Douglas (*Debt*, 31) suggests two key questions when assessing the function of this social institution: (a) whether the institution of debt is necessary and sufficient to preserve the social goods necessary to maintain one's social status, and (b) whether *always* paying one's debts is the best way to support the institution itself.

41. 4Q416.2.3.8. The *Leitwort* נחלה ("inheritance") appears over thirty times in 4QInstruction, sometimes meaning *l'héritage humain* and sometimes *l'héritage divine* (Rey, *Sagesse*, 56–57).

ואל תתבלע בה פן תסיג גבולכה	But do not obsess about it,[42] lest you displace your boundary stone.[43]
ואם ישיבכה לכבוד בה התהלך	So if he restores your wealth,[44] utilize it,
וברז נהיה דרוש מולדיו	Scrutinizing its foundations in light of the coming mystery.[45]
ואז תדע נחלתו ובצדק תתהלך	Then you will know *his* inheritance and walk in *his* justice,
כי מראש הרים ראושכה	For he has lifted your head from poverty,[46]
ועם נדיבם הושיבכה	Seated you among nobles,
ובנחלת כבוד המשילכה	And bestowed upon you a rich inheritance.[47]

Loan Guarantees

אל תקל ערובת רעיכה	Do not default on your neighbor's pledge,[48]

42. 4Q416.2.3.8 (lit., "do not be swallowed up by it").

43. 4Q416.2.3.8–9. Displacing a boundary stone is a violation not only of Hebrew (Deut 19:14; cf. Prov 15:25), but of Babylonian (*kudurru*, "boundary stone," *BBSt* 3.6.21 et *passim*), Greek (ὅριον, Plutarch, *Arist.* 11.8), and Roman law (*saxum antiquum ingens*, "huge ancient stone," *Aen.* 12.897). Cf. Hershkowitz (*Madness*, 108).

44. 4Q416.2.3.9. Heb כבוד often means "glory/honor," but in socioeconomic contexts it refers to "wealth" (Gen 31:1; Isa 10:3; cf. *HAL* 436–37). Given the context here, it may well be intentionally polysemantic.

45. 4Q416.2.3.9. Whether or not רז נהיה is an eschatological expression is questionable (cf. above).

46. 4Q416.2.3.11.

47. 4Q416.2.3.11–12.

48. 4Q416.2.2.3. Restoring תק]ל ("default"), Goff (*4QInstruction*, 59, 69) reads this line as an admonition to the מבין not to "mistreat" (קלל) the pledge he has provided for his neighbor, *contra* Rey (*Sagesse*, 64, 70) and Tigchelaar (*DSSSE* 849), who restore תק]ח and read the line as a warning not to "take back" (לקח) his pledge. In contrast to, say, Judah's pledge to secure his brother Benjamin (Gen 44:32), the book of Proverbs issues a similar warning: אדם חסר לב תוקע כף ערב ערבה לפני רעהו, "It is senseless (lit., 'lack of mind') for a man to donate a pledge (lit., 'to clasp hands') to guarantee a loan for a neighbor" (Prov 17:18; cf. Job 17:3). So, where 4QInstruction "forbids as well as cautions against the practice of standing surety for others" (Murphy, *Wealth*, 165), Goff (*4QInstruction*, 26) posits that Sirach "encourages his students to be ethical creditors who should lend money to those in need, even though the loan may not be repaid" (cf. Sir 29:1–14; cf. Luke 6:35), a practice Gregory (*Generosity*, 292) files under "essential acts of mercy."

פן תכשול בה	Lest you be ruined by it[49]
ובחרפתו תכסה פניכה	And cover your face with his shame,
ובאולתו מאסור כמהו	Becoming like him a prisoner in his folly.[50]

With regard to the moneylending *process*, the role of the debtor takes center stage:

אם בהון הנושה בו ישה	If a creditor loans you money,[51]
ומהר שלם	Then compensate him quickly,[52]
ואתה תשוה בו	That you may secure from him a clean slate.[53]
כי כיס צפונ'כה פקדתה לנושה בכה	For if you have entrusted your fortune to your creditor,[54]
בעד רעיכה נתתה כל חייכה בו	And lent out your life-savings for your neighbor's use,[55]
מהר תן אשר לוא יקח כיסכה	Repay it quickly, before your creditor seizes it.[56]

Since trust is so essential to maintaining a healthy bond between debtor and creditor, the sage advises the מבין not to abuse it:

49. 4Q416.2.2.3. Heb כשל ("to stumble") in the nominal pl. form מכשלות can mean "ruins" (Zeph 1:3, Vg *ruinae*). Sirach (29:14) parallels this proverb with an antonymous counterpart: ἀνὴρ ἀγαθὸς ἐγγυήσεται τὸν πλησίον καὶ ὁ ἀπολωλεκὼς αἰσχύνην ἐγκαταλείψει αὐτόν, "A good man will stand surety for his neighbor, but the shameless will abandon him."

50. 4Q416.2.2.3–4. Cf. Ug *asr* ("prisoner") in El's response to Yam, *`bdk b`l yymm . . . bn dgn asrkm*, "Ba`al is your slave, O Yam . . . the son of Dagan your 'prisoner,'" *CAT* 1.2.1.36–37). Chirichigno (*Debt-Slavery*, 344–45) insists that the pervasiveness of debt-slavery cannot be overstated.

51. 4Q416.2.2.4 (reconstructed from 4Q418.8.1, emending בו to בכה). Heb הון usually means "wealth" (1QpHab 8.3), a term Murphy (*Wealth*, 163) finds originally "deriving from sapiential strata of the Hebrew Bible" (cf. Harrington, "רז נהיה," 549–53; Wold, *Women*, 20–23).

52. On שלם as "compensation" (*Aḥq* 131), cf. Gerleman (*Wurzel*, 1–2) and above.

53. 4Q416.2.2.4 (lit., "become equal with him"). Other translations read "be even with him" (Tigchelaar, *DSSSE* 849); and "like him" (Goff, *4QInstruction*, 59).

54. Lit., "a bag of your treasure."

55. Goff (*4QInstruction*, 71) contends that, while the מבין is not as well-off as, say, one of Sirach's students, he is not "destitute." That being said, the מבין probably "does not have an ample or sturdy safety net of resources to fall back on if he were to lose the bag and its contents."

56. 4Q416.2.2.4–6. Unlike Qohelet, Sirach, and most of Proverbs, 4QInstruction speaks more to the needs of debtors than creditors.

ובדבריכה אל תמעט רוחכה	Do not demean your spirit by your behavior,[57]
בכל הון אל תמר רוח קודשך	Nor exchange your holy spirit for wealth of any kind,[58]
כי אין מחיר שוה	For no sum will be enough.[59]

Debt-Slavery

Much like the warning issued by the Jewish governor Nehemiah,[60] 4QInstruction warns the מבין not to try to exploit the debtor-creditor relationship to his own advantage:

אם איש לא יטכה ברצון	If he (the "creditor") treats you unfavorably[61]
שחר פניו וכלשונו דבר	Seek him out and speak to him in his own tongue,[62]
ואז תמצא חפצכה מחרפתכה	So that you may experience delight instead of shame.[63]

57. 4Q416 2.2.6. Cf. the expression רע לנפשו, "bad to his soul" (Sir 14:5–6).

58. 4Q416 2.2.6. Whereas Nötscher (*Terminologie*, 42) and Sekki (*Meaning*, 71–72) regard the "holy spirit" as an impersonal power at Qumran, Charlesworth ("Scrolls," 19–62) defines it as a hypostatic/angelic being; i.e., not the Holy Spirit *of* God, but a holy spirit *from* God.

59. 4Q416.2.2.7 (i.e., to justify such behavior). Cf. Ps 49:8, ויקר פדיון נפשם וחדל לעולם, "For the redemption of their souls is valuable, and does not change," and Prov 3:15, וכל חפציך לא ישוו בה, "for no desirable thing is comparable to her." In GNT the Nazarene asks, τί γὰρ ὠφεληθήσεται ἄνθρωπος ἐὰν τὸν κόσμον ὅλον κερδήσῃ τὴν δὲ ψυχὴν αὐτοῦ ζημιωθῇ ἢ τί δώσει ἄνθρωπος ἀντάλλαγμα τῆς ψυχῆς αὐτοῦ "What does it 'profit' a person if he gains the whole world and loses his 'soul' (cf. נפש in *Aḥq* 131), or what will someone give in exchange for their soul?" (Mark 8:36–37).

60. Neh 5:1–5; cf. Chirichigno (*Debt-Slavery*, 101–43); Moore (*WealthWarn*, 136–39). Warning Mohammed not to judge infidels by himself without community support, the deity asks him to question his motives: تسلهم اجر فهم من معرم مثقلون, "Do you ask for a payment so that they become burdened down by debt?" (Q 68.46).

61. 4Q416.2.2.7 (lit., "does not reach out to you with favor").

62. 4Q416.2.2.7–8. Tigchelaar (*DSSSE* 851) and Goff (*4QInstruction*, 59) read "speech." "Tongue" (לשון) here may refer to (a) a second language (cf. 2 Kgs 18:26// Isa 36:11); (b) an isogloss within the same language (Judg 12:6); or (c) the creditor's habitual *style* of speaking.

63. 4Q416.2.2.8. Cf. Heb חרפה ("shame") above in 2.3.

אל ת[מ]ר לו וחוקיכה אל תרף	Do not embitter him by forsaking your duties,[64]
וברזיכה השמר [מאו]דה	But carefully[65] monitor your mysteries.[66]
אם עבודתו יפקיד לכה	When he assigns you a task,
אל מנוח בנפשכה ואל תנומה לעיניכה	Give no rest to your soul or sleep to your eyes
עד עשׂותכה מצותיו	Until you carry out its directives.[67]
אל תוסף	But do not overdo it.[68]
אם יש להצניע	If anything lies hidden,[69]
ואל תותר לו אף הון בלי	Do not seek to profit[70] from the (funds) set aside for taxes,[71]
פן יאמר בזני	Lest your master think, "He despises me."[72]

64. 4Q416.2.2.8. Reconstructing with Tigchelaar (*DSSSE* 851).

65. 4Q416.2.2.8–9. For the reconstruction [מאו]דה, cf. Tigchelaar (*DSSSE* 851), *contra* Strugnell and Harrington (נפשכה, "for your soul," DJD 34.90), and Rey (לחייכה, "for the sake of your life," *Sagesse*, 64).

66. 4Q416.2.2.8 (lit., "guard your mysteries"); cf. התבונן ברזיכה, "understand your mysteries" (4Q417 1.1.25). On Heb רז ("secret, mystery") Goff (*4QInstruction*, 78) plausibly suggests that "the term 'mysteries' likely signifies the teachings which the מבין has received in a general sense." In other words, "the fact that he is a debt-slave does not mean he should abandon the instruction he has been given." Cf. τὸ μυστήριον τῆς πίστεως, "the mystery of the faith" (1 Tim 3:9).

67. 4Q416.2.2.9–10. Paul similarly advises Christian slaves at Colossae to attend to motive as well as action (Col 3:22).

68. 4Q416.2.2.10 (lit., "do not add on, increase").

69. 4Q416.2.2.10. Heb צנע can mean either (a) "to be humble" (Mic 6:8) or (b) "to hide, conceal, deposit"; e.g., הן אטו אמורים מצנעי ישׂראל לא מצנעי, "So, are you saying that the Amorites do 'conceal' (coins, jewelry, important documents, etc. in walls for safekeeping), but that Israel does not 'conceal?'" (*b. B. Meṣ* 25b).

70. 4Q416.2.2.10. Heb יתר can mean (a) "to leave over, go beyond, be profitable" or in some cases (b) "do too much" (e.g., "if you omit one letter or write 'one too many,'" *b. `Erub.* 13a). Cf. Qoh 1:3 *et passim* (above).

71. 4Q416.2.2.10. Strugnell and Harrington (DJD 34.101) emend בלי to בלו, a term referencing a particular kind of tax, the "produce tax" (Ezra 4:13, 20).

72. 4Q416.2.2.10. Frymer-Kensky ("Israel," 257) mentions two Tanak texts likely alluding to creditor-debtor relationships gone sour: (a) Jephthah's raiding army consists of אנשים ריקים ("empty men"; so Syr and OG; Vg *viri inopes*, "worthless men," Judg 11:3)—i.e., "people emptied of their property, landless"; and (b) David's raiding army consists of כל איש אשר לו נשה, "everyone obligated to a creditor" (1 Sam 22:2).

Should this advice be taken seriously, then who knows what good might result?

תועצנו והייתה לו בן בכר	You may advise him and become his firstborn son,[73]
וחמל עליכה כאיש על יחידו	So that he might empathize with you like a man with his only son,[74]
כי אתה עבדו ובחירו	Because you are his servant, his chosen one.[75]

Then again, it's always wise to be cautious:

ואתה אל תבטח למה תשׂנא	But you, do not become overconfident, lest you suffer disgrace.
ואל תשקוד ממדהבבכה	Do not fret or lose sleep over the taxman,[76]
ואתה דמה לו לעבד משׂכיל	But focus on becoming your master's "sensible servant."[77]

73. 4Q416.2.2.13. Whether this is metaphorical or not is not clear. N.B. the socioeconomic responsibilities Abraham assigns to his servant Eleazar (Gen 24:2–67), as well as the warning in the Babylonian Theodicy that not all *bukrū* ("firstborn") automatically grow up to be "prosperous . . . wealthy lords" (*ešērū . . . bēl mešrū*, *BWL* 70.19–20).

74. Sirach (29:15) goes so far as to advise the debtor, χάριτας ἐγγύου μὴ ἐπιλάθῃ ἔδωκεν γὰρ τὴν ψυχὴν αὐτοῦ ὑπὲρ σοῦ, "Do not forget the kindness of your guarantor, for he has given his soul for you," even to the point of calling him a ῥυσάμενον ("rescuer").

75. 4Q416.2.2.14. Harrington (*Wisdom*, 46) and Murphy (*Wealth*, 182) see the material in lines 9–15 referring to a labor crisis perhaps brought on by debt-slavery. For Wold (*4QInstruction*, 44–45) this text has to do with how the מבין relates to someone "who is not equal to him," and that "by relating appropriately to others during times of hardship (i.e., not striking them or lowering himself to their level) the addressee becomes like, or relates as, a father to them. When . . . line 17 turns to the subject of wealth, instruction occurs on how to relate to one's financial oppressor. Therefore, in becoming as a firstborn son to God the addressee relates to weaker members of his community as a father by modeling the appropriate way of dealing with financial matters."

76. 4Q416.2.2.14. Heb מדהבה occurs only once in Tanak (Isa 14:4; OG ἐπισπουδαστής, "taskmaster"; Sym/Theo φορολογία, "tribute/tax-collector") and two other times in 4QInstruction (4Q18.176.3 and 4Q18a.16.3). Strugnell and Harrington (DJD 34.104) read "oppressive tax-gatherer"; Elgvin ("Analysis," 212) reads "creditor." Noting the cognate מדהוב in CD 13.10, Goff (*4QInstruction*, 82–83) notes that the CD passage also "deals with the alleviation of economic distress."

77. 4Q416.2.2.15 (cf. עבד משׂכיל in Prov 17:2; Sir 10:25). Strugnell and Harrington (DJD 34.244) translate "servant of an intelligent man," but Hempel ("Rule," 287), noting this expression in other wisdom texts (Prov 14:35: 17:2; Sir 7:21), translates "wise servant" (cf. גבר חכמה, "wise man," in 7:26).

Most importantly, the מבין needs to learn how to tell the difference between "slavery" and "service":[78]

וגם אל תשפל נפשכה לאשר לא ישוה	Do not crudely demean yourself.[79]
לאשר אין כוחכה אל תגע	Do not jockey for positions you cannot handle
פן תשכל וחרפתכה תרבה מאודה	Lest faltering, you incur shame.[80]
אל תמכור נפשכה בהון	Do not sell your soul for money,[81]
טוב היתכה עבד ברוח	For it is good to be a spiritually-minded servant
וחנם תעבוד נוגשיכה	Serving your supervisors without expecting compensation.[82]
ובמחיר אל תמכור כבודכה	So do not barter your birthright for a fee
ואל תערבהו בנחלתכה	Or otherwise endanger your inheritance.[83]

Recognizing (a) that "some Qumran texts identify the elect as 'the poor,'"[84] and (b) that "4QInstruction's refrain of the phrase 'you are poor' is without exact parallel in Second Temple literature," and (c) that it "shows

78. Del Olmo Lete and Sanmartín (*DULAT* 139) argue that Ugaritic *`bd* can mean "slave" in some contexts and "servant" in others, but it's doubtful that the same distinction applies to Heb עבד.

79. 4Q416.2.2.15. Cf. ומי יכבד מקלה נפשו, "Who will honor a man who demeans his own soul?" (Sir 10:29; cf. 14:6).

80. Elsewhere at Qumran the nature of this shame is juristically spelled out: "if someone fails to care for the property of the 'community' (יחד), thereby 'causing its loss' (לאבדו) he shall fully 'compensate it,' שלמו). But if he cannot compensate it, he shall be punished for sixty days" (1QS 7.5–7; cf. Schmidt, *Wealth*, 93). Olyan ("Honor," 217) argues that the ANE/Mediterranean honor-shame polarity is part of a "larger complex of ideas related to covenant, a complex characterized by notions of reciprocity" (cf. Lau, *Shame*).

81. "Indebtedness is portrayed as a loss of one's spirit, which has more value than something which can be bought for money" (Goff, *Worldly*, 164).

82. 4Q416.2.2.17. Goff (*4QInstruction*, 73) suggests that the "claim . . . that he is to serve his 'oppressors' without wages suggests that the addressee is not paid for his labor." N.B. the centrality of this motif in Job (חנם recurs in the Prosecutor's question in Job 1:9, above) and Luke's Sermon on the Plain (Luke 6:35, below).

83. 4Q416.2.2.17. N.B. the recurrence of עבר in the epithet יום עברה (lit., "day of 'passing over,'" Sir 5:8). Q 3.77 clarifies the language of this saying, warning that anyone "selling" (يشترون) the divine "covenant" (بعهد) or their own "oaths" (ايمانهم), regardless of "price" (ثمنا), forfeits their "share" (خلاق) in the hereafter.

84. E.g., CD 19.9 and 1QM 13.12–14.

concern for the addressee's economic situation" by "giving him practical advice to ensure that he does not face destitute poverty," Matthew Goff concludes that the poverty motif in 4QInstruction is designed "to teach the מבין about his elect status."[85] Agreeing with this conclusion, Jean-Sébastien Rey adds that the sage's goal is to "punctuate his teaching on poverty with theological conclusions related to the acquisition of learning or eschatological judgment."[86] Curtis Hutt, however, suggests that even though the מבין is "economically poor," there is enough evidence in 4QInstruction to suggest that he might also be an administrative trainee—a moneychanger-in-training, so to speak—who, unlike the moneychangers working for the Wicked Priest in Jerusalem,[87] follows a strong ethical code rooted in a sturdy religious faith.[88]

Whatever its range and scope, the socioeconomic melody-line in 4QInstruction (unlike that in, say, CD and 1QS) modulates into a non-sectarian key whenever the sage admonishes his readers to live within their means, avoid indebtedness, accept whatever "poverty" comes their way, and most importantly, accept every gift as coming from the heart of a deity willing to "clarify anything unclear about his kindness."[89]

The Wisdom of Ben Sira

The Wisdom of Ben Sira (Sirach) is by far the longest sapiential text in Second Temple Judaism, a text Robert Balgarnie Young Scott refers to as a "latter-day book of Proverbs."[90] Benjamin Wright calls it a "very difficult

85. Goff, *Wisdom*, 127.

86. Rey, *Sagesse*, 134 ("L'auteur ponctue son enseignement sur la pauvreté par des conclusions théologiques relatives à l'acquisition de la connaissance ou au jugement eschatologique"). To quote another Hebrew sage, "poverty is evil only in the opinion of the ungodly," ἡ πτωχεία ἐν στόματι ἀσεβοῦς (Sir 13:24).

87. Lim ("Priest," 973–76); Atkinson ("Wicked," 68–83). Köstenberger (*John*, 106) implausibly proposes that the Nazarene's main problem in John 2:14–16 is not that moneychangers turn the Temple into a "house of trade" (οἶκον ἐμπορίου), but that by doing so they take away the only place where God-fearing Gentiles might lawfully worship, the "court of the Gentiles."

88. Hutt, "Money," 118–19.

89. למל]א כול מחסורי אוטו (4Q416.2.2.1; cf. 4Q417.2+23.3). Cf. the similar comment in the Epistle of James, πᾶσα δόσις ἀγαθὴ καὶ πᾶν δώρημα τέλειον ἄνωθέν, "Every good endowment, with every perfect gift, is from above" (Jas 1:17, cf. below).

90. Scott, *Wisdom*, 201–2. The volume of essays edited by Joosten and Rey (*Texts and Versions*) is one of the better sources for learning about Sirach's complex textual history.

book,"[91] and Gerhard von Rad thinks it "defies all attempts to impose upon it a scheme."[92] More to the point, Robert Gnuse recognizes that Sirach "speaks frequently of economic oppression,"[93] even though Brad Gregory also sees in it a positive portrayal of "blameless wealth,"[94] calling it a "marvelous work for appreciating the way Second Temple Jews appropriate earlier traditions about generosity."[95] Along with "generosity,"[96] however, Sirach manipulates several other motifs to formulate his rather byzantine understanding of the poverty-wealth polarity.[97]

How Not to Treat the Poor (Sir 4:1–6)

One of the first items on his socioeconomic agenda is "How Not to Treat the Poor."[98]

בני אל תלעג לחיי עני	My child, do not cheat[99] the poor out of their livelihood;[100]
ואל תדאיב נפש עני ומר נפש	Nor goad them into becoming indigent, bitter souls.[101]

91. Wright, *Signet*, 241.

92. Von Rad, *Wisdom*, 240.

93. Gnuse, *Steal*, 89.

94. Cf. below on Sir 31:1–11.

95. Gregory, *Sirach*, 1.

96. ἐλεημοσύνη // צדקה. Anderson (*Charity*, 19) recognizes that almsgiving receives "pride of place" among acts of charity in Early Judaism (cf. Moore, *WealthWarn*, 148–50, 161–62, 192).

97. Cf. Asencio ("Poverty," 151–78); Beentjes ("Waisen," 51–64); Wright and Camp ("Gold," 153–73); and Gilbert ("Poor," 153–69; "Prêt," 179–89). *Pace* Geller ("Wisdom," 176) Sirach is hardly the termination point of the Hebraic wisdom trajectory.

98. N.B. that Sirach pronounces a blessing on those who attend בית מדרשי, "my house of instruction" (Sir 51:23): אשרי איש באלה יהגה, "Happy is the one who meditates on these things" (50:28), the "things" here referring to the teachings laid down throughout the scroll which Davis ("Sirach," 999) dubs the "written form (of) the results of decades of oral instruction." In short, as the Prologue clearly states (1.13), the target audience is the φιλομαθεῖς ("lovers of learning").

99. Sir 4:1 (lit., "to mock"). Syr ܬܒܙܚ ("to mock"); OG ἀποστερήσῃς ("to cheat"); Vg *fraudes* ("defraud").

100. Sir 4:1 (cf. 34:25–26). Vg *elemosynam* is a transliteration of ἐλεημοσύνη ("alms").

101. Sir 4:1 (cf. Prov 30:9). Cf. OG μὴ παρελκύσῃς ὀφθαλμοὺς ἐπιδεεῖς ("do not keep needy eyes waiting"). The opposite of this is simple to understand, but as any "overseer" can attest (ἐπισκοπῆς, 1 Tim 3:1), it is often quite difficult to implement; i.e., "'to oversee' (ἐπισκέπτεσθαι) the care of orphans and widows in their distress" (Jas

רווח נפש חסירה אל פוח	Never drive the spirits of needy souls into despair,[102]
ואל תתעלם ממדכדך נפש	Nor get dragged into plots to crush their souls.[103]
אל [תאביל] מעי דך	Do not cause the afflicted to mourn within,[104]
וקרב עני אל תכאיב	Nor cause the needy to grieve internally.[105]
אל תמנע מתן ממסכינך	Never withhold gifts from the poor in your care;
ולא תבזה שאולות דל	Do not reject their petitions,[106]
ולא תתן לו מקום לקללך	Or give them a reason to curse you.[107]

Lest these mandates be ignored, OG Sirach later restates them in stronger terms:

θύων υἱὸν ἔναντι τοῦ πατρὸς αὐτου	Like someone who kills a son in front of his father[108]

1:27; see below). Reflecting on this difficulty, Metz (*Poverty*, 32–33) suggests that the only valid way to respond is via *sacrament*; i.e., that since "every authentic religious act is directed toward the concreteness of God in our human neighbors and their world . . . our human neighbor now becomes a 'sacrament' of God's hidden presence among us."

102. Sir 4:2 (lit., "a soul of scarcity"; cf. חסר in 4Q416.2.2.1, discussed above). Syr ܢܦܫܐ ܕܚܣܝܪ ܠܗ ("the soul of scarcity to it"); OG ψυχὴν πεινῶσαν ("a hungry soul"); Vg *animam esurientem ne despexeris* ("do not disdain a starving soul").

103. Sir 4:2. Cf. the warnings against joining pirate-gangs at the beginning of Proverbs (Prov 1:11–13).

104. Sir 4:3. Reconstructing causative אבל (Syr ܬܒܠܐ) to parallel causative כאב in the next line (cf. Job 14:22).

105. Sir 4:3. OG καρδίαν παρωργισμένην μὴ προσταράξῃς καὶ μὴ παρελκύσῃς δόσιν προσδεομένου, "Do not provoke the hearts of the desperate, or delay giving to the needy."

106. Sir 4:4. Syr ܒܥܘܬܐ ܕܡܣܟܢܐ ܠܐ ܬܒܣܘܢ, "do not dismiss the petitions of the poor"; OG ἱκέτην θλιβόμενον μὴ ἀπαναίνου καὶ μὴ ἀποστρέψῃς τὸ πρόσωπόν σου ἀπὸ πτωχοῦ, "do not reject a suppliant in distress or turn your face away from the poor."

107. Sir 4:5 (lit., "place to curse"). OG ἀπὸ δεομένου μὴ ἀποστρέψῃς ὀφθαλμὸν καὶ μὴ δῷς τόπον ἀνθρώπῳ καταράσασθαί σε, "Do not avert your eye from the needy and give no one reason to curse you"; Syr ܘܠܐ ܬܬܠ ܠܗ ܐܬܪܐ ܕܠܘܛܟ, "do not let him seize an opportunity to curse you."

108. Sir 34:24. Vg adds *quasi* ("like").

ὁ προσάγων θυσίαν ἐκ χρημάτων πενήτων	Is the person who offers sacrifice from the possessions of the poor.[109]
ἄρτος ἐπιδεομένων ζωὴ πτωχῶν	The bread of the needy is the life of the poor;
ὁ ἀποστερῶν αὐτὴν ἄνθρωπος αἱμάτων	Only a bloodthirsty beast would deprive them of it.[110]
φονεύων τὸν πλησίον ὁ ἀφαιρούμενος ἐμβίωσιν	Whoever takes away his neighbor's livelihood is a murderer,[111]
καὶ ἐκχέων αἷμα ὁ ἀποστερῶν μισθὸν μισθίου	And whoever holds back his wages is a shedder of blood.[112]

Wicked Wealth (Sir 4:27—5:8)

Like 4QInstruction and the Letter of James, Sirach is not averse to manipulating various types of socioeconomic motifs operating in contexts taut with

109. Sir 34:24. Oesterley (*Sirach*, 220) interprets this to mean that "sacrifices which the rich are enabled to offer because they have grown wealthy by oppressing the poor are as heart-rending to God as the sight of his son's murder would be to a father." Pointing out parallels to Amos 2:6–7, Horsley and Tiller (*Wisdom*, 50) suggest that this verse refers to creditors inclined toward the practice of "debt foreclosure."

110. Sir 34:25. Standing within the mob responsible for expelling King David from Jerusalem, Shimei ben Gera calls David a איש דמים, "man of blood" (2 Sam 16:8); cf. איש דמים יתעב יהוה, "Yhwh abhors the man of blood" (Ps 5:7).

111. Sir 34:26. Johnson (*Possessions*, 85–86) points out that "what is most striking about this sort of oppression is its theological placement . . . . The claim that idolatry leads to the murder of the innocent (Deut 12:30–31) is literally true for oppression as an extension of idolatry: those who oppress the needy and poor have murder on their hands."

112. Sir 34:27. Ezekiel (18:10, 12) also associates the שפך דם ("shedder of blood") with עני ואביון הונה ("oppressing the poor and needy"), and Witherington (*Homilies*, 511) recognizes the parallel between this text and James 5:1–12 (cf. below).

eschatological tension.[113] In this section,[114] for example, the sage issues several אל-commands[115] to prepare readers for the coming "day":[116]

אל יהי ידך מושטת לשאת	Do not hold your hand out to accept,[117]
ובעת השב פקודה	Then squeeze it shut when it's time to provide.[118]
אל תשען על חילך	Do not rely upon your own wealth,[119]
ואל תאמר יש לאל ידי	Or say, "I am self-sufficient."[120]
אל תשען על כוחך	Do not rely upon your own strength,
ללכת אחר תאות נפשך	Or pursue the cravings of your soul.[121]

A few admonitions later he warns:

113. Cf. Moore (*Babbler*, 166–79); Goff (*4QInstruction*, 15–17); Rey (*Sagesse*, 228–76); Murphy (*Wealth*, 166–74). Blomberg (*Poverty*, 242) argues that the sapiential/lyric literature "sows the seeds for a doctrine that becomes clearer" in the Second Temple period—viz., that "judgment day and a life to come are the only true and equitable solutions to this world's injustice."

114. Skehan and Di Lella (*Ben Sira*, 181) read this section as three poems focused on the dangers of *presumption* (Sir 5:1–8), *duplicity* (5:9—6:1) and *unruly passions* (6:2–4).

115. The negative particle אל occurs some 16 times in this section.

116. Sir 5:8; Cf. Argall (*Sirach*, 211–47); Goff ("Wisdom," 58, n. 4); Moore (*Babbler*, 45–57; 166–79).

117. Sir 4:31 (MS C). MS A reads פתוחה לקחת, "open to taking"; Syr ܦܫܝܛܐ ܠܡܣܒ, "stretched out to take"; OG ἐκτεταμένη εἰς τὸ λαβεῖν, "extended to take"; Vg *porrecta ad accipiendum*, "stretched out to accept."

118. Sir 4:31 (MS C). MS A reads פקוצה בתוק מתן, "closed at the time for giving"; Syr ܩܦܝܨܐ ܠܡܬܠ, "closed for giving"; OG ἐν τῷ ἀποδιδόναι συνεσταλμένη, "contracted for giving"; Vg *reddendum collecta*, "returning the contribution." Cf. Did. 4.5; Barn. 19.9; and Moore (*WealthWarn*, 193) on the use of this "give-vs.-take" polarity in Plutarch (*Mor.* 778c) and GNT (Acts 20:35).

119. Sir 5:1. Syr ܠܐ ܬܬܟܠ ܥܠ ܢܟܣܝܟ, "Do not rely upon your wealth"; OG μὴ ἔπεχε ἐπὶ τοῖς χρήμασίν σου, "do not hold fast to your possessions"; Vg adds *possessiones iniquas*, "wrongful possessions." Cf. אל תבטח על נכסי שקר, "Do not trust in wicked wealth" (5:8). Philo (*Det.* 136) insists that "there is no ground for rejoicing over 'abundance of wealth and possessions' (χρημάτων ἢ κτημάτων περιουσίᾳ), or over brilliant position, or over anything outside us, since these things are 'soulless' (ἀψύχων)."

120. Sir 5:1 (lit., "there is to God my hand"). OG αὐτάρκη μοί ἐστιν, "I am self-sufficient"; Syr ܝܘܬܪܢ ܐܝܬ ܠܝ, "abundance is mine"; Vg *est mihi sufficiens vita nihil enim proderit in tempore vindictae et obductionis*, "life is sufficient for me without making a profit in a time of vengeance and darkness."

121. Sir 5:1. The Hebrew and Latin traditions add/preserve this couplet; Syr and OG omit. Cf. the "cravings/addictions" of the rabble in the wilderness (תאות, Num 11:4).

אל תבטח על נכסי שקר	Do not trust in wicked wealth,[122]
כי לא יועילו ביום עברה	For it profits nothing on the "day of distress."[123]

Haustafeln (Sir 7:18–21)

Whereas the Pauline *Haustafeln* owe their identity to influences as Hebraic as they are Hellenistic,[124] the same appears to apply to Sirach's *Haustafeln*:

אל תמיר אוהב במחיר	Do not trade a loved one for money,[125]
ואח תלוי בזהב אופיר	Or barter a brother for gold from Ophir.[126]
אל תמאס אשה משכיל	Do not dismiss a sensible wife,[127]
וטובת חן מפנינים	For she is a bequest more valuable than gemstones.[128]
אל תדע באמת עובד אמת	Do not abuse an honest, reliable worker,[129]

122. Sir 5:8; Syr ܢܟܣܐ ܕܥܘܠܐ, "evil wealth" (lit., "riches of wickedness"). Presumably the sage here speaks of a "wealth" procured through wrongful and/or illicit activity like that described by Wright and Camp ("Gold," 155–58). Mathews (*Riches*, 72) recognizes that whether the problem is "wicked wealth" (5:8) or simply "wealth" (5:1) "the text clearly denounces trusting in wealth."

123. Sir 5:8 (lit., "day of passing over," Exod 12:27; Ezek 10:18). Syr ܝܘܡܐ ܕܥܩܬܐ, "day of distress"; OG ἡμέρᾳ ἐπαγωγῆς, "day of visitation" (Sir 2:2 reads καιρῷ ἐπαγωγῆς, "moment of visitation"); Vg *die obductionis et vindictae*, "day of clouds and vengeance." Cf. Exod 12:12 and Moore (*Babbler*, 45–57).

124. Lohmeyer (*Briefe*, 155–56); cf. Hering (*Haustafeln*, 20–22); Schroeder ("*Haustafeln*," 102–3). *Haustafeln* ("household codes on how to treat various members of the family, including slaves") tend to occur in didactic and epistolary texts.

125. Sir 7:18 (doubtless a covert reference to debt-slavery). N.B. that twice these *Haustafeln* refer to a "loved one" (7:18, 21; cf. Lohmeyer, *Haustafeln*, 1–2).

126. Sir 7:18. Syr ܠܐ ܬܫܚܠܦ ܪܚܡܐ ܒܡܡܘܢܐ ܘܐܚܐ ܕܐܝܬ ܠܟ ܒܕܗܒܐ ܕܐܘܦܝܪ, "Do not barter a friend for *mammon*, or a brother for the gold of Ophir"; OG μὴ ἀλλάξῃς φίλον ἕνεκεν διαφόρου μηδὲ ἀδελφὸν γνήσιον ἐν χρυσίῳ Σουφιρ, "Do not barter a friend for money, or a brother for the gold of Ophir"; Vg *fratrem carissimum*, "a dear brother." Christidès ("Ophir," 240–47) notes that in spite of several proposals the location of Ophir remains a mystery.

127. Sir 7:18. N.B. that משכיל reappears in the expression עבד משכיל ("sensible servant," 7:21; cf. Balla, "Sirach," 107–26).

128. Sir 7:19 (cf. פנינים in Prov 31:1 and N.B. that וטובת goes not with the words *preceding*, but with those *succeeding*).

129. Sir 7:20 (lit., "do not know"); Syr ܠܐ ܬܛܪܦ, "do not slap"; OG μὴ κακώσῃς, "do not abuse"; Vg *non laedas*, "do not hurt."

וכן שוכר נותן נפשו	Or a hired laborer who gives his all.[130]
עבד משכיל חביב כנפש	A sensible servant,[131] a beloved soul—
אל תמנע ממנו חפש	Do not suppress his autonomy.[132]

Wealth and Anxiety (Sir 11:10–19)

Sirach 11:7–28 includes six "mini-poems," the last two of which focus on the "futility of unwarranted anxiety" (vss 10–13) and the "gift of riches" (vss 14–19).[133]

בני למה תרבה עשקך	My child, why do you multiply your misfortunes?[134]
ואץ להרבות לא ינקה	Stirring up your anxiety will not make you blameless.[135]
בני אם לא תרוץ תגיע	My child, if you do not hurry you will not arrive,[136]

130. Sir 7:20 (lit., "his soul"). Explaining why employers should pay their workers on time, Torah states, כי עני הוא ואליו הוא נשׂא את נפשו, "because he is poor and sets his soul upon his 'wages'" (שׂכר, Deut 24:15). Talmud explains that (a) the employee's soul depends on this שׂכר, even as (b) the employer holding it back forfeits *his* soul (*b. B. Meṣ* 112a).

131. Sir 7:21. N.B. the parallel אשה משכיל ("prudent wife") in 7:18, not to mention the recurrence of עבד משׂכיל in Prov 14:35; 17:2; Sir 10:25; and 4Q416.2.2.15.

132. Sir 7:21. Syr ܚܐܪܘܬܐ ("freedom"); OG ἐλευθερίας ("liberty"); Vg *non defraudes illum libertate neque inopem derelinquas illum* ("neither defraud him of freedom nor leave him needy"). Cf. החפשית בית, "house of freedom" (2 Kgs 15:5), where the leprous king Azariah/Uzzah is either (a) "freed/separated" in quarantine (Barnes, *Kings*, 299), or (b) "freed" of his royal duties (Gray, *Kings*, 618–20).

133. Skehan and Di Lella, *Ben Sira*, 238.

134. Sir 11:10 (lit., "oppression"); Syr ܒܪܝ، ܠܡܢܐ ܡܣܓܐ ܐܢܬ ܒܫܘܚܩܟ ܘܕܪܫܬ ܠܡܣܓܝܘܬܐ ("My child, why do you increase your misfortune by disputing over abundance?"); OG τέκνον μὴ περὶ πολλὰ ἔστωσαν ("Child, do not busy yourself with so many things").

135. Sir 11:10 (lit., "innocent"); OG πράξεις σου ἐὰν πληθύνῃς οὐκ ἀθῳωθήσῃ καὶ ἐὰν διώκῃς οὐ μὴ καταλάβῃς καὶ οὐ μὴ ἐκφύγῃς διαδράς ("Increasing your activities will not make you blameless"). Alongside *death* (40:2) and *daughters* (7:24; 42:9–14), Sirach finds *wealth* a prominent producer of anxiety (cf. Collins, *Wisdom*, 71–72, 77, 94, 168).

136. Sir 11:10 (cf. Esth 4:14; Qoh 8:14; Ezek 7:12); Vg *adprehendes* ("overtake, apprehend"). Syr ܒܪܝ، ܐܢ ܠܐ ܬܪܗܛ ܠܐ ܬܕܪܟ ("My child, if you do not scurry you will not comprehend"); OG καταλάβῃς ("arrive"). Rabbi Neḥunya ben Hakana's daily prayer consists of contrasting his behavior with that of his enemies: אני רץ לחיי העולם והם רצים לבאר שחת ("I run to the life of the world-to-come, but they hasten to the pit of destruction," *b. Ber.* 28b).

ואם לא תבקש לא תמצא	And if you do not seek you will not find.[137]
יש עמל ויגע ורץ	Some labor, struggle, and scurry about,
וכדי כן הוא מתאחר	Yet still fall behind.[138]
יש רשש ואבד מהלך	Others are beaten down, lost, and adrift,[139]
חסר כל ויותר א[ו]נש	Devoid of strength and stung by weakness.[140]
ועין יי צפתהו לטוב	Yet Yhwh's eye looks kindly upon them
וינעריהו מפער צחנה	As he shakes off the flecks of their filth,
נשא בראשו וירממהו	Raises their heads, and points them skyward,[141]
ויתמהו עליו רבים	To the amazement of many.[142]
טוב ורע חיים ומות ריש ועושר	Good and bad, life and death, poverty and wealth—
מיי הוא	All come from Yhwh.[143]
ב[גד] ע[שיר] בחוקר	The rich can be vindictive in their pursuits,[144]

137. Sir 11:10. Cf. Deut 4:29; Prov 8:17; and Sir 6:18; 32:14. Also cf. ζητεῖτε καὶ εὑρήσετε ("seek and you will find," Matt 7:7).

138. Sir 11:11. OG καὶ τόσῳ μᾶλλον ὑστερεῖται ("and fall even more behind"). Horsley (*Scribes*, 55) thinks Sirach here shows contempt for manual laborers, but Ellis (*Gender*, 130) questions this in light of 7:15–22.

139. Sir 11:12. OG ἔστιν νωθρὸς προσδεόμενος ἀντιλήμψεως ("Some are weak and need help"). Schmidt (*Sirach*, 331) thinks that "Ben Sira's observations about manual laborers are not necessarily meant to be negative."

140. Sir 11:12, reading כח (OG ἰσχύι) for כל (MS A).

141. Sir 11:13 (lit., "exalts him"). Cf. מקימי מעפר דל, "He lifts the poor from the dust" (Ps 113:7).

142. Sir 11:13. Malchow ("Justice," 121) argues that while some sages "engage in self-serving justification to promote their own status by maligning the poor, Sirach and others show that such sages "are in the minority . . . . In fact, the wise express many opinions that move in the opposite direction."

143. Sir 11:14 (cf. 10:31; 18:25). N.B. that the monotheistic timbre of Isa 45:7 depicts Yhwh as the deity responsible for "forming light and creating darkness, 'making recompense' (עשׂה שלום) and 'creating evil' (בורא רע)." Philo (*Det.* 122) argues that "the nature of justice in the first place creates rest in the place of toil' (ἀνάπαυλαν ποιεῖν ἀντὶ καμάτου), owing to its complete indifference to objects on the borderland between vice and virtue, such as wealth, fame, official posts, honours, and everything of that sort which preoccupy the majority of humankind."

144. Sir 11:18. Reconstructed from OG ἔστιν πλουτῶν ἀπὸ προσοχῆς καὶ σφιγγίας αὐτου ("Some grow rich through diligence and greed"); Syr ܐܝܬ ܕܥܬܪ ܡܢ ܡܣܟܢܘܬܗ ("Some say to prepare for poverty").

ושיתה דתכאלמבו עש[ר]ה ובו	And even if there is wickedness in them, *they* are the ones who will manage your affairs in your old age.[145]
אל תתמה ב[חוקריו	So do not be surprised by their behavior;[146]
ות]רוץ ליי וקוה לאורו	Run to Yhwh and take refuge in his radiance.[147]

Rich vs. Poor (Sir 13:1—14:2)

This section includes several "rivalry" vignettes, some sociological, some moral, some obvious, some not-so-obvious—all relating differences between the rich and the poor:[148]

עשיר יענה הוא יתנוה	Frequently the rich are oppressive,[149]
ועל דל נעוה הוא יתחנן	So the poor bend the knee to their power.[150]
אם תכשר לו יעבד בך	If you are *kosher* the rich tolerate you,[151]
ואם תכרע יחמל עליך	But if you bend the knee they really warm up.[152]

145. Sir 11:18. Reconstructed from OG καὶ αὕτη ἡ μερὶς τοῦ μισθοῦ αὐτοῦ ("and this is his allotted reward") and Syr ܘܐܝܬ ܕܠܐ ܠܘܐ ܠܗ ܡܘܬܪܐ ("for his wealth comes without preparation").

146. Sir 11:19. Reconstructing on the basis of בחוקר in the previous verse (11:18). OG ἐν τῷ εἰπεῖν αὐτόν εὗρον ἀνάπαυσιν καὶ νῦν φάγομαι ἐκ τῶν ἀγαθῶν μου ("When he says, 'Now that I have found rest, I will feast on my goods'").

147. Sir 11:19.

148. Johnson (*James*, 190) suggests that "'lowliness' can be seen as a form of 'testing' from the side of the world's evaluation and as a 'blessing' from the side of God's election," and Stagg ("James," 394) contends that "*eudaemonism*, the vulgar idea that one's wealth is a sign of divine favor," should be "rejected." Nickelsburg ("Social," 651) suggests that the poor to whom Sirach often alludes reappear often in 1 Enoch.

149. Sir 13:3; OG πλούσιος ἠδίκησεν καὶ αὐτὸς προσενεβριμήσατο ("The rich person does wrong and threatens"); Syr ܥܬܝܪܐ ܚܛܐ ܘܡܬܡܗܐ ("The rich man sins and it is disregarded"); Vg *dives iniuste egit et fremebit* ("the rich are unjust and angry").

150. Sir 13:3; OG πτωχὸς ἠδίκηται καὶ αὐτὸς προσδεηθήσεται ("the poor person does wrong and is bound"). Syr ܘܡܣܟܢܐ ܚܛܐ ܘܡܬܕܚܐ ("but the poor man sins and is pushed aside"); Vg *pauper autem laesus tacebit* ("but the poor man endures injury in silence").

151. Sir 13:4. Cf. Syr ܐܢ ܬܗܘܐ ܥܬܝܪ ܢܦܠܚܘܢ ܥܡܟ ("If you are successful they will not work with you"); OG ἐὰν χρησιμεύσῃς ἐργᾶται ἐν σοί ("If you are useful they will work with you"); Vg *si largitus fueris adsumet te* ("If you offer them a bribe they will work with you").

152. Sir 13:4; Syr ܘܐܢ ܬܬܡܣܟܢ ܢܫܒܩܘܢܟ ("If you are poor they will abandon you");

אם שלך ייטיב דבריו עמך	When summoning you they use pleasant words,[153]
וירששך ולא יכאב לו	Then crush you suddenly with no regrets.[154]
צריך לו עסך והשיע לך	Your people may stand in need of them, and they may "deliver" you,[155]
ושוחק לך והבטיחך	But even as they welcome your trust, they pummel you,[156]
עד אשר יועיל יהתל בך	Exploiting you until they can turn a profit.[157]

Then there are the Aesop-like folk sayings:

מאיש שלום צבוע אל כלב	What peace can there be between a hyena and a dog?
מאין שלום עשיר אל רש	What peace can there be between rich and poor?[158]
מאכל ארי פראי מדבר	Just as lions feed on prey in the savannah
כן מרעית עשיר דלים	So the poor are a feeding-ground for the rich.[159]

OG καὶ ἐὰν ὑστερήσῃς καταλείψει σε ("But if you are needy he will abandon you"); Vg *et si non habueris derelinquet te* ("But if you do not offer them bribes they will abandon you").

153. Sir 13:5; Syr ܐܢ ܐܫܬܟ ܠܟ ܢܥܒܕ ܒܫܘܬܦܘܬܐ ܥܡܟ ("If they find you pleasing they will engage you"); OG ἐὰν ἔχῃς συμβιώσεταί σοι ("If you have something they will cohabitate with you").

154. Sir 13:5; Syr ܢܣܚ ܠܐ ܗܘܐ ܡܬܬܘܝܐ ("and bleed you dry without a qualm"); OG καὶ ἀποκενώσει σε καὶ αὐτὸς οὐ πονέσει ("they will eviscerate you and not care").

155. Sir 13:6; OG χρείαν ἔσχηκέν σου καὶ ἀποπλανήσει σε ("When he has need of you he will beguile you"); Syr ܟܕ ܥܒܕܐ ܢܣܒܗ ܥܡܟ ܢܬܪܥܐ ܠܟ ("When a servant takes delight in you").

156. Sir 13:6; OG καὶ προσγελάσεταί σοι καὶ δώσει σοι ἐλπίδα, λαλήσει σοι καλὰ καὶ ἐρεῖ τίς ἡ χρεία σου ("and deceive you, and a man who gets results will summon you and say good things to you before asking, 'What do you need?'").

157. Sir 13:7. Wischmeyer (*Kultur*, 50) recognizes that Sirach's "principle interest" focuses on "the upper classes of society," where he is most "at home" and where "he recruits his pupils," but Minissale ("Sirach," 261) sees Sirach as "critical of the rich and showing himself to be sensitive in dealing with the dignity and the hardships of the poor."

158. Sir 13:18. Vg *quae communicatio sancto homini ad canem aut quae pax bona diviti ad pauperem*, "What communication is there between a pious man and a dog, or what peace is there between a good rich man and a poor man?"

159. Sir 13:19. Wright and Camp ("Gold," 160) recognize that "in addition to the difficulties inherent in a life of poverty . . . , those who are rich often make the lot of the

תועבת גאוה ענוה	Just as the humble are loathsome to the proud,[160]
ותועבה עשיר אביון	So the poor are loathsome to the rich.[161]
עשיר מוט בסמך רע	The rich who stumble find support from their friends,[162]
ודל נמוט נדחה מרע אל רע	But the floundering poor are passed from friend to friend.[163]
עשיר מדבר ועזרין רבים	When the rich speak it is to many supporters,[164]
ודבריו מכוערין מהופין	Even when their words are crude and perverse.[165]
דל נמוט גע גע ושא	But when the poor flounder the crowds pile on.[166]

poor worse." Roth (*Blind*, 130) finds in this passage an example of "sarcasm worthy of Juvenal or Lucian." Asencio ("Poverty," 159) posits that "a society oriented to the search of wealth and profit, established on the grounds of social injustice and crime, sooner or later becomes a jungle where the law of the strongest always prevails."

160. Sir 13:20 (cf. Jas 4:6). Mathews (*Riches*, 72) agrees with Wright and Camp ("Gold," 172) that poverty and wealth are not necessarily signs of piety or impiety in Sirach, only that the sage is in "contact with traditions that use the *language* of rich and poor to make these distinctions." Goff (*Worldly*, 137) finds this "dualistic" language to be "sharper" here than in, say, Proverbs.

161. Sir 13:20. From Montero's perspective (*Plain*, 41) "Sirach claims that the rich will always exploit the poor, and that the poor are victims of this oppression—leading to the conclusion that there cannot be any peace between the rich and the poor" because the rich are "proud, deceitful, cruel and selfish." James unapologetically presumes this same pedestrian portrayal (Jas 1:10).

162. Sir 13:21 (Minissale, "Sirach," 261, emends מוט to נמוט to match the use of the latter in later lines). OG πλούσιος σαλευόμενος στηρίζεται ὑπὸ φίλων, "When the rich person stumbles he is supported by friends."

163. Sir 13:21. OG ταπεινὸς δὲ πεσὼν προσαπωθεῖται ὑπὸ φίλων, "But when the poor man falls, he is pushed away by his 'friends'" (cf. Job and *his* "friends"). Minissale ("Sirach," 262) wants to make the argument that the metaphor of "falling" (OG πίπτω) is central to the entire book of Sirach.

164. Sir 13:22. OG πλουσίου σφαλέντος πολλοὶ ἀντιλήμπτορες, "If a rich person stumbles, many come to the rescue." Rabbi Samuel ben Naḥmani comments that "whereas the 'wealthy' (עשירים) show a smiling face to their friends, the poor (lit., 'those unwealthy') tend to hide their face in shame (lit., 'put their face on the earth')" (*Gen. Rab.* 91.5).

165. Sir 13:22. OG ἐλάλησεν ἀπόρρητα καὶ ἐδικαίωσαν αὐτόν, "He speaks inappropriately, but they justify him."

166. Sir 13:22, reading with OG προσεπετίμησαν αὐτῷ, "they criticize him."

ודבר משכיל ואין לו מקום	No one listens, not even when their words make good sense.[167]
עשיר דובר הכל נסכתו	When the rich speak everyone falls silent[168]
ואת שכלו עד עב יגיעו	As they vaunt their "wisdom" to the clouds.
דל דובר מי זה יאמרוו	When the poor speak someone says, "Who is this?"[169]
ואם נתקל גם הם יהדפוהו	And if they flounder, they are summarily dismissed.[170]
טוב העושר אם אין עון	*Conclusion:* So wealth, if it is not wicked, is good.[171]

Generosity vs. Stinginess (Sir 14:3–19)

Reflecting on the generosity-stinginess polarity, Sirach comes to an important insight: stinginess has less to do with greed than with self-hatred.[172]

167. Sir 13:22. In Aristophanes' play, *Wealth,* a frustrated slave, unable to get his master's attention, suddenly turns to the audience and cries, "What an unhappy fate, O gods, to be the slave of a fool! A servant may give the best of advice, but if his master does not follow it, the poor slave must inevitably take his part in the disaster which follows" (*Plut.* 4–5).

168. Sir 13:23, reading with OG ἐσίγησαν, "they are silent."

169. Philo (*Sobr.* 1.38) recognizes that some of the best ideas are never heard: "Those who are prudent, and temperate, and manly, and just men in their dispositions are infinite in number, having a happy portion in nature, and institutions in accordance with the law, and exerting themselves in invincible and unhesitating labors; but the good which encompasses the ideas in their minds they are not able to display because of their 'poverty' (πενία)."

170. Sir 13:23 (lit., "they push him away"; cf. Schmidt, *Sirach*, 338–40). Gowan ("Wealth," 344) recognizes that "lack of status, lack of respect" makes the poor "an easy mark for the powerful and unscrupulous."

171. Sir 13:24. Cf. Jas 2:1–9 (below). Corley (*Friendship*, 117) argues that the purpose of this section (esp. 13:15–23) is "to explain why Sirach considers friendship between rich and poor to be impossible."

172. Explaining Alcoff's (*Identities*, 223) attempt to explain how dominant groups interface with minorities, La Caze (*Wonder*, 82–83) argues that Alcoff's notion of "double consciousness" (e.g., where whites accept responsibility for a racist past while recognizing at the same time that some whites challenge it) "involves generosity . . . rather than self-loathing."

Bluntly put, stinginess—the opposite of generosity—is one of the inevitable results of being "bad to one's soul":[173]

ללב קטן לא נאוה עושר	Wealth is bewildering to a small mind,[174]
ולאיש רע עין לא נאוה חרוץ	But perilous for someone caught by the evil eye.[175]
מונע נפשו יקבץ לאחר	Anyone who hates his own soul[176] soon gleans for another,
ובטובתו יתבעבע זר	Warehousing his goods for strangers.[177]
רע לנפשו למי ייטיב	If he hates himself,[178] to whom can he be generous[179]
ולא יקרה בטובתו	When he does not appreciate his own gifts?[180]

173. Sir 14:5–6 (רע לנפשו). Cf. Gregory, *Generosity*, 291–94. Philo (*Conf.* 1.18) voices a different opinion, remarking that what protects a person from attack are three δορυφόροι ("bodyguards"); viz., πλοῦτος, εὐδοξία, τιμαί ("wealth, glory and honors"), who guard against his worst enemies: ἀτιμία, ἀδοξία, πενία ("dishonor, contempt, and poverty"), and Josephus (*AJ* 6.149) juxtaposes the two categories when he speaks of τῆς πενίας . . . τὴν τιμὴν ("the poverty honor").

174. Sir 14:3 (lit., "small heart"). OG ἀνδρὶ μικρολόγῳ, "petty man" (lit., "small-worded man"); Syr ܠܒܐ ܕܚܣܝܪܐ, "weak mind"; Vg *viro cupido et tenaci*, "greedy and stingy man."

175. Sir 14:3; Syr ܓܒܪܐ ܕܒܝܫܬܐ, "man of wickedness"; OG ἀνθρώπῳ βασκάνῳ, "devious man"; Vg *homini livido*, "spiteful man." According to Elliott (*Beware*, 1–76), the "evil eye" motif appears in ANE literature as early as the fourth millennium.

176. Sir 14:4 (מנע, lit., "to diminish, withhold). OG ὁ συνάγων ἀπὸ τῆς ψυχῆς αὐτοῦ ("that which he gathers for his soul"); Syr ܕܟܠܗ ܡܢ ܢܦܫܗ ܡܟܢܫ ܠܐܚܪܢܐ ("from all which his soul gather for others"); Vg *qui acervat ex animo suo iniuste aliis* ("whatever he unjustly heaps up from his soul for others"). Vg and Syr appear to follow OG. By way of illustration, N.B. that Talmud posits seven things "ostracized by heaven," one of which is המונע מנעלים מרגליו, "withholding sandals from the feet," *b. Pes.* 113b).

177. Sir 14:4; Pitt-Rivers ("Honour," 21–27) argues that "honor" is "the value of a person in his own eyes (and) in the eyes of his society," so if "the way to acquire the wisdom which promises honor, prestige, wealth, and a noble end is straightforward" (DeSilva, "Honor," 443), then it is to be expected that the "honor-shame" polarity underlying Sirach and other Second Temple texts organically correlates with (and exercises profound influence over) the way in which the sage imagines the "stinginess-generosity" polarity.

178. Sir 14:5 (lit., "is bad to his soul"); Syr ܕܒܝܫ ܠܢܦܫܗ ("is bad to his soul"); OG ὁ πονηρὸς ἑαυτῷ ("the one who is bad/evil to himself").

179. Sir 14:5 (lit., "make himself good"); ܠܡܢ ܛܐܒ ("to whom is he good").

180. Sir 14:5 (lit., "recite, call out"); Syr ܢܘܕܐ, "acknowledge"; OG εὐφρανθήσεται, "enjoy"; Vg *iucundabitur*, "take delight."

Conclusion: No hatred is worse than self-hatred,	רע לנפשו אין רע ממנו
For with it comes payback for one's evil deeds.[181]	ועמו תשלומת רעתו

Blameless Wealth (Sir 31:1–11)

The section in 30:14—31:11 contains four poems addressing "the blessing of good health" (30:14–20), "the benefits of cheerfulness" (30:21–27), "the anxiety of the wealthy" (31:1–7),[182] and "the blessedness of the blameless rich" (31:8–11).[183]

The anxiety of the rich rots their flesh away,[184]	שקד עשיר ימחה שארו
And worry over wherewithal[185] drives away sleep,[186]	דאגת מחיה תפריע נומה
While the prospect of (debt-) forgiveness drives it far away.[187]	ומחלי חזק תפריע נומה
The task of the rich is to manage wealth,[188]	עמלי עשיר לקבל הון

181. Sir 14:6; Syr ܡܩܒܠ ܦܘܪܥܢܐ ܒܒܝܫܬܐ, "receptacle of payment for his wickedness." Cf. τὰ γὰρ ὀψώνια τῆς ἁμαρτίας θάνατος, "the compensation for sin is death" (Rom 6:23). Qur'an describes the unfaithful as those who تكذبون بالدين "deny the recompense" (Q 82.9).

182. Gregory (*Sirach*, 323) succinctly summarizes the textual problems in this section of the book.

183. Skehan and Di Lella, *Ben Sira*, 381. That Sirach speaks at all of "the blameless rich" sharply distinguishes his depiction of the wealthy from that of, say, the Letter of James (cf. below).

184. Sir 31:1. The "anxiety-of-the-wealthy" motif occurs repeatedly in the sapiential texts (cf. Sir 11:10; 31:2; Prov 15:16–17; Ross, "Proverbs," 141).

185. Sir 31:1. Cf. יש לו מחיה, "he has left 'wherewithal' for himself" (*y. Pe'ah* 3.17d bottom; cited in *DTTM* 760).

186. Sir 31:1. OG ἀγρυπνία ("sleepless"). To Socrates' question, "Why did you not wake me?" Crito answers, "I was wondering at you for some time, seeing how sweetly you sleep; so I purposely refrained from waking you," adding "I only wish that I were not so 'sleepless' (ἀγρυπνία)" (Plato, *Crito* 43b).

187. Sir 31:2 (cf. Ps 73). On מחל as "remit/forgive," cf. מוכר שטר חוב לחבירו וחזר ומחלו מחול, "if someone sells a writ of indebtedness to his comrade, then returns and forgives it, it is forgiven" (*b. Ket.* 85b).

188. Sir 31:3. N.B. the contrast between the "task" (עמל) of the rich and the "task" (עמל) of the poor (31:4), and cf. Job's lament over the wretchedness of *his* עמל (Job

ואם ינוח לקבל תענוג	And when they calm down, disseminate serenity.[189]
יגע עני לחסר ביתו	Economic scarcity stretches the poor thin,[190]
ואם ינוח יהיה צריך	But when *they* calm down desperation sets in.[191]
רודף הרוץ לא ינקה	Those who pursue gold are not blameless,
ואוהב מחיר בו ישגה	But those in love with money are by it led astray.[192]
רבים היו חבולי זהב	Many fall to their ruin over gold;[193]
והבוטח על פנינים	Not to mention those who trust in gemstones.
ולא מצאו להנצל מרעה	For eventually they discover that none of these things delivers from evil,
וגם להושע ביום ערבה	Nor do they save on the day of distress.[194]
כי תקלה הוא לאויל	Indeed, that will be a terrifying moment
וכל פותה יוקש בו	When everything suddenly comes to a halt.[195]

3:10; 7:3). Philo (*Spec.* 4:74) admonishes the wealthy: "Let not the rich man collect in his house vast quantities of silver and gold, and store them up, but let him bring them forward freely in order by his cheerful bounty to soften the hard condition of the poor."

189. Sir 31:3. N.B. that קבל (repeated twice here) occurs in explicitly economic texts; e.g., המקבל שדה מחברו, "If one leases (lit., "contracts, takes on, receives, embraces") a field from his comrade . . ." (m. *B. Meṣ* 9:1). For Philo (*Post.* 114–15), "it is a fact that those who obtain 'health and wealth' (πλουθυγείαν), the coupling of which is proverbial, imagine that they have secured absolutely all things."

190. Sir 31:4a (lit., "the scarcity of his house"). Haspecker's attempt (*Gottesfurcht*, 187–88) to position Sirach primarily as a defender of the poor tilts too far to one side of the poverty-wealth continuum.

191. Sir 31:4a. "Rest" (נוח) is a transient thing because, according to Otto (*Krieg*, 14), the "world of the gods is not a peaceful place."

192. Sir 31:5. Philo (*Spec.* 1.24) scolds "all poor men" not to become "possessed of that terrible disease, 'money-love' (φιλαργυρία)," and Saul of Tarsus (1 Tim 6:10) uses this same term to warn his pupil Timothy that "'money-love' is the root of all evil." Cf. *Sib. Or.* 2.111: "The love of profit is the mother of all evil."

193. Sir 31:6a. Gregory (*Sirach*, 52) sees this verse arguing that "those who pursue gold and place their confidence in luxury end up being bound over as debt-slaves to gold itself."

194. Sir 13:6b. Gregory (*Signet*, 51) comments: "Indeed, the love of money is deceptive; it would seem to promise security, but only results in entrapment." Sirach often references a "day" of "distress" (cf. 3:15; 5:8; 18:24; 40:2; cf. יום עברה in 5:8).

195. Sir 13:6c.

Commercial activity in the marketplace makes “blamelessness” especially difficult:

μόλις ἐξελεῖται ἔμπορος ἀπὸ πλημμελείας	A merchant is hardly blameless[196]
καὶ οὐ δικαιωθήσεται κάπηλος ἀπὸ ἁμαρτίας	Nor a huckster sinless.[197]

On Managing Possessions (Sir 33:19–22)

שמעו אלי שרי עם רב	Listen to me, O leaders of a great people;
ומשלי קהל ה[אזינוני	Leaders of the assembly, give ear to me.[198]
בן ואשה אהב ורע	Son, beloved wife, friend,
אל תמשיל בחייך	Do not forfeit control over your life.[199]
עד עודך חי ונשמה הבך	As long as you have in you life and breath
אל תשלט בך כל	Do not let anyone take your place.[200]
אל תתן שלך לאחר	Do not relinquish your property to others
לשוב לחלות א[ ]	Lest you have to return to them and ask for it back.[201]
כי טוב לחלות בניך פניך	For it is better for your children to plead with you

196. Sir 26:29. Syr ܒܥܡܝܠܘܬܐ ܪܒܬܐ ܡܬܦܨܐ ܥܪܘܩܐ ܡܢ ܚܛܗܐ, “With great difficulty is a fugitive free from sin”; Vg *difficile exuitur negotians a neglegentia*, “Difficult is it for a merchant (“negotiator”) to be divested of negligence.” Cf. *CH* §104 above (17.68—18.14).

197. Sir 26:29. Lysias (*Against the Grain Dealers* 22.21) uses this word-pair (ἔμπορος // κάπηλος) to denounce the grain-dealers (σιτόπωλοι) gouging the populace with overpriced products.

198. Sir 33:19. On the basis of OG ἐνωτίσασθε (“give ear”), Skehan and Di Lella (*Ben Sira*, 405) reconstruct ה]אזינו (“give ear”), but Syr ܨܘܬܘܢܝ includes a 1st c. sg. suff. on ܨܘܬ (“to give ear”).

199. Sir 33:20. On משל, cf. Talmud: “There are three who cry out and are not answered, as they are responsible for their own troubles: (a) one who has money and lends it not in the presence of witnesses, (b) one who acquires a master for himself, and (c) ומי שאשתו מושלת עליו, “one whose wife rules over him,” (*b. B. Meṣ* 75b).

200. Sir 33:21a. Cf. במשלטת על נכסיו, “when she manages his (her husband’s) business” (*y. Naz.* 4.53b). The word “sultan” is a transliteration of שׁלטן.

201. Sir 33:21b; restoring with Syr ܠܡܗܦܟܘ ܘܠܡܒܥܐ ܡܢܗܘܢ. Cf. Q 17.31, “Do not kill your children ‘for fear of poverty’ (خشيه ملق), for we will ‘provide for them and for you’ (نحن نرزقهم واياكم).”

מהביטך על ידי [בניך	Than for you to have to plead with your children.[202]

Engagement with the community adds another dimension:

πίστιν κτῆσαι ἐν πτωχείᾳ μετὰ τοῦ πλησίον	Acquire the trust of your neighbor in his poverty[203]
ἵνα ἐν τοῖς ἀγαθοῖς αὐτοῦ ὁμοῦ πλησθῇς	So that you may together share in his prosperity.[204]
ἐν καιρῷ θλίψεως διάμενε αὐτῷ	Persevere with him in times of distress
ἵνα ἐν τῇ κληρονομίᾳ αὐτοῦ συγκληρονομήσῃς	So that you may share in *his* inheritance.[205]

On Tithes, Gifts, and Bribes (Sir 35:10–15)

Whether chapters 35 and 36 are designed to be read separately or together,[206] Sirach's decision to link Israel's plight to the plight of the poor is no accident:[207]

בטוב עין הללו יי	Praise the Lord with a bountiful eye,[208]

202. Sir 33:22 (lit., "than for you to look to the hands of"). The key idea of this section is not to surrender control to anyone with regard to the managing of one's inheritance, even family members.

203. Sir 22:23. Syr ܣܡܘܟ ܠܪܚܡܟ ܒܡܣܟܢܘܬܗ, "Support your friend in his poverty."

204. Sir 22:23 (lit., "his good things"). Should the socioeconomic concerns of the community not be taken seriously, Qur'an warns, a hostile outcome may occur (Q 33.60): "If the hypocrites, the diseased of heart, and the gossips do not stop spreading rumors in the city . . . 'they will no longer be your neighbors' (يجاورونك)."

205. Sir 22:23 (lit., "co-inherit with his inheritance); Syr ܒܥܘܬܪܗ ܬܐܪܬ "share his profits." The irony, of course, is that Sirach elsewhere staunchly warns *against* "co-inheritance" (e.g., 33:19–22).

206. Collins (*Wisdom*, 23, 111) thinks the prayer in chapter 36 "is so alien to the thought-world of Ben-Sira that it must be regarded as a secondary addition," but Bradley disagrees ("Relationship," 311–27).

207. Fuller (*Restoration*, 35–36) argues that "it is within the wider argument for the significance of Israel, especially the Temple as the cultural and sapiential center of the occupied world, that Sirach stakes out the claim for Israel's restoration."

208. Sir 35:10. Reconstructed from OG, ἐν ἀγαθῷ ὀφθαλμῷ (cf. the opposite phrase רע עין, "evil eye," in 14:3).

And do not sully the first fruits of your hands.[209]	ואל תמעט בכורי ידיך
With every intrepid prayer at your disposal[210]	בכל מעשיך ה[ ]אים
Consecrate your tithe with joy.[211]	ובששון הקדש מעשר
Give back [to God] what he has given to you[212]	תן לו [לאל] מתנתו לך
With a good eye and generous hand.[213]	בטוב עין ובהשגת יד
For God is the Paymaster	כי אלוה תשלומות הוא
Who pays you back seven-fold.[214]	ושבעתים ישיב לך
Do not try to bribe him, for he will not accept it,[215]	אל תשחד כי לא יקח
And do not put your trust in sacrifice-via-extortion.[216]	ואל תבטח על זבח מעשק

209. Sir 35:10. Reconstructed from OG, μὴ σμικρύνῃς ἀπαρχὴν χειρῶν σου. Cf. this same command (אל תמעט, "do not demean") in 4Q416 2.2.6. Rabbi Meir says, הוי ממעט בעסק ועסק בתורה, "Engage but little in business, but instead be busy with Torah" (*m. 'Abot* 4.10).

210. Sir 35:11, reading with Syr ܘܒܪܘܚܝܗܘܢ ܕܗܘܝܢܐ ܠܟܠܬܐ ܕܩܘܪܒܢܝܗܘܢ. On Sirach's approach to prayer, cf. Crenshaw ("Prayer," 81–97) and Petrany (*Prayer*, 62–69).

211. Sir 35:11 (cf. Tob 1:6–8). Keener (*Commentary*, 514) sees this text influencing the "cheerful giver" passage in 2 Cor 9:7, but it seems prudent to remember that not everyone sees tithing as a "joy." Rabbi Yoḥanan (*b. Ber.* 35b), in fact, remembers a time when former generations brought their produce through the city gate, where the tithe could be calculated and "consecrated," but how later generations avoid paying tithes by hoisting their produce over the roofs of private homes adjoined to the city wall.

212. Sir 35:12. OG ὑψίστῳ, "Most High." Omitting any reference to deity, Syr specifies that giving should be ܠܡܣܟܢܐ, "for the poor." Cf. above note on Prov 19:17, and Garrison (*Almsgiving*, 46–59).

213. Sir 35:12 (lit., "enlarged hand"); Syr ܒܥܝܢܐ ܛܒܬܐ ܗܒ ܠܡܣܟܢܐ ܘܠܐ ܬܬܒܥܐ ܒܡܘܗܒܬܟ ("Give to the poor with a good eye and do not seek to gain something by your gifts").

214. Sir 35:13. OG ἀνταποδιδούς ("in exchange for"). Herodotus (*Hist.* 1.18.3) tells a story of a battle against Miletus when no one comes to the aid of the Milesians except the Chians, who "lend their aid 'in exchange for' (ἀνταποδιδόντες) similar services rendered to them."

215. Sir 35:14. Torah describes Yhwh as an impartial deity who לא יקח שחד, "takes no bribe" (Deut 10:19). The psalmist depicts the "unshakeable" person as someone who לא נתן בנשך ושחד על נקי לא לקח, "charges no interest and never takes a bribe against the innocent" (Ps 15:5). And Isaiah praises those who מאס בבצע מעשקות נער כפיו מתמך בשחד, "resist the making of profits through extortion, tossing out bribes rather than accepting them" (Isa 33:15).

216. Sir 35:15. Cf. the linkages in the Babylonian Theodicy (*BWL* 74.55) and

כי אלהי משפט הוא	For he is a God of judgment
ואין עמו משוה פנים	Who plays no favorites.[217]

Sirach has a good deal to say about the poverty-wealth polarity, yet contemporary interpretation of the book runs in very different directions. Some, like Victor Asensio, see here a sharp dichotomy between rich and poor, imagining that the sage depicts the poverty-wealth polarity as a simple conflict between (to use the outdated language of the twentieth century) "proletarians" and "bourgeoisie."[218] This view is problematic for several reasons, of course, but not least because it fails to take into account Sirach's profound ambivalence about things economic.[219] Sensitive to this ambivalence, Ben Wright and Claudia Camp read the book through a wider lens, identifying it as a daring, yet flawed attempt to apply the deuteronomic standard of retributive justice to the socioeconomic realities of Second Temple life.[220] Appreciative of their work, Brad Gregory nevertheless concludes that even though this retributional approach presumes the "righteous" always to experience success and the "wicked" always to suffer deprivation, the fact remains that such polarization rarely, if ever, occurs in the real world.[221]

Dialogue of Pessimism (*BWL* 146.55). Ezekiel condemns those who שחד לקחו בך למען שפך דם נשך ותרבית לקחת ותבצעי רעיך בעשק, "take bribes to shed blood, charge interest and surcharges, and extort their neighbors" (Ezek 22:12). Citing dozens of disturbing case-studies, Hatcher (*Poverty*, 1) documents how twenty-first century predators in the "poverty industry" "strip-mine billions in federal aid from impoverished families, abused and neglected children, and the disabled and elderly poor."

217. Sir 35:14 (lit., "lifting up of the face," *DTTM* 777). James also addresses the problem of "favoritism" (προσωπολημψία, Jas 2:1; cf. below).

218. Asencio ("Poverty," 151–78); cf. Jaruzelska (*Amos*, 167); Marx and Engels (*Manifesto*, 12–28). Boer (*Bible*) usefully critiques the presumptions, methods, and conclusions of a dozen Marxist thinkers.

219. Von Rad (*Wisdom*, 242) sees the scroll "dealing with this strangely ambivalent phenomenon of wisdom." Bredenhof (*Failure*, 121) points out that Sirach is hardly alone in his ambivalence; even a text so "uniform" as Deuteronomy "may be understood as relaying a mixed message on the future of poverty."

220. Wright and Camp ("Gold," 153–73). Argall (*Sirach*, 160) thinks that "1 Enoch takes phenomena at home in Sirach's doctrine of opposites and shows, via paradox, that reality is more complex," but the phrase "doctrine of opposites" seems a bit simplistic.

221. Gregory, *Signet*, 292. Sider (*Christians*, 57) argues that "God does not have class enemies. But he hates and punishes both oppression and neglect of the poor. And the rich, if we accept the repeated warnings of Scripture, are frequently guilty of one or both."

The Wisdom of Solomon

Maurice Gilbert points out that the Wisdom of Solomon not only shows "the sapiential biblical world opening itself up to hellenistic culture,"[222] but it denounces all oppressors of the poor (regardless of class profile, cultural bias, or financial status), mocking them via a "diatribe style"[223] depicting them as autocratic powerbrokers trusting in the jungle mantra "might makes right." Speaking in the first person,[224] he tries to expose this trust to the light of reason:

καταδυναστεύσωμεν πένητα δίκαιον	"Let us oppress the righteous poor[225]
μὴ φεισώμεθα χήρας μηδὲ πρεσβύτου ἐντραπῶμεν πολιὰς πολυχρονίους	Let us spare not the widow nor show respect to the grey-haired elder.[226]
ἔστω δὲ ἡμῶν ἡ ἰσχὺς νόμος τῆς δικαιοσύνης	Let the justice system (instead) be shaped by *our* power,
τὸ γὰρ ἀσθενὲς ἄχρηστον ἐλέγχεται	Even as the uselessness of the weak is confirmed."[227]

Later, however, as such thinking begins to bear its ugly fruit, they start—at least in the sage's mind—to ask:

222. Gilbert ("Sagesse," 38): "Le monde sapientiel biblique s'ouvre à la cultur hellénistique."

223. Winston ("Wisdom," 120) finds the "hypothesis that Wisdom is a translation of a Hebrew original virtually untenable" (*Wisdom*, 17). Jerome (*PL* 28.1242) feels the *style* of this "great text" to be "redolent of Greek eloquence."

224. Pioske (*Memory*, 29) recognizes "the fluctuations between first and third person discourse" in historical texts, but wisdom appears to be another matter altogether.

225. Wis 2:10. Like the Epistle of James, the Wisdom of Solomon does not recognize the "unrighteous poor." Levin ("Amosbuch," 411) argues that for many Second Temple Jews "righteous poor" designates a socio-religious category in which "poverty is as much a given as an effect," even to the point of delineating "their social status as well as the self-understanding to which they hold."

226. Wis 2:10. OG πολυχρονίους ("long-lived"); Vg *canos* ("grey-haired"); Syr adds ܐܦܠܐ ܥܠ ܝܬܡܐ ("make things fall for the orphan"). Reflecting on the differences between children and adults, Philo (*Abr.* 1.271) contends that those "who spend a long life in that existence which is subject to the body, apart from all virtue, we must call only 'long-lived' (πολυχρονίους) children, having never been instructed in those branches of education befitting the grey-haired."

227. Wis 2:11. N.B. that ἄχρηστον (alpha privitive + χρηστός, "monied, wealthy") hardly seems coincidental in defining this particular type of "uselessness" (i.e. "moneylessness").

τί ὠφέλησεν ἡμᾶς ἡ ὑπερηφανία	"What does our arrogance profit us?[228]
καὶ τί πλοῦτος μετὰ ἀλαζονείας συμβέβληται ἡμῖν	What does the pretense of our wealth acquire for us[229]
παρῆλθεν ἐκεῖνα πάντα ὡς σκιὰ	Seeing that all these things will vanish like a shadow,[230]
καὶ ὡς ἀγγελία παρατρέχουσα	Like a rumor running its course?"[231]

Speaking in the voice of "King Solomon,"[232] the sage recalls his "first encounter" with Sophia:

διὰ τοῦτο εὐξάμην καὶ φρόνησις ἐδόθη μοι	So I prayed and understanding was given to me;
ἐπεκαλεσάμην καὶ ἦλθέν μοι πνεῦμα σοφίας	I called out and the spirit of Sophia came to me.[233]

Like the sages before him, he highlights his loyalty to Sophia by comparing her to valuable treasure, even as he realizes the futility of such comparison:

228. Wis 2:11. Cf. the Nazarene's question, "'What does it profit' (τί γὰρ ὠφεληθήσεται, Matt 16:26/Mark 8:36/Luke 9:25) a person to gain the whole world, but lose their own soul?" and Sirach's admonition, "Do not trust in wicked wealth, for it brings no 'profit'" (ὠφελήσει, Sir 5:8, יועילו, ipf causative of יעל usually translated as ὠφελέω; cf., e.g., OG Isa 30:6; Jer 2:11; Prov 10:2).

229. Wis 5:8. Plato (*Gorg.* 525a) lists ψεύδους (falsehood) and ἀλαζονεία ("pretension") as characteristics of σκόλια ("crookedness"), and Philo (*Conf.* 1.44, 48) criticizes those opposed to the "lover of virtue (φιλαρέτων), "for every one of them, proposing riches or glory as their object, aim all the actions of their lives at it like so many arrows, neglecting equality, pursuing inequality, rejecting fellowship, and laboring to acquire for themselves all the possessions properly belonging to everyone," thus "making a hypocritical 'pretense of goodwill' (ὑποκρινόμενος εὔνοιαν)."

230. Wis 5:8. Cf. the description of the deity in the Epistle of James as a deity "devoid of shadow" (ἀποσκίασμα, Jas 1:17).

231. Wis 5:9. Philo's (*Leg.* 1.103) notion that "the peculiar task of wisdom is to "alienate" (ἀλλοτριόω) itself from the body" is likely indebted to Plato's notion of "alienation" (ἀλλοτριόω, *Tim.* 64e).

232. 1 Kgs 3:5–14 (cf. Moore, *Faith*, 269–75). Another common moniker for this hellenistic Jewish writer is "Pseudo-Solomon."

233. Wis 7:7. Doubtless it's important to remember that what Solomon asks from the deity is a לב שמע ("listening/ obedient mind," 1 Kgs 3:9), after which he receives a לב חכם ונבון ("wise and discerning mind," 3:12).

προέκρινα αὐτὴν σκήπτρων καὶ θρόνων	I prefer her to scepters and thrones
καὶ πλοῦτον οὐδὲν ἡγησάμην ἐν συγκρίσει αὐτῆς	I consider wealth as nothing in comparison to her.[234]
οὐδὲ ὡμοίωσα αὐτῇ λίθον ἀτίμητον	Nor do I compare her to any precious gemstone,
ὅτι ὁ πᾶς χρυσὸς ἐν ὄψει αὐτῆς ψάμμος ὀλίγη	Because to her all gold is like grains of sand,
καὶ ὡς πηλὸς λογισθήσεται ἄργυρος ἐναντίον αὐτῆς	And silver is like clay.[235]

Perhaps the most that can be said about her in this regard is that economic prosperity is one of her most gracious gifts:

ἦλθεν δέ μοι τὰ ἀγαθὰ ὁμοῦ πάντα μετ᾽ αὐτῆς	Along with her come all good things to me,
καὶ ἀναρίθμητος πλοῦτος ἐν χερσὶν αὐτῆς	With immeasurable wealth in her hands.[236]

Question: What makes *this* wealth "blameless" instead of "wicked?" *Answer:*

εὐφράνθην δὲ ἐπὶ πᾶσιν ὅτι αὐτῶν ἡγεῖται σοφία	I take joy in all of it because Sophia is in charge,
ἠγνόουν δὲ αὐτὴν γενέτιν εἶναι τούτων	Though I was once unaware that she is the source.[237]
τὸν πλοῦτον αὐτῆς οὐκ ἀποκρύπτομαι	I do not conceal her wealth,

234. Wis 7:8. Alongside political power ("thrones and scepters"), πλοῦτος ("wealth") is the yardstick to which Sophia is primarily compared, a fact underlined by the ἀναρίθμητος πλοῦτος ("uncountable wealth," 7:11) in her hands.

235. Wis 7:9.

236. Wis 7:11. Significantly, the Queen of Sheba (Sophia's *Doppelgänger*?) gives to King Solomon "great wealth" (1 Kgs 10:10; cf. Matthews, *Sophia*, 31–32).

237. Wis 7:12. Allegorically presuming her to be the "mother of all things" (τὴν μητέρα τῶν συμπάντων, *Leg.* 2.49; cf. *Det.* 1.54) and the "husband" (ἀνήρ) of "the Father" (*Cher.* 1.49), Philo (*Opif.* 1.45; *Cher.* 1.9) repeatedly distinguishes σοφία ("Sophia/wisdom") from σοφιστεία ("sophistry").

ἀνεκλιπὴς γὰρ θησαυρός ἐστιν ἀνθρώποις	For it confers inexhaustible treasure to humanity.[238]
ὃν οἱ κτησάμενοι πρὸς θεὸν ἐστείλαντο φιλίαν	Those who acquire it develop a love for God
διὰ τὰς ἐκ παιδείας δωρεὰς συσταθέντες	Sustained by the training conditioned via her gifts.[239]

In light of all this the path forward is clear:

ταῦτα λογισάμενος ἐν ἐμαυτῷ	Considering these things inwardly,
καὶ φροντίσας ἐν καρδίᾳ μου	And pondering in my heart
ὅτι ἀθανασία ἐστὶν ἐν συγγενείᾳ σοφίας	That kinship with Sophia is equivalent to immortality,[240]
καὶ ἐν φιλίᾳ αὐτῆς τέρψις ἀγαθὴ	That pure delight accompanies her love,
καὶ ἐν πόνοις χειρῶν αὐτῆς πλοῦτος ἀνεκλιπὴς	And inexhaustible wealth emerges from the labor of her hands.[241]

Compared to other sapiential texts, Wisdom allots much less attention to the poverty-wealth polarity,[242] in part because its conception of wealth is something of a two-edged sword: a blessing when used under Sophia's guidance, a curse when not. Like Eliphaz's critique of Job, Wisdom's engagement with socioeconomic issues tends to be shallow and

238. Wis 7:13.

239. Wis 7:14. Later the rescue of the patriarch Joseph is listed as a prime example (10:13–14).

240. Wis 8:17. Collins (*Wisdom*, 187) argues that since Wisdom shows no "practical difference between immortality and incorruptibility . . . it is not clear whether the wicked simply perish." At the very least, "the things upon which the wicked base their hopes, such as wealth and posturing, leave no trace."

241. Wis 8:18 (cf. ἀναρίθμητος πλοῦτος, "uncountable wealth" in 7:11). N.B. that ἀνεκλιπὴς ("inexhaustible") here occurs elsewhere in Sirach to describe Sophia's θησαυρός ("treasure" (7:14). One recipient of this wealth is Jacob, a patriarch she delights in "making rich" (ἐπλούτισεν αὐτόν, 10:10–11; cf. Glicksman, *Wisdom*, 123–34).

242. N.B. that Sophia not only "prospers (εὐόδωσεν) Israel . . . by the hand of a holy prophet," but "in every generation passes into holy souls and makes them God's friends and prophets" (Wis 11:1; 7:27).

conventional, perhaps because he imagines himself to be speaking, like the *išḫuil* texts, to "the rulers of the world."[243]

Summary

From what is presently known, then, even the most casual survey of socio-economic motifs in Second Temple wisdom shows how deeply and broadly Jewish sages manipulate the motifs of *poverty, wealth, moneylending, alms-giving, tithing, taxes, bribery, debt-recovery, inheritance, self-loathing-vs.-generosity,* and *wicked-vs.-blameless wealth.*

Question: How do Nazarene sages manipulate these motifs?

243. Wis 1:1; cf. Gilbert ("Sagesse," 39) and above on the *išḫuil* texts.

5

Socioeconomic Motifs in New Testament Wisdom

For the needy shall not always be forgotten,
nor the hope of the poor forever falter.[1]

Having successfully traversed the Hellenistic gauntlet,[2] the Hebrew wisdom tradition goes on to impact GNT in at least three ways.[3] *First*, some writers view Yeshu`a of Nazareth as the terminus of a Sophia trajectory winding its way through Proverbs, Sirach, Wisdom, and other texts,[4] thereby generating a christological trajectory which, while significant, says nothing about the socioeconomic motifs contributing to it.[5] *Second*, some readers

1. Ps 9:19.

2. Cf. above and Hengel (*"Hellenization,"* 53–56); Koester (*Introduction* 1.41–96). Gese ("Prologue," 167–222) argues that the λόγος-tradition in the prologue to the Fourth Gospel (John 1:1–18) fundamentally derives not from Graeco-Roman philosophy, but from Hebrew wisdom.

3. GNT references didactic wisdom, but not pessimistic, the most obvious example being James' memory of Job not as "suffering sceptic," but as "patient hero" (Jas 5:11; i.e., as depicted in *T. Job*; cf. Gray, "James," 406–24; Richardson, "Job," 213–29).

4. The texts most cited in this vein are Luke 11:49 and Mark 6:2. Broekhoven ("Wisdom," vi) argues that "the sapiential Christology of Col 1:15–20 "is rooted to history and to the formation and maintenance of the community," but the Coptic text known as Sophia of Jesus Christ (NHC 3.4) depicts Christ as "the latest incarnation of the gnostic savior" (Parrott, "Sophia," 220). Aware of this variety, Cahana-Blum ("Sophia," 472) admits that GNT (a) "only mentions Wisdom/Sophia sporadically," and (b) that "an argument can be made that she is almost never personified."

5. Cf. Bartholomew and O'Dowd ("Jesus," 231–60); Jobes ("Christology," 226–50). Scott (*Sophia*, 83–173) traces this trajectory into the Fourth Gospel, and Paffenroth (*Wisdom*, xi) traces it into the work of Augustine, Shakespeare, Goethe and other writers, remarking that "when I first read about Lady Wisdom in Proverbs, I found the image beautiful and intriguing, but I don't think I really knew what it meant until I met Gretchen in Goethe's *Faust* or Monica in Augustine's *Confessions*."

view "wisdom" as a socioliterary force formulating what Gerald Sheppard calls a "hermeneutical construct"; i.e., a sapiential literary prism fostering "an understanding of canon forming a perspective from which to interpret Torah and the prophetic traditions."[6] *Third*, wisdom's impact measurably decelerates in GNT because no "book" in this twenty-seven-book collection enacts so prominent a role as that enacted by Proverbs, Qohelet, and Job (in MT), and Sirach and Wisdom (in OG).[7] Due to these and other factors,[8] the analysis below cautiously confines itself to just two texts: (a) Luke's Sermon on the Plain, and (b) the Letter of James.

Luke's Sermon on the Plain

Roughly one-third the size of Matthew's Sermon on the Mount,[9] Luke's chiastically-structured Sermon on the Plain highlights,[10] as does Luke-Acts generally,[11] a set of socioeconomic concerns highly influenced by those

6. Sheppard (*Wisdom*, 45; cf. πνεῦμα σοφίας, "spirit of wisdom" in Eph 1:17). Finding this thesis helpful, Gottwald ("Matrix," 18) nevertheless warns against ignoring "the tremendous social systemic tensions and conflicts integral to the final outcome of the community's canonical decisions," and Fontaine (*Wisdom*, 117), while agreeing that "canon consciousness may exercise a special role in 'religious discourse' where it opens up possibilities for interpretation of texts heard synthetically (or 'pre-critically'!), yet circumscribes the number of hermeneutical possibilities available, is sound, even though one may not care to endorse particular exegetical conclusions or precise statements about the state of canonical 'awareness' on the part of any given author."

7. Bartholomew and O'Dowd (*Wisdom*, 259) admit that "wisdom is not *the* key to interpreting the New Testament," but that "one cannot understand Jesus, his kingdom, or his redemption without it."

8. E.g., texts like Luke 16:19–31 (the "*Parable* of Dives and Lazarus," according to Nickelsburg, "Riches," 324) presume the existence of a poverty-wealth polarity, but as (Bredenhof (*Prospect*, 117) points out, "no explicit moral judgment is passed on the rich man for the manner in which he lives or for how his wealth is acquired." Further, texts like 1 Cor 1–3 clearly contribute to the wisdom trajectory, but without the aid of a noticeable socioeconomic component. Texts like 2 Cor 2:17 and 8–9 *do* engage socioeconomic questions and concerns, but within a context only minimally linked to the wisdom trajectory. Finally, another delimitation arises from the fact that Luke's stewardship parables, a goldmine of socioeconomic motifs, are already engaged in the first volume of this series (Moore, *WealthWatch*, 204–22).

9. Matt 5–7. Cf. Strecker (*Bergpredigt*, 181–90); Carter (*Sermon*, 127–29); Evans (*BKBC* 101–62); Moore (*WealthWarn*, 160–66).

10. Luke 6:20–49. Cf. Bovon (*Lukas*, 309). Marshall (*Luke*, 243–44) lists other structural possibilities.

11. Cf. Moxnes (*Economy*, 154–59); Giambrone (*Economy*, 279–82); Johnson (*Possessions*, 13–25); Hays (*Wealth*, 264–69); Metzger (*Consumption*, 183–200); and Moore (*WealthWatch*, 202–21; *WealthWarn*, 180–95). Barton ("Money," 37–59) observes in GNT (a) that economic practices are not marginal to Christianity; (b) that early

influencing older sapiential texts;[12] viz., (a) the practical impossibility of ignoring the poverty-wealth polarity;[13] (b) the categorical value of almsgiving without the expectation of compensation;[14] (c) the categorical value of moneylending without the expectation of compensation;[15] and (d) the practical difficulty of producing "good things" from "wicked wealth."[16]

The Poverty-Wealth Polarity

Arriving at a "flat place" near Capernaum traditionally known as Gennesaret,[17] Yeshu`a lays out for his disciples a contrapuntal list of blessings and woes, using a paradigm Joel Green calls a "topos of transition,"[18] but Julia van den Brink intertextually recognizes as "antithetical covenant blessing and curse."[19] Most of the items on this list attend in some way to socioeconomic concerns:[20]

Christianity represents a "re-narration" of what really counts and how to attain it; (c) that the Christian message *radicalizes, intensifies, confounds*, and *disrupts* culturally dominant economic notions and systems; and (d) that continuity and discontinuity exist "between the Testaments" with regard to socioeconomic questions.

12. Ringe (*Luke*, 91) recognizes that both Matthew and Luke "exercise considerable freedom in constructing their collections of Jesus' teachings to meet their own literary and theological purposes."

13. Cf. 4QInstruction (esp. 4Q416.2.3.2, 8, 12, 19). Gardner ("Giving," 16–41) documents the depth of this impossibility in some detail.

14. Luke 6:27–30. Cf. *Aḥq* 131; 4Q416.2.2.4–5; Job 1:9 (חנם, "for nothing").

15. Luke 6:31–38. Cf. 4Q416.2.2.17. Betz (*Sermon*, 602) wonders why Luke addresses the issue of (money)lending, attributing its likely engagement to the prevalence of hellenistic debates about benevolence, but Giambrone (*Charity*, 107) finds such reasoning "twisted."

16. Luke 6:43–45. One is tempted, with Sirach, to say "impossibility" (אל תבטח על נכסי שקר, "Do not trust in wicked wealth," Sir 5:8), were it not for the commendation Yeshu`a gives to the protagonist in the Parable of the Shrewd Manager (Luke 16:1–13). Giambrone (*Charity*, 261) argues that if Enoch's attitude toward "wicked wealth" is "relentless" (e.g., 1 En 94.8–10), then Luke's is "tempered."

17. Heb כנרת ("stringed harp"; cf. כנרות in 1 Kgs 15:20). Luke 5:1 (*BAGD* s.v. Γεννησαρέτ); ἐπὶ τόπου πεδινοῦ (6:17). Today this plain is called لاغور (El-Ghuweir).

18. Green (*Luke*, 270) defines this as a Greco-Roman construct involving "a stable configuration of motifs sketching a reversal of fortune."

19. Focusing on Deut 28, van den Brink ("Beatitudes," 13) calls this a "Jewish concept," but appears to ignore the extensive presence of the blessing-curse polarity as it recurs in ANE treaties (e.g., the treaty of Birga'yah with Mat`i'el, *KAI* 222–24; cf. Barré, "Treaties," 653–56).

20. Displaying the closeness of its relationship to Luke (*contra* Matthew), the Gospel of Thomas engages blessings extended to (a) the "poor" (Gos. Thom. 54), and (b) the "hungry" (Gos. Thom. 69b; cf. Boring, "Beatitudes," 25–26).

μακάριοί οἱ πτωχοί	Blessed are the beggars,[21]
ὅτι ὑμετέρα ἐστὶν ἡ βασιλεία τοῦ θεοῦ	For yours is the kingdom of God.[22]
μακάριοί οἱ πεινῶντες νῦν	Blessed are those who hunger now,
ὅτι χορτασθήσεσθε	For you will be filled.[23]
μακάριοι οἱ κλαίοντες νῦν	Blessed are those who weep now,
ὅτι γελάσετε	For you will laugh.[24]
μακάριοί ἐστε ὅταν μισήσωσιν ὑμᾶς οἱ ἄνθρωποι	Blessed are you when people hate you,
καὶ ὅταν ἀφορίσωσιν ὑμᾶς καὶ ὀνειδίσωσιν	When they exclude and revile you,[25]
καὶ ἐκβάλωσιν τὸ ὄνομα ὑμῶν ὡς πονηρὸν	And repudiate your name as evil
ἕνεκα τοῦ υἱοῦ τοῦ ἀνθρώπου	On account of the Son of Man.[26]
χάρητε ἐν ἐκείνῃ τῇ ἡμέρᾳ καὶ σκιρτήσατε	Rejoice on that day and leap for joy

21. Luke 6:20; Syr ܡܣܟܢܐ ("poor/needy/wretched"); Vg *pauperes* ("paupers"). Esler (*Community*, 164) contends that "'beggars' . . . is the correct rendering of πτωχοί . . . a word whose force is eviscerated by the translation 'the poor' (*LSJ* s.v. πτωχός)." Baarda ("Poor," 43) suggests that Gos. Thom. 54.6, "Blessed are the poor, for yours is the kingdom of heaven" is more likely based on Luke 6:20 than *vice versa*. Cf. Bammel (πτωχός, 885–86); and Mongstad-Kvammen (*James*, xiv).

22. Luke 6:20–26. Johnson (*Luke*, 106) argues that in this text "the 'poor' are not spiritualized; they are the economically impoverished," an assessment upon which Hron (*Mirage*, 3) thoughtfully reflects: "Cynicism is a shiny toy—sometimes it's a lot of fun to play with, but we have a lot to lose if we let it into the nursery of social justice."

23. Luke 6:21. N.B. that the beggar Lazarus ἐπιθυμῶν χορτασθῆναι ἀπὸ τῶν πιπτόντων ἀπὸ τῆς τραπέζης τοῦ πλουσίου, "longs to be filled with the things falling from the rich man's table" (16:21).

24. Luke 6:21. In the Testament of Judah, "Judah" promises that "those who die in grief will arise in joy, and those who are poor for the Lord's sake will be made rich, and the poor will be fed, and the weak will be made strong" (*T. Jud.* 25:4).

25. Luke 6:22. Osburn ("Poor," 113–32) points out that Sirach (esp. 13:21) also reflects on the social isolationism suffered by the poor (cf. above).

26. Luke 6:22. What distinguishes this saying from that in Sir 13:20–21 is *motivation*; i.e., suffering for the sake of the Son of Man is not *exactly* the same as being reviled for being poor, esp. when a theologian no less competent than Bonhoeffer (*Discipleship*, 50) contends that "suffering and rejection are not the same." Whether the title "Son of Man" signifies suffering or sovereignty is a question over which there is no little debate (cf., e.g., Burkett, *Debate*, 58–59).

ἰδοὺ γὰρ ὁ μισθὸς ὑμῶν πολὺς ἐν τῷ οὐρανω	For truly your reward will be great in heaven,[27]
κατὰ τὰ αὐτὰ γὰρ ἐποίουν τοῖς προφήταις οἱ πατέρες αὐτῶν	For thus their ancestors abused the prophets.[28]

The lines immediately following re-engage these same motifs from an "other-side-of-the-tracks" perspective:[29]

πλὴν οὐαὶ ὑμῖν τοῖς πλουσίοις	But woe to you who are wealthy,[30]
ὅτι ἀπέχετε τὴν παράκλησιν ὑμῶν	For you have received your support.[31]
οὐαὶ ὑμῖν, οἱ ἐμπεπλησμένοι νῦν	Woe to you who are now full,[32]
ὅτι πεινάσετε	For you will be hungry.
οὐαί, οἱ γελῶντες νῦν	Woe to those who now laugh,[33]
ὅτι πενθήσετε καὶ κλαύσετε	For you will mourn and weep.[34]

27. Luke 6:23. Syr ܐܓܪܐ ("wage/fee/fare"); Vg *merces* ("reward/wage/hire"). N.B. (a) that the promise of "compensation/wage" (μισθὸς) in this first section foreshadows its recurrence in the second and third sections; and (b) that whereas Bonaventure imagines this transaction as *acceptatio* ("acceptance"), Aquinas imagines it in terms of *ordinatio* ("order," cited from Colberg, *Wayfarer*, 233–34).

28. Luke 6:23. Stephen's speech (Acts 7:39–53) straightforwardly describes this ancestral behavior (cf. Moore, *Reconciliation*, 12–13; *WealthWarn*, 184–86).

29. This phrase arises from the custom in nineteenth-century, American towns to install railroad lines segregating the homes of poor residents from all others (cf. Carlotti, *Flashbacks*, 7–8).

30. Luke 6:24. Syr ܥܬܝܪܐ ("wealthy/rich"; cf. Aram עתיר). Westermann (*Speech*, 190–98) posits the origin of the woe-oracle in prophecy (*a là* Whybray, *Intellectual*, 21), but Gerstenberger ("Woe-Oracles," 257) thinks it more likely that it comes "from the same stratum of popular ethos as do the wisdom accounts." Morris (*Luke*, 148) argues that "wealth predisposes people to think that they have need of nothing. They then rely on riches, not on God."

31. Sirach (13:21) observes that in stark contrast to the poor, even "a stumbling rich man is supported by friends" (πλούσιος σαλευόμενος στηρίζεται ὑπὸ φίλων; cf. above).

32. Luke 6:25. Elsewhere Luke contrasts the rich man's "fullness" with the beggar's "emptiness" (16:19).

33. Luke 6:25. The warning here is not against laughter *per se*, but against what Fitzmyer (*Luke*, 636) calls "the carefree expression of contentment with the success of the present."

34. Luke 6:25. Hatcher ("Gold," 277), recognizes that the context of The Rich Man and Lazarus parable (16:19–31) comes "laced with caveats against the lure of lucre. In his censure of greed (11:39–41; 12:15), his command to turn temporal treasure into

οὐαὶ ὅταν ὑμᾶς καλῶς εἴπωσιν πάντες οἱ ἄνθρωποι	Woe to you when everyone says nice things,
κατὰ τὰ αὐτὰ γὰρ ἐποίουν τοῖς ψευδοπροφήταις οἱ πατέρες αὐτῶν	For thus the false prophets seduced their ancestors.[35]

(Alms)Giving Without Compensation

Picking up where the Joban Prosecutor leaves off,[36] Yeshu`a refocuses attention on the question of "compensation":

αλλ᾽ ὑμῖν λέγω τοῖς ἀκούουσιν	But I say to you who would listen:
ἀγαπᾶτε τοὺς ἐχθροὺς ὑμῶν	Love your enemies.[37]
καλῶς ποιεῖτε τοῖς μισοῦσιν ὑμᾶς	Do good to those who hate you.[38]
εὐλογεῖτε τοὺς καταρωμένους ὑμᾶς	Bless those who curse you.[39]

eternal equities through almsgiving (12:33), and his call to relinquish riches as a prerequisite for discipleship (14:33; 18:18–24), Jesus depicts wealth as a potential stumbling block to participation in the in-breaking reign of God."

35. Luke 6:26. Well-known is the warning in Didache that any "missionary/apostle" (ἀπόστολος) asking for more than two nights of free room and board is a ψευδοπροφήτη ("false prophet," Did. 11.4–6).

36. Job 1:9 (cf. above).

37. Luke 6:27. In the Testament of Issachar, "Issachar" voices the cultural maxim dominant among Second Temple Jews: "Love the Lord and your neighbor, and show mercy to the poor and weak" (*T. Iss.* 5.2), but says nothing about "loving enemies." Schofttroff and Stegemann (*Poor*, 112) define Yeshu`a's saying as Luke "explaining the command of the love of enemies as an exhortation to prosperous and respected Christians. They are to do good to their fellow Christians, even if the latter hate them. They are to exercise charity without expecting a return; to lend, for example, without demanding a return of what is loaned, or to lend without expecting a full repayment, or to cancel debts."

38. Luke 6:27. In the Testament of Job, "Job" is careful to "command my house servants that the doors be open, since I was concerned lest anyone seeking alms might see me sitting at the door and turn back ashamed, having taken nothing" (*T. Job* 9.8–9).

39. Luke 6:28. Though admired by a few rabbis (e.g., *Derek 'Ereṣ Rabbah* 2.13), the Nazarene ἀγάπη-ethic contrasts sharply with the retributional ethic taught in priestly Israel (Deut 27:15–27), Qumran (1QS 2.4–8), Greece (Hesiod, *Op.* 342), and Rome (Seneca, *De Otio* 1.4).

προσεύχεσθε περὶ τῶνἐπηρεαζόντων ὑμᾶς	Pray for those who threaten you.[40]
τῷ τύπτοντί σε ἐπὶ τὴν σιαγόνα	To the one who strikes you on the cheek
πάρεχε καὶ τὴν ἄλλην	Offer the other as well.[41]
καὶ ἀπὸ τοῦ αἴροντός σου τὸ ἱμάτιον	And from anyone who would take your jacket
καὶ τὸν χιτῶνα μὴ κωλύσῃς	Withhold not your shirt.[42]
παντὶ αἰτοῦντί σε δίδου	Give to anyone who asks of you,[43]
καὶ ἀπὸ τοῦ αἴροντος τὰ σὰ μὴ ἀπαίτει	And if someone takes something of yours away, do not ask for it back.[44]

(Money)Lending Without Compensation

With the following remarks the Nazarene "sets the bar" for his disciples very high:

40. Luke 6:28. To quell the Ionian revolt, the Persians advise the Greeks that the only way to make people stop fighting is to "threaten" them (ἐπηρεαζόντες, *Hdt.* 6.9.4).

41. Luke 6:29. That Matt 5:39 specifies the "right" cheek is significant to Wink (*Powers*, 176–84), who reasons that since punching with the left hand is unlikely (i.e., the "defiled" hand), the only way to strike the right cheek is to use the back of the right hand, a universal gesture of insult.

42. Luke 6:29. Wink (*Nonviolence*, 18) argues that "indebtedness is the most serious social problem in first-century Palestine. Jesus' parables are full of debtors struggling to salvage their lives. The situation is not, however, a natural calamity that has overtaken the incompetent. It is the direct consequence of Roman imperial policy. Emperors tax the wealthy ruthlessly to fund their wars. Naturally, the rich seek non-liquid investments to secure their wealth . . . . It is in this context that Jesus speaks" to "hearers" who "share a rankling hatred for a system that subjects them to humiliation by stripping them of their lands, their goods, and finally even their outer garments."

43. Otzen (*Tobit*, 35–37) emphasizes that "almsgiving" is one of Tobit's primary concerns (cf. Moore, *WealthWarn*, 142–55).

44. Luke 6:30. Cf. how Sirach warns his students not to relinquish any of their possessions lest they find themselves having to ask for it back (33:21). Philo (*Virt.* 183–84) distinguishes between "giving" and "lending," but only to a point: "If a person is not willing wholly to give, then by all means let him lend, so as to give the temporary use of what is wanted freely and cheerfully, without expecting to receive anything beyond the principal. For in this way the poor will not become poorer." The Nazarene, however, teaches *his* students not to bother asking for *anything* back (even the principal) since releasing the debtor from debt-slavery is simply one more opportunity to reflect the *imago Dei*.

καὶ καθὼς θέλετε ἵνα ποιῶσιν ὑμῖν οἱ ἄνθρωποι	Whatever you want people to do for you,
ποιεῖτε αὐτοῖς ὁμοίως	Do likewise for them.[45]
καὶ [γὰρ] ἐὰν ἀγαθοποιῆτε τοὺς ἀγαθοποιοῦντας ὑμᾶς	If you love those who love you,
ποία ὑμῖν χάρις ἐστίν	What credit is that to you?[46]
καὶ οἱ ἁμαρτωλοὶ τὸ αὐτὸ ποιοῦσιν	Even outsiders do the same.[47]
καὶ ἐὰν δανίσητε παρ᾽ ὧν ἐλπίζετε λαβεῖν	And if you lend[48] to those from whom you hope to receive,[49]
ποία ὑμῖν χάρις ἐστίν	What credit is that to you?[50]

45. Luke 6:31. Often called the "Golden Rule," this saying is a simple transposition into sapiential language of the priestly command, "Love your neighbor as yourself" (Lev 19:18)—the edict James calls the "royal law" (Jas 2:8; cf. Kloppenberg, *Democracy*, 26).

46. Luke 6:32 (NRSV, NIV, NJB). Syr ܛܝܒܘܬܐ ("benefit, goodness"); Vg *gratia* ("credit, gratitude"). Gk χάρις ("grace/credit") covers a relatively wide semantic field (cf. *BAGD* and *LSJ*, s.v. χάρις). Montero (*Manifesto*, 84) argues that "to love those that love you fits perfectly with traditional Hellenistic ethics where friendship, at bottom, is an exchange," but "the term used here for "credit" is χάρις, which is used in this context as the response, or the thanks, for generosity or benefaction."

47. Luke 6:33 (lit., "sinners"). Syr ܚܛܝܐ ("sinners"); Vg *peccatores* ("sinners"). Gk ἁμαρτωλοὶ recurs four times in this sermon (6:32, 33, 34), and though some still interpret the word as a *moral* term (e.g., Adams, *Sinner*, 181), others highlight its *social* connotations (e.g., Pilgrim, *Poor*, 80–83).

48. Luke 6:34. Syr ܡܘܙܦܝܢ ("lend"; lit., "cause to borrow"—causative m pl ptc of ܝܙܦ, "to borrow"). Philo (*Spec.* 2.75) draws on δανίζω to ask, "O you creditors, why do you seek to disguise your unsociable disposition by an apparent pretense of good fellowship? And why do you in words, indeed, pretend to be a humane and considerate person, while in your actions you exhibit a want of humanity and a terrible hardness of heart, exacting more than you give, and sometimes even doubling your original loan, so as to make the poor man an even poorer man?"

49. Luke 6:34. Denoted here by the root ἐλπίζομαι, "hope" stands at the center of every loan agreement, for, as Andreau (*Banking*, 25) observes, creditors basically "hope" for two things: (a) "to recoup interest from their money," and (b) "to diversify their sources of income."

50. Luke 6:34. Philo asks (*Somn.* 1:98), "Is any 'creditor' (δανειστής) so 'covetous of riches' (βαθύπλουτός, lit., "deep in wealth"), or so very cruel, or so perverse, as not to be willing to contribute a tetradrachm, or even less, to one in distress? Or is anyone so stingy as to be willing to lend it, but to refuse to give it?" The Nazarene goes a step further by basing his teaching not on ἔρος, but on the Torah principle of אהבה/ἀγάπη "love" (Lev 19:18; cf. Moran, "Love," 77–78).

καὶ ἁμαρτωλοὶ ἁμαρτωλοῖς δανίζουσιν	Even outsiders lend to outsiders,[51]
ἵνα ἀπολάβωσιν τὰ ἴσα	In order that they may later recover it.[52]
πλὴν ἀγαπᾶτε τοὺς ἐχθροὺς ὑμῶν καὶ ἀγαθοποιεῖτε	So love your enemies, do good,
καὶ δανίζετε μηδὲν ἀπελπίζοντες	And lend, expecting nothing in return.[53]
καὶ ἔσται ὁ μισθὸς ὑμῶν πολύς	Then your reward will be great[54]
καὶ ἔσεσθε υἱοὶ ὑψίστου	And you will become children of the Most High,
ὅτι αὐτὸς χρηστός ἐστιν ἐπὶ τοὺς ἀχαρίστους καὶ πονηρούς	For he is kind to the ungrateful and the wicked.[55]

51. In Hodayot the writer contrasts the "sons of your truth" (בני אמתכה, 1QH 18.27) with the "strongmen" (גבורים) of this world, men whose main interest is the "excess of luxuries" (רוב עדנים, 18.24).

52. Luke 6:34. The Nazarene is hardly the first to address this socioeconomic question (cf. above). Philo (*Somn.* 1.95) observes that "debtors are poor, some might say, and it is right to pity them." Then he asks, "would it not then have been more reasonable to enact a law in accordance with which a 'contribution' (ἐρανιοῦσι) might be made to assist their necessities, rather than force them to languish in debt?"

53. Luke 6:35 (cf. Job 1:9). In Aristophanes' play, *Wealth,* Chremylus brags to his friend Blepsidemus that because he has "captured" Plutus (Gk god of wealth), wealthy people will now be limited to men of "sharp" (δεξιός) and "sound" (σώφρων) mind. To this Penia ("Poverty") replies that making only "righteous" (δίκαιος) men wealthy is dangerously short-sighted (*Plut.* 386–87, 473–75).

54. Luke 6:35. The irony, of course, is that right after articulating the "no-expectation-of-compensation" principle, the Nazarene promises that the "compensation" for "expecting no compensation" will be "great." Theissen (*Religion*, 92) tries to explain this by suggesting that the earliest churches embrace a "circular theory" of giving "according to which the poor are rich with God (cf. πλουσίους ἐν πίστει, 'rich in faith,' Jas 2:5), whereas the rich hold with God a debit balance (cf. the الله قرضا, 'goodly loan to Allah,' Q 5.12). Now if the rich who do not have much to say to God support the poor, the poor pray for them—and God then sees that the wealth of the rich does not cease, so that they can continue to give to the poor." This "vertical solidarity" later shifts into balance with "horizontal solidarity," as evidenced by the admonition here, presumably to both rich and poor, to "lend without expecting anything back."

55. Luke 6:35 (cf. Sir 10:31; 11:14; 18:25). Regaining his sight in the temple of Asclepius, Plutus (god of wealth) pleads, "Let me prove to humanity that if I *did* give to the wicked, it was against my will" (Aristophanes, *Plut.* 780–81). Cf. Sir 11:11–13 (above): "Some labor, struggle, and scurry about, yet still fall behind; others are beaten down, lost, and adrift, devoid of strength and stung by weakness. Yet the eye of Yhwh looks kindly upon them as he shakes off the dust of their filth, lifting up their heads and pointing them skyward, to the amazement of many."

δίδοτε, καὶ δοθήσεται ὑμῖν	Give, and it will be given to you,[56]
μέτρον καλὸν πεπιεσμένον σεσαλευμένον ὑπερεκχυννόμενον	Good measure, pressed down, shaken together, running over,[57]
δώσουσιν εἰς τὸν κόλπον ὑμῶν	They will put[58] into your lap,[59]
ᾧ γὰρ μέτρῳ μετρεῖτε ἀντιμετρηθήσεται ὑμῖν	For the measure you give will be the measure you get.[60]

Wicked Wealth

Like Sirach, the Nazarene sage finds it obvious that nothing good can come from an evil source, or, to put it in the words of his brother James:

μήτι ἡ πηγὴ ἐκ τῆς αὐτῆς ὀπῆς βρύει τὸ γλυκὺ καὶ τὸ πικρόν	Does a spring bring forth salty water as well as sweet?[61]

Simple contrasts like this describe what the sages believe to be universally obvious:

Οὐ γάρ ἐστιν δένδρον καλὸν ποιοῦν καρπὸν σαπρόν	No good tree bears bad fruit,

56. Learning that some of his debtors have been robbed, "Job" responds by "crowning the transaction as cancelled, saying, 'Inasmuch as I trust you, in benefit of the poor, I will receive from you nothing.' Then I would accept nothing from my debtor" (*T. Job* 11.11–12).

57. Cf. Mal 3:10: בחנוני נא בזות אמר יהוה צבאות אם לא אפתח לכם את ארבות שמים והריקתי לכם ברכה עד בלי די, "Test me on this, says Yhwh of Hosts, and see if I do not open up the windows of heaven for you, and pour down upon you an incredible blessing."

58. Luke 6:38. With the exception of KJV and ASV, most ETs translate this clause as pass. sg., even though it is fut. act. 3rd pers. pl. (so Vg *dabunt*), perhaps to eliminate the possibility that these gift-givers might be among the "ungrateful and wicked" (6:35).

59. Luke 6:38. N.B. that Lazarus moves at his death εἰς τὸν κόλπον Ἀβραάμ, "into Abraham's lap" (16:22).

60. Luke 6:38. Cf. the admonition in *Sib. Or.* 2.86–89: "To the fallen give a hand, and save the man who stands without defense. Suffering is the great common denominator. Life is a wheel and riches are unstable. But if you *are* wealthy, reach out your hand to the poor and bestow what God gives you on the needy."

61. Jas 3:11.

οὐδὲ πάλιν δένδρον σαπρὸν ποιοῦν καρπὸν καλόν	Nor does a bad tree bear good fruit.[62]
ἕκαστον γὰρ δένδρον ἐκ τοῦ ἰδίου καρποῦ γινώσκεται	For each tree is known by its own fruit:
οὐ γὰρ ἐξ ἀκανθῶν συλλέγουσιν σῦκα	Figs are not gathered from thorns,
οὐδὲ ἐκ βάτου σταφυλὴν τρυγῶσιν	Nor grapes from hedgerows.[63]
ὁ ἀγαθὸς ἄνθρωπος ἐκ τοῦ ἀγαθοῦ θησαυροῦ τῆς καρδίας προφέρει τὸ ἀγαθόν	The good person out of the good treasure of the heart produces that which is good,[64]
καὶ ὁ πονηρὸς ἐκ τοῦ πονηροῦ προφέρει τὸ πονηρόν	But the wicked person out of the wicked (treasure of the heart) produces that which is wicked.[65]

Read alongside the didactic sayings about (alms)giving and (money-) lending in Proverbs, Sirach, and 4QInstruction, the Sermon on the Plain—in spite of several claims to the contrary—is structurally balanced,[66] intertextually active,[67] and ethically deliberate.[68] Like the rest of the Nazarene

62. Luke 6:43 (cf. Matt 7:15–17). Philo (*Spec.* 1:277) contends that "a good man will not receive gifts from a wicked person, not even though he may be poor and the other rich, and he himself perhaps in actual want of what he would so receive."

63. Luke 6:45. Elsewhere Luke speaks of μαμωνᾶ τῆς ἀδικίας, the "*mammon* of wickedness" (Luke 16:9). Cf. Sandoval (*Discourse*, 156–580); Moore (*WealthWatch*, 219–20).

64. Luke 6:45. Philo's (Spec. 1.277) approach to this "good-vs-evil" polarity is utilitarian: "A good man will not receive gifts from a wicked person, not even though he may be poor and the other rich, and he himself perhaps in actual want of what he would so receive."

65. Luke 6:45. Cf. *Sib. Or.* 2.102: "Possession of lawful wealth is useful, but unwarranted profits are worthless."

66. I.e., due to its chiastic structure (Bovon, *Lukas*, 309).

67. Armitage (*Poverty*, 244–46) contends that the variegated witnesses in GNT build on the Jewish foundation initiated by Tanak, but only as it is strained through Graeco-Roman filters.

68. Contemporary interpreters contest each of these attributes. Convinced, for example, that the Sermon's primary *raison d'être* is to show the necessity of divine grace in the face of "impossible ethical demands," Protestant reformer Martin Luther ("Sermon," 291) contends that it says "nothing about how we become Christians, but only about the works and fruit that no one can do unless he is already a Christian and in a state

curriculum, the taproot of this text extends all the way down to the concrete bedrock of the "Great Commandment,"[69] i.e., the Torah text which prioritizes in no uncertain terms the axiomatic principle of אהבה/ἀγάπη "love."[70] That this principle is habitually diluted, perverted, dismissed, and/or ignored—even by those who claim to champion it—hardly challenges its centrality within the Judeo-Christian tradition.[71]

The Letter of James

Of the 105 verses making up the Letter of James, no less than forty-seven allude to "wealth and its use,"[72] a ratio prompting Mariam Kamell to surmise that "one's relationship to money" in this text is a "litmus text for one's relationship to God."[73] Recent study of James, however, tends to ignore this statistic,[74] assigning to the poverty-wealth polarity no more importance than that assigned to the motifs of double-mindedness, self-deception, true-vs.-false religion, arrogant teaching, or the irrepressible tongue.[75] Indeed, some

---

of grace." The fact that Luther also calls the Letter of James an "epistle of straw" (*LW* 35.362) appears to demonstrate, if nothing else, a fundamental lack of appreciation for the Hebrew wisdom tradition. Cf. Stassen (*Peacemaking*, 33–88); Murphy ("Enemies," 123–29).

69. Matt 22:38. Pleading for a definition of "economic science" which presumes that human beings (including economists) are made in the *imago Dei*, Tiemstra (*Economics*, 58–59) believes that "the assertion that all relevant human motivation stems from a natural and laudable drive to maximize one's standard of living" does not comport well with "the Christian social ethics implied by the Great Commandment."

70. Deut 6:4; Lev 19:18; Mark 12:30; Jas 2:8. Cf. Jauss (*Liebe*); Moore (*Liebe*). Philo (*Opif.* 1.70) thinks that ἔρος-"love" is the σοφίας ποδηγετοῦντι ("guide to wisdom").

71. Goodchild's (*Money*, 241–56) notion of "evaluative credit" is a promising response to the Sermon on the Plain because "economics and theology are disciplines in crisis . . . . Economics aspires to scientific status basing its models on evidence, but it is largely unable to predict major economic events and so inspire stability and confidence. Theology aspires to provide a universal and comprehensive vision of life, yet finds it impossible to unite believers from the same tradition in a single vision, let alone the wider world." Still, "in spite of appearances, economics and theology do share a common domain: the ordering of trust" (Goodchild, *Credit*, 3).

72. Davids, "Wealth," 355.

73. Kamell, "Economics," 157.

74. Allison (*James*, 192) suggests that discussion of this question in Jas 1:9–11, "judging by the relatively low number of relevant sermons and academic articles, has garnered less attention than any other part of James."

75. Puzzled by its multiplicity of traditional themes, Dibelius (*James*, 2–3) suggests that "the entire document lacks continuity in thought," an assessment leading Palmer (*James*, 13–16) to portray James as a "new book of Proverbs."

have come to believe, with Dan McCartney, that "almost every aspect of interpretation" in this short epistle is dismally "tangled together."[76]

However (in)accurate this characterization, various readers propose various theories with regard to the epistle's literary structure.[77] Unanimity remains elusive, of course, but what *does* command consensus is (a) the fact that this epistle preserves one of the densest patches of Hebrew wisdom in GNT,[78] seeing as it is a series of sapiential admonitions highly congruent with (and doubtless influenced by) those shaping the Sermons on the Plain[79] and Mount;[80] and (b) that unlike Proverbs, Qohelet, and Sirach, James rather simplistically presumes[81] the "rich" always to be "bad" and the "poor" always to be "good."[82]

Beginning with a preamble praising the deity as Prime Giver,[83] James introduces the letter's theological rationale:

εἰ δέ τις ὑμῶν λείπεται σοφίας	If any of you lack[84] wisdom
αἰτείτω παρὰ τοῦ διδόντος θεοῦ πᾶσιν	Let him petition the God who gives to all

76. McCartney, *James*, 2. Citing Deissmann (*Studies*, 52), Jackson-McCabe (*James*, 1) ranks "the Letter of James . . . as one of the most enigmatic works of early Christian literature."

77. Allison (*James*, 1–2) lists most of the major suggestions.

78. Baasland ("Jakobusbrief," 123–25), contends that forty of these 105 verses allude to the Hebrew wisdom trajectory.

79. Knox ("James," 16) argues that the initial beatitudes and final exhortation in the letter show a form identical to that found in the Sermon on the Plain (cf. Adamson, *James*, 22).

80. Schmid (*Theology*, 364) contends that "James not only agrees with numerous passages in Matthew's Gospel . . . , but also with that great body of precepts which Matthew gives as a whole, the Sermon on the Mount."

81. Batten ("Poor," 65–77) thinks this presumption is rooted in the fact that most Mediterranean economies in the first century CE are zero-sum in orientation (cf. Beinhocker, *Wealth*, 1–78).

82. Even 4QInstruction is more open to "wealthy benevolence" than James (cf. above). Most attempts to "rescue the rich" in James, as shown by Allison (*James*, 192), allot little or no attention to the ANE/OT poverty-wealth trajectory, but instead interpret the epistle against ideological contexts framed by Paulinist ("flesh-vs.-spirit") and medievalist polarities ("faith-vs-works").

83. Jas 1:5. Jackson-McCabe (*James*, 1) recognizes that some readers think James is "originally a Jewish work only subsequently 'Christianized' by the insertion of references to Jesus Christ, who is in fact explicitly mentioned only twice" (Jas 1:1; 2:1).

84. Jas 1:5. Syr ܚܣܝܪ ("to lack/want," cf. Heb חסר, "to be scarce"); Vg *indiget* ("to lack, be in want of"); cf. the main theme of 4QInstruction, למלא כל מחסרי אוטו, "to fill up anything 'lacking' in his tenderness" (4Q416.2.2.1).

ἁπλῶς καὶ μὴ ὀνειδίζοντος	Liberally[85] and without censure,[86]
καὶ δοθήσεται αὐτῷ	And it will be given to him.[87]
πᾶσα δόσις ἀγαθὴ καὶ πᾶν δώρημα τέλειον	All "good giving"[88] and every perfect gift
ἄνωθέν ἐστιν	Is from above,
καταβαῖνον ἀπὸ τοῦ πατρὸς τῶν φώτων	Descending from the father of lights,
παρ᾽ ᾧ οὐκ ἔνι παραλλαγὴ ἢ τροπῆς ἀποσκίασμα	In whom is no (ex)change or flickering of shadow.[89]

Then attention turns to the "fate of the rich":

καυχάσθω δὲ ὁ ἀδελφὸς ὁ ταπεινὸς ἐν τῷ ὕψει αὐτου	Let the lowly brother boast in his ascension,[90]
ὁ δὲ πλούσιος ἐν τῇ ταπεινώσει αὐτοῦ	And the rich (brother) in his descension,[91]
ὅτι ὡς ἄνθος χόρτου παρελεύσεται	For like a flower of the field he will pass away.[92]

85. Jas 1:5. Syr ܦܫܝܛܐܝܬ ("simply, directly, liberally"); Vg *affluenter* ("affluently").

86. Jas 1:5. Hesiod (*Op.* 718) warns: μηδέ ποτ᾽ οὐλομένην πενίην θυμοφθόρον ἀνδρὶ τέτλαθ᾽ ὀνειδίζειν, "Never dare to censure someone with the sort of contemptible poverty which breaks the spirit."

87. Jas 1:5. Kirk ("Wisdom," 24–38) suggests that the role of "wisdom" in James parallels the role(s) enacted elsewhere in GNT by the Holy Spirit.

88. Jas 1:17. This phrase denotes the polar opposite of "wicked wealth" in Sir 5:8; 1 En 94.8–10; Luke 6:45; 16:9.

89. Jas 1:17. The root of παραλλαγὴ is ἀλλάσσω, "to exchange, barter"; cf. the declaration of Prometheus to Hermes about his future: "I do not barter/negotiate" (οὐκ ἂν ἀλλάξαιμ᾽ ἐγώ, Aes., *Prom.* 967), and N.B. that in dramatic contrast to the constant bargaining between the gods in pagan pantheons, Torah straightforwardly testifies to the "oneness" of the deity (אחד, Deut 6:4).

90. Jas 1:10. N.B. the simple alternation in these lines between "ascension" (1:10) and "descension" (καταβαῖνον, 1:17, 1:10).

91. Jas 1:10. Whether the πλούσιος ("rich man") here is an ἀδελφός ("brother") is not crystal clear, but in all likelihood he, too, is a Christian. Cf. the opinions voiced in Maynard-Reid (*Poverty*, 1–12); Davids ("Wealth," 357); Friesen ("Poverty," 247); and Stulac ("Rich," 89–102); and N.B. (a) that Sirach (13:20) lays out a similar contrast between the "proud" and the "humble"; and (b) Vassiliadis ("John," 416) interprets the foot-washing scene in John 13 as another example of "social role inversion."

92. Jas 1:10. This verb (παρέρχομαι) is the first of four synonyms in 1:10–11, each conveying a different aspect of the rich man's fate: παρέρχομαι ("to pass away"); ξηραίνω

ἀνέτειλεν γὰρ ὁ ἥλιος σὺν τῷ καύσωνι	The sun rises with its scorching heat,
καὶ ἐξήρανεν τὸν χόρτον	And the field withers up;
καὶ τὸ ἄνθος αὐτοῦ ἐξέπεσεν	Its petals fall,
καὶ ἡ εὐπρέπεια τοῦ προσώπου αὐτοῦ ἀπώλετο	And the beauty of its appearance fades.[93]
οὕτως καὶ ὁ πλούσιος	So also the wealthy[94]
ἐν ταῖς πορείαις αὐτοῦ μαρανθήσεται.	Will fade away in the midst of their pursuits.[95]

Socioeconomic Prejudice

Like the Corinthian churches,[96] the congregations targeted by this encyclical[97] practice a radically selfish socioeconomic prejudice.[98] So insidious is the problem, in fact, James finds it necessary to write a letter to challenge it on three fronts. These diaspora churches need (a) to *recognize* socioeconomic prejudice for what it is; (b) to *reflect* on the unbreakable link between "mistreatment of the poor" and "transgression of the royal law";[99] and (c) to *ridicule* the irony of believers acting as "oppressors-of-the-poor."

("to dry out/wither"); μαραίνω ("to be quenched"); and ἀπόλλυμι ("to be destroyed). N.B. that the moniker of the angel in charge of the bottomless pit is Ἀπολλύων, "the Destroyer" (Rev 9:12).

93. Jas 1:11 (alluding to Isa 40:7–8; Job 7:9; Ps 90:6). Observing a fleet sailing off to battle, Thucydides (*Hist.* 6.31.3) notes how "every sailor strives to make *his* ship the one most excellent in swiftness and 'beauty/majesty/appearance' (εὐπρέπεια)."

94. Like James, Ps.-Phocylides (1.62) believes that "great wealth is conceited and prone to insolence."

95. Jas 1:11. Preparing a meal for Odysseus, Achilles and Patroclus cook several portions of meat until "the fire dies down and the flame 'extinguishes' (ἐμαράνθη)," after which Odysseus continues his attempt to convince Achilles to rejoin Agamemnon (*Il.* 9.212).

96. 1 Cor 11:22. Martin (*Body*, xvii) posits that "although the Corinthian church contains no one from the highest levels of Greco-Roman culture—which, incidentally, produces most of the extant literature of the period—it does comprise a range of socioeconomic positions which . . . prompt theological conflicts."

97. Bauckham (*James*, 13) calls the epistle—addressed to "the twelve tribes in the dispora"—a "paranetic encyclical" (i.e., a circular letter/sermon).

98. Contrast the so-called Apocryphon of James (NHC 1.2), a pseudonymous Coptic text containing no reference to the poverty-wealth polarity at all, not even metaphorically.

99. Lev 19:18 (cf. Martin, *James*, 79). Moo (*James*, 108–9) similarly sees three

ἀδελφοί μου	My brothers,
μὴ ἐν προσωπολημψίαις ἔχετε	Do you not practice prejudice[100]
τὴν πίστιν τοῦ κυρίου ἡμῶν Ἰησοῦ Χριστοῦ τῆς δόξης	With regard to the Faith of our glorious Lord Jesus Christ?[101]
ἐὰν γὰρ εἰσέλθῃ εἰς συναγωγὴν ὑμῶν ἀνὴρ	For if someone enters your meeting-place
χρυσοδακτύλιος ἐν ἐσθῆτι λαμπρᾷ	With a gold ring and fine clothes,[102]
εἰσέλθῃ δὲ καὶ πτωχὸς ἐν ῥυπαρᾷ ἐσθῆτι	And a beggar[103] with dirty clothes enters,
ἐπιβλέψητε δὲ ἐπὶ τὸν φοροῦντα τὴν ἐσθῆτα τὴν λαμπρὰν	And you take notice of the one wearing fine clothes,
καὶ εἴπητε σὺ κάθου ὧδε καλῶς	Saying, "Take a seat here, please,"[104]
καὶ τῷ πτωχῷ εἴπητε· σὺ στῆθι	But to the beggar you say, "Stand over there,"[105]

sections, finding each section organically linked to the "rich oppressors" motif.

100. Jas 2:1. The word προσωπολημψίαις (προσωπολημπτέω in 2:9) consists of πρόσωπον ("face") + λημπτέω ("to receive"). Inserting an alpha-privative before the word προσωπολημψίαις ("a common way of negating a word in Greek," Parry, *Word*, 115), Clement (1 Clem. 1.3) apophatically "praises" the Corinthians for "doing everything *without* prejudice" (ἀπροσωπολήμπτως γὰρ πάντα ἐποιεῖτε) before firmly taking them to task for it.

101. Jas 2:1. Doubtless πίστις here signifies not the Nazarene's personal faith, but the Faith as a socioreligious movement. N.B. that no "great chasm" (χάσμα μέγα, Luke 16:26) exists here between religious belief and socioeconomic practice, something Johnson (*Brother*, 166) underlines by observing that "in James' covenantal perspective, religion and ethics are inseparable."

102. Jas 2:2. The sibylline oracle admonishes, "Do not unjustly cast out the poor, nor judge by outward show" (*Sib. Or.* 2.62).

103. Jas 2:2 (cf. Luke 6:20 above). Philo (*Spec.* 2.75) distinguishes between different levels of poverty. Speaking to creditors, he asks why they try to "exact more than you give, and sometimes even double your original loan, so as to make the 'poor' (πένης) even 'poorer' (πενιχρότερον)?"

104. Jas 2:3. This may well be a reference to the "Moses Chair" reserved for dignitaries (Matt 23:2) in many synagogues, or perhaps the spirit of Moses, the latter possibility due to the fact that the Moses Chairs found in the excavated synagogues at Chorazin, Ein Gedi, and elsewhere are contiguous with the alcove where the Torah ark rests (cf. Rousseau and Arav, "Moses," 204).

105. Jas 2:3. N.B. that in the Testament of Job, Satan disguises himself as a beggar to deceive Job's wife (*T. Job* 6.4).

ἢ κάθου ἐκεῖ ὑπὸ τὸ ὑποπόδιόν μου	Or "Sit here, under my footstool,"
καὶ οὐ διεκρίθητε ἐν ἑαυτοῖς	Have you not discriminated among yourselves[106]
καὶ ἐγένεσθε κριταὶ διαλογισμῶν πονηρῶν	And become censors with wicked intentions?[107]

To answer this question he lays out his "theology of the poor":

ἀκούσατε, ἀδελφοί μου ἀγαπητοί	Listen, my beloved brothers:
οὐχ ὁ θεὸς ἐξελέξατο τοὺς πτωχοὺς τῷ κόσμω	Has not God chosen the poor in the world
πλουσίους ἐν πίστει καὶ κληρονόμους τῆς βασιλείας	To be rich in faith and heirs of the kingdom
ἧς ἐπηγγείλατο τοῖς ἀγαπῶσιν αὐτόν	Which he promises to those who love him?[108]

Socioeconomic Abuse of Laborers

Doubtless aware of the sapiential preoccupation with *labor* (see above), he warns:

ἰδοὺ ὁ μισθὸς τῶν ἐργατῶν τῶν ἀμησάντων τὰς χώρας ὑμῶν	Behold, the wages of the workers who tend your fields,[109]

106. Jas 2:4. Syr ܐܬܦܠܓܬܘܢ ("you have divided yourselves"); Vg *iudicatis* ("to adjudicate, judge"). Rather than (re)define "poverty" along "party lines," one Hittite prince asks his father's cronies, "Do you ever seek to 'redeem the blood' of the poor? Do you ever try to engage your servants, or do you just do the rich man's bidding? You go to his house, eat, drink, and accept his gifts, but the plight of the poor man you ignore" (*KBo* 22.1.24′–30′; cf. above).

107. Jas 2:4. N.B. the persistent repetition of the root κριτ- in these lines. The sybilline oracle instructs, "You will not shut your door when a stranger comes to you to curb the hunger generated by his poverty, but taking hold of that person you shall sprinkle him with water and pray three times . . . , 'I do not long for wealth'" (*Sib Or.* 7:85–89).

108. Jas 2:5. Finding it problematic to call poor people "rich" and rich people "poor" (*Prob.* 1.8–9), Philo (*Fug.* 1.16) suggests that "those who are free both in name and also in their minds do not consider any foolish person as either rich or famous, but look upon all such people, so to say, as 'infamous and poor' (ἀδόξους καὶ πένητας), even if their fortune exceeds that of wealthy kings."

109. Jas 5:4. In the Testament of Job, "Job" receives a request from someone not

ὁ ἀπεστερημένος ἀφ᾽ ὑμῶν	Which you fraudulently withhold,[110]
κράζει	Cry out,[111]
καὶ αἱ βοαὶ τῶν θερισάντων	And the harvesters' cries
εἰς τὰ ὦτα κυρίου σαβαὼθ εἰσεληλύθασιν	Enter the ears of the Lord of Hosts.[112]
ἐτρυφήσατε ἐπὶ τῆς γῆς καὶ ἐσπαταλήσατε	Is your life on earth about sumptuous pleasure
ἐθρέψατε τὰς καρδίας ὑμῶν ἐν ἡμέρᾳ σφαγῆς	As you fatten your hearts for a day of slaughter?[113]

The Royal Law

Norman T. Wright imagines the "royal law" to be "the law which King Jesus himself endorses and insists upon":[114]

εἰ μέντοι νόμον τελεῖτε βασιλικὸν κατὰ τὴν γραφήν	If you truly fulfill the royal law[115] according to the scripture,

wealthy enough to give alms, yet who still wishes to serve. So Job gives him a job serving the guests at his table. So "when evening comes he receives payment from me, but he refuses to take it. So I compel him, saying, 'I know that you are a working man expecting and counting on your wages, so you must accept.' In this way I refuse to allow the wage of a wage-earner to remain with me in my house" (*T. Job* 12:1–4).

110. Jas 5:4. Sirach (7:20) admonishes his students, אל תדע באמת עובד אמת, "Do not abuse an honest, reliable worker," reminding them that ἐκχέων αἷμα ὁ ἀποστερῶν μισθὸν μισθίου, "to defraud a worker of his wages is to shed blood" (34:22). In his comedy "The Birds," Aristophanes has Poseidon disparage Herakles with the words, "You are a glutton . . . who 'defrauds' (ἀποστερεῖς) his father" (*Av.* 1605).

111. Jas 5:4. In the Testament of Asher, "Asher" points out what "fraud" actually is: "He who defrauds his neighbor provokes God and swears falsely against the Most High, yet *pities* the poor; Yhwh commands the law and provokes, yet *refreshes* the poor" (*T. Ash.* 2:6).

112. Jas 5:4. Townsend (*James*, 95) thinks that James here speaks to the problem of "fair world trade and political liberty," even when it involves "paying high prices" for consumer goods and "higher taxes." Reyes ("Grito," 79–97) sees here a pointed critique of global economies in which *acquisition* is more important than *protection*, esp. the protection of loyal workers (cf. Sir 7:20; Moore, *WealthWatch*, 224).

113. Jas 5:5. Cf. יום עברה, "day of distress" (Sir 5:8; 13:6).

114. Wright, *James*, 30.

115. Jas 2:8. Reflecting on Torah, Philo (*Spec.* 2.107) asks how appropriate it is "to love these laws . . . by which the rich are taught to 'share' (μεταδίδωμι) the blessings

ἀγαπήσεις τὸν πλησίον σου ὡς σεαυτόν	"Love your neighbor as yourself,"[116]
καλῶς ποιεῖτε	You do well.
εἰ δὲ προσωπολημπτεῖτε, ἁμαρτίαν ἐργάζεσθε	But if you play favorites, you commit sin
ἐλεγχόμενοι ὑπὸ τοῦ νόμου ὡς παραβάται	And are convicted by the law as transgressors.[117]

The Irony of Behaving Like Rich Oppressors

Daring to reveal his personal middle-class history, George Orwell takes a firsthand, unadorned look at wartime poverty in northern England, then concludes: "I had reduced everything to the simple theory that the oppressed are always right and the oppressors are always wrong: a mistaken theory, but the natural result of being one of the oppressors yourself."[118] James' understanding of the poverty-wealth polarity, though similarly simplistic, leads him to ask the "How-is-this-profitable?" question:

ὑμεῖς δὲ ἠτιμάσατε τὸν πτωχόν	You disenfranchise the poor,[119]
οὐχ οἱ πλούσιοι καταδυναστεύουσιν ὑμῶν	But is it not the rich who oppress you?[120]

which they have, . . . and the poor are comforted because they no longer have to frequent the 'upscale houses' (ταῖς τῶν εὐπόρων οἰκίαις, lit., 'houses of the wealthy') to have their needs supplied."

116. Jas 2:8. Paul says basically the same thing to Galatian believers: ὁ γὰρ πᾶς νόμος ἐν ἑνὶ λόγῳ πεπλήρωται ἐν τῷ ἀγαπήσεις τὸν πλησίον σου ὡς σεαυτόν, "the whole law is fulfilled in one statement, 'You shall love your neighbor as yourself'" (Gal 5:14).

117. Jas 2:9. Ward ("Partiality," 87–97) imagines this conviction actually taking place in a "church court" where the beggar and the rich man are litigants.

118. Orwell, *Pier*, 148.

119. Jas 2:6. Syr ܫܛܬܘܢܝܗܝ ("you mistreat"); Vg *exhonorastis* ('you dishonor"). Gk ἀτιμάζω, often translated "dishonor," can also mean "disenfranchise." Dio Cassius (*Hist.* 38.13.2), e.g., tells how one of Cicero's strongest enemies, Publius Clodius Pulcher, in an attempt to win over the Roman Senate, revives the *collegiae* in order to "forbid the enfranchisers/censors (τιμηταῖς) from removing anybody or 'disenfranchising' (ἀτιμάζειν) anyone."

120. Jas 2:6.Gk καταδυναστεύω (lit., "to make you power down," κατα + δυναμις). Cf. κατεδυνάστευον οἱ Αἰγύπτιοι τοὺς υἱοὺς Ισραηλ, "the Egyptians oppressed the children of Israel" (OG Exod 1:13).

καὶ αὐτοὶ ἕλκουσιν ὑμᾶς εἰς κριτήρια	Is it not the rich who drag you into court?[121]
οὐκ αὐτοὶ βλασφημοῦσιν τὸ καλὸν ὄνομα	Are they not the ones who blaspheme the good name
τὸ ἐπικληθὲν ἐφ' ὑμᾶς	Which was invoked over you?[122]
τί τὸ ὄφελος, ἀδελφοί μου	How is this "profitable," my brothers?[123]
ἐὰν ἀδελφὸς ἢ ἀδελφὴ γυμνοὶ ὑπάρχωσιν	If a brother or sister is naked
καὶ λειπόμενοι ὦσιν τῆς ἐφημέρου τροφῆς	And lacks daily food[124]
εἴπῃ δέ τις αὐτοῖς ἐξ ὑμῶν	And one of you says to them,
ὑπάγετε ἐν εἰρήνῃ, θερμαίνεσθε καὶ χορτάζεσθε	"Go in peace. Be warmed and filled."[125]
μὴ δῶτε δὲ αὐτοῖς τὰ ἐπιτήδεια τοῦ σώματος	But attend not to their bodily needs,
τί τὸ ὄφελος	How is this "profitable?"[126]

121. Jas 2:6. McCartney (*James*, 142) suggests that "drag you into court" may "refer to the common experience of a rich creditor hauling a poor debtor into court." Keenan (*Wisdom*, 70) suggests that James here "addresses himself not to the poor, but to an audience he accuses of dishonoring the poor. He reminds them that it is not only the poor, but they themselves who are oppressed and dragged into court."

122. Jas 2:7 (cf. 5:10, 14; Luke 6:22; 2 Tim 1:6–8). The term ἐπικαλέω indicates a divine "calling/summons" (cf., e.g., the "calling/summons" of Artemis, Ar. *Lys.* 1280).

123. Jas 2:14. This paragraph begins (2:14) and ends (2:16) with the same question about ὄφελος ("profit"), calling to mind the similar question in the Wisdom of Solomon, τί ὠφέλησεν ἡμᾶς ἡ ὑπερηφανία, "What has our arrogance profited us?" (Wis 2:11), not to mention (a) the depiction of Šamaš as the "profits provider" in the Šamaš Hymn (*balāṭa uttar*, *BWL* 132.106), and (b) Sirach's admonition not to trust in "wicked wealth" because of its "unprofitability" (Sir 5:8).

124. Jas 2:15. "When I feed the hungry they call me a saint; when I ask why the hungry don't have enough food, they call me a communist" (attributed to Dom Hélder Câmara).

125. Jas 2:16. Swartley (*Peace*, 260) argues, in light of the epistle's preoccupation with socioeconomic conflict (3:17—4:7), that "the 'sickness' in the community marked by the arrogance of the rich and the humiliation of the poor (chaps. 2 and 5) is rooted not in a wisdom that comes from above, but in the basest of human vices, envy."

126. Jas 2:16. Pointed socioeconomic questioning is a staple of Hebrew pedagogy; e.g., "What 'profit' (בצע) is it if we kill our brother and conceal his blood?" (Gen 37:26); "What 'profit' (יתרון) is it to a person for all his labor?" (Qoh 1:3); "What 'profit' (ὠφεληθήσεται) is it for a person to gain the whole world, but lose his soul?" (Matt

The Fate of the Wealthy

Compared to previous sages, James is by far the least optimistic about the "fate of the wealthy."[127]

ἄγε νῦν οἱ λέγοντες	Come now, you who say,
σήμερον ἢ αὔριον πορευσόμεθα εἰς τήνδε τὴν πόλιν	"Today or tomorrow we will go into this or that town,
καὶ ποιήσομεν ἐκεῖ ἐνιαυτὸν,	And spend a year there,
καὶ ἐμπορευσόμεθα καὶ κερδήσομεν	Doing business and making money,"[128]
οἵτινες οὐκ ἐπίστασθε τὸ τῆς αὔριον	Yet you know nothing about tomorrow.[129]
ποία ἡ ζωὴ ὑμῶν	What is your life?[130]
ἀτμὶς γάρ ἐστε ἡ πρὸς ὀλίγον φαινομένη	You are a vapor[131] which appears for a moment,
ἔπειτα καὶ ἀφανιζομένη	Then vanishes.
ἄγε νῦν οἱ πλούσιοι	Come now, you rich,[132]

16:26). Qur'an warns unbelievers that "neither their 'wealth' (اموالهم) nor their children will 'profit' (يغن) them" (Q 3.10).

127. Collins (*Wages*, 244) sees "the epistle rejecting the biblical Wisdom tradition that prosperity is a blessing from God and espousing the Jesus tradition's view that wealth is problematic," but as the present survey makes clear, the "biblical Wisdom tradition" as a whole is much more ambivalent about wealth.

128. Jas 4:13 (cf. above discussion on ענין, "business," in Qoh 5:13 *et passim*). In the Testament of Job, "Job" is grateful to report that "some strangers who, having seen my eagerness, were also eager to assist in this service. Some others without resources, and unable to undertake, came entreating and saying, 'We beg you, since we could also engage in this service, but be merciful to us and lend us money, so that even in faraway cities engaging in business we might still be able to serve the poor'" (*T. Job* 11.1–3).

129. εἶπεν δὲ αὐτῷ ὁ θεός· ἄφρων, ταύτῃ τῇ νυκτὶ τὴν ψυχήν σου ἀπαιτοῦσιν ἀπὸ σοῦ· ἃ δὲ ἡτοίμασας, τίνι ἔσται, "Then God said to him, 'Fool! This very night your soul is required from you, and the things you have prepared, what is to become of them?'" (Luke 12:20).

130. For all intents and purposes, this is the third "How-is-this-profitable?" question.

131. Jas 4:14. Syr ܠܗܓܐ ("vapor, steam"); Vg *vapor*. Although OG Qohelet tends to translate the *Leitwort* הבל with ματαιότης ("futility, emptiness, meaninglessness, Qoh 1:2 and *passim*), Aquila, Symmachus and Theodotion use the term found here, ἀτμίς ("vapor"; cf. Seow, "Grasp," 1–3).

132. Jas 5:1. McKnight (*James*, 380) thinks that "James uses the language 'rich people' . . . as 'code' for the oppressors of the messianic community," a suggestion well taken as long as it does not ignore or dismiss the wisdom trajectory's overt concern with things socioeconomic.

κλαύσατε ὀλολύζοντες	Weep and wail
ἐπὶ ταῖς ταλαιπωρίαις ὑμῶν ταῖς ἐπερχομέναις	Over the hardships coming your way.[133]
ὁ πλοῦτος ὑμῶν σέσηπεν	Your wealth is rotten,[134]
καὶ τὰ ἱμάτια ὑμῶν σητόβρωτα γέγονεν	Your clothes are moth-eaten.[135]
ὁ χρυσὸς ὑμῶν καὶ ὁ ἄργυρος κατίωται	Your gold and silver is corroded,
καὶ ὁ ἰὸς αὐτῶν εἰς μαρτύριον ὑμῖν ἔσται	And their poison testifies against you,[136]
καὶ φάγεται τὰς σάρκας ὑμῶν ὡς πῦρ	Devouring your flesh like fire.
ἐθησαυρίσατε ἐν ἐσχάταις ἡμέραις	You are laying up "treasure" for the last days.[137]

In his Emory dissertation Wesley Hiram Wachob calls the Letter of James "a deliberative discourse in the guise of a letter using the sayings of Jesus to persuade an audience to think and act in ways that have significant social consequences."[138] Prominent among these "consequences" is the dreadful fate he sees awaiting those "brothers"[139] who refuse to renounce their ingrained socioeconomic prejudices, even as they go on pretending to participate in communities allegedly devoted to upholding the "royal

133. Jas 5:1. Cf. "Woe unto you rich, for you have put your trust in your wealth . . . for during your affluence you practiced oppression" (1 En 94.8–9). "Woe unto you who acquire silver and gold by unjust means, who say, 'We have grown rich by accumulating all these goods, so now we can do whatever we like'" (1 En 97.8–9).

134. Jas 5:2 (σήπω, lit., "rotting"). Pitching his dream of conquering Troy to a council of intransigent Greeks, Agamemnon laments that their procrastination is causing many of their "ships' timbers . . . to rot" (δοῦρα σέσηπε νεῶν, *Il.*, 2.135).

135. Jas 5:2. N.B. that Job laments the fact that *his* clothes have become "moth-eaten" (Job 13:28).

136. Jas 5:3. Gold and silver can "rust" (Crane, *Gold*, 493), but when the epistle earlier uses ἰὸς ("poison, rust") to describe the ἰὸς saturating the tongue as "deadly" (θανατηφόρου, 3:8), most likely the term here also refers to "poison."

137. Jas 5:3.

138. Wachob, *Voice*, 22–23. Achtemeier et al. (*Introducing*, 503) similarly conclude that "the epistle of James represents the application of Jesus' messianic interpretation of the law."

139. Whereas Paul addresses his readers as "children" (e.g., Gal 4:19), James prefers the term "brothers" (e.g., Jas 5:19).

law."[140] Whether or not James extends the promise of "repentance" to these "brothers,"[141] or whether this epistle is applicable to any institution other than the Christian church,[142] the fact remains that for James, greed and oppression are just as lethal as adultery or deception or murder.[143] In Dan McCartney's opinion, in fact, James argues that "if someone who professes faith in Christ is participating in corporate greed or self-indulgent consumerism . . . , then the genuineness of that person's faith surely is called into question."[144] This catholic epistle may not yet indicate it fully, but "Christian reformulation" of the "practice of wealth and poverty," in Helen Rhee's opinion, soon becomes "indispensable for shaping Christian self-definitions *vis-à-vis* the Greco-Roman and Jewish worlds."[145]

Summary

GNT focuses less on socioeconomic questions than 4QInstruction or Sirach, yet Luke's Sermon on the Plain and the Letter of James provide two clear examples of (a) the fleshing out of socioeconomic concerns first introduced in ANE and Tanak sapiential texts, and (b) the condemnation of any and all "Christians" who would hypocritically oppress the poor. Whereas the Sermon on the Plain champions the giving of alms and the lending of money apart from the expectation of compensation, the Letter of James testifies to how "one's relationship to money" can be, in Mariam Kamell's estimation, a reliable "litmus text" for determining the true disposition of "one's relationship to God."[146]

140. Among many others, Jackson-McCabe (*Logos*, 153) sees the phrase "royal law" in Jas 2:8 applying to *all* of Torah, not just the "love your neighbor" edict in Lev 19:18.

141. Maynard-Reid (*James*, 81) argues that nothing in James is designed to lead the rich to "repentance" because, in his view, the wealthy "are no more part of the listening congregation than the nations and peoples addressed in Isa 34:1."

142. McCartney, *James*, 74.

143. Jas 4:2, 4.

144. McCartney, *James*, 74.

145. Rhee, *Wealth*, xiii.

146. Kamell, "Economics," 157.

6

Summary and Conclusions

May he defend the poor, deliver the needy,
and crush the oppressor.[1]

Textual Observations

Sometimes a Greek, Syriac, Aramaic, or Latin translator misunderstands a Hebrew phrase,[2] or the wording of the translation betrays the existence of a social, historical, political, or ideological filter.[3] To such common possibilities must now be added another because, as the pages above clearly show, ancient translators sometimes react to a socioeconomic text not so much by *translating* it as by *targeting* it to a specific socioeconomic concern.[4] For example:

Prov 1:13

MT reads נמלא בתינו שלל ("fill our houses with plunder"), but Syr (ܙܝܬܐ) and Tg (זיתא) do not so much translate this text as use it to target a particular *type* of "plunder," in this case "olives"; i.e., "fill our houses with olives." Perhaps this is because there is a preoccupation here with an immediate need, perhaps a requisition for produce stockpiled in, say, a government

1. Ps 72:4.

2. Cf. Tov ("Syriac," 85–86). Occasionally Qur'an adopts the same basic take on a biblical text as one of the vss (cf. examples cited in Hossein et al., *Economics*).

3. McCarter (*Criticism*, 26–38) and Tov ("'Alterations,'" 1–20) discuss the most common "filters."

4. All of the following texts are cited, translated, and discussed above, and are worthy of much deeper analysis than can be provided here.

warehouse[5] or village granary like those mentioned in the Babylonian and Hittite texts.[6]

Prov 3:9

MT reads כבד את־יהוה מהונך ("treasure Yhwh more than your wealth"), but instead of a generic word for "wealth" (e.g. πλοῦτος), OG reads δικαίων πόνων ("righteous labors"). Syr reads ܥܢܝܢ ("business"),[7] and Vg *substantia* ("substance"). Alongside this varied list of options Tg reads ממון, "*mammon*," an Aramaic term often tainted with negative connotations in the Second Temple period.[8] Whether MT is intentionally vague or the versions intentionally specific (or both), Tg's choice echoes that of other translators; e.g., פרח in Isa 5:24 ("blossom") becomes ממון ("mammon"); צו in Hos 5:11 ("vanity") becomes שקר ממון ("deceptive mammon"); and Sir 7:18 אל תמיר אוהב במחיר ("Do not trade a loved one for money") becomes ܠܐ ܬܫܠܦ ܪܚܡܐ ܒܡܡܘܢܐ ("Do not barter a friend for *mammon*").[9] Rainer Kessler believes that texts like these force translators (ancient and modern) to wrestle with specific questions, like whether or not the "poor" in a given context are socioeconomically or spiritually "poor."[10]

5. Clermont-Ganneau ("Note," 204–9) suggests that the *lmlk* seals from Iron Age Judah (cf. Welten, *Stempel*) are (a) all that remains of governmentally-stamped clay pots designed to store wine, oil, and/or grain, and (b) likely represent taxes in kind payed to royal storehouses at Socoh, Hebron, Ziph and *mmšt* (cf. Moore, "Judah," 18).

6. Cf. above discussion on *CH* §113; *KUB* 13.9+40.62.3–10; and *KBo* 16.24+16.25.1.41–45.

7. Cf. the discussion above on Heb ענין ("business") in Qoh 2:26; 5:13. Based on Aram עינין (*CAP* 26.22) and Syr ܥܢܝܢ ("business, toil," *PSD* 420), Wagner (*Aramäismen*, 222) identifies this Heb term as an Aramaic loanword.

8. Rather than translate, Luke 16:9, 13 transliterates ממון (μαμωνᾶς), thereby prompting Hauck ("μαμωνᾶς," 389) to suggest that "the community does not render ממון by a Gk word (e.g., οὐσία)" because of its "untranslatable ethical and religious nuance." Krämer (*Rätsel*, 234) suggests that the "Parable of the Prudent Manager" invites disciples either (a) to distribute their worldly goods before deciding to follow the Nazarene, or (b) to avoid contact with ממון altogether (cf. Moore, *WealthWatch*, 219–20).

9. As is well known, ממון does not appear in Tanak, yet the first two words in Sanhedrin read ממונות דיני ("Now in cases involving *mammon*," *m. Sanh.* 1.1), and the covenanters at Qumran are warned that והאי[ש א]ש[ר (יש)קר בממון והוא יודע וה[בדילוהו] מן הטהרה ("the one who knowingly lies about *mammon* will be excluded from the pure food," CD 14.20).

10. Kessler, *Statt*, 22. Distinguishing between these two types of "poverty" can be difficult to ascertain, but Hoppe's attempt (*Poverty*, 72, 75, 171) simply to choose one instead of the other seems more reactionary than judicious.

Prov 3:14

MT reads כי טוב סחרה מסחר כס ומחרוץ תבואתה ("for trading with her is better than trading with silver or the revenue generated by refined gold"), but Tg is (again) socioeconomically specific: מטול דטבא תגרותה מן תגרותא דסמא ומן דהבא סנינא עללתה ("for business with her is preferable to the discovery of treasure-chests or warehouses of refined gold").[11]

Prov 5:9

MT reads פן תתן לאחרים הודך ושנותיך לאכזרי ("lest she hand your wealth over to others and your years to the ruthless"). OG reads ζωήν σου καὶ σὸν βίον ἀνελεήμοσιν ("your life and its merciless existence"); Syr ܫܢܝܟ ܠܐܠܗܐ ܠܐ ܡܪܚܡܢܐ ("your years to unmerciful gods"); and Tg לנוכראין ("to foreigners"). Syr and Tg are more specific than MT, and OG may be reading a Heb text different from MT,[12] but all seem committed to bleaching out the socioeconomic component in this saying.[13]

Prov 11:15

MT reads רע ירוע כי ערב זר, "Anyone securing loans for strangers courts trouble," but Syr omits all reference to the practice of moneylending: ܒܝܫܐ ܡܒܐܫ ܡܐ ܕܐܙܠ ܠܒܥܠܕܒܒܐ ܥܡ ܙܕܝܩܐ ܕܨܒܐ ܕܢܬܚܙܐ ܠܡܣܟܢܐ ("Quite evil is it when an adversary fights with a righteous person because he wants to portray himself as poor").[14] Vg comes closest to MT: *adfligetur malo qui fidem facit pro extraneo qui autem cavet laqueos securus erit* ("Those who put their faith in others by guaranteeing them loans put themselves in danger by wrapping

11. Cf. Snell ("Proverbs," 72–74).

12. Following painstaking comparative work on the biblical text-fragments found in Cave 4, Cross ("Evolution," 309–15) concludes that there are three "local text-types" contributing to the preservation of Tanak: Babylonian, Alexandrian, and Palestinian.

13. OG Zech 4:14 goes in the opposite direction, unequivocally describing Joshua and Zerubbabel as "sons of prosperity" (υἱοὶ τῆς πιότητος) whereas MT merely calls them "anointed ones" (בני היצהר, lit. "sons of oil"). As Ahearne-Kroll points out ("Portrayal," 188), the usual OG translation for יצהר is the same as that for שמן (ἔλαιον, "oil"), but like Sym, OG here translates πιότης, a term pregnant with socioeconomic meaning. Why? Evidently because OG wants to emphasize that these "sons" are not so much "anointed ones" as "promoted by divine approval to assist in God's restoration of the temple and establishment of security in the land."

14. Omission is just as significant as commission when assessing the socioeconomic inclinations of a translation.

a noose around their neck"), but OG πονηρὸς κακοποιεῖ ὅταν συμμείξῃ δικαίῳ ("An evil person does evil when he confuses the righteous person")[15] attempts either (a) to convey the basic underlying meaning of MT, or (b) bleach out (with Syr) the text's socioeconomic component.[16]

Sir 5:1

The Hebrew text reads יש לאל ידי (lit., "there is to God my hand"), an idiomatic expression like the many others built around the common term יד ("hand, power").[17] OG reads αὐτάρκη μοί ἐστιν ("I am self-sufficient"), but more overtly socioeconomic are the translations of Syr ܪܘܚܐ ܐܝܬ ܠܝ ("abundance is mine") and Vg *est mihi sufficiens vita nihil enim proderit in tempore vindictae et obductionis* ("life is sufficient for me without making a profit in times of vengeance and darkness"). Each takes a stab at the idiom, but Vg evidently cannot resist the urge to use this verse to condemn the pursuit of "profit" *per se*.[18]

Sir 13:3

The Hebrew text reads עשיר יענה הוא יתנוה, "frequently the rich are oppressive," but the versions raise the moral temperature, OG reading πλούσιος ἠδίκησεν καὶ αὐτὸς προσενεβριμήσατο ("the rich do wrong and threaten"), Syr reading ܥܬܝܪܐ ܚܛܐ ܫܠܐ ܘܡܬܒܣܪܐ ("the rich sin and it is disregarded"), and Vg reading *dives iniuste egit et fremebit* ("the rich are unjust and angry").[19]

Many more examples may be cited, but suffice it to say with Emmanuel Tov that each textual version operates in the shade of its own "umbrella"—philological, historical, political, ideological—just to name a few

15. Banerjee and Duflo (*Economics*, 268) observe that poor people are the most vulnerable segment of society to thefts and scams because they "often lack critical pieces of information and believe things that are not true."

16. Maloney ("Usury," 20) observes (a) that the maximum interest for OB loans is twenty percent for money and thirty-three percent for grain; (b) that the temples are the most common creditors; and (c) that in Assyria the normal rate of interest is twenty-five percent for money and as high as fifty percent for grain.

17. E.g., *yd.il* ("hand of El," *CAT* 1.23.33). Cf. Isa 57:8; Roberts ("Hand," 244–51).

18. Ambrose of Milan condemns "profit" because "avarice generally dulls people's senses and pervert judgments, so that they think of profit as piety and money as the reward of prudence" (Letter to Bishop Constantius, cited in Rhee, *Christianity*, 113).

19. Cf. Rhee, *Christianity*, xvii–xxii.

of the most obvious.[20] The point here is simply to recognize that alongside these umbrellas stands a *socioeconomic* "umbrella" midrashically pressuring translators as much as any other.[21] In short, the fact that translators often feel driven to specify a particular socioeconomic concern in their translations is significant, even when it is unclear (a) what that concern might be or (b) from what source it might ultimately derive.

Socioeconomic Motif Trajectories

Like the versions, the motifs identified above stand in the shadow of several types of "umbrellas." The following chart freely classifies them according to source and type:

	Poverty	Wealth	Property	Trade	Debt	Labor	Fraud	Giving	Inheritance
IŠ		success wealth supplies				labor			
CH				trade	debt dowry bridewealth	labor slavery			inheritance
Lud		productivity wealth							
BT	poverty	prosperity			taxation		banditry		
ŠH		abundance capital	property	trade profits	taxation		fraud		inheritance
DP		loans		investment			consumerism	sacrifice	
AT	poverty		property land	redemption compensation		labor oppression slavery	bribery theft	giving	
TD	poverty begging scarcity	treasure productivity mammon loans wealth prosperity supplies luxury	land property	trade profits interest compensation reward enterprise redemption business	pledge tribute withholding debt creditor debtor taxation	oppression labor laziness diligence negligence slavery workaholism lethargy proficiency skill	theft corruption banditry greed bribery hedonism addiction hoarding materialism	giving generosity almsgiving	legacy inheritance
TP	widows orphans	fertility		compensation wagering					
4QI	"the poor"	assets			debt-slavery loan guarantees pledge debtor creditor				inheritance
WBS	gleaning	wicked wealth blameless wealth		compensation trade profit		labor slavery vs. service	fraud exploitation	gifts tithes generosity	firstborn birthright bequest
WS	scarcity hucksterism	wherewithal first fruits	property	merchant					
GNT	begging	credit profit		compensation		labor	fraud	almsgiving giving	

As this chart indicates, the socioeconomic motifs identified above readily fall into several broad categories: *poverty, wealth, property, trade, debt, labor, fraud, giving*, and *inheritance*. None of these motifs appear in every

20. Tov, "'Alterations,'" 1–20.

21. Tov (*Criticism*, 128–33) lists several "midrashic tendencies," but nothing socioeconomic in nature.

surveyed source, yet each makes a vital contribution to the development of the Judeo-Christian wisdom tradition.

Poverty

From the sources surveyed above Lud implicitly alludes to poverty in the complaints of the "pious sufferer,"[22] but it is not until BT that the poverty motif becomes explicit.[23] In Anatolia, however, the evidence is forthright and compelling, particularly in the royal edict of the young prince chiding his lieutenants for oppressing the poor and camouflaging it.[24] "Poverty," "begging," and "scarcity" find frequent mention in TD, and TP shows a "gentleman" (Job) defending his benevolence toward widows and orphans. The Aramaic sage Aḥiqar posits that "nothing is more bitter than poverty,"[25] but it is not until 4QI that a Hebrew sage addresses the question of poverty *from the perspective of the poor themselves.* Except for 4QI and GNT,[26] this ANE trajectory discusses disenfranchisement solely from the perspective of the enfranchised.[27]

Wealth

One of the oldest socioeconomic motifs in ANE wisdom, *wealth* is something in which ANE sages take interest as early as the third millennium in IŠ. Afterwards it recurs in Lud, BT, ŠH, and DP, but in TD it branches out considerably, birthing various offshoot-motifs like "treasure," "prosperity," and "productivity." 4QI focuses on the "poverty" side of the poverty-wealth polarity, but not so that the latter might simply be ignored. What WBS does with "wealth" is similar to what covenanters do with the "two spirits" treatise in the Scroll of the Rule from Qumran Cave 1.[28] Just as the "two spirits" treatise reflects the dualistic mindset beginning to shape Second Temple thinking,[29] so WBS finds it helpful, if not necessary to explain *wealth* to its

22. Cf. *er-ru-ub é-uš-šu,* "I will impound his house" (*Lud* 1.62).

23. E.g., cf. *BWL* 72.79: *ku-bu-uk-ku i-te-niš ba-ṭi-il iš-di-ḫu,* "(My) power dwindles, (my) income fades." The earliest ANE sources tend to focus on prosperity instead of poverty.

24. *KBo* 22.1.3′–30′ (cf. above).

25. לא איתי [מ]ריר מן ענות (*Aḥq* 105).

26. Cf. Goff (*4QInstruction*, 23–27); Pilgrim (*Poor*, 39–63).

27. Cf. Levin (*Essays*, 287–300); Armitage (*Poverty*, 157–91).

28. שתי רוחות; cf. 1QS 3.13—4.26 (esp. 3.18; cf. Frey, "Spirit," 401).

29. Cf. 4Q473; *T. Ash.* 3.1–5; *T. Jud.* 20–1–2; Nickelsburg ("Ways," 95–108);

hellenized audience by subdividing the motif into two parts: "wickedness" vs. "blamelessness."[30] In GNT Yeshu`a gravitates to the "credit" and "profit" motifs when challenging students to reimagine their lives in modes beyond the merely mercenary.[31]

Property

ŠH contrasts the behavior of good and bad merchants, warning the latter to change their ways or else "their brothers will not inherit their estates."[32] Whether "estates" refers to land or livestock or both is not clear, but in the texts surveyed above ŠH seems to preserve the earliest explicit reference to the *property* motif. In Anatolia, the theft of a "field" (A.ŠÀ) is serious enough to require compensation, but not as much as, say, murder.[33] Unlike other motifs, *property* does not generate a multitude of synonyms in TD before its fleeting appearance in WS. In short, prophets seem to have a good deal more to say about *property* than sages.[34]

Trade

Of the texts examined above the earliest to engage the *trade* motif is CH, particularly in its laws for reining in dishonest merchants. A few of these laws find reinforcement in ŠH, and the DP "master" flirts with the idea of investment before denying its tenability (because the process of waiting for a profit is similar to that of romancing a spouse; i.e., both take too much time). In Anatolia, several edicts and laws focus on how to deal responsibly with criminals, demanding (a) various levels of compensation for individuals redeemed of their crimes, as well as (b) the survivors forced by these criminals to lose their spot on the socioeconomic ladder. In TD the floodgates open up (again), displaying synonymous socioeconomic motifs like "compensation," "reward," "profits," "enterprise," and "business." TP hosts

Duhaime ("Dualism," 216–17).

30. In other words, Sirach gives considerable attention to the ideological profile of his hellenized Jewish audience (cf. Coggins, *Sirach*, 50–53).

31. Johnson (*Luke*, 109) points out that in contrast to Matthew's use of μισθός ("wage," Matt 5:46), Luke's use of χάρις ("gift," Luke 6:32) is "an added nuance" because it denotes "the 'gift' quality of what Jesus demands"; i.e., he wants them to go *beyond* mere reciprocity into gift-giving."

32. *a-na bīti-šú ul ir-ru-bu šu-nu aḫḫu*^{MEŠ}*-šú* (*BWL* 132.117).

33. *KUB* 13.9+40.62.1.11.

34. Cf. Gottwald ("Class," 5); Gnuse (*Property*, 63); Moore (*WealthWarn*, 200–1).

the complementary motifs of "wagering" and "compensation," the latter of which figuring prominently in both WBS and GNT.

Debt

In the texts surveyed above CH preserves the oldest mention of *debt*-related concerns, referencing it as a vital component of family law, particularly with regard to the socioeconomic conventions of "bridewealth" and "dowry."[35] BT and SH are the first to utilize the "taxation" motif before TD draws greater attention to it alongside "tribute," "pledging," and "withholding." Despite its fragmented state, 4QI details the duties and responsibilities of "debtors," "creditors," "debt-slaves," and "pledgers." In short, *debt* is a persistent socioeconomic issue with which no ANE sage can afford to be unaware.[36]

Labor

Alongside *wealth*, the *labor* motif helps fashion one of the longest ANE wisdom trajectories, appearing as early as the third millennium in IŠ. Early on, Anatolian and Mesopotamian edicts consistently distinguish "labor" from "slavery," and 4QI parallels this distinction with injunctions to the מבין to differentiate between "slavery" and "service."[37] As expected, TD fleshes out this motif to include a number of corollary sayings about "negligence," "laziness," "diligence," "lethargy," "proficiency," "skill," "oppression," even "workaholism." GNT's attention to *labor* is thus nothing new, even in James' message of hope to oppressed "laborers."[38]

Fraud

The "sufferer/sceptic's" threat at the end of BT with regard to a life of "banditry" is one of the earliest ANE references to *fraud* in the texts above, and DP follows this by attending to *fraud* and ŠH attends to it with warnings against rank "consumerism."[39] AT engages the problems of "bribery" and

35. Cf. Goody and Tambiah (*Bridewealth*, 14); Westbrook (*Marriage*, 24–25); Lemos (*Marriage*, 1–19); Moore (*WealthWarn*, 47–51).

36. Cf. Finkelstein ("*Misharum*," 233–46); Chirichigno (*Debt-Slavery*, 97–100); Frymer-Kensky ("Israel," 251–64).

37. 4Q416.2.2.15–16.

38. Jas 5:1–5 (cf. Collins, *Wages*, 243–62).

39. Cf. also Zophar's speech in TP (Job 20:21). Stearns (*Consumerism*, 15) begins

"theft," but things really heat up in TD, with its numerous sayings about "theft," "corruption," "banditry," "greed," "bribery," "hedonism," "addiction," "hoarding," and "consumerism." WBS recognizes the link between "fraud" and "exploitation," but GNT more explicitly incorporates the motif in James' condemnation of wealthy employers defrauding their employees.[40]

Giving

With the brief exception of DP[41] and AT,[42] the motif of *(alms)giving* enters the ANE sapiential trajectory with repeated references to "(alms)giving" and "generosity" in TD,[43] followed by several attempts in WBS to refocus the "stinginess-generosity" polarity along quasi-dualistic lines,[44] followed by Yeshu`a's teachings in GNT to give (and lend!) without expecting any sort of compensation.[45]

Inheritance

The oldest mention of the *inheritance* motif occurs in CH, a second millennium lawcode which dares to judge heirs by their behavior as much as their biology.[46] In ŠH, on the other hand, the merchant who fraudulently manipulates the scales and cheats poor debtors eventually makes it impossible for his biological heir to inherit anything from the family estate.[47] As with the *property* motif, TD's interest in *inheritance* is relatively meager, but 4QI displays a vigorous interest by utilizing the term נחלה ("inheritance") no

---

his history of consumerism with 18th century Europe, but one does not need to look too far in the ANE texts to realize the shallowness of this approach (cf. Moore, *Wealth-Watch*, 21–22).

40. Jas 5:4 (cf. Collins, *Wages*, 243–62).

41. *BWL* 146.55.

42. Cf. the edict in *KUB* 13.4.2.41″–42″ where gifts to the king are distinguished from bribes by making them subject to strict governmental controls.

43. Cf. Ps 112:3, translating צדקה as "almsgiving/charity," as in 4Q200.2.6–9 (Tob 4:7–8); Prov 11:24; 31:20.

44. Cf. Sir 3:30; Sir 4:3 (OG); 4:31; 14:5 (cf. Bradley, *Generosity*).

45. Cf. Luke 6:30, 35, 38.

46. E.g., *šumma awīlum ana mārišu nasāḫim panam ištakan ana dayāni māri anassaḫ iqtabi dayānū warkassu iparrasūma*, "If a gentleman decides to disown his son, and states before the judges, 'I disown my son,' the judges shall make a decision about his estate" (*CH* 28.16).

47. *BWL* 132.116 reads *makkur-šú ul i-be-el* IBILA-*šú*, "his heir will assume no control over his property."

less than thirty times, and WBS suggests that the decision to help poverty-stricken neighbors easily leads to situations in which "you might share in their inheritance."[48]

Final Remarks

Since the sages of the ancient Near East tend to be ambivalent about anything having to do with "wealth," simplistic approaches championing one extreme over another tend to be highly problematic. The hypothesis "wealth-is-a-sign-of-divine-favor" represents a worldview just as extremist as "all-rich-people-are-oppressors" or "all-poor-people-are-righteous." If the present study says anything, it is that false polarities like these are too simplistic to be taken seriously even though they embarrassingly define the thinking of many businesspeople, politicians, and televangelists. Poverty and wealth are not so neatly segregated into opposing "camps." The sages responsible for preserving these ancient instructions can help anyone learn how to live "successfully," yet resisting the desire to cut corners in our understanding of them never comes easy, especially for incredibly privileged readers living in the wealthiest economy in history.

48. ἵνα ἐν τῇ κληρονομίᾳ αὐτοῦ συγκληρονομήσῃς (Sir 22:23).

Bibliography

Achtemeier, Paul J., et al. *Introducing the New Testament: Its Literature and Theology*. Grand Rapids: Eerdmans, 2001.

Adams, Dwayne. *The Sinner in Luke*. ETSMS. Eugene: Pickwick, 2008.

Adams, Samuel L. "Rethinking the Relationship between 4QInstruction and Ben Sira." *RevQ* 24 (2010) 555–83.

———. *Wisdom in Transition: Act and Consequence in Second Temple Instructions*. Leiden: Brill, 2008.

Adamson, James B. *The Epistle of James*. NICNT. Grand Rapids: Eerdmans, 1976.

Ahearne-Kroll, Patricia. "LXX/OG Zechariah 1–6 and the Portrayal of Joshua Centuries After the Restoration of the Temple." In *Septuagint Research: Issues and Challenges in the Study of the Greek Jewish Scriptures*, edited by W. Kraus and R. G. Wooden, 179–92. SBLSCS 53. Atlanta: SBL, 2006.

Aiken, Bill. "The Challenge of Unmarried Cohabitation—The New Zealand Response." *FLQ* 37 (2003) 303–25.

Aimers, Geoffrey J. "'Give the Devil His Due': The Satanic Agenda and Social Justice in the Book of Job." *JSOT* 37 (2012) 57–66.

Alaura, Silvia. "Proverbs and Rhetorical Strategies in §7′ of the *Hittite Instructions for Priests and Temple Personnel* (*CTH* 264)." In *Audias Fabulas Veteres: Anatolian Studies in Honor of Jana Součková-Siegelová*, edited by Šarká Velhartická, 1–16. CHANE 79. Leiden: Brill, 2016.

Albertz, Rainer. "*Ludlul bēl nēmeqi*—eine Lehrdichtung zur Ausbreitung und Vertiefung der persönlichen Mardukfrömmigkeit." In *Ad ben et fideliter seminandum: Festgabe for Karlheinz Deller*, edited by G. Mauer and U. Magen, 25–53. AOAT 220. Neukirchen-Vluyn: Neukirchener, 1988.

———. "Der sozialgeschichtliche Hintergrund des Hiobbuches und der 'Babylonischen Theodizee.'" In *Die Botschaft und die Boten. Festschrift für Hans Walter Wolff*, edited by J. Jeremias and L. Perlitt, 349–72. Neukirchen-Vluyn: Neukirchener, 1981.

Albright, William F. "The Mouth of the Rivers." *AJSL* 35 (1919) 161–95.

Alcoff, Linda Martin. *Visible Identities: Race, Gender, and the Self*. Oxford: Oxford University Press, 2006.

Allen, James P. *The Debate Between a Man and His Soul: A Masterpiece of Ancient Egyptian Literature*. CHANE 44. Leiden: Brill, 2011.

Allison, Dale C., Jr. *A Critical and Exegetical Commentary on the Epistle of James*. ICC. New York: Bloomsbury, 2013.

Al-Rawi, Farouk N. H., and Andrew F. George. "Tablets from the Sippar Library III. Two Royal Counterfeits." *Iraq* 56 (1994) 135–48.

Alster, Bendt. "Early Dynastic Proverbs and Other Contributions to the Study of Literary Texts from Abū Ṣalābīkh." *AfO* 38 (1993) 1–45.

———. *Proverbs of Ancient Sumer*. Bethesda: CDL, 2005.

———. *Wisdom of Ancient Sumer*. Bethesda: CDL, 2005.

Alster, Bendt, and H. L. J. Vanstiphout. "Lahar and Ashnan: Presentation and Analysis of a Sumerian Debate Poem." *AcSum* 9 (1987) 1–43.

Alster, Bendt, and Takayoshi Oshima. "A Sumerian Proverb Tablet with Some Thoughts on Sumerian Proverb Collections." *Or* 75 (2006) 31–72.

Alter, Robert. *The Art of Biblical Narrative*. New York: Basic, 1980.

———. *The Wisdom Books: Job, Proverbs, and Ecclesiastes (A Translation with Commentary)*. New York: Norton, 2010.

Andersen, Francis I. *Job*. TOTC. Downers Grove: InterVarsity, 1976.

Anderson, Gary A. *Charity: The Place of the Poor in the Biblical Tradition*. New Haven: Yale University Press, 2013.

Andreau, Jean. *Banking and Business in the Roman World*. Translated by J. Lloyd. KTAH. Cambridge: Cambridge University Press, 1999.

Annus, Amar, and Alan Lenzi. *Ludlul bēl nēmeqi: The Standard Babylonian Poem of the Righteous Sufferer*. SAACT 7. Helsinki: The Neo-Assyrian Text Corpus Project, 2010.

Ansberry, Christopher B. *Be Wise, My Son, and Make My Heart Glad: An Exploration of the Courtly Nature of the Book of Proverbs*. BZAW 422. Berlin: de Gruyter, 2010.

Aphergis, Gerassimos George. *The Seleukid Royal Economy: The Finances and Financial Administration of the Seleukid Empire*. Cambridge: Cambridge University Press, 2004.

Archi, Alfonso. "L'humanité des Hittites." In *Florilegium Anatolicum. Mélanges offerts à Emmanuel Laroche*, edited by E. Akurgal et al., 37–48. Paris: Boccard, 1979.

Argall, Randal A. *1 Enoch and Sirach: A Literary Comparative and Conceptual Analysis of the Themes of Revelation, Creation, and Judgment*. SBLEJL 8. Atlanta: Scholars, 1995.

Armitage, David J. *Theories of Poverty in the World of the New Testament*. WUNT 423. Tübingen: Mohr Siebeck, 2016.

Asencio, Victor Morla. *Libro de Job: Récondito Armonía*. San Bernadino: Editorio Verbal Divino, 2017.

———. "Poverty and Wealth: Ben Sira's View of Possessions." In *Der Einzelne und seine Gemeinschaft bei Ben-Sira*, edited by R. Egger-Wenzel and I. Krammer, 151–78. BZAW 270. Berlin: de Gruyter, 1998.

Askari, Hossein, et al. *Introduction to Islamic Economics: Theory and Application*. Hoboken: Wiley and Sons, 2015.

Assmann, Jan. *Ma'at: Gerechtigkeit und Unsterblichkeit im alten Ägypt*. Munich: Beck, 1990.

———. *The Mind of Egypt: History and Meaning in the Time of the Pharaohs*. Translated by A. Jenkins. Cambridge: Harvard University Press, 2002.

———. *The Search for God in Ancient Egypt*. Translated by D. Lorton. Ithaca: Cornell University Press, 2001.

Atkinson, Kenneth. "The Identification of the 'Wicked Priest' Reconsidered: the Case for Hyrcanus II. In *Sybils, Scriptures and Scrolls: John Collins at Seventy*, edited by J. Baden et al., 68–83. Leiden: Brill, 2017.

Atkinson, Tyler. "Overcoming Competition through Kairological Enjoyment: The Implications of Qohelet's Theology of Time for the Ethics of Work." *SCE* 26 (2013) 395–409.

Audet, J. P. "Origines comparées de la double tradition de la loi et de la Sagesse dans le Proche-Orient ancien." *International Congress of Orientalists* 1 (1964) 352–57.

Baarda, Tjitze. "'Blessed Are the Poor . . .': Concerning the Provenance of Logion 54 in 'Thomas.'" *ARC* 33 (2005) 32–51.

Baasland, Ernst. "Der Jakobusbrief als neutestamentliche Weisheitschrift." *ST* 36 (1982) 119–39.

Bailey, Clinton. *Bedouin Culture in the Bible*. New Haven: Yale University Press, 2018.

Bales, Kevin. *Disposable People: New Slavery in the Global Economy*. Berkeley: University of California Press, 2004.

Balentine, Samuel E. *Have You Considered My Servant Job? Understanding the Biblical Archetype of Patience*. SPOT. Columbia: University of South Carolina Press, 2015.

———. *Prayer in the Hebrew Bible: The Drama of Divine-Human Dialogue*. OBT. Minneapolis: Fortress, 1993.

Balla, Ibolya. *Ben Sira on Family, Gender, and Sexuality*. DCLS 8. Berlin: de Gruyter, 2011.

———. "The Relationship Between Husband and Wife According to Sirach 25–26, 36." In *Family and Kinship in the Deuterocanonical and Cognate Literature*, edited by A. Passaro, 107–26. Berlin: de Gruyter, 2013.

Bammel, Ernst. "πτωχός." In *TDNT* 6.885–915.

Banerjee, Abhijit V., and Esther Duflo. *Poor Economics: A Radical Rethinking of the Way to Fight Global Poverty*. New York: PublicAffairs, 2011.

Barbalet, Jack M. "Power and Resistance." *BJSoc* 4 (1985) 531–48.

Barclay, John M. G. *Jews in the Mediterranean Diaspora: From Alexander to Trajan (323 BCE- 117 CE)*. Berkeley: University of California Press, 1996.

Barré, Michael L. "'Fear of God' and the World View of Wisdom." *BTB* 11 (1981) 41–43.

———. "Treaties in the Ancient Near East." In *ABD* 6.653–56.

Bartholomew, Craig G. *Ecclesiastes*. Grand Rapids: Baker Academic, 2009.

Bartholomew, Craig G., and Ryan P. O'Dowd. "Jesus, the Wisdom of God." In *Old Testament Wisdom Literature: A Theological Introduction*, 231–60. Downers Grove: InterVarsity, 2011.

Barton, Stephen C. "Money Matters: Economic Relations and the Transformation of Value in Early Christianity." In *Engaging Economics: New Testament Scenarios and Early Christian Reception*, edited by B. Longenecker and K. Liebegood, 37–59. Grand Rapids: Eerdmans, 2009.

Barnes, William H. *1–2 Kings*. CBC 4b. Carol Stream: Tyndale, 2012.

Batten, Alicia J. "The Degraded Poor and the Greedy Rich: Exploring the Language of Poverty and Wealth in James." In *The Social Sciences and Biblical Translation*, edited by D. Neufeld, 65–77. Atlanta: SBL, 2008.

Bauckham, Richard. *James: Wisdom of James, Disciple of Jesus the Sage*. NTR. London: Routledge, 1999.

Beal, Richard H. "The ^{GIŠ}TUKUL-Institution in Second Millenium Ḫatti." *AoF* 15 (1988) 269–305.

Beaulieu, Paul-Alain. "The Social and Intellectual Setting of Babylonian Wisdom Literature." In *Wisdom Literature in Mesopotamia and Israel*, edited by R. J. Clifford, 3–19. SBLSS 36. Atlanta: SBL, 2007.

Beckert, Jens. *Inherited Wealth*. Translated by T. Dunlap. Princeton: Princeton University Press, 2008.

Beckman, Gary M. "The Hittite Assembly." *JAOS* 102 (1982) 435–42.

———. "Hittite Literature." In *From an Antique Land: An Introduction to Ancient Near Eastern Literature*, edited by C. Freilich, 215–54. Lanham: Rowman & Littlefield, 2009.

———. "Hittite Proverbs." In *COS* 1.215.

———. "The Old Woman: Female Wisdom as a Resource and a Threat in Hittite Anatolia." In *Audias Fabulas Veteres: Anatolian Studies in Honor of Jana Součková-Siegelová*, edited by Šarká Velhartická, 48–57. CHANE 79. Leiden: Brill, 2016.

Beentjes, Pancratius C. *The Book of Ben Sira in Hebrew*. VTSup 68. Leiden: Brill, 2006.

———. "'Full Wisdom is from the Lord': Sir 1:1–10 and Its Place in Israel's Wisdom Literature." In *The Wisdom of Ben Sira: Studies on Tradition, Redaction, and Theology*, edited by A. Passaro and G. Bellia, 139–54. DCLS 1. Berlin: de Gruyter, 2008.

———. "'Sei den Waisen wie ein Vater und die Witwen wei en Gatte.' Ein kleiner Kommentar zu Ben-Sira 4,1–10." In *Der Einzelne und seiner Gemenschaft bei Ben Sira*, edited by R. Egger-Wenzel and I. Krammer, 51–64. BZAW 270. Berlin: de Gruyter, 1998.

Beinhocker, Eric D. *The Origin of Wealth: Evolution, Complexity, and the Radical Remaking of Economics*. Cambridge: Harvard Business School, 2006.

Bellah, Robert N., et al. *Habits of the Heart: Individualism and Commitment in American Life*. Berkeley: University of California Press, 1985.

Ben Zvi, Ehud. "The 'Successful, Wise, Worthy Wife' of Prov 31:10–31 as a Source for Reconstructing Aspects of Thought and Economy in the Late Persian/Early Hellenistic Period." In *The Economy of Ancient Judah in its Historical Context*, edited by M. L. Miller et al., 27–49. Winona Lake: Eisenbrauns, 2015.

Berges, Ulrich. "Die Knechte im Psalter. Ein Beitrag zu seiner Kompositionsgeschichte." *Bib* 81 (2000) 153–78.

Berjak, Rafik. "*Hulul*." In *QE* 276–77.

Berquist, Jon. "Resistance and Accomodation in the Persian Empire." In *In the Shadow of Empire: Reclaiming the Bible as a History of Faithful Resistance*, edited by R. Horsley, 41–58. Louisville Westminster John Knox, 2008.

Berry, Donald K. "Agur." In *ABD* 1.100.

Betz, Hans Dieter. *The Sermon on the Mount: A Commentary on the Sermon on the Mount, Including the Sermon on the Plain (Matt 5:3–7:27 and Luke 6:20–49)*. Minneapolis: Fortress, 1995.

Biggs, Robert D. "The Instructions of Shuruppak." In *ANET* 594–96.

Black, Jeremy, et al. *The Literature of Ancient Sumer*. Oxford: Oxford University Press, 2004.

Bland, Dave. *Proverbs and the Formation of Character*. Eugene: Cascade, 2015.

———. *Proverbs, Ecclesiastes and Song of Songs*. CPNIV. Joplin: College, 2002.

Bland, Richard Murray. "The Arabic Commentary of Yephet ben Ali on the Book of Ecclesiastes." PhD diss., University of California, 1966.

Bledsoe, Seth. "Can *Aḥiqar* Tell Us Anything About Personified Wisdom?" *JBL* 132 (2013) 119–37.

Blenkinsopp, Joseph. *Sage, Priest, Prophet: Religious and Intellectual Leadership in Ancient Israel*. Louisville: Westminster John Knox, 1995.

———. "The Social Context of the 'Outsider Woman' in Proverbs 1–9." *BI* 42 (1991) 457–73.

———. *Wisdom and Law in the Old Testament: The Ordering of Life in Israel and Early Judaism*. Oxford: Oxford University, 1983.

Blomberg, Craig L. *Neither Poverty nor Riches: A Biblical Theology of Possessions*. NSBT. Downers Grove: InterVarsity, 1999.

Boadt, Lawrence E. "Proverbs." In *The Collegeville Bible Commentary: Old Testament*, edited by D. Bergant, 644–74. Collegeville: Liturgical, 1992.

Boccaccini, Gabriele. *Roots of Rabbinic Judaism: An Intellectual History, from Ezekiel to Daniel*. Grand Rapids: Eerdmans, 2002.

Boda, Mark J., et al. *Riddles and Revelations: Explorations into the Relationship Between Wisdom and Prophecy in the Hebrew Bible*. LHBOTS 634. London: T&T Clark, 2018.

Bodi, Daniel. "The Aramaic Proverbs of Aḥiqar and Some Akkadian and Hebrew Parallels." *Aliento* 2 (2011) 13–25.

Boer, Roland. *Criticism of Heaven: On Marxism and Theology*. Leiden: Brill, 2007.

———. *Marxist Criticism of the Hebrew Bible*. London: T&T Clark, 2015.

Böhl, Franz Marius Theodor de Liagre. "Die Religion der Babylonier un Assyrier." In *Christus und die Religionen der Erde 2*, edited by F. König, 441–98. Vienna: Herder, 1951.

Bonhoeffer, Dietrich. *Discipleship*. Minneapolis: Fortress, 2015.

Borger, Rykle. "Die Weihe eines Enlil-Priesters." *BO* 30 (1973) 163–76.

Boring, M. Eugene. "The Historical-Critical Method's 'Criteria of Authenticity': The Beatitudes in Q and Thomas as a Test Case." *Sem* 44 (1988) 9–44.

Bottéro, Jean. "Le 'Dialogue de Pessimiste' et la transcendance." *RTP* 16 (1996) 4–24.

———. *Mesopotamia: Writing, Reasoning, and the Gods*. Translated by Z. Bahraini and M. van de Mieroop. Chicago: University of Chicago Press, 1992.

———. *La plus vieille religion. En Mésopotamie*. FH 82. Paris: Gallimard, 1998.

Boström, Gustav. *Proverbiastudien: Die Weisheit und das fremde Weib*. Lund: Gleerup, 1935.

Botha, Phil J. "'Wealth and Riches Are in His House' (Psa 112:3): Acrostic Wisdom Psalms and the Development of Anti-Materialism." In *The Shape and Shaping of the Book of Psalms: the Current State of Scholarship*, edited by N. deClaissé-Walford, 105–28. AIL 20. Atlanta: SBL, 2014.

Bovon, François. *Evangelischer-Katholischer Kommentar zum Neuen Testament, III.1. Das Evangelium Nach Lukas (Luke 1:1–9:50)*. Zurich: Benziger und Neukirchener, 1989.

Bowler, Kate. *Blessed: A History of the American Prosperity Gospel*. Oxford: Oxford University Press, 2013.

Brainard, Lael, et al. "The Tangled Web: The Poverty-Insecurity Nexus." In *Too Poor for Peace? Global Poverty, Conflict, and Security in the 21st Century*, edited by L. Brainard and D. Chollet, 1–30. Washington: Brookings Institution, 2007.

Brake, Elizabeth. *Minimizing Marriage: Marriage, Morality, and the Law*. Oxford: Oxford University Press, 2012.

Breck, John. *The Shape of Biblical Language: Chiasmus in the Scriptures and Beyond.* Crestwood: St. Vladimir's Seminary, 1994.

Bredenhof, Reuben. *Failure and Prospect: Lazarus and the Rich Man (Luke 16:19–31) in the Context of Luke-Acts.* LNTS 603. London: T&T Clark, 2019.

Brichto, Herbert Chanan. "Kin, Cult, Land and Afterlife—A Biblical Complex." *HUCA* 44 (1973) 1–54.

Brinkman, J. A. "The Western Asiatic Seals Found at Thebes in Greece." *AfO* 28 (1981) 73–78.

Brodersen, Alma. *The End of the Psalter: Psalms 146–150 in the Masoretic Text, the Dead Sea Scrolls, and the Septuagint.* BZAW 505. Berlin: de Gruyter, 2017.

Broekhoven, Harold C., Jr. "Wisdom and World: The Functions of Wisdom Imagery in Sirach, Pseudo-Solomon and Colossians." PhD diss., Boston University, 1988.

Brown, Jeannine K. "Genre Criticism and the Bible." In *Words and the Word: Explorations in Biblical Interpretation and Literary Theory*, edited by D. Firth and J. Grant, 111–50. Nottingham: Apollos, 2008.

Brown, William P. *Character in Crisis: A Fresh Approach to the Wisdom Literature of the Old Testament.* Grand Rapids: Eerdmans, 1996.

———. *Ecclesiastes.* Interpretation. Louisville: Westminster John Knox, 2011.

Brueggemann, Walter. *Abiding Astonishment: Psalms, Modernity, and the Making of History.* LCBI. Louisville: Westminster John Knox, 1991.

Bryce, Trevor. *Letters of the Great Kings of the Ancient Near East: The Royal Correspondence of the Late Bronze Age.* New York: Routledge, 2003.

———. *Life and Society in the Hittite World.* Oxford: Oxford University Press, 2002.

Buccellati, Giorgio. "Wisdom and Not: The Case of Mesopotamia." *JAOS* 101 (1981) 35–47.

Bulgakov, Sergei. *Philosophy of Economy: The World as Household.* Translated by C. Evtuhov. New Haven: Yale University Press, 2000.

Burkett, Delbert. *The Son of Man Debate: A History and Evaluation.* Cambridge: Cambridge University Press, 2004

Cahana-Blum, Jonathan. "Sophia." In *The Oxford Handbook of New Testament, Gender, and Sexuality*, edited by B. Dunning, 469–84. Oxford: Oxford University Press, 2019

Cammarosano, Michele. *Hittite Local Cults.* WAW 40. Atlanta: SBL, 2018.

Camp, Claudia V. *Wisdom and the Feminine in the Book of Proverbs.* Sheffield: Almond, 1985.

———. *Wise, Strange, and Holy: The Strange Woman and the Making of the Bible.* JSOTSup 320. Sheffield: Sheffield Academic, 2000.

Carlotti, Gino. *Flashbacks: From the Other Side of the Tracks.* New York: Media, 2015.

Carter, Warren. *What Are They Saying About Matthew's Sermon on the Mount?* Mahwah: Paulist, 1994.

Cartledge, Tony W. *Vows in the Hebrew Bible and the Ancient Near East.* JSOTSup 147. Sheffield: Sheffield Academic, 1992.

Ceresko, Anthony R. *Introduction to Old Testament Wisdom: A Spirituality for Liberation.* Maryknoll: Orbis, 1999.

Charlesworth, James H. "The Dead Sea Scrolls and the Historical Jesus." In *Jesus and the Dead Sea Scrolls*, edited by J. Charlesworth, 19–62. New York: Doubleday, 1992.

Charpin, Dominique. *Hammurabi of Babylon*, 2003. London: Tauris and Co., 2012.

———. "I Am the Sun of Babylon": Solar Aspects of Royal Power in Old Babylonian Mesopotamia." *In Cosmos, Politics, and the Ideology of Kingship in Ancient Egypt and Mesopotamia*, edited by J. A. Hill et al., 65–96. Philadelphia: University of Pennsylvania Press, 2013.

———. *Writing, Law, and Kingship in Old Babylonian Mesopotamia*. Translated by J. M. Todd. Chicago: University of Chicago Press, 2010.

Chavalas, Mark W. "Code of Hammurabi." In *HEWS* 1.330–31.

Cheung, Simon Chi-Chung. *Wisdom Intoned: A Reappraisal of the Genre "Wisdom Psalms."* LHBOTS 613. New York: Bloomsbury, 2015.

Chirichigno, Gregory C. *Debt-Slavery in Israel and the Ancient Near East*. JSOTSup 141. Sheffield: Sheffield Academic, 1993.

Christidès, Vassilios. "L'énigme d'Ophir." *RB* 77 (1970) 240–47.

Christianson, Eric S. *A Time to Tell: Narrative Strategies in Ecclesiastes*. JSOTSup 280. Sheffield: Sheffield Academic, 1998.

Civil, Miguel. "Išme-Dagan and Enlil's Chariot." *JAOS* 88 (1967) 3–14.

———. "Notes on the 'Instructions of Šuruppak.'" JNES 4 (1984) 281–98.

Clements, Ronald E. "Proverbs." In *Eerdmans Commentary on the Bible*, edited by J. D. G. Dunn and J. Rogerson, 437–66. Grand Rapids: Eerdmans, 2003.

Clermont-Ganneau, Ch. "Note on the Inscribed Jar-Handle and Weight found at Tell Zakarîya." *PEQ* 31 (1899) 204–9.

Clifford, Richard J. "Introduction." In *Wisdom Literature in Mesopotamia and Israel*, edited by R. J. Clifford, xi–xiii. Atlanta: SBL, 2007.

———. *Proverbs: A Commentary*. OTL. Louisville: Westminster John Knox, 1999.

———. *The Wisdom Literature*. IBT. Nashville: Abingdon, 1998.

Clines, David J. M. *Interested Parties: The Ideology of Writers and Readers of the Hebrew Bible*. Sheffield: Sheffield Academic, 1995.

———. *Job 1–20*. WBC 17. Grand Rapids: Zondervan, 1989.

Clines, David J. M., and David M. Gunn. "'You Tried to Persuade Me' and 'Violence! Outrage!' in Jeremiah 20:7–8." *VT* 28 (1978) 20–27.

Clines, David J. M., et al., eds. *Weisheit im Israel*. Münster: LIT, 2003.

Coggins, Richard J. *Sirach*. GAP. Sheffield: Sheffield Academic, 1998.

Cohen, Harold R. *Biblical Hapax Legomena in the Light of Akkadian and Ugaritic*. SBLDS 37. Missoula: Scholars, 1978.

Cohen, Yoram. "The Problem of Theodicy: A Mesopotamian Perspective." In *Colères et repentirs divins*, edited by J.-M. Durand et al., 243–70. OBO 278. Göttingen: Vandenhoeck & Ruprecht, 2015.

———. *Wisdom from the Late Bronze Age*. WAW 34. Atlanta: SBL, 2013.

———. "Why 'Wisdom?' Copying, Studying, and Collecting Wisdom Literature in the Cuneiform World." In *Teaching Morality in Antiquity: Wisdom Texts, Oral Traditions, and Images*, edited by T. Oshima and S. Kohlhaas, 41–59. Tübingen: Mohr Siebeck, 2018.

Colberg, Shawn M. *The Wayfarer's End: Bonaventure and Aquinas on Divine Rewards in Scripture and Sacred Doctrine*. Washington: Catholic University of America Press, 2020.

Cole, Stephen W. *The Early Neo-Babylonian Governor's Archives from Nippur*. Chicago: University of Chicago Press, 1996.

Coleman, Robb. Review of *An Obituary for "Wisdom Literature": The Birth, Death, and Intertextual Reintegration of a Biblical Corpus*, by W. Kynes. *CTR* 17 (2019) 113–15.

Collins, Billie Jean. "Animals in Hittite Literature." In *A History of the Animal World in the Ancient Near East*, edited by B. J. Collins, 237–50. Leiden: Brill, 2002.

———. "Divine Wrath and Divine Mercy of the Hittite and Hurrian Deities." In *Divine Wrath and Divine Mercy in the World of Antiquity*, edited by R. Kratz and H. Spieckermann, 67–77. FAT 33. Tübingen: Mohr Siebeck, 2008.

Collins, John J. *Jewish Wisdom in the Hellenistic Age*. OTL. Louisville: Westminster John Knox, 1997.

———. "Wisdom and Torah." In *Pedagogy in Ancient Judaism and Early Christianity*, edited by K. M. Hogan et al., 59–80. Atlanta: SBL, 2017.

Collins, Raymond F. *Wealth, Wages, and the Wealthy: New Testament Insight for Preachers and Teachers*. Collegeville: Liturgical, 2017.

Conybeare, Frederick C., et al. *The Story of Aḥiqar from the Aramaic, Syriac, Arabic, Armenian, Old Turkish, Greek and Slavonic Versions*. Cambridge: Cambridge University Press, 1913.

Cooper, Jerrold S. *The Curse of Agade*. Baltimore: Johns Hopkins University Press, 1983.

Corley, Jeremy. *Ben Sira's Teaching on Friendship*. BJS. Atlanta: Scholars, 2002.

Couturier, Guy. "La vie familiale comme source de la sagesse et la loi." *ScEs* 32 (1980) 177–92.

Cowan, Robin, and Mario J. Rizzo, eds. *Profits and Morality*. Chicago: University of Chicago Press, 1995.

Crane, Walter R. *Gold and Silver*. New York: Wiley and Sons, 1908.

Creach, Jerome F. D. *Yahweh as Refuge and the Editing of the Hebrew Psalter*. JSOTSup 217. Sheffield: Sheffield Academic, 1996.

Crenshaw, James L. "The Contemplative Life in the Ancient Near East." In *CANE* 2445–57.

———. "Ecclesiastes." In *ABD* 2.271–80.

———. "Method in Determining Wisdom Influence Upon 'Historical Literature.'" *JBL* 88 (1969) 129–42.

———. *Old Testament Wisdom: An Introduction*. Louisville: Westminster John Knox, 2010.

———. "Proverbs, Book of." In *ABD* 5.513–20.

———. *Reading Job: A Literary and Theological Commentary*. Macon: Smith & Helwys, 2011.

———. "The Restraint of Reason, The Humility of Prayer." In *The Echoes of Many Texts: Reflections on Jewish and Christian Traditions: Essays in Honor of Lou H. Silberman*, edited by W. Dever and J. E. Wright, 81–97. BJS. Atlanta: Scholars, 1997.

———. Review of *Vorwurf gegen Gott. Ein religiöses Motiv im Alten Orient (Ägypten und Mesopotamien)*, by D. Sitzler. *JBL* 116 (1997) 327–29.

Cross, Frank Moore. "The Evolution of a Theory of Local Texts." In *1971 Proceedings, International Organization of Septuagint and Cognate Studies*, 108–26. Missoula: SBL, 1972.

Crüsemann, Frank. *Studien zur Formgeschichte von Hymnus und Danklied in Israel*. Neukirchen-Vluyn: Neukirchener, 1968.

Dahood, Mitchell J. "Canaanite and Phoenician Influence on Qoheleth." *Bib* 33 (1952) 30–52, 191–221.
Dalley, Stephanie. *Myths from Mesopotamia*. New York: Oxford University Press, 2000.
———. "Old Babylonian Dowries." *Iraq* 1 (1980) 53–74.
Dalman, Gustaf. *Arbeit und Sitte in Palästina, Vols. 1–7*. Gütersloh: Bertelsmann, 1928–42.
D'Amato, Anthony A. *International Law Studies: Collected Papers, Vol. 2*. Cambridge: Kluwer Law International, 1997.
D'Andrade, Kendall. "Bribery." *JBE* 4 (1985) 239–48.
Dardano, P. "'La main est coupable,' 'le sang devient abondant': Sur quelques expressions avec de noms de parties et d'éléments du corps humain dans la littérature juridico-politique de l'Ancien et du Moyen Royaume hittite." *Or* 71 (2002) 333–92.
———. "Per l'etimo dell'ittito *maškan*." *RAnt* 6 (2009) 3–12.
Davids, Peter H. "The Test of Wealth." In *The Missions of James, Peter, and Paul: Tensions in Early Christianity*, edited by B. Chilton and C. Evans, 355–84. Leiden: Brill, 2005.
Davis, Stacy. "Sirach." In *The Old Testament and Apocrypha: Fortress Commentary on the Bible*, edited by G. Yee et al., 999–1025. Minneapolis: Fortress, 2014.
Dawson, Kirsten. "'Did Not He Who Made Me in the Belly Make Him, and the Same One Fashion Us in the Womb?' (Job 31:15): Violence, Slavery, and the Book of Job." *BI* 21 (2013) 435–68.
Day, Peggy L. *An Adversary in Heaven: śāṭān in the Hebrew Bible*. HSM 43. Atlanta: Scholars, 1988.
Deissmann, Adolf. *Bible Studies*, 1895. Translated by A. Grieve. Edinburgh: T&T Clark, 1901.
Delekat, Lienhard. "Zum hebräischen Wörterbuch." *VT* 14 (1964) 7–66.
Delitzsch, Franz. *Biblical Commentary on the Proverbs of Solomon*. 2 vols. Translated by M. G. Easton. Edinburgh: T&T Clark, 1875.
———. *Hoheslied und Koheleth*. Leipzig: Dörffling und Franke, 1875.
———. *Proverbs, Ecclesiastes, Song of Solomon*. Translated by M. G. Easton. Edinburgh: T&T Clark, 1891.
Delkurt, Holger. *Ethische Einsichten in der alttestamentlichen Spruchweisheit*. BThS 21. Neukirchen-Vluyn: Neukirchener, 1993.
Dell, Katherine J. "'I Will Solve My Riddle to the Music of the Lyre' (Psalm 49:4): A Cultic Setting for Wisdom Psalms?" *VT* 54 (2004) 445–58.
Denning Bolle, Sara. *Wisdom in Akkadian Literature: Expression, Instruction, Dialogue*. Mededelingen en verhandelingen van het Vooraziatisch-Egyptisch Genootschap "Ex Oriente Lux" 28. Leiden: Ex Oriente Lux, 1992.
Dibelius, Martin. *A Commentary on the Epistle of James*. Translated by M. A. Williams. Hermeneia. Philadelphia: Fortress, 1976.
Dick, Michael B. "The Legal Metaphor in Job 31." *CBQ* 41 (1979) 37–50.
Di Lella, Alexander A. "Wisdom of Ben-Sira." In *ABD* 6.931–45.
Dnes, Antony W., and Robert Rowthorn. "Introduction." In *The Law and Economics of Marriage and Divorce*, edited by A. Dnes and R. Rowthorn, 1–9. Cambridge: Cambridge University Press, 2002.
De Jong, Stephan. "Qohelet and the Ambitious Spirit of the Ptolemaic Period." *JSOT* 19 (1994) 85–96.

De Soto, Hernando. *The Mystery of Capital: Why Capitalism Triumphs in the West and Fails Everywhere Else*. New York: Basic, 2000.

Douglas, Alexander X. *The Philosophy of Debt*. London: Routledge, 2016.

Driver, Geoffrey R., and John C. Miles. *Babylonian Laws*. Oxford: Oxford University Press, 1960.

Duhaime, Jean. "Dualism." In *EDSS* 215–20.

Dumbrell, William J. *The Faith of Israel: A Theological Survey of the Old Testament*. Grand Rapids: Baker Academic, 2002.

Dunham, Kyle C. *The Pious Sage in Job: Eliphaz in the Context of Wisdom Theodicy*. Eugene: Wipf & Stock, 2016.

Dunn, James D. G. *Christology in the Making: A New Inquiry into Origins of the Doctrine of the Incarnation*. Grand Rapids: Eerdmans, 1989.

———. *The Theology of Paul the Apostle*. Grand Rapids: Eerdmans, 1998.

Eaton, Michael C. *Ecclesiastes: An Introduction and Commentary*. TOTC 18. Downers Grove: IVP Academic, 1983.

Ebeling, Erich. "Quellen zur Kenntnis der Babylonischen Religion." *MVAG* 23 (1919) 50–70.

Ehrlich, Arnold B. "Die Sprüche." In *Randglossen zur hebräischen Bibel: textkritisches, sprachliches und sachliches, Vol. 6*. Leipzig: Hinrichs, 1913.

Eissfeldt, Otto. *Der Mashal im Alten Testament*. BZAW 24. Giessen: Töpelmann, 1913.

Elgvin, Torleiff. "An Analysis of 4QInstruction." PhD diss., Hebrew University Jerusalem, 1997.

———. "The Mystery to Come: Early Essene Theology of Revelation." In *Qumran Between the Old and New Testaments*, edited by F. H. Cryer and T. L. Thompson, 113–50. JSOTSup 290. Sheffield: Sheffield Academic, 1998.

———. "Reconstruction of Sapiential Work A." *RevQ* 16 (1995) 559–80.

Elliott, John H. *Beware the Evil Eye*. 4 vols. Eugene: Cascade, 2015–17.

Ellis, Teresa Ann. *Gender in Book of Ben Sira: Divine Wisdom, Erotic Poetry, and the Garden of Eden*. Berlin: de Gruyter, 2013.

Emerton, John. Review of *Wisdom and the Book of Proverbs: An Israelite Goddess Redefined*, by B. Lang. *VT* 37 (1987) 127.

Engle, Cynthia L. "I Delight in Your Law: A Study of Psalm 119." PhD diss., Cambridge University, 2005.

Erman, Adolf. "Eine agyptische Quelle der 'Sprüche Salomos.'" *Sitzungsberichte der Preussischen Akademie der Wissenschaften, philologisch-historische Klasse* 15 (1924) 86–93.

Esler, Philip Francis. *Community and Gospel in Luke-Acts: The Social and Political Motivations of Lucan Theology*. SNTSMS 57. Cambridge: Cambridge University Press, 1987.

Evans, Craig A. Review of *The Syriac Peshitta Bible with English Translation: John*, by Jeff Childers et al. *BBR* 28 (2018) 678–80.

Fafchamps, Marcel, and Agnes R. Quisumbing. "Household Formation and Marriage Markets in Rural Areas." In *Handbook of Development Economics*, vol. 4, edited by T. P. Schultz and J. Strauss, 3187–248. Radarweg: North-Holland, 2008.

Farber Flügge, Gertrud. *Der Mythos "Inanna und Enki" unter besonderer Berücksichtigen der Lister der* ME. SP 10. Rome: Biblical Institute, 1973.

Farmer, Kathleen A. *Who Knows What Is Good? A Commentary on the Books of Proverbs and Ecclesiastes*. ITC. Grand Rapids: Eerdmans, 1991.

Fassel, Diane. *Working Ourselves to Death: The High Cost of Workaholism and the Rewards of Recovery*. San Francisco: Harper, 1990.

Fee, Gordon. *The Disease of the Health and Wealth Gospels*. Vancouver: Regent College Publishing, 1996.

Finkelstein, Jacob J. "Some New *Misharum* Material and Its Implications." In *Studies in Honor of Benno Landsberger on his Seventy-Fifth Birthday*, edited by H. Güterbock and T. Jacobsen, 233–46. AS 16. Chicago: University of Chicago Press, 1965.

Finn, Jennifer. *Much Ado About Marduk*. Berlin: de Gruyter, 2017.

Firth, David. Review of *An Obituary for "Wisdom Literature": The Birth, Death, and Intertextual Reintegration of a Biblical Corpus*, by W. Kynes. *RBL* https://www.bookreviews.org/pdf/12981_14477.pdf.

Fischer, Johannes. "Human Dignity and Human Rights." In *Religion and Human Rights*, edited by L. Charbonnier and W. Gräb, 71–86. Berlin: de Gruyter, 2015.

Fitzmyer, Joseph A. *The Gospel According to Luke: Introduction, Translation, and Notes*. AB 28. New York: Doubleday, 1982.

Fontaine, Carole R. Review of *Wisdom as a Hermeneutical Construct: A Study in the Sapientalizing of the Old Testament*, by Gerald Sheppard. *CBQ* 43 (1981) 116–17.

Foster, Benjamin R. *The Age of Agade: Inventing Empire in Ancient Mesopotamia*. London: Routledge, 2016.

———. "Agriculture and Accountability in Ancient Mesopotamia." In *The Origin of Cities in Dry-Farming Syria and Mesopotamia in the Third Millenium BC*, edited by H. Weiss, 109–28. Guilford: Four Quarters, 1986.

———. *Before the Muses: An Anthology of Akkadian Literature*. Bethesda: CDL, 2005.

———. "In Search of Akkadian Literature." In *Before the Muses: An Anthology of Akkadian Literature*, 1–47. Bethesda: CDL, 2005.

———. "A Sufferer's Salvation." In *COS* 1.486.

———. "Wool in the Economy of Sargonic Mesopotamia." In *Wool Economy in the Ancient Near East and the Aegean: From the Beginnings of Sheep Husbandry to Institutional Textile Industry*, edited by C. Breniquet and C. Michel, 115–23. Oxford: Oxbow, 2020.

Fowler, Alistair. *Kinds of Literature: An Introduction to the Theory of Genres and Modes*. Cambridge: Harvard University Press, 1982.

Fox, Michael V. *Ecclesiastes*. JPSBC. Philadelphia: Jewish Publication Society, 2004.

———. *Proverbs: A New Translation with Introduction and Commentary*. AB 18A/B. New Haven: Yale University Press, 2000, 2009.

———. "Three Theses on Wisdom." In *Was There a Wisdom Tradition? New Prospects in Israelite Wisdom Studies*, edited by M. Sneed, 69–86. AIL 23. Atlanta: SBL, 2015.

———. Wisdom in Qoheleth." In *In Search of Wisdom: Essays in Memory of John G. Gammie*, edited by L. G. Perdue et al., 115–31. Louisville: Westminster John Knox, 1993.

Foxvog, Daniel A. Review of *The Instructions of Šuruppak: A Sumerian Proverb Collection*, by B. Alster. *Or* 45 (1976) 371–74.

Frahm, Echart. "The Latest Sumerian Proverbs." In *Opening the Tablet Box: Near Eastern Studies in Honor of Benjamin R. Foster*, edited by S. Melville and A. Slotsky, 155–84. CHANE 42. Leiden: Brill, 2010.

Franke, Judith. "Nippur." In *ABD* 4.1119–22.

Frey, Jörg. "Flesh and Spirit in the Palestinian Jewish Sapiential Tradition and in the Qumran Texts: An Inquiry into the Background of Pauline Usage." In *The Wisdom Texts from Qumran and the Development of Sapiential Thought*, edited by C. Hempel et al., 367–404. Leuven: Leuven University Press, 2002:

———. "'Judaism' and 'Hellenism': Martin Hengel's Work in Perspective." In *Jewish Cultural Encounters in the Ancient Mediterranean and Near Eastern World*, edited by M. Popović et al., 96–118. Leiden: Brill, 2017.

Fried, Lisbeth. "Exploitation of Depopulated Land in Achaemenid Judah." In *The Economy of Ancient Judah in Its Historical Context*, edited by M. L. Miller et al., 151–64. Winona Lake: Eisenbrauns, 2015.

Friesen, Steven J. "Injustice or God's Will: Explanations of Poverty in Proto-Christian Communities." In *A People's History of Christianity, Vol. 1: Christian Origins*, edited by R. Horsley, 240–60. Minneapolis: Fortress, 2005.

Frow, John. *Genre: The New Critical Idiom*. London: Routledge, 2006.

Frymer-Kensky, Tikva. *In the Wake of the Goddesses: Women, Culture, and the Biblical Transformation of Pagan Myth*. New York: Free, 1992.

———. "Israel." In *Security for Debt in Ancient Near Eastern Law*, edited by R. Westbrook and R. Jasnow, 251–64. CHANE 9. Leiden: Brill, 2001.

Fuller, Michael E. *The Restoration of Israel: Israel's Re-Gathering and the Fate of the Nations in Early Jewish Literature and Luke-Acts*. BZNW 138. Berlin: de Gruyter, 2006.

Gardner, Gregg. "Giving to the Poor in Early Rabbinic Judaism." PhD diss., Princeton University, 2009.

Garelli, Paul. *Les Assyriens en Cappadoce*. Paris: Librairie Adrien-Maisonneuve, 1963.

Garfinkle, Steven J. "Shepherds, Merchants, and Credit: Some Observations on Lending Practices in Ur III Mesopotamia." *JESHO* 47 (2004) 1–30.

Garrison, Roman. *Redemptive Almsgiving in Early Christianity*. Sheffield: Sheffield Academic, 1993.

Geller, Stephen A. "'Where is Wisdom?' A Literary Study of Job 28 in Its Settings." In *Judaic Perspectives on Ancient Israel*, edited by J. Neusner et al., 155–88. Minneapolis: Fortress, 1987.

Gemser, Berend. *Sprüche Salomos*. HAT 16. Tübingen: Mohr, 1963.

George, Andrew R. *The Babylonian Gilgamesh Epic*. 2 vols. New York: Oxford University Press, 2003.

———. *Babylonian Topographical Texts*. OLA 40. Leuven: Peeters, 1992.

Gerhards, Meik. *Der undefinierbare Gott: Theologische Annäherrungen an alttestamentliche und altorientalische Texte*. RTS 24. Berlin: LIT, 2011.

Gerleman, Gillis. "Die Wurzel Öìí." *ZAW* 85 (1973) 1–14.

Gerstenberger, Erhard. *Israel in the Persian Period: The Fifth and Fourth Centuries BCE*. Translated by S. Schatzmann. BE 8. Atlanta: SBL, 2011.

———. *Wesen und Herkunft des "apodiktischen Rechts."* WMANT 20. Neukirchen-Vluyn: Neukirchener, 1965.

———. "Woe-Oracles of the Prophets." *JBL* 81 (1962) 249–63.

———. "òðä." In *TDOT* 11.230–52.

Gese, Hartmut. "The Prologue to John's Gospel." In *Essays on Biblical Theology*, 167–222. Minneapolis: Augsburg Fortress, 1981.

Giambrone, Anthony. *Sacramental Charity, Creditor Christology, and the Economy of Salvation in Luke's Gospel*. WUNT 439. Tübingen: Mohr Siebeck, 2017.

Gilbert, Maurice. "À l'école de la sagesse. La pédagogie des sages dans l'ancien Israël." *Greg* 85 (2004) 20–42.

———. "Prêt, aumône et caution." In *Der Einzelne und seine Gemeinschaft bei Ben Sira*, edited by R. Egger-Wenzel and I. Krammer, 179–89. BZAW 270. Berlin: de Gruyter, 1998.

———. "Wisdom of the Poor: Ben Sira 10,19–11,6." In *The Book of Ben Sira in Modern Research. Proceedings of the First International Ben Sira Conference 28–31 July 1996*, edited by P. Beentjes, 153–69. BZAW 255. Berlin: de Gruyter, 1997.

Giovino, Mariana. *The Assyrian Sacred Tree: A History of Interpretations*. OBO 230. Göttingen: Vandenhoeck & Ruprecht, 2007.

Glatt-Gilad, David A. "Reflections on the Intersection Between 'Song' and Wisdom in the Hebrew Bible." In *Marbeh Hokmah: Studies in the Bible and the Ancient Near East in Loving Memory of Victor Avigdor Hurowitz*, edited by S. Yona et al., 229–35. Winona Lake: Eisenbrauns, 2015.

Glicksman, Andrew T. *Wisdom of Solomon 10: A Jewish Hellenistic Reinterpretation of Early Israelite History through Sapiential Lenses*. DCLS 9. Berlin: de Gruyter, 2011.

Gnuse, Robert. *You Shall Not Steal: Community and Property in the Biblical Tradition*. Maryknoll: Orbis, 1985.

Goetze, Albrecht. *Kulturgeschichte Kleinasiens*. Munich: Beck, 1957.

Goetzmann, William N. *Money Changes Everything: How Finance Made Civilization Possible*. Princeton: Princeton University Press, 2016.

Goff, Matthew J. *4QInstruction*. WLAW 2. Atlanta: SBL, 2013.

———. "The Mystery of Creation in 4QInstruction." *DSD* 10 (2003) 163–86.

———. "Wisdom, Apocalypticism, and the Pedagogical Ethos in 4QInstruction." In *Conflicted Boundaries in Wisdom and Apocalypticism*, edited by B. Wright and L. Wills, 57–68. SBLSS 35. Atlanta: SBL, 2005.

———. *The Worldly and Heavenly Wisdom of 4QInstruction*. STDJ 50. Leiden: Brill, 2003.

Goldingay, John. "The Arrangement of Sayings in Proverbs 10–15." *JSOT* 61 (1994) 75–83.

———. *Psalms*. Grand Rapids: Baker, 2006.

———. "Proverbs." In *NBC: 21st Century Edition*, edited by G. Wenham et al., 584–608. Downers Grove: InterVarsity, 1994.

Goodchild, Philip. *Economic Theology: Credit and Faith II*. Lanham: Rowman and Littlefield, 2020.

———. *Theology of Money*. Durham: Duke University Pres, 2009.

Goody, Jack, and S. J. Tambiah. *Bridewealth and Dowry*. CPSA 7. Cambridge: Cambridge University Press, 1973.

Gordis, Robert. *Koheleth: The Man and his World*. New York: Schocken, 1968.

———. "A Note on *Yad*." *JBL* 62 (1943) 341–44.

———. "Quotations in Wisdom Literature." *JQR* 30 (1939) 123–47.

Gordon, Edmund I. *Sumerian Proverbs: Glimpses of Everyday Life in Ancient Mesopotamia*. Westport: Greenwood, 1969.

Görg, Manfred. "Öëï." In *TDOT* 14.691–702.

Gorman, Frank H., Jr. *The Ideology of Ritual: Space, Time and Status in the Priestly Theology*. JSOTSup 91. Sheffield: JSOT Press, 1990.

Gottwald, Norman K. *The Hebrew Bible: A Brief Socio-Literary Introduction*. Minneapolis: Fortress, 2009.

———. "Social Class as an Analytic and Hermeneutical Category in Biblical Studies." JBL 112 (1993) 3–22.

———. "Social Matrix and Canonical Shape." *ThTo* 42 (1985) 301–21.

Gowan, Donald E. "Wealth and Poverty in the Old Testament." *Int* 41 (1987) 341–53.

Grabbe, Lester L. "The Jews and Hellenization: Hengel and His Critics." In *Second Temple Studies III: Studies in Politics, Class, and Material Culture*, edited by P. R. Davies and J. M. Halligan, 52–66. JSOTSup 340. Sheffield: Sheffield Academic, 2002.

Gray, Patrick. "Points and Lines: Thematic Parallelism in the Letter of James and the Testament of Job." *NTS* 50 (2004) 406–24.

Grayson, A. Kirk. "Mesopotamia, History of (Babylonia)." In *ABD* 4.755–77.

Greenfield, Jonas C. "The Background and Parallel to a Proverb of Aḥiqar." In *Hommages à André Dupont-Sommer*, edited by A. Caquot and M. Philonenko, 49–59. Paris: Maisonneuve, 1971.

Gregory, Bradley C. *Like an Everlasting Signet Ring: Generosity in the Book of Sirach*. DCLS 2. Berlin: de Gruyter, 2010.

———. "The Relationship Between the Poor in Judea and Israel under Foreign Rule: Sirach 35:14–26 among Second Temple Prayers and Hymns." *JSJ* 42 (2011) 311–27.

Grelot, Pierre. *Documents araméens d'Égypte: introduction, traduction et presentation*. Paris: Éditions du Cerf, 1972.

———. "Les proverbes d'Aḥîqar." *RB* 104 (2001) 511–28.

Groneberg, Brigitte."Towards a Definition of Literature as Applied to Akkadian Literature." In *Mesopotamian Poetic Language: Sumerian and Akkadian*, edited by M. E. Vogelzang and H. L. J. Vanstiphout, 59–84. Groningen: Styx, 1996.

Grünewald, Thomas. *Bandits in the Roman Empire: Myth and Reality*. Translated by J. Drinkwater. London: Routledge, 2004.

Guillaume, Philippe. *Land, Credit and Crisis: Agrarian Finance in the Hebrew Bible*. Sheffield: Equinox, 2012.

Gunkel, Hermann. *Einleitung in die Psalmen*. Göttingen: Vandenhoeck und Ruprecht, 1933.

Gurney, Oliver R. *The Middle Babylonian Legal and Economic Texts from Ur*. Baghdad: British School of Archaeology in Iraq, 1983.

Güterbock, Hans. "Noch einmal die Formel *parnaššea šuwaizzi*." *Or* 52 (1983) 73–80.

Gutiérrez, Gustavo. *On Job: God-Talk and the Suffering of the Innocent*. Maryknoll: Orbis, 1987.

Gutmann, Peter M. "The Subterranean Economy, Redux." In *The Economics of the Shadow Economy*, edited by W. Gaertner and A. Wenig, 2–18. New York: Springer, 1985.

Haag, Ernst. *Das hellenistische Zeitalter. Israel und die Bibel im 4. bis 1. Jahrhundert vor Chr.* Stuttgart: Kohlhammer, 2003.

Habel, Norman C. *The Book of Job: A Commentary*. OTL. Philadelphia: Westminster, 1985.

Halivni, David Weiss. *Midrash, Mishnah, and Gemara: the Jewish Predilection for Justified Law*. Cambridge: Harvard University Press, 1986.

Halliday, Daniel. *Inheritance of Wealth: Justice, Equality, and the Right to Bequeath*. Oxford: Oxford University Press, 2018.

Hallo, William W. Review of *The Instructions of Šuruppak: A Sumerian Proverb Collection*, by Bendt Alster. *JNES* 37 (1978) 269–73.

———. *Origins: The Ancient Near Eastern Background of Some Modern Western Institutions*. Leiden: Brill, 1996.

———. *The World's Oldest Literature: Studies in Sumerian Belles-Lettres*. CHANE 35. Leiden: Brill, 2010.

Hamilton, Mark A. "Elite Lives: Job 29–31 and Traditional Authority." *JSOT* 32 (2007) 69–89.

Harper, Robert Francis. *The Code of Hammurabi, King of Babylon*. Chicago: University of Chicago Press, 1904.

Harrington, Daniel J. "The øæ ðäéä in a Qumran Wisdom Text: (1Q26, 4Q415–18, 423)." *RevQ* 17 (1996) 49–53.

———. "Two Early Jewish Approaches to Wisdom: Sirach and Qumran Sapiential Work A." In *The Wisdom Texts from Qumran and the Development of Sapiential Thought*, edited by C. Hempel et al., 263–76. BETL 159. Leuven: Leuven University Press, 2002.

———. "Wisdom Texts." In *EDSS* 976–80.

———. *Wisdom Texts from Qumran*. London: Routledge, 1996.

Harris, Rivkah. "The Case of Three Babylonian Marriage Contracts." *JNES* 33 (1973) 363–69.

Hartley, John E. *The Book of Job*. NICOT. Grand Rapids: Eerdmans, 1988.

———. "Job 2: Ancient Near Eastern Background." In *Dictionary of the Old Testament Writings: Wisdom, Poetry, and Writings*, edited by T. Longman and P. Enns, 346–61. Downers Grove: InterVarsity, 2008.

Harvey, David. *Marx, Capital, and the Madness of Economic Reason*. New York: Oxford University Press, 2018.

Haspecker, Josef. *Gottesfurcht bei Jesus Sirach. Ihre religiöse Struktur und ihre literarische und doctrinäre Bedeutung*. Rome: Papstliches Bibelinstitut, 1967.

Hatcher, Daniel L. *The Poverty Industry: The Exploitation of America's Most Vulnerable Citizens*. New York: New York University Press, 2016.

Hatcher, Karen M. "In Gold We Trust: The Parable of the Rich Man and Lazarus (Luke 16:19–31)." *RevExp* 109 (2012) 277–83.

Hauck, Friedrich. "μαμωνᾶς." In *TDNT* 4.389.

Hausmann, Jutta. *Studien zum Menschenbild der älteren Weisheit*. FAT 7. Tübingen: Mohr, 1995.

Hawley, Lance. "The Rhetoric of Condemnation in the Book of Job." *JBL* 139 (2020) 459–78.

Hayes, Elizabeth. "The Unity of the Egyptian Hallel: Psalm 113–118." *BBR* 9 (1999) 145–56.

Hayes, Katherine Murphey. *The Earth Mourns: Prophetic Metaphor and Oral Aesthetic*. SBLAB 8. Leiden: Brill, 2002.

Heim, Knut Martin. *Ecclesiastes*. TOTC. Downers Grove: InterVarsity, 2019.

Hempel, Charlotte. "The Qumran Sapiential Texts and the Rule Books." In *The Wisdom Texts from Qumran and the Development of Sapiential Thought*, edited by C. Hempel et al., 277–96. BETL 159. Leuven: Peeters, 2002.

Hendon, Donald W., et al. *Cross-Cultural Business Negotiations*. London: Quorum, 1996.

Hengel, Martin. *Judaism and Hellenism: Studies in Their Encounter in Palestine during the Early Hellenistic Period*, 1973. Translated by J. Bowden. Philadelphia: Fortress, 1974.

———. *The "Hellenization" of Judea in the First Century After Christ*, 1989. Translated by J. Bowden. Eugene: Wipf & Stock, 2003.

Hering, James P. *The Colossian and Ephesian* Haustafeln *in Theological Context: An Analysis of their Origins, Relationship, and Message.* AUS 7.260. New York: Lang, 2007.

Hershkowitz, Debra. *The Madness of Epic: Reading Insanity from Homer to Statius.* OCM. Oxford: Clarendon, 1998.

Hertzberg, Hans Wilhelm. *Der Prediger.* KAT 17.4. Gütersloh: Mohn, 1963.

Hildebrandt, Ted. "Proverbial Pairs: Compositional Units in Proverbs 10–29." *JBL* 107 (1988) 207–24.

Hilton, Rodney H. "The Origins of Robin Hood." 1958. Reprinted in *Robin Hood: An Anthology of Scholarship and Criticism*, edited by S. T. Knight, 197–210. Cambridge: Brewer, 1999.

Hoffman, Yair. *A Blemished Perfection: The Book of Job in Context.* JSOTSup213. Sheffield: Sheffield Academic, 1996.

———. "The Concept of 'Other Gods' in the Deuteronomistic Literature." In *Politics and Theopolitics in the Bible and Postbiblical Literature*, edited by H. G. Reventlow et al., 66–84. Sheffield: Sheffield Academic, 1994.

Hoffner, Harry A. "Hittite Laws." In *Law Collections from Mesopotamia and Asia Minor*, edited by M. T. Roth, 213–40. SBLWAW 6. Atlanta: Scholars, 1997.

———. *Hittite Myths.* SBLWAW 2. Atlanta: Scholars, 1990.

———. "The King's Speech: Royal Rhetorical Language." In *Beyond Hatti: A Tribute to Gary Beckman*, edited by B. J. Collins and P. Michalowski, 137–54. Atlanta: Lockwood, 2013.

———. "Legal and Social Institutions of Hittite Anatolia." In *CANE* 555–69.

———. "Studies in Hittite Grammar." In *Kaniššuwar: A Tribute to Hans G. Güterbock on His 75th Birthday*, edited by H. Hoffner and G. Beckman, 83–94. AS 23. Chicago: Oriental Institute of the University of Chicago, 1986.

Holland, Glenn S. *Gods of the Desert: Religions of the Ancient Near East.* New York: Rowman and Littlefield, 2009.

Hoppe, Leslie J. *There Shall Be No Poor Among You: Poverty in the Bible.* Nashville: Abingdon, 2004.

Hornborg, Alf. *Global Ecology and Unequal Exchange.* London: Routledge, 2011.

Horsley, Richard A. *Scribes, Visionaries, and the Politics of Second Temple Judea.* Louisville: Westminster John Knox, 2007.

Horsley, Richard A., and Patrick Tiller. *After Apocalyptic and Wisdom: Rethinking Texts in Context.* Eugene: Cascade, 2012.

Horwitz, William James. "The Ugaritic Scribe." *UF* 11 (1979) 389–94.

Hossfeld, Frank-Lothar. "Der gnädige Gott und der arme Gerechte: Anthropologische Akzente in der Psalmengruppe 113–118." In *Kircheneinheit und Welverantwortung. Festschrift für Peter Neuner*, edited by C. Böttigheimer and H. Filser, 51–63. Regensburg: Pustet, 2006.

Hossfeld, Frank-Lothar, and Erich Zenger. *Die Psalmen*, I-III. Würzberg: Echter, 1993.

House, Robert S., Jr. "An Economic Profile of Silver." In *Precious Metals 1981*, edited by E. D. Zysk, 29–40. Toronto: Pergamon, 1982.

Howard, Vicki. *Brides, Inc.: American Weddings and the Business of Tradition.* Philadelphia: University of Pennsylvania Press, 2006.

Hron, Ondrej. *The Mirage Shall Become a Pool: A New Testament Theology of Social Justice and Charity.* Eugene: Pickwick, 2012.

Hubbard, David A. "Principles of Financial Investment: Ecclesiastes 11:1–8." In *Reflecting with Solomon: Selected Studies on the Book of Ecclesiastes*, edited by R. B. Zuck, 341–46. Eugene: Wipf & Stock, 2003.

Hundley, Michael B. *Gods in Dwellings: Temples and the Divine Presence in the Ancient Near East.* WAWSup 3. Atlanta: SBL, 2013.

Hunter, Alisdair G. Review of *Wisdom Intoned*, by S. Cheung. *JSOT* 40 (2016) 102.

Hurowitz, Victor Avigdor. "An Allusion to the *Šamaš Hymn* in *Dialogue of Pessimism*." In *Wisdom Literature in Mesopotamia and Israel*, edited by R. J. Clifford, 33–36. Atlanta: SBL, 2007.

———. "^{D}Narru and ^{D}Zulummar in the Babylonian Theodicy (*BWL* 88.276–77)." *JAOS* 124 (2004) 777–78.

Hutt, Curtis. "1Q/4QInstruction: Training for a Money Changer?" In *Wealth and Poverty in Jewish Tradition*, edited by L. Greenspoon, 101–25. SJC 26. West Lafayette: Purdue University Press, 2015.

Isaksson, Bo. *Studies in the Language of Qoheleth, with Special Emphasis on the Verbal System.* Uppsala: Uppsala University, 1987.

Izre'el, Shlomo. *Adapa and the South Wind: Language Has the Power of Death.* MC 10. Winona Lake: Eisenbrauns, 2001.

Jackson-McCabe, Matt A. *Logos and Law in the Letter of James: The Law of Nature, the Law of Moses, and the Law of Freedom.* NTSup 100. Leiden: Brill, 2000.

Jacobsen, Thorkild, and Kirsten Nielsen. "Cursing the Day." *SJOT* 6 (1992) 187–204.

Jameson, Fredric. *Postmodernism: The Cultural Logic of Late Capitalism.* Durham: Duke University Press, 1991.

Janssen, Jac J. "The Role of the Temple in the Egyptian Economy During the New Kingdom." In *State and Temple Economy in the Ancient Near East, Vol. 2*, edited by E. Lipiński, 505–15. Leuven: Departement Oriëntalistiek, 1979.

Janzen, Gerald J. *Job.* Interpretation. Atlanta: John Knox, 1985.

———. "Qohelet on Life 'Under the Sun.'" *CBQ* 70 (2008) 465–83.

Jaruzelska, Izabela. *Amos and the Officialdom in the Kingdom of Israel: The Socio-Economic Position of the Officials in the Light of the Biblical, the Epigraphic, and Archaeological Evidence.* Poznan: Wydawnictwo Naukowe Uniwersytetu im. Adama Mickiewicza, 1998.

Jastrow, Morris. *The Civilization of Babylonia and Assyria: Its Remains, Language, History, Religion, Commerce, Law, Art and Literature.* Boston: Ginn & Company, 1898.

———. *A Gentle Cynic: Being a Translation of the Book of Koheleth.* Philadelphia: Lippincott, 1919.

Jauss, Hannelore. *Der liebebedürftige Gott und die gottbedürftige Liebe des Menschen: Ursprung und Funktion der Rede von der Liebe des Menschen zu Gott als alttestamtentlicher Beitrag zur Gotteslehre.* BVB 25. Münster: LIT, 2014.

Jefferies, Daryl. *Wisdom at Qumran: A Form-Critical Analysis of the Admonitions of 4QInstruction.* GDNES 3. Piscataway: Gorgias, 2002.

Jensen, David H. *Responsive Labor: A Theology of Work.* Knoxville: Westminster John Knox, 2006.

Jiménez, Enrique. *The Babylonian Disputation Poems.* CHANE 87. Leiden: Brill, 2017.

Jobes, Karen H. "Sophia Christology: The Way of Wisdom?" In *The Way of Wisdom: Essays in Honor of Bruce K. Waltke*, edited by J. I. Packer and S. Soderlund, 226–50. Grand Rapids: Zondervan, 2000.

Jodock, Darrell. *The Church's Bible: Its Contemporary Authority*. Minneapolis: Augsburg Fortress, 1989.

Johnson, Luke Timothy. *Brother of Jesus, Friend of God: Studies in the Letter of James*. Grand Rapids: Eerdmans, 2004.

———. *The Gospel of Luke*. SP 3. Collegeville: Liturgical, 1991.

———. *The Letter of James: A New Translation with Introduction and Commentary*. AB 37A. New York: Doubleday, 1995.

———. *Sharing Possessions: What Faith Demands*. Grand Rapids: Eerdmans, 2011.

Johnston, Robert K. "Confessions of a Workaholic: A Reappraisal of Qoheleth." In *Reflecting with Solomon: Selected Studies on Ecclesiastes*, edited by R. B. Zuck, 133–48. Eugene: Wipf & Stock, 2003.

Jones, Robert G., ed. *Nepotism in Organizations*. New York: Routledge, 2012.

Jones, Scott C. *Rumors of Wisdom: Job 28 as Poetry*. Berlin: de Gruyter, 2009.

———. Review of *Wisdom Intoned: A Reappraisal of the Genre "Wisdom Psalms,"* by Simon Chi-Chung Cheung. *RBL* (2019).

Joosten, Jan. *People and Land in the Holiness Code: An Exegetical of the Ideational Framework of the Law in Leviticus 17–26*. VTSup 67. Leiden: Brill, 1996.

Joosten, Jan, and Jean-Sébastien Rey, eds. *Texts and Versions of the Book of Ben Sira*. Leiden: Brill, 2011.

Kamell, Mariam. "The Economics of Humility: The Rich and Humble in James." In *Engaging Economics: New Testament Scenarios and Early Christian Reception*, edited by B. Longenecker and K. Liebengood, 157–75. Grand Rapids: Eerdmans, 2009.

Karavites, Peter. *Promise-Giving and Treaty-Making: Homer and the Near East*. Leiden: Brill, 1992.

Karenga, Maulana. *Maat: The Moral Ideal in Ancient Egypt*. London, Routledge, 2004.

Kassis, Riad Aziz. *The Book of Proverbs and Arabic Proverbial Works*. Leiden: Brill, 1999.

Kayatz, Christa. *Studien du Proverbien 1–9. Eine form- und motivgeshichtlice Untersuchung*. Neukirchen-Vluyn: Neukirchener, 1966.

Keener, Craig S. *The IVP Bible Background Commentary: New Testament*. Downers Grove: IVP Academic, 2014.

Kellermann, Diether. "בצע." In *TDOT* 2.205–8.

———. "כשר." In *TDOT* 7.367–70.

Kessler, Rainer. *Staat und Gesellschaft im vorexilischen Juda: Vom 8. Jahrhundert bis zum Exil*. VTSup 47. Leiden: Brill, 1992.

Khanjian, John. "Wisdom in Ugarit and in the Ancient Near East with Particular Emphasis on Old Testament Wisdom Literature." PhD diss., Claremont Graduate School, 1973.

Kim, Jimyung. *Reanimating Qohelet's Contradictory Voices: Studies of Open-Ended Discourse on Wisdom in Ecclesiastes*. Leiden: Brill, 2018.

Kim, Seenam. *The Coherence of the Collections in the Book of Proverbs*. Eugene: Pickwick, 2007.

Kirk, James A. "The Meaning of Wisdom in James: Examination of an Hypothesis." *NTS* 16 (1970) 24–38.

Kloppenberg, James T. *Toward Democracy: The Struggle for Self-Rule in European and American Thought*. Oxford: Oxford University Press, 2016.

Knox, Wilfred L. "The Epistle of St. James." *JTS* 46 (1945) 10–17.

Koester, Helmut. *Introduction to the New Testament, Vol. 1: History, Culture, and Religion of the Hellenistic Age*. Berlin: de Gruyter, 1995.

Köstenberger, Andreas J. *John*. BECNT. Grand Rapids: Baker Academic, 2004.

Kottsieper, Ingo. "Aramaic Literature." In *From an Antique Land: An Introduction to Ancient Near Eastern Literature*, edited by C. S. Ehrlich, 393–443. Lanham: Rowman & Littlefield, 2009.

_______. "The Aramaic Tradition: Aḥiqar." In *Scribes, Sages, and Seers: The Sage in the Eastern Mediterranean World*, edited by L. G. Perdue, 109–24. FRLANT 219. Göttingen: Vandenhoeck & Ruprecht, 2009.

Kramer, Samuel Noah. "The Sage in Sumerian Literature: A Composite Portrait." In *The Sage in Israel and the Ancient Near East*, edited by J. Gammie and L. Perdue, 31–37. Winona Lake: Eisenbrauns, 1990.

———. *The Sumerians: Their History, Culture, and Character*. Chicago: University of Chicago Press, 1963.

Krämer, Michael. *Das Rätsel der Parabel vom ungerechten Verwalter, Lk 16:1–13: Auslegungsgeschichte - Umfang - Sinn. Eine Diskussion der Probleme und Lösungsvorschläge der Verwalterparabel von den Vätern bis heute*. Zurich: Pas-Verlag, 1972.

Kraus, Hans-Joachim. *Die Psalmen 1*. BKAT 15. Neukirchener: Neukirchen-Vluyn, 1960.

Kreeft, Peter. *Three Philosophies of Life*. San Francisco: Ignatius, 1989.

Kronholm, Tryggve. "יתר." In *TDOT* 6.482–91.

———. "קדים." In *TDOT* 12.501–5.

Kruger, Paul A. "A World Turned on Its Head in Ancient Near Eastern Prophetic Literature: A Powerful Strategy to Depict Chaotic Scenarios." *VT* 62 (2012) 58–76.

Krüger, Thomas. "Morality and Religion in Three Babylonian Poems of Pious Sufferers." In *Teaching Morality in Antiquity: Wisdom Texts, Oral Traditions, and Images*, edited by T. Oshima and S. Kohlhaas, 182–88. Tübingen: Mohr Siebeck, 2018.

———. Review of *Proverbs 1–9*, by J. A. Loader. *RBL* 2 (2016).

Kugel, James L. "Qohelet and Money." *CBQ* 51 (1989) 32–49.

Kuntz, J. Kenneth. Review of *Wisdom Intoned*, by Simon Cheung. *Bib* 98 (2017) 138–40.

Kuran, Timur. *The Long Divergence: How Islamic Law Held Back the Middle East*. Princeton: Princeton University Press, 2011.

Kynes, Will. *An Obituary for "Wisdom Literature": The Birth, Death, and Intertextual Reintegration of a Biblical Corpus*. New York: Oxford University Press, 2019.

Laato, Antti, and Johannes Cornelis de Moor, eds. *Theodicy in the World of the Bible: The Goodness of God and the Problem of Evil*. Leiden: Brill, 2003.

La Caze, Marguerite. *Wonder and Generosity: Their Role in Ethics and Politics*. Albany: State University of New York Press, 2013.

Lambert, W. G. "Some New Babylonian Wisdom Literature." In *Wisdom in Ancient Israel: Essays in Honour of J. A. Emerton*, edited by J. Day et al., 30–42. Cambridge: Cambridge University Press, 1995.

Landsberger, Bruno. "Die babylonische Theodizee (akrostichisches Zwiegespräch; sog. 'Kohelet')." *ZA* 43 (1936) 32–76.

Lange, Armin. *Weisheit und Prädestination. Weisheitlich Urordnung und Prädestination in den Textfunden von Qumran*. STDJ 18. Leiden: Brill, 1995.

Langdon, Stephen H. *Babylonian Wisdom*. London: Luzac, 1923.

Larcher, C. *Le livre de Job. Bible de Jerusalem: La sainte Bible*. Paris: Les Éditions du Cerf, 1950.

Larrimore, Mark J. *The Book of Job: A Biography*. Princeton: Princeton University Press, 2013.

———. "The Ethics of Leibniz' 'Theodicy.'" PhD diss., Princeton University, 1994.

Lau, Te-Li. *Defending Shame: The Formative Power in Paul's Letters*. Grand Rapids: Baker Academic, 2020.

Lee, Eunny P. *The Vitality of Enjoyment in Qohelet's Theological Rhetoric*. BZAW 353. Berlin: de Gruyter, 2005.

Leibniz, Gottfried Wilhelm. *Essais de Théodicée sur la bonté de Dieu, la liberté de l'homme, et l'origine du mal*. 1701. Reprint, Dresden: Andersseitig, 2017.

Leick, Gwendolyn. *Mesopotamia: The Invention of the City*. New York: Penguin, 2001.

Lemos, Tracy Maria. *Marriage Gifts and Social Change in Ancient Palestine 1200 BCE—200 CE*. Cambridge: Cambridge University Press, 2010.

———. *Violence and Personhood in Ancient Israel and Comparative Contexts*. Oxford: Oxford University Press, 2017.

Lenzi, Alan. "A Hymn to Marduk: *Ludlul bēl nēmeqi* 1.1–40." In *Akkadian Hymns and Prayers: A Reader*. Edited by A. Lenzi, 483–501. SBLANEM 3. Atlanta: SBL, 2011.

———. "The Language of Akkadian Prayers in *Ludlul Bēl Nēmeqi* and its Significance Within and Beyond Mesopotamia." In *Mesopotamia in the Ancient World: Impact, Continuities, Parallels*, edited by R. Rollinger and E. van Dongen, 67–106. Münster: Ugarit, 2015.

———. "Proverbs 8:22–31: Three Perspectives on Its Composition." *JBL* 125 (2006) 687–714.

———. "Scribal Hermeneutics and the Twelve Gates of *Ludlul bēl nēmeqi*." *JAOS* 135 (2015) 733–49.

———. *Secrecy and the Gods: Secret Knowledge in Ancient Mesopotamia and Biblical Israel*. SAAS 19. Helsinki: Neo-Assyrian Text Corpus Project, 2008.

Levin, Christoph. "Das Amosbuch der Anawim." *ZTK* 94 (1997) 407–36.

———. *Re-Reading the Scriptures: Essays on the Literary History of the Old Testament*. FAT 87. Tübingen: Mohr Siebeck, 2013.

Lewis, C. S. *The Weight of Glory and Other Addresses*, 1949. Reprint, New York: HarperCollins, 2000.

Lichtheim, Miriam. *Late Egyptian Wisdom in the International Context: A Study of Demotic Instructions*. OBO 52. Göttingen: Vandenhoeck und Ruprecht, 1983.

Lie, Arthur G. *The Inscriptions of Sargon II, King of Assyria*. Paris: Geuthner, 1929.

Lim, Timothy. "Wicked Priest." In *EDSS* 973–76.

Lindblom, Johannes. "Wisdom in the Old Testament Prophets." In *Wisdom in Israel and in the Ancient Near East: Presented to Professor Henry Harold Rowley in Celebration of his Sixty- Fifth Birthday*, edited by M. Noth and D. W. Thomas, 192–204. Leiden: Brill, 1955.

Lindenberger, James M. *The Aramaic Proverbs of Ahiqar*. Baltimore: Johns Hopkins University Press, 1983.

———. "Ahiqar." In *OTP* 2.479–507.

Lipiński, Eduard. "מהר." In *TDOT* 8.142–49.

Liverani, Mario. "The Trade Network of Tyre According to Ezekiel 27." In *Ah, Assyria . . . !: Studies in Assyrian History and Ancient Near Eastern Historiography Presented to Ḥayim Tadmor*, edited by M. Cogan and I. Eph`al, 65–79. Jerusalem: Hebrew University Press, 1991.

Livingstone, Alasdair. *Court Poetry and Literary Miscellanea*. SAA 3. Helsinki: Neo-Assyrian Text Corpus Project, 1989.

Lo, Alison. *Job 28 as Rhetoric: An Analysis of Job 28 in the Context of Job 21–31*. Leiden: Brill, 2003.

Loader, James A. *Polar Structures in the Book of Qohelet*. BZAW 152. Berlin: de Gruyter, 1979.

———. *Proverbs 1–9*. HCOT. Leuven: Peeters, 2014.

———. "Wisdom by (the) People for (the) People." *ZAW* 111 (1999) 211–33.

Lohfink, Norbert. "ירשׁ." In *TDOT* 6.368–96.

———. *Qoheleth: A Continental Commentary*, 1980. Translated by S. McEvenue. Minneapolis: Fortress, 2003.

Lohmeyer, Ernst. *Die Briefe an die Philipper, an die Kolosser, und an Philemon*. KEK 9. Göttingen: Vandenhoeck & Ruprecht, 1964.

Longenecker, Richard N. *Biblical Exegesis in the Apostolic Period*. Grand Rapids: Eerdmans, 1999.

Longman, Tremper, III. *The Book of Ecclesiastes*. NICOT. Grand Rapids: Eerdmans, 1998.

———. *Proverbs*. Grand Rapids: Baker Academic, 2006.

Longman, Tremper, III, and John H. Walton. *The Lost World of the Flood: Mythology, Theology, and the Deluge Debate*. Downers Grove: InterVarsity, 2018.

Loretz, Oswald. *Qohelet und der alte Orient. Untersuchungen zu Stil und theologischer Thematik des Buches Qohelet*. Freiburg: Herder, 1964.

Luther, Martin. "Sermon on the Mount." In *LW* 21, edited by J. Pelikan. St. Louis: Concordia, 1956.

Luukko, M. "The Administrative Roles of the 'Chief Scribe' and the 'Palace Scribe' in the Middle Assyrian Period." *SAAB* 16 (2007) 227–56.

Lyu, Sun Myung. *Righteousness in the Book of Proverbs*. FAT 55. Tübingen: Mohr Siebeck, 2012.

MacGinnis, John D. A. "The Use of Writing Boards in the Neo-Babylonian Temple Administration at Sippar." *Iraq* 64 (2002) 217–36.

Maier, Christl. *Die "fremde Frau" in Proverbien 1–9. Eine exegetische und sozialgeschichtliche Studie*. OBO 144. Göttingen: Vandenhoeck und Ruprecht, 2000.

———. "Good and Evil Women in Proverbs and Job: The Emergence of Cultural Stereotypes." In *The Writings and Later Wisdom Books*, edited by C. Maier and N. Calduch- Benages, 77–92. Atlanta: SBL, 2014.

Malchow, Bruce V. "Social Justice in the Wisdom Literature." *BTB* 12 (1982) 120–24.

Maloney, Robert P. "Usury and Restrictions on Interest-Taking in the Ancient Near East." *CBQ* 36 (1974) 1–20.

Marazzi, Massimiliano. "Note in margine all'editto reale *KBo* 22.1." In *Studi de storia e di filologia anatolica dedicate a Giovanni Pugliese Carratelli*, edited by F. Imparati, 119–29. Eothen 1. Firenze: Elite, 1988.

Marazzi, Massimiliano, and Holger Gzella. "Bemerkungen zu SAG.DU-*ZU waš*- und *wašše*- in CTH 258 und HG §198/*84." *SMEA* 45 (2003) 71–78.

Marcel, Gabriel. *Philosophy of Existentialism*. New York: Citadel, 2002.
Markter, Florian. *Transformationen. Zur Anthropologie des Propheten Ezechiel unter besonderer Berücksichtigung des Motivs "Herz."* FB 127. Würzburg: Echter, 2013.
Marshall, I. Howard. *The Gospel of Luke: A Commentary on the Greek Text*. NIGTC. Grand Rapids: Eerdmans, 1978.
Marsman, Hennie J. *Women in Ugarit and Israel: Their Social and Religious Position in the Context of the Ancient Near East*. Leiden: Brill, 2003.
Martin, Dale B. *The Corinthian Body*. New Haven: Yale University Press, 1995.
Martin, Ralph. *James*. WBC 48. Waco: Word, 1988.
Marx, Karl, and Frederick Engels. *Manifesto of the Communist Party*. Translated by F. Engels. Chicago: Kerr and Co., 1906.
Mathews, Mark D. *Riches, Poverty, and the Faithful: Perspectives on Wealth in the Second Temple Period and the Apocalypse of John*. SNTSMS 154. Cambridge: Cambridge University Press, 2013.
Mathewson, Dan. *Death and Survival in the Book of Job: Desymbolization and Traumatic Experience*. LHBOTS 450. New York: T&T Clark, 2006.
Matthews, Caitlin. *Sophia: Goddess of Wisdom, Bride of God*. Wheaton: Quest, 2001.
Matusova, Ekaterina. *The Meaning of Aristeas in Light of Biblical Traditional and Grammatical Tradition, and with Reference to Its Historical Context*. Göttingen: Vandenhoeck & Ruprecht, 2015.
al-Maydânî, Ibrahim. *Collection of Proverbs* (مجمع الامثال), *1120–1124 CE*. Edited by N. Zarzûr. Beirut: Dâr al-Kutub al-`Ilmiyya, 1988.
Maynard-Reid, Pedrito. *Poverty and Wealth in James*. Maryknoll: Orbis, 1987.
Mays, James L. "The Place of the Torah-Psalms in the Psalter." *JBL* 106 (1987) 3–12.
———. *Psalms*. Interpretation. Louisville: Westminster John Knox, 1994.
McCarter, P. Lyle. *Textual Criticism: Recovering the Text of the Hebrew Bible*. Philadelphia: Fortress, 1986.
McKane, William. *Proverbs: A New Approach*. London: SCM, 1980.
———. *Prophets and Wise Men*. 1965. Reprint, Eugene: Wipf & Stock, 2010.
McKnight, Scot. *The Letter of James*. NICNT. Grand Rapids: Eerdmans, 2011.
McLaughlin, John L. *An Introduction to Israel's Wisdom Traditions*. Grand Rapids: Eerdmans, 2018.
Meek, Theophile J. "The Code of Hammurabi." In *ANET* 163–80.
Meier, Samuel A. *The Messenger in the Ancient Semitic World*. HSM 44. Atlanta: Scholars, 1988.
Meinhold, Arndt. *Die Sprüche*. Zurich: Theologischer, 1991.
Méndez-Montoya, Angel F. *The Theology of Food: Eating and the Eucharist*. Malden: Wiley-Blackwell, 2009.
Mercer, Samuel A. B. *The Oath in Babylonian and Assyrian Literature*. Paris: Geuthner, 1912.
Metz, Johannes. *Poverty of Spirit*, 1968. Translated by J. Drury. Mahwah: Paulist, 1998.
Metzger, James A. *Consumption and Wealth in Luke's Travel Narrative*. Leiden: Brill, 2007.
Michel, Cécile. *Women of Assur and Kanesh: Texts from the Archives of Assyrian Merchants*. WAW. Atlanta: SBL, 2020.
Miles, Johnny E. *Wise King—Royal Fool: Semiotics, Satire, and Proverbs 1–9*. London: T&T Clark, 2004.
Miller, Carolyn. "Genre as Social Action." *QJS* 70 (1984) 151–67.

Miller, Jared. *Royal Hittite Instructions and Related Administrative Texts*. WAW 31. Atlanta: SBL, 2013.
Minissale, Antonino. "The Metaphor of 'Falling': Hermeneutic Key to the Book of Sirach." In *The Wisdom of Ben Sira: Studies on Tradition, Redaction, and Theology*, edited by A. Passaro and G. Bellia, 253–75. DCLS 1. Berlin: de Gruyter, 2008.
Moberly, R. Walter L. *The Bible, Theology, and Faith: A Study of Abraham and Jesus*. Cambridge: Cambridge University Press, 2000.
Mongstad-Kvammen, Ingeborg. *Toward a Postcolonial Reading of the Epistle of James: James 2:1–13 in Its Roman Imperial Context*. BibInt 119. Leiden: Brill, 2013.
Montero, Roman A. *Jesus's Manifesto: The Sermon on the Plain*. Eugene: Resource, 2019.
Moo, Douglas J. *The Letter of James*. PiNTC. Grand Rapids: Eerdmans, 2000.
Moore, Michael S. "1 Maccabees." In *The Old Testament and Apocrypha: Fortress Commentary on the Bible*, edited by G. Yee et al., 1055–63. Minneapolis: Fortress, 2014.
———. "הגאל: The Cultural Gyroscope of Ancient Hebrew Society." *RestQ* 23 (1980) 27–35.
———. *The Balaam Traditions: Their Character and Development*. SBLDS 113. Atlanta: Scholars, 1988.
———. "Divine Presence." In *DOTPr* 166–70.
———. *Faith Under Pressure: A Study of Biblical Leaders in Conflict*. Abilene: Abilene Christian University Press, 2003.
———. "Introduction to the Wisdom and Lyric Literature." In *The Transforming Word*, edited by M. Hamilton, 9–15. Abilene: Abilene Christian University Press, 2009.
———. "The Judean *lmlk* Stamps: Some Unresolved Issues." *ResQ* 28 (1985/86) 17–26.
———. *Reconciliation: A Study of Biblical Families in Conflict*. Joplin: College, 1994.
———. Review of *Abiding Astonishment*, by W. Brueggemann. *CBQ* 54 (1992) 740–41.
———. Review of *An Adversary in Heaven: śāṭān in the Hebrew Bible*, by P. L. Day. *JBL* 109 (1990) 508–10.
———. Review of *The Church's Bible: Its Contemporary Authority*, by D. Jodock. *ResQ* 32 (1990) 236–38.
———. Review of *Der liebebedürftige Gott und die gottbedürftige Liebe des Menschen: Ursprung und Funktion der Rede von der Liebe des Menschen zu Gott als a alttestamentlicher Beitrag zur Gotteslehre*, by H. Jauss. *RBL* (2017).
———. Review of *Enūma Eliš: The Standard Babylonian Creation Myth*, by P. Talon. *CBQ* 69 (2007) 800–2.
———. Review of *There Shall Be No Poor Among You*, by L. Hoppe. *JHS* 5 (2004/05).
———. Review of *Theology of the Old Testament: Testimony, Dispute, Advocacy*, by W. Brueggemann. *PSB* 19 (1998) 212–15.
———. Review of *Wealth in the Dead Sea Scrolls and in the Qumran Community*, by C. Murphy. *JHS* 4 (2003).
———. *WealthWarn: A Study of Socioeconomic Conflict in Hebrew Prophecy*. Eugene: Pickwick, 2019.
———. *WealthWatch: A Study of Socioeconomic Conflict in the Bible*. Eugene: Pickwick, 2011.
———. *What Is This Babbler Trying to Say? Essays on Biblical Interpretation*. Eugene: Pickwick, 2016.
Moran, William L. "The Ancient Near Eastern Background of Love of God in Deuteronomy." *CBQ* 25 (1963) 77–87.

———. "Notes on the Hymn to Marduk in *Ludlul bēl nēmeqi*." *JAOS* 103 (1983) 255–60.

Morenz, Siegfried. *Egyptian Religion*, 1960. Translated by A. E. Keep. Ithaca: Cornell University Press, 1973.

Morley, Neville. *Theories, Models, and Concepts in Ancient History: Approaching the Ancient World*. London: Routledge, 2004.

Morris, Leon. *Luke: An Introduction and Commentary*. Downers Grove: InterVarsity, 1988.

Mouton, Alice. "Le rituel de Walkui (*KBo* 32.176): quelques réflexions sur la déesse de la nuit et l'image du porc dans le monde hittite." *ZA* 94 (2004) 85–105.

Moxnes, Halvor. *The Economy of the Kingdom: Social Conflict and Economic Relations in Luke's Gospel*. Minneapolis: Augsburg Fortress, 1988.

Mowinckel, Sigmund. *Psalmenstudien*. 6 vols. Oslo: Det Norske Videnskaps- Akademi, 1921–24.

———. "Psalms and Wisdom." In *Wisdom in Israel and in the Ancient Near East: Presented to Professor Henry Harold Rowley in Celebration of his Sixty-Fifth Birthday*, edited by M. Noth and D. W. Thomas, 205–44. Leiden: Brill, 1955.

Mugerauer, Robert. "Literature as Reconciliation: The Art of Hypothetical Vision." *Soundings* 58 (1975) 407–15.

Müller, Hans-Peter. "חכם." *TDOT* 4.370–85.

Murphy, Catherine M. *Wealth in the Dead Sea Scrolls and in the Qumran Community*. STDJ 40. Leiden: Brill, 2002.

Murphy, Nancey. "When Jesus Said 'Love Your Enemies' I Think He Probably Meant Don't Kill Them." *PRSt* 40 (2013) 123–29.

Murphy, Roland E. "A Consideration of the Classification Wisdom Psalms." *VTSup* 9. Leiden: Brill, 156–67.

———. "The Personification of Wisdom." In *Wisdom in Ancient Israel: Essays in Honour of John Emerton*, edited by J. Day et al., 222–33. Cambridge: Cambridge University Press, 1995.

———. *Proverbs*. WBC 22. Nashville: Thomas Nelson, 1998.

———. *The Tree of Life: An Exploration of Biblical Wisdom Literature*. Grand Rapids: Eerdmans, 1990.

———. "Wisdom in the OT." *ABD* 6.920–31.

Nakata, Ichiro. "Mesopotamian Merchants and Their Ethos." *JANES* 3 (1970/71) 90–100.

Nemet-Nejat, Karen. "Akkadian Wisdom Literature." In *Women in the Ancient Near East: A Sourcebook*, edited by M. Chavalas, 75–100. London: Routledge, 2014.

Neusner, Jacob. *Understanding the Talmud: A Dialogic Approach*. Jersey City: KTAV, 2004.

Neville, Richard. "A Reassessment of the Radical Nature of Job's Ethic in Job 31:13–15." *VT* 53 (2003) 181–200.

Newsom, Carol A. *The Book of Job: A Contest of Moral Imaginations*. New York: Oxford University Press, 2003.

———. "Job." In *Women's Bible Commentary*, edited by C. Newsom et al., 208–15. Louisville: Westminster John Knox, 2012.

Nickelsburg, George W. "Riches, the Rich, and God's Judgment in 1 Enoch 92–105 and the Gospel According to Luke." *NTS* 25 (1979) 324–44.

———. "Seeking the Origin of the Two Ways Tradition in Jewish and Christian Ethical Texts." In A *Multiform Heritage: Studies on Early Judaism and Christianity in Honor of Robert A. Kraft*, edited by B. G. Wright. SPHS 24. Atlanta: Scholars, 1999.

———. "Social Aspects of Palestinian Jewish Apocalypticism." In *Apocalypticism in the Mediterranean World and the Near East*, edited by D. Hellholm, 641–54. Tübingen: Mohr Siebeck, 1983.

Nolan, Patrick, and Gerhard Lenski. *Human Societies: An Introduction to Macrosociology*. New York: Oxford University Press, 2014.

Nötscher, Friedrich. *Zur theologischen Terminologie der Qumrantexte*. BBB 10. Bonn: Hanstein, 1956.

Nougayrol, Jean. "'Juste Soufrant' (RS 25.460)." In *Ugaritica* V. Paris: Geuthner, 1968.

O'Connor, Kathleen M. *The Wisdom Literature*. MBS 5. Collegeville: Liturgical, 1988.

Oeming, Manfred. "Wisdom as a Hermeneutical Key to the Book of Psalms." In *Scribes, Sages, and Seers: The Sage in the Eastern Mediterranean World*, edited by L. G. Perdue, 154–62. Göttingen: Vandenhoeck & Ruprecht, 2008.

Oesterley, William Oscar Emil. *The Wisdom of Jesus the Son of Sirach, or Ecclesiasticus*. Cambridge: Cambridge University Press, 1912.

Olyan, Saul M. "Honor, Shame, and Covenant Relations in Ancient Israel and Its Environment." *JBL* 115 (1996) 201–18.

———. *Social Inequality in the World of the Text: The Significance of Ritual and Social Distinctions in the Hebrew Bible*. Göttingen: Vandenhoeck & Ruprecht, 2011.

Oppenheim, A. Leo. *Ancient Mesopotamia: Portrait of a Dead Civilization*. Chicago: University of Chicago Press, 1977.

———. "The Seafaring Merchants of Ur." *JAOS* 74 (1954) 6–17.

Orlin, Louis L. *Assyrian Colonies in Cappadocia*. Paris: Mouton, 1970.

Ortlund, Robert C. *Proverbs: Wisdom that Works*. Wheaton: Crossway, 2012.

Orwell, George. *The Road to Wigan Pier*. New York: Harcourt, 1958.

Osburn, Carroll D. "James, Sirach, and the Poor." *ExAud* 22 (2006) 113–32.

Oshima, Takayoshi. *Babylonian Poems of Pious Sufferers: Ludlul bēl nēmeqi and the Babylonian Theodicy*. ORA 14. Tübingen: Mohr Siebeck, 2014.

———. *The Babylonian Theodicy*. SAACT 9. Helsinki: Neo-Assyrian Text Corpus Project, 2013.

———. "How 'Mesopotamian' was Aḥiqar the Wise? A Search for Aḥiqar in Cuneiform Texts." In *Wandering Arameans: Arameans Outside Assyria: Textual and Archaeological Perspectives*, edited by A. Berlejung et al., 148–67. Wiesbaden: Harrassowitz, 2017.

Osing, Jürgen. "Die Worte von Heliopolis." In *Fontes atque Pontes. Eine Festgabe für Hellmut Brunner*, edited by M. Görg, 347–61. Wiesbaden: Harrassowitz, 1983.

Otto, Eberhard. *Der Vorwurf an Gott. Zur Entstehung der ägyptischen Auseinandersetzungsliteratur*. Hildesheim: Gerstenberg, 1951.

Otto, Eckhart. *Krieg und Frieden in der Hebräischen Bibel und im Alten Orient*. Aspekte fur eine Friedensordnung in der Moderne. Stuttgart: Kohlhammer, 1999.

Otzen, Benedikt. "עמל." In *TDOT* 11.196–202.

———. *Tobit and Judith*. GAP 11. London: Sheffield Academic, 2002.

Paffenroth, Kim. *In Praise of Wisdom: Literary and Theological Reflections on Faith and Reason*. New York: Continuum, 2004.

Palmer, Earl F. *The Book that James Wrote*. Grand Rapids: Eerdmans, 1997.

Paper, Herbert H. "Proverbs in Judeo-Persian." In *Irano-Judaica*, edited by S. Shaked, 12.2–47. Jerusalem: Ben-Zvi Institute, 1982.

Pardee, Dennis. "A New Aramaic Inscription from Zincirli." *BASOR* 356 (2009) 51–71.

Parrott, Douglas M. "Eugnostos the Blessed and the Sophia of Jesus Christ." In *The Nag Hammadi Library in English*, edited by J. M. Robinson, 220–43. Leiden: Brill, 1988.

Parry, Kenneth. *Depicting the Word: Byzantine Iconophile Thought of the Eighth and Ninth Centuries*. Leiden: Brill, 1996.

Pascal, Blaise. *Pensées*. Translated by W. F. Trotter. Mineola: Dover, 2018.

Patterson, Orlando. *Slavery and Social Death: A Comparative Study*. Cambridge: Harvard University Press, 2018.

Patterson, Richard. *Aristotle's Modal Logic: Essence and Entailment in the* Organon. Cambridge: Cambridge University Press, 1995.

Paul, Shalom M. "Euphemism and Dysphemism." In *EncJud* 959–62.

———. "Vain Imprecations on Having Been Born in Job 3 and Mesopotamian Literature." In *Marbeh Hokmah: Studies in the Bible and the Ancient Near East in Loving Memory of Victor Avigdor Hurowitz*, edited by S. Yona et al., 401–6. Winona Lake: Eisenbrauns, 2015.

Peake, Arthur S. *Job*. NCB. Edinburgh: T. C. and E. C. Jack, 1905.

Pecchioli Daddi, Francesca. "A Song of Release from Hattic Tradition." In *Akten des IV Internationalen Kongresses für Hethitologie*, edited by G. Wilhelm, 552–60. Wiesbaden: Harrassowitz, 2001.

Pemberton, Glenn. *A Life That Is Good: The Message of Proverbs in a World Wanting Wisdom*. Grand Rapids: Eerdmans, 2018.

Penchansky, David. *Understanding Wisdom Literature: Conflict and Dissonance in the Hebrew Text*. Grand Rapids: Eerdmans, 2012.

Perdue, Leo G. *Proverbs*. Interpretation. Louisville: Westminster John Knox, 2000.

———. "The Riddles of Psalm 49." *JBL* 93 (1974) 533–42.

———. *The Sword and the Stylus: An Introduction to Wisdom in the Age of Empires*. Grand Rapids: Eerdmans, 2008.

———. *Wisdom and Cult*. SBLDS 30. Missoula: Scholars, 1977.

Perry, Theodore A. *Dialogues with Kohelet: The Book of Ecclesiastes*. University Park: Pennsylvania State University Press, 1993.

Peterson, Brian Neil. *Qoheleth's Hope: The Message of Ecclesiastes in a Broken World*. Lanham: Fortress Academic, 2019.

Petrany, Catherine. *Pedagogy, Prayer, and Praise: The Wisdom of the Psalms and Psalter*. FAT 83. Tübingen: Mohr Siebeck, 2015.

Pfeiffer, Robert H. "A Pessimistic Dialogue Between Master and Servant." In *ANET* 437–38.

Pilgrim, Walter E. *Good News to the Poor: Wealth and Poverty in Luke-Acts*. Minneapolis: Augsburg Fortress, 1981.

Pioske, Daniel D. *Memory in a Time of Prose: Studies in Epistemology, Hebrew Scribalism, and the Biblical Past*. Oxford: Oxford University Press, 2018.

Pippin, Tina. "Wisdom and Apocalypse in the Apocalypse of John: Desiring Sophia." In *In Search of Wisdom: Essays in Memory of John G. Gammie*, edited by L. G. Perdue et al., 285–96. Louisville: Westminster John Knox, 1993.

Pitt-Rivers, Julian. "Honour and Social Status." In *Honour and Shame: The Values of Mediterranean Society*, edited by J. G. Peristiany, 21–77. Chicago: University of Chicago Press, 1966.

Pleins, J. David. "Poor, Poverty." In *ABD* 5.402–14.
———. *The Social Visions of the Hebrew Bible: A Theological Introduction*. Louisville: Westminster John Knox, 2001.
Plöger, Otto. *Sprüche Salomos (Proverbia)*. BKAT 17/2–4. Neukirchen-Vluyn: Neukirchener, 1984.
Polanyi, Karl. "Marketless Trading in Hammurabi's Time." In *Trade and Market in the Early Empires: Economies in History and Theory*, edited by K. Polanyi et al., 12–26. New York: Free, 1957.
Pope, Marvin. *Job: Introduction, Translation, and Notes*. AB 15. Garden City: Doubleday, 1965.
———. *Song of Songs: Introduction Translation, and Notes*. AB 7C. Garden City: Doubleday, 1977.
Porter, Barbara N. *Trees, Kings, and Politics: Studies in Assyrian Iconography*. OBO 197. Göttingen: Vandenhoeck & Ruprecht, 2003.
Potts, Daniel T. "Distant Shores: Ancient Near Eastern Trade with South Asia and Northeast Africa." In *CANE* 1451–63.
Powell, Marvin A. *Labor in the Ancient Near East*. AOS 68. New Haven: American Oriental Society, 1987.
———. "Money in Mesopotamia." *JESHO* 39 (1996) 224–42.
Preuss, Horst Dietrich. "יעל." In *TDOT* 6.144–47.
Puech, Émile. Review of *The Aramaic Proverbs of Aḥiqar*, by James Lindenberger. *RB* 95 (1988) 588–92.
Rabin, Chaim. "Discourse Analysis and the Dating of Deuteronomy." In *Interpreting the Hebrew Bible: Essays in Honour of Erwin I. J. Rosenthal*, edited by J. Emerton and S. Reif, 171–77. Cambridge: Cambridge University Press, 1982.
Rachman, Gideon. *Zero-Sum Future: American Power in an Age of Anxiety*. New York: Simon & Schuster, 2011.
Rapson, W. S. "The Development and Promotion of Markets for Gold." In *Precious Metals 1981*, edited by E. D. Zysk, 61–68. Toronto: Pergamon, 1982.
Reiner, Erika. "Die akkadische Literatur." In *Neues Handbuch der Literatur-Wissenschaft: Altorientalische Literaturen*, edited by Wolfgang Röllig, 1.151–210. Wiesbaden: Athenaion, 1978.
———. "First Millennium Babylonian Literature." In *CAH* 3.2.293–321.
Reines, Chaim W. "Koheleth on Wisdom and Wealth." *JJS* 5 (1954) 80–84.
Reiterer, Friederich V. "The Sociological Significance of the Scribe as the Teacher of Wisdom in Ben Sira." In *Scribes, Sages, and Seers: The Sage in the Eastern Mediterranean World*, edited by L. Perdue, 218–43. Göttingen: Vandenhoeck and Ruprecht, 2008.
———. "Das Verhältnis der חכמה zur תורה im Buch Ben Sira: Kriterien zur gegenseitigen Bestimmung." In *Studies on the Book of Ben Sira: Papers of the Third International Conference on the Deuterocanonical Books, Shim'on Center, Pápa, Hungary, 18–20 May, 2006*, edited by G. Xeravits et al., 97–133. JSJSup 127. Leiden: Brill, 2008.
Renfrew, Jane. "Vegetables in the Ancient Near Eastern Diet." In *CANE* 191–202.
Resnick, Judith, and Dennis Curtis. *Representing Justice: Invention, Controversy, and Rights in City-States and Democratic Courtrooms*. New Haven: Yale University Press, 2011.
Rey, Jean-Sébastien. *4QInstruction: Sagesse et eschatologie*. STDJ 81. Leiden: Brill, 2009.

Reyes, George. "El Grito del Salario." *Recursos Teológicos* 5 (2004) 79–97.

Rhee, Helen. *Loving the Poor, Saving the Rich: Wealth, Poverty, and Early Christian Formation*. Grand Rapids: Baker Academic, 2012.

———. *Wealth and Poverty in Early Christianity*. Minneapolis: Fortress, 2017.

Richardson, Kurt Anders. "Job as Exemplar in the Epistle of James." In *Hearing the Old Testament in the New Testament*, edited by S. Porter, 213–29. Grand Rapids: Eerdmans, 2006.

Richardson, Mervyn E. J. *Hammurabi's Laws: Text, Translation, and Glossary*. 2000. Reprint, London: T&T Clark, 2004.

Ringe, Sharon H. *Luke*. WBiC. Louisville: Westminster John Knox, 1995.

Ristvet, Lauren. *Ritual, Performance, and Politics in the Ancient Near East*. Cambridge: Cambridge University Press, 2015.

Ro, Johannes Unsok. *Poverty, Law, and Divine Justice in Persian and Hellenistic Judah*. AIL 32. Atlanta: SBL, 2018.

Roberts, J. J. M. "The Ancient Near Eastern Environment." In *The Hebrew Bible and Its Modern Interpreters*, edited by D. Knight and G. Tucker, 75–121. Chico: Scholars, 1985.

———. *The Earliest Semitic Pantheon: A Study of the Semitic Deities Attested in Mesopotamia Before Ur III*. Baltimore: John Hopkins University Press, 1972.

———. "The Hand of Yahweh." *VT* 21 (1971) 244–51.

Robertson, John F. "The Social and Economic Organization of Ancient Mesopotamian Temples." In *CANE* 443–54.

Roche-Hawley, Carole, and Robert Hawley, eds. *Scribes et érudits dans l'orbite de Babylone: Travaux réalisés dans le cadre du projet ANR Mespériph 2007–2011*. Paris: De Boccard, 2012.

Rogers, Jessie. "'It Overflows Like the Euphrates with Understanding': Another Look at the Relationship Between Law and Wisdom in Sirach." In *Of Scribes and Sages: Early Jewish Interpretation and Transmission of Scripture, Vol. 1: Ancient Versions and Traditions*, edited by C. Evans, 114–21. New York: T&T Clark, 2004.

Rosenzweig, Franz. *The Star of Redemption*, 1921. Translated by B. Galli. Madison: University of Wisconsin Press, 2005.

Rositani, Annunziata. "Work and Wages in the Code of Hammurabi." *EVO* 40 (2017) 47–72.

Ross, Allen P. *A Commentary on the Psalms: Vol. 1: 1–41*. KEL. Grand Rapids: Kregel, 2011.

———. "Proverbs." In *The Expositor's Bible Commentary, Vol 6: Proverbs-Isaiah*, edited by T. Longman and D. Garland, 21–251. Grand Rapids: Zondervan, 2008.

Roth, Martha T. *Law Collections from Mesopotamia and Asia Minor*. WAW 6. Atlanta: SBL, 1997.

———. "The Neo-Babylonian Widow." *JCS* 43/45 (1991–1993) 1–26.

Roth, S. John. *The Blind, The Lame, and The Poor: Character Types in Luke-Acts*. JSNT 144. Sheffield: Sheffield Academic, 1997.

Rousseau, John J., and Rami Arav. "Moses' Seat." In *Jesus and His World: An Archaeological and Cultural Dictionary*, 203–6. Minneapolis: Fortress, 1995.

Rowe, Ignacio Márquez. "Scribes, Sages, and Seers in Ugarit." In *Scribes, Sages, and Seers: The Sage in the Eastern Mediterranean World*, edited by L. Perdue, 95–108. Göttingen: Vandenhoeck & Ruprecht, 2008.

Rudman, Dominic. "A Contextual Reading of Ecclesiastes 4:13–16." *JBL* 116 (1997) 57–73.

———. "Determinism in the Book of Ecclesiastes." PhD diss., University of St. Andrews, 1997.

Sachau, Eduard. *Aramäische Papyrus und Ostraka aus einer jüdischen Militär-Kolonie zu Elephantine.* 2 vols. Leipzig: Hinrichs'sche, 1911.

Sack, Ronald H. "Nabonidus." In *ABD* 4.973–76.

Sadler, Rodney. "Genesis." In *Fortress Commentary on the Bible: The Old Testament and Apocrypha*, edited by G. Yee et al., 89–136. Minneapolis: Fortress, 2014.

Saebø, Magnes. "רוּשׁ." In *TDOT* 13.422–26.

Sallaberger, Walther. "Der 'Prolog' des Codex Lipit-Ishtar." In "*Gerechtigkeit und Recht zu üben" (Gen 18,19). Studien zur altorientalischen und biblischen Rechtsgeschichte, zur Religionsgeschichte Israels und zur Religionssoziologie. Festschrift für Eckart Otto zum 65 Geburtstag*, edited by R. Achenbach and M. Arneth, 7–33. BZABR 13. Wiesbaden: Harrassowitz, 2009.

Salters, Robert B. "Acrostics and Lamentations." In *On Stone and Scroll: Essays in Honour of Graham Ivor Davies*, edited by J. K. Aitken et al., 425–40. Berlin: de Gruyter, 2011.

Salyer, Gary Dean. "Vain Rhetoric: Implied Author/Narrator/Narratee/Implied Reader Relationships in Ecclesiastes' Use of First-Person Discourse." PhD diss., University of California, 1997.

Sandmel, Samuel. "Parallelomania." *JBL* 81 (1962) 1–13.

Sandoval, Timothy J. *The Discourse of Wealth and Poverty in the Book of Proverbs.* BIS 77. Leiden: Brill, 2006.

Schifferdecker, Kathryn. *Out of the Whirlwind: Creation Theology in the Book of Job.* HTS 61. Cambridge: Harvard University Press, 2008.

Schipper, Bernd U. *Hermeneutik der Tora. Studien zur Traditionsgeschichte von Prov 2 und zur Komposition von Prov 1–9.* BZAW 432. Berlin: de Gruyter, 2012.

———. *Proverbs 1–15.* Hermeneia. Minneapolis: Fortress, 2019.

Schmid, Christian Friedrich. *Biblical Theology of the New Testament.* Edinburgh: T&T Clark, 1877.

Schmid, Hans Heinrich. *Wesen und Geschichte der Weisheit. Eine Untersuchung zur altorientalischen und israelitischen Literatur.* BZAW 101. Berlin: Töpelmann, 1966.

Schmid, Konrad. "The Authors of Job and Their Historical and Social Setting." In *Scribes, Sages, and Seers: The Sage in the Eastern Mediterranean World*, edited by L. Perdue, 145–53. Göttingen: Vandenhoeck and Ruprecht, 2008.

Schmidt, A. Jordan. *Wisdom, Cosmos, and Cultus in the Book of Sirach.* DCLS 42. Berlin: de Gruyter, 2019.

Schmidt, Thomas E. *Hostility to Wealth in the Synoptic Gospels.* JSNT 15. Sheffield: Sheffield Academic Press, 1987.

Schnabel, Eckhard J. *Law and Wisdom from Ben Sira to Paul.* Tübingen: Mohr and Siebeck, 1985.

Schneider, Thomas. "Knowledge and Knowledgeable Persons in Ancient Egypt: Queries and Arguments About an Unsettled Issue." In *Scribes, Sages, and Seers: The Sage in the Eastern Mediterranean World*, edited by L. Perdue, 35–46. FRLANT 219. Göttingen: Vendenhoek & Ruprecht, 2008.

Schoors, Anton. *The Preacher Sought to Find Pleasing Words: A Study of the Language of Qoheleth, Part II: Vocabulary.* OLA 143. Leuven: Peeters, 2004.

Schottroff, Luise, and Wolfgang Stegemann. *Jesus and the Hope of the Poor*. Translated by M. J. O'Connell. Maryknoll: Orbis, 1986.

Schroeder, David. "Die Haustafeln des Neuen Testaments. Ihre Herkinft und ihr theologischer Sinn." PhD diss., Universität Hamburg, 1959.

Schwartz, Seth. *The Ancient Jews from Alexander to Muhammad*. Cambridge: Cambridge University Press, 2014.

Schwemer, Daniel. Review of *Hittite Priesthood*, by A. Taggar-Cohen. *Or* 78 (2009) 96–105.

Scott, Robert B. Y. *Proverbs, Ecclesiastes: Introduction, Translation, and Notes*. AB 18. Garden City: Doubleday, 1965.

———. *The Way of Wisdom in the Old Testament*. New York: MacMillan, 1971.

Scott, Martin. *Sophia and the Johannine Jesus*. JSNTSup 71. Sheffield: Sheffield Academic, 1992.

Seitz, Christopher. *The Elder Testament: Canon, Theology, Trinity*. Waco: Baylor University Press, 2018.

Sekki, Arthur E. *The Meaning of* רוּחַ *at Qumran*. SBLDS 110. Atlanta: Scholars, 1989.

Seow, Choon Leong. "Beyond Mortal Grasp: The Usage of הבל in Ecclesiastes." *ABR* 48 (2000) 1–16.

———. *Ecclesiastes: A New Translation with Commentary*. AB 18C. New York: Doubleday, 1997.

———. *Job 1–21: Interpretation and Commentary*. Illuminations. Grand Rapids: Eerdmans, 2013.

———. "The Social World of Ecclesiastes." In *Scribes, Sages, and Seers: The Sage in the Eastern Mediterranean World*, edited by L. Perdue, 189–217. Göttingen: Vandenhoeck & Ruprecht, 2008.

———. "The Socioeconomic Context of the Preacher's Hermeneutic." *PSB* 17 (1996) 168–95.

Seri, Andrea. "The Fifty Names of Marduk in *Enūma eliš*." *JAOS* 126 (2006) 507–19.

Sheldon, Linda Jean. "The Book of Job as Hebrew Theodicy: An Ancient Near Eastern Intertextual Conflict Between Law and Cosmology." PhD diss., University of California, 2002.

Sheppard, Gerald T. *Wisdom as a Hermeneutical Construct: A Study in the Sapientializing of the Old Testament*. BZAW 151. Berlin: de Gruyter, 1980.

Shipp, R. Mark. *Of Dead Kings and Dirges: Myth and Meaning in Isaiah 14:4b-21*. AcBib 11. Leiden: Brill, 2002.

Shupak, Nili. "The Contribution of Egyptian Wisdom to the Study of Biblical Wisdom Literature." In *Was There a Wisdom Tradition? New Prospects in Israelite Wisdom Studies*, edited by M. Sneed, 265–304. AIL 23. Atlanta: SBL, 2015.

———. "The Instruction of Amenemope and Proverbs 22:17–24:22 from the Perspective of Contemporary Research." In *Seeking Out the Wisdom of the Ancients: Essays Offered to Michael V. Fox on the Occasion of his Sixty-Fifth Birthday*, edited by R. Troxel et al., 203–20. Winona Lake: Eisenbrauns, 2005.

Shutt, R. James H. "Aristeas, Letter of." In *ABD* 1.380–82.

Sider, Ronald J. *Rich Christians in an Age of Hunger: Moving from Affluence to Generosity*. Nashville: Thomas Nelson, 2015.

Sidursky, Michael. "A Tablet of Prayers for a King? (K. 2279)." *JRAS* 37 (1920) 565–72.

Siegfried, Carl G. *Prediger und Hoheslied*. HKAT 2.3.2. Göttingen: Vandenhoeck & Ruprecht, 1898.

Sinding, Michael. "After Definitions: Genre, Categories, and Cognitive Science." *Genre* 35 (2002) 181–220.
Singer, Ithamar. *Hittite Prayers*. WAW 11. Leiden: Brill, 2002.
Sinnott, Alice M. *The Personification of Wisdom*. 2005. Reprint, SOTSMS, New York: Routledge, 2017.
Sitzler, Dorothea. *"Vorwurf gegen Gott." Ein religiöses Motiv im Alten Orient (Ägypten und Mesopotamien)*. SOR 32. Wiesbaden: Harrassowitz, 1995.
Skehan, Patrick. *Studies in Israelite Poetry and Wisdom*. CBQMS 1. Washington, DC: Catholic Biblical Association, 1971.
Skehan, Patrick, and Alexander Di Lella. *The Wisdom of Ben Sira: Introduction, Translation, and Notes*. AB 39. New York: Doubleday, 1987.
Smith, Mark S. *The Ugaritic Ba'al Cycle, Vol. 1: Introduction with Text, Translation, and Commentary on* CAT *1.1–1.2*. Leiden: Brill, 1994.
Sneed, Mark R. "'Grasping After the Wind': The Elusive Attempt to Define and Delimit Wisdom." In *Was There A Wisdom Tradition? New Prospects in Israelite Wisdom Studies*, edited by M. Sneed, 39–68. AIL 23. Atlanta: SBL, 2015.
———. "Is the 'Wisdom Tradition' a Tradition?" *CBQ* 73 (2011) 50–71.
———. "Methods, Muddles, and Modes of Literature: The Question of Influence Between Wisdom and Prophecy." *In Riddles and Revelations: Explorations into the Relationship Between Wisdom and Prophecy in the Hebrew Bible*, edited by M. J. Boda et al., 30–44. LHBOTS 634. London: T&T Clark, 2018.
———. *The Politics of Pessimism in Ecclesiastes: A Social-Science Perspective*. AIL 12. Atlanta: SBL, 2012.
———. *The Social World of the Sages*. Minneapolis: Fortress, 2015.
———. *Was There a Wisdom Tradition? New Prospects in Israelite Wisdom Studies*. AIL 23. Atlanta: SBL, 2015.
Snell, Daniel. "The Activities of Some Merchants of Umma." *Iraq* 39 (1977) 45–50.
———. *Ledgers and Prices*. New Haven: Yale University Press, 1982.
———. "The Relation Between the Targum and the Peshitta of Proverbs." *ZAW* 110 (1998) 72–74.
Sommerfeld, Walter. *Der Aufstieg Marduks. Die Stellung Marduks in der babylonischen Religion des zweiten Jahrtausends v. Chr.* Kevelaer: Butzon & Bercker, 1982.
Speiser, Ephraim A. "The Case of the Obliging Servant." *JCS* 8 (1954) 98–105.
Spieckermann, Hermann. *Gottes Liebe zu Israel: Studien zur Theologie des Alten Testaments*. FAT 33. Tübingen: Mohr Siebeck, 2004.
———. "Wrath and Mercy as Crucial Terms of Theological Hermeneutics." In *Divine Wrath and Mercy in the World of Antiquity*, edited by R. Kratz and H. Spieckermann, 3–16. FAT 33. Tübingen: Mohr Siebeck, 2008.
Spielvogel, Jackson J. *Western Civilization*. Boston: Cengage Learning, 2018.
Stagg, Frank. "Exegetical Themes in James 1 and 2." *RevExp* 66 (1969) 391–402.
Stassen, Glen. *Just Peacemaking: Transforming Initiatives for Justice and Peace*. Louisville: Westminster John Knox, 1992.
Stearns, Peter N. *Consumerism in World History: The Global Transformation of Desire*. London: Routledge, 2001.
Steck, Odil Hannes. "Theological Streams of Tradition." In *Tradition and Theology in the Old Testament*, edited by D. A. Knight, 183–214. 1977. Reprint, Sheffield: JSOT Press, 1990.

Steiner, Richard C. *Disembodied Souls: The Nefesh in Israel and Kindred Spirits in the Ancient Near East, with an Appendix on the Katumuwa Inscription*. ANEM 11. Atlanta: SBL, 2015.

Stern, David. "Introduction: On Comparative Biblical Exegesis—Interpretation, Influence, Appropriation." In *Jewish Biblical Interpretation and Cultural Exchange*, edited by N. Dohrmann and D. Stern, 1–19. Philadelphia: University of Pennsylvania Press, 2008.

Stewart, Alander Coe. Review of *Wisdom Intoned*, by Simon Cheung. *JHS* 17 (2017).

Stokes, Ryan E. *The Satan: How God's Executioner Became the Enemy*. Grand Rapids: Eerdmans, 2019.

Stol, Marten. *Women in the Ancient Near East*. Berlin: de Gruyter, 2016.

Stoner, Katherine E., and Shae Irving. *Prenuptial Agreements: How to Write a Fair and Lasting Contract*. Berkeley: NOLO, 2016.

Story, Cullen I. K. "The Book of Proverbs and Northwest Semitic Literature." *JBL* 64 (1945) 319–37.

Strack, Hermann L. *Die Sprüche Salomos*. Nördlingen: Beck, 1888.

Strecker, George. *Die Bergpredigt: Ein exegetische Kommentar*. Göttingen: Vandenhoeck & Ruprecht, 1985.

Strugnell, John, et al. *Discoveries in the Judean Desert XXXIV, Sapiential Texts Part 2: 4QInstruction* (מוסר למבין)*: 4Q415ff. with a Re-edition of 1Q26 by J. Strugnell and D. Harrington and an Edition of 4Q423 by T. Elgvin, in consultation with J. A. Fitzmyer*. DJD 34. Oxford: Clarendon, 1999.

Stuckenbruck, Loren. "4QInstruction and the Possible Influence of Early Enochic Traditions: An Evaluation." In *The Wisdom Texts from Qumran and the Development of Sapiential Thought*, edited by C. Hempel et al., 245–62. BETL 159. Leuven: Peeters, 2002.

Stulac, George M. "Who Are the 'Rich' in James?" *Pres* 16 (1990) 89–102.

Stulman, Louis. *The Other Text of Jeremiah: A Reconstruction of the Hebrew Text Underlying the Greek Version of the Prose Sections of Jeremiah, with English Translation*. Lanham: University Press of America, 1985.

Sunkara, Bhaskar. *The Socialist Manifesto: The Case for Radical Politics in an Age of Extreme Inequality*. New York: Basic, 2020.

Swartley, Willard M. *Covenant of Peace: The Missing Peace in New Testament Theology and Ethics*. Grand Rapids: Eerdmans, 2006.

Taggar-Cohen, Ada. "Biblical Covenant and Hittite *išḫiul* Reexamined." *VT* 61 (2011) 461–88.

———. "Biblical Wisdom Literature and Hittite Didactic Texts in the Ancient Near Eastern Literary Context." *JISMOR* 14 (2019) 45–64.

Talisse, Ribert B., and Scott F. Aiken. "Why Pragmatists Cannot Be Pluralists." *TCSPS* 41 (2005) 101–18.

Talon, Philippe, *Enūma Eliš: The Standard Babylonian Creation Myth*. SAACT 4. Helsinki: Neo-Assyrian Text Corpus Project, 2005.

Tan, Nancy Nam Hoon. *The "Foreignness" of the Foreign Woman in Proverbs 1–9: A Study of the Origin and Development of a Biblical Motif*. BZAW 381. Berlin: de Gruyter, 2008.

Taylor, Jon. "The Sumerian Proverb Collections." *RA* 99 (2005) 13–38.

Teeter, D. Andrew. "Torah, Wisdom, and the Composition of Rewritten Scripture: *Jubilees* and 11QPsa in Comparative Perspective." In *Wisdom and Torah: The Reception of "Torah" in the Wisdom Literature of the Second Temple Period*, edited by B. U. Schipper and D. A. Teeter, 233–72. JSJSup 163. Leiden: Brill, 2013.

Terkel, Studs. *Working: People Talk About What They Do All Day and How they Feel About What They Do*. New York: New, 1974.

Theissen, Gerd. *The Religion of the Earliest Christian Churches: Creating a Symbolic World*. Translated by J. Bowden. Minneapolis: Augsburg Fortress, 1999.

Thurow, Lester. *The Zero-Sum Society: Distribution and the Possibilities for Change*. New York: Basic, 1980.

Ticciati, Susannah. *Job and the Disruption of Identity: Reading Beyond Barth*. New York: T&T Clark, 2005.

Tiemstra, John P. *Stories Economists Tell: Studies in Christianity and Economics*. Eugene: Pickwick, 2012.

Tigchelaar, Eibert J. C. *To Increase Learning for the Understanding Ones: Reading and Reconstructing the Fragmentary Early Jewish Sapiential Text 4QInstruction*. Leiden: Brill, 2002.

———. "Towards a Reconstruction of the Beginning of 4QInstruction (4Q416 Fragment 1 and Parallels)." In *The Wisdom Texts from Qumran and the Development of Sapiential Thought*, edited by C. Hempel et al., 99–126. Leuven: Peeters, 2002.

Tov, Emanuel. "The Aramaic, Syriac, and Latin Translations of Hebrew Scripture *vis-à-vis* the Masoretic Text." In *Textual Criticism of the Hebrew Bible, Qumran, Septuagint: Collected Essays, Vol. 3*, 82–94. Leiden: Brill, 2015.

———. "The Rabbinic Tradition Concerning the 'Alterations' Inserted into the Greek Translation of the Torah and their Relation to the Original Text of the Septuagint." In *The Greek and Hebrew Bible: Collected Essays on the Septuagint, Vol. 1*, 1–20. Leiden: Brill, 1999.

———. *Textual Criticism of the Hebrew Bible*. Minneapolis: Fortress, 2001.

Townsend, Michael J. *The Epistle of James*. ECS. London: Epworth, 1994.

Toy, Crawford H. *A Critical and Exegetical Commentary on the Book of Proverbs*. ICC. Edinburgh: T&T Clark, 1899.

Treier, Daniel J. *Proverbs and Ecclesiastes*. BTCB. Grand Rapids: Brazos, 2011.

Tsafrir, Nurit. *Collective Liability in Islam: The `Aqila and Blood-Money Payments*. Cambridge: Cambridge University Press, 2019.

Tsai, Daisy Yulin. *Human Rights in Deuteronomy: With Special Focus on Slave Laws*. BZAW 464. Berlin: de Gruyter, 2014.

Tur-Sinai, Naphtali H. משלי שלמה. Tel Aviv: Yavneh, 1947.

Ünal, Ahmet. "Zum Status der 'Augures' bei den Hethitern." *RHA* 31 (1973) 27–56.

Unger, Eckhard. *Babylon: Die heilige Stadt nach der Beschreibung der Babylonier*. Berlin: de Gruyter, 1931.

Ungnad, A. "Zur babylonischen Lebensphilosophie." *AfO* 15 (1945–1951) 74–75.

Uusimäki, Elisa. Review of *Wisdom Intoned*, by Simon Cheung. *JSS* 63 (2018) 273–75.

van de Mieroop, Marc. *The Ancient Mesopotamian City*. Oxford: Oxford University Press, 1999.

———. *King Hammurabi of Babylon: A Biography*. Oxford: Blackwell, 2005.

van den Brink, Julia. "Luke's Beatitudes and Woes: Are They Covenant Blessings and Curses?" *Stimulus* 23 (2016) 12–17.

van der Toorn, Karel. "In the Lions' Den: the Babylonian Background of a Biblical Motif." *CBQ* 60 (1998) 626–40.

———. "Theodicy in Akkadian Literature." In *Theodicy in the World of the Bible*, edited by A. Laato and J. de Moor, 57–89. Leiden: Brill, 2003.

———. "Why Wisdom Became a Secret: On Wisdom as a Written Genre." In *Wisdom Literature in Mesopotamia and Israel*, edited by R. J. Clifford, 21–32. SBLSymS 36. Atlanta: SBL, 2007.

Van Dijk, Johannes Jacobus Adrianus. *La sagesse suméro-accadienne: Recherches sur les genres littéraires des textes sapientiaux*. Leiden: Brill, 1993.

———. "Theodicy in Akkadian Literature." In *Theodicy in the World of the Bible: The Goodness of God and the Problem of Evil*, edited by A. Laato and J. C. de Moor, 57–89. Leiden: Brill, 2003.

Van Leeuwen, Raymond C. "Wealth and Poverty: System and Contradiction in Proverbs." *HS* 33 (1992) 25–36.

Vanstiphout, Herman L. J. "Some Thoughts on Genre in Mesopotamian Literature." In *Keilschriftliche Literaturen. Ausgewahlte Vortrage der XXXII Recontre Assyriologique Internationale*, edited by K. Hecker and W. Sommerfeld, 1–11. BBVO 6. Berlin: Reimer, 1986.

Vassiliadis, Petros. "John in an Orthodox Perspective." In *Global Bible Commentary*, edited by D. Patte, 412–18. Nashville: Abingdon, 2004.

Vayntrub, Jacqueline E. "The Book of Proverbs and the Idea of Ancient Israelite Education." *ZAW* 128 (2016) 96–114.

Veenhof, Klaas R. *Aspects of Old Assyrian Trade and Its Terminology*. Leiden: Brill, 1972.

Veldhuis, Niek. "Sumerian Proverbs in Their Curricular Context." *JAOS* 120 (2000) 383–99.

Venter, Pieter. "An Ideology of Poverty in 4QInstruction." In *Wisdom Poured Out Like Water: Studies on Jewish and Christian Antiquity in Honor of Gabriele Boccaccini*, edited by J. H. Ellens et al., 215–31. DCLS 38. Berlin: de Gruyter, 2018.

Vermeylen, Jacques. *Métamorphoses: Les rédactions successives du livre de Job*. Leuven: Peeters, 2015.

Vesely, Patricia. *Friendship and Virtue Ethics in the Book of Job*. Cambridge: Cambridge University Press, 2019.

Volgger, David. "Die Adressaten des Weisheitsbuches." *Bib* 82 (2001) 153–77.

Volk, Konrad. "Edubba'a und Edubba'a-Literatur: Rätsel und Lösungen." *ZA* 90 (2000) 1–30.

von Klinger, Friedrich Maximilian. *Sturm und Drang*. A play first performed in 1777 by the Abel Seyler Theatre Company in Hamburg, Germany.

von Rad, Gerhard. *Wisdom in Israel*. Translated by J. D. Martin. Harrisburg: Trinity, 1972.

von Schuler, Einar. "Hethitische Königserlässe als Quellen der Rechtsfindung und ihr Verhältnis zum kodifizierten Recht." In *Festschrift Johannes Friedrich zum 65 Geburtstag*, edited by R. von Kienle et al., 446–72. Heidelberg: Winter, 1959.

von Soden, Wolfram. *The Ancient Orient: An Introduction to the Study of the Ancient Near East*, 1985. Translated by D. G. Schley. Grand Rapids: Eerdmans, 1994.

———. "'Weisheitstexte' in akkadischer Sprache." In *Texte aus der Umwelt des Alten Testaments Band III. Weisheitstexte, Mythen und Epen*, edited by B. Günter et al., 110–88. Gütersloh: Mohn, 1990.

Wachob, Wesley Hiram. *The Voice of Jesus in the Social Rhetoric of James*. SNTS 106. Cambridge: Cambridge University Press, 2000.

Wagner, Max. *Die lexikalischen und grammatikalischen Aramäismen im alttestamentlichen Hebräisch*. BZAW 96. Berlin: Töpelmann, 1966.

Walker, Christopher, and Michael Dick. *The Induction of the Cult Image in Ancient Mesopotamia: The Mesopotamian* Mis Pî *Ritual*. SAALT 1. Helsinki: Neo-Assyrian Text Corpus Project, 2001.

Waltke, Bruce K. *An Old Testament Theology: An Exegetical, Canonical, and Thematic Approach*. Grand Rapids: Zondervan, 2007.

———. *Proverbs 1–15*. NICOT. Grand Rapids: Eerdmans, 2004.

Walton, John H. *Ancient Near Eastern Thought and the Old Testament: Introducing the Conceptual World of the Hebrew Bible*. Grand Rapids: Baker Academic, 2018.

Ward, Roy B. "Partiality in the Assembly: James 2:2–4." *HTR* 62 (1969) 87–97.

Washington, Harold C. "The 'Strange Woman' of Proverbs 1–9 and Post-Exilic Judaean Society." In *Second Temple Studies 2: Temple Community in the Persian Period*, edited by T. Eskenazi and K. Richards, 217–45. JSOTSup 175. Sheffield: JSOT Press, 1994.

———. *Wealth and Poverty in the Instruction of Amenemope and the Hebrew Proverbs: A Comparative Case Study in the Social Location and Function of Ancient Near Eastern Wisdom Literature*. Atlanta: Scholars, 1994.

Watson, Duane F. Review of *Restoring the Diaspora: Discursive Structure and Purpose in the Epistle of James*, by T. Cargal. *JBL* 114 (1995) 348–51.

Watson, Wilfred G. E. *Traditional Techniques in Classical Hebrew Verse*. JSOTSup 170. Sheffield: Sheffield Academic, 1994.

Wazana, Nili. "A Case of the Evil Eye: Qohelet 4:4–8." *JBL* 126 (2007) 685–702.

Weeks, Stuart. *Ecclesiastes and Scepticism*. New York: T&T Clark, 2012.

———. *An Introduction to the Study of Wisdom Literature*. New York: T&T Clark, 2010.

———. *Early Israelite Wisdom*. New York: Oxford University Press, 1994.

———. *Instruction and Imagery in Proverbs 1–9*. New York: Oxford University Press, 2007.

Weigel, Sigrid. "Inheritance Law, Heritage, Heredity: European Perspectives." *LL* 20 (2008) 279–87.

Weigl, Michael. *Die aramäischen Achikar-Sprüche aus Elephantine und die alttestamentliche Weisheitsliteratur*. BZAW 399. Berlin: de Gruyter, 2010.

Weinfeld, Moshe. "Job and Its Mesopotamian Parallels—A Typological Analysis." In *Text and Context: Old Testament and Semitic Studies for F. C. Fensham*, edited by W. Claasen, 217–26. JSOTSup 48. Sheffield: JSOT Press, 1988.

———. "The Origin of the Apodictic Law: An Overlooked Source." *VT* 23 (1973) 63–75.

Wells, Bruce. "Law and Practice." In *A Companion to the Ancient Near East*, edited by D. Snell, 196–210. Oxford: Blackwell, 2005.

Welten, Peter. *Die Königs Stempel*. Wiesbaden: Harrassowitz, 1969.

Welz, Claudia. *Love's Transcendence and the Problem of Theodicy*. RPT 30. Tübingen: Mohr Siebeck, 2008.

Westbrook, Raymond. "The Character of Ancient Near Eastern Law." In *A History of Ancient Near Eastern Law*, edited by R. Westbrook, 1.1–91. HdO 72/1. Leiden: Brill, 2003.

———. "Cuneiform Law Codes and the Origins of Legislation." *ZA* 79 (1989) 201–22.

———. "The Old Babylonian Period." In *Security for Debt in Ancient Near Eastern Law*, edited by R. Westbrook and R. Jasnow, 63–92. Leiden: Brill, 2001.

———. *Old Babylonian Marriage Law*. Horn: Berger, 1988.

Westbrook, Raymond, and Roger D. Woodard. "The Edict of Tudḫaliya IV." *JAOS* 110 (1990) 641–59.

Westermann, Claus. *Basic Forms of Prophetic Speech*, 1960. Translated by H. C. White. Louisville: Westminster John Knox, 1991.

———. *Der Psalter*. Stuttgart: Calver, 1967.

———. *The Roots of Wisdom. The Oldest Proverbs of Israel and Other Peoples*. Translated by J. D. Charles. Louisville: Westminster John Knox, 1995.

Whitley, Charles F. *Koheleth: His Language and Thought*. BZAW 148. Berlin: de Gruyter, 1979.

Whybray, Roger N. *The Book of the Proverbs: A Survey of Modern Study*. Leiden: Brill, 1995.

———. *The Composition of the Book of Proverbs*. JSOTSup 168. Sheffield: Sheffield Academic, 1994.

———. "The Identification and Use of Quotations in Ecclesiastes." *VTSup* 32 (1981) 435–51.

———. *The Intellectual Tradition in the Old Testament*. BZAW 135. Berlin: de Gruyter, 1974.

———. *Wealth and Poverty in the Book of Proverbs*. JSOTSup 99. Sheffield: JSOT Press, 1990.

———. "Wisdom Psalms." In *Wisdom in Ancient Israel*, edited by J. Day et al., 152–60. Cambridge: Cambridge University Press, 1995.

Wilcke, Claus. *Early Ancient Near Eastern Law: A History of Its Beginnings. The Early Dynastic and Sargonic Periods*. Winona Lake: Eisenbrauns, 2007.

Wilson, Andrew P. *Critical Entanglements: Postmodern Theory and Biblical Studies*. Leiden: Brill, 2019.

Wilson, John A. "A Dispute Over Suicide." In *ANET* 405–7.

———. "The Oath in Ancient Egypt." *JNES* 7 (1948) 129–56.

Wilson, Lindsay. *Proverbs: An Introduction and Commentary*. TOTC 17. Downers Grove: InterVarsity, 2018.

Wink, Walter. *Engaging the Powers: Discernment and Resistance in a World of Domination*. Minneapolis: Fortress, 1992.

———. *Jesus and Nonviolence: A Third Way*. Minneapolis: Fortress, 2003.

Winston, David. "Solomon, Wisdom of." In *ABD* 6.120–27.

———. *The Wisdom of Solomon: A New Translation with Introduction and Commentary*. AB 43. Garden City: Doubleday, 1979.

Wischmeyer, Oda. *Die Kultur des Buches Jesus Sirach*. BZAW 77. Berlin: de Gruyter, 1995.

Witherington, Benjamin. *Letters and Homilies for Jewish Christians: A Socio-Rhetorical Commentary on Hebrews, James and Jude*. Downers Grove: IVP Academic, 2007.

Witte, John. *Church, State, and Family: Reconciling Traditional Teachings and Modern Liberties*. Cambridge: Cambridge University Press, 2019.

Wittgenstein, Ludwig. *Philosophical Investigations*. Translated by G. E. M. Anscombe et al. London: Basil Blackwell, 1958.

Wold, Benjamin G. *4QInstruction: Division and Hierarchies*. Leiden: Brill, 2018.

———. "Metaphorical Poverty in *Musar leMevin*." *JJS* 58 (2007) 140–53.

———. *Women, Men and Angels: The Qumran Wisdom Document* "Musar leMevin" *and Its Allusions to Genesis Creation Traditions*. WUNT 2/201. Tübingen: Mohr Siebeck, 2005.

Wolff, Richard D., and Stephen A. Resnick. *Contending Economic Theories: Neoclassical, Keynesian, and Marxian*. Cambridge: MIT Press, 2012.

Wright, Addison G. "The Riddle of the Sphinx: The Structure of the Book of Qoheleth." In *Reflecting with Solomon: Selected Studies on the Book of Ecclesiastes*, edited by R. B. Zuck, 45–66. Eugene: Wipf & Stock, 2003.

Wright, Benjamin G., III. *The Letter of Aristeas: "Aristeas to Philocrates," or "On the Translation of the Law of the Jews."* CEJL. Berlin: de Gruyter, 2015.

———. Review of *Like an Everlasting Signet Ring: Generosity in the Book of Sirach*, by B. Gregory. *DSD* 22 (2015) 240–42.

———. "Torah and Sapiential Pedagogy in the Book of Ben Sira." In *Wisdom and Torah: The Reception of "Torah" in the Wisdom Literature of the Second Temple Period*, edited by B. Schipper and D. A. Teeter, 157–86. Leiden: Brill, 2013.

———. "What Does India Have to Do with Jerusalem? Ben Sira, Language, and Colonialism." In *Jewish Cultural Encounters in the Ancient Mediterranean and Near Eastern World*, edited by M. Popović et al., 136–56. Leiden: Brill, 2017.

Wright, Benjamin G., III, and Claudia V. Camp. "Who Has Been Tested By Gold and Found Perfect? Ben Sira's Discourse of Riches and Poverty." *Henoch* 23 (2001) 153–73.

Wright, David P. *Inventing God's Law: How the Covenant Code of the Bible Used and Revised the Laws of Hammurabi*. Oxford: Oxford University Press, 2009.

———. *Ritual in Narrative: The Dynamics of Feasting, Mourning, and Retaliation Rites in the Ugaritic Tale of Aqhat*. Winona Lake: Eisenbrauns, 2001.

Wright, Norman T. *James*. Downers Grove: InterVarsity, 2012.

Wunsch, Cornelia. *Urkunden zum Ehe-, Vermögens- und Erbrecht aus verschiedenen neubabylonischen Archiven*. Dresden: Islet, 2003.

Yadin, Yigael. *Hazor: The Rediscovery of a Great Citadel of the Bible*. New York: Random, 1975.

Yoder, Christine R. *Proverbs*. AOTC. Nashville: Abingdon, 2009.

———. *Wisdom as a Woman of Substance: A Socioeconomic Reading of Proverbs 1–9 and 31:10–31*. BZAW 304. Berlin: de Gruyter, 2001.

———. "The 'Woman of Substance' (אשת־חיל): A Socioeconomic Reading of Proverbs 31:10–31." *JBL* 122 (2003) 427–47.

Zabán, Bálint Károly. *The Pillar Function of the Speeches of Wisdom: Proverbs 1:20–33, 8:1–36, and 9:1–6 in the Structural Framework of Proverbs 1–9*. BZAW 429. Berlin: de Gruyter, 2012.

Zaccagnini, Carlo. "Nuzi." In *Security for Debt in Ancient Near Eastern Law*, edited by R. Westbrook and R. Jasnow, 223–36. CHANE 9. Leiden: Brill, 2001.

Zenger, Erich. "Die Komposition der sog. Kleinen Hallel bzw. Schluss-Hallel Ps. 146–150," in *Psalmen 101–150*, 807–10. HThKAT. Freiburg: Herder, 2008.

Žižek, Slavoj. *Violence: Six Sideways Reflections*. London: Profile, 2008.

Zuckerman, Bruce. *Job the Silent: A Study in Historical Counterpoint*. Oxford: Oxford University Press, 1991.

Subject Index

1 Enoch, 149n148, 159n220, 167n16, 186n133
4QInstruction, 5, 130, 130n6, 131, 131n14, 131n17, 132, 132n26, 133n31, 134n41, 135n48, 136n56, 137, 139n76, 140, 141, 144, 167n13, 175, 177n82, 177n84, 187, 194

Aesop, 150
Aḥiqar, 2n9, 5, 55, 55n344, 55n345, 55n347, 55n348, 55n349, 56n352, 68, 194
alms(giving), 71n96, 74n114, 76n133, 81n165, 84n184, 85n192, 92, 97n280, 134n35, 142n96, 158n212, 164, 167, 170, 170n34, 170n38, 171n43, 175, 182n109, 187, 197, 197n43
Ambrose, 192n18
Amen-em-opet, 59n4, 73n107, 77n138, 82n170, 82n172, 88n209
Amos, 32n186, 111n360, 118n404, 119n414, 120n422
Anatolia, 46, 47n294, 48n304, 50n316, 53, 54, 58, 59, 59n7, 69n81, 70n82, 194, 195, 196
Aquinas, 169n27
Aramaic, 40n253, 51n320, 54, 54n343, 55n348, 55n349, 57n368, 58, 62n22, 107n338, 189, 190, 190n7
Aristeas, 130, 130n8
Aristophanes, 152n167, 173n53, 182n110
Aristotle, 3n17
Assyria(n), 13, 25n134, 25n135, 42n261, 55n347, 192n16
Atraḫasis, 16, 47n294, 90n226, 115n390
Augustine, 165n5

Babylon(ian), 2, 2n10, 13, 15n67, 21n94, 22, 25, 25n131, 30n168, 31n174, 38, 38n241, 39n244, 42, 43n267, 47n294, 50n316, 62n22, 111n265, 135n43, 190
Babylonian Theodicy, 5, 23, 28n151, 31, 31n173, 31n174, 31n175, 34n204, 35n212, 37n223, 38, 43, 43n269, 56n354, 60, 63n32, 98, 99n292, 111n365, 117, 127, 139n73, 158n216
Balaam, 41n260, 73n112
betrothal, 12, 18, 18n84, 21, 22, 58
Bonaventure, 169n27
bribe(ry), 30n165, 37, 48n303, 51, 51n321, 51n323, 52n327, 54, 74n115, 89, 90, 90n222, 90n223, 90n225, 90n226, 90n229, 102n310, 120, 120n418, 123, 150n152, 157, 158, 158n215, 159n216, 164, 196, 197, 197n42
bridewealth, 18, 20, 196

business, 8, 8n14, 33n192, 34n201, 38n239, 48n300, 52n324, 63n33, 64n40, 65n47, 65n48, 69n75, 69n81, 75, 86n201, 88n211, 89n217, 92, 99, 101, 106n334, 107, 107n338, 107n339, 107n341, 107n342, 108, 108n346, 109, 118n409, 119n411, 122, 130, 158n209, 185, 185n128, 190, 190n7, 191, 195

Clement, 180n100
compensation/reward/wage(s), 19, 19n85, 34, 34n201, 34n202, 48n301, 49, 50, 50n314, 51, 51n319, 53, 53n337, 54, 57n364, 62n27, 81, 101n306, 112n367, 113n376, 119, 119n416, 121n430, 124n448, 126n466, 127, 128, 136, 136n52, 140, 140n78, 144, 147n130, 148n143, 154, 154n181, 158, 167, 169, 169n27, 170, 172, 173, 173n54, 182n109, 188, 195, 196, 197
consumer(ism), 20n93, 90, 120n418, 122, 123, 124, 127n472, 187, 196, 197, 197n39
corruption/fraud, 28n152, 47, 47n295, 48, 51n321, 54, 57, 57n364, 58, 63, 70n87, 96n266, 130, 197, 70n87, 83n175, 89, 96n266, 118n411, 130, 182n111, 196, 197
creditor, 16n70, 16n72, 41n259, 58, 68n65, 68n73, 80, 81n161, 82, 94n253, 110, 135n48, 136, 136n56, 137, 137n62, 138n72, 139n76, 144n109, 172, 172n46, 172n48, 172n49, 176n71, 180n103, 184n121, 192n16, 195, 196

Daniel, 26n138, 26n139, 77n140, 121n425
debt(or), 9, 12, 15, 15n66, 15n67, 16, 16n70, 16n72, 17, 17n73, 17n74, 17n79, 22, 26n137, 30n164, 44n276, 45n282, 45n284, 50n314, 56, 57n361, 58, 68, 68n72, 68n73, 69n77, 80, 81n161, 82, 82n167, 109n352, 110, 125n454, 132, 134, 134n38, 134n40, 136, 136n50, 136n56, 137, 137n60, 138n66, 138n72, 139n74, 139n75, 140n81, 141, 144n109, 146n125, 154n187, 155n193, 164, 170n37, 171n42, 171n44, 173n52, 174n56, 184n121, 196, 197
Dialogue of Pessimism, 5, 42, 43n267, 46, 46n288, 60, 87n203, 98, 99n293, 114n383, 127, 159n216
didactic, 6, 6n5, 7, 7n8, 53n336, 59, 90n227, 93, 98, 129, 130, 146n124, 165n3, 175
diligence, 70n88, 79, 82n168, 84, 85, 86, 90, 92, 148n144, 196
Dio Cassius, 183n119
divorce, 12, 18, 20, 20n93, 22, 58
dowry, 19, 19n87, 20, 196

Ea/Enki, 24n122, 37, 37n224
economic, 1, 6, 7, 10, 11, 12, 18, 19n85, 24, 24n124, 28n151, 30, 31, 34n204, 40n251, 40n255, 41n258, 43, 44n278, 45n281, 46, 48n301, 49, 52, 53, 54, 57n367, 57n369, 58, 59, 59n8, 60, 64n41, 67n59, 67n60, 69n77, 70n82, 71n96, 72, 72n105, 73n113, 75n123, 75n124, 81n162, 82n167, 91, 93, 94n253, 97, 99, 100, 102n308, 102n310, 108, 111n361, 114n382, 115, 117, 117n397, 118n407, 119, 123, 127n470, 130, 131, 133, 133n31, 135n44, 139n76, 141, 142, 144, 155, 155n189, 162, 163, 165, 166, 167n11, 173n52, 176n69, 176n71, 179, 180n101, 187, 189, 193
Egypt(ian), 6, 6n4, 22, 23, 52n332, 59, 59n4, 61, 62n22, 72, 72n103, 98n283, 100n298, 102, 130, 184n120
Enkidu, 24n120, 27n146, 36n219
Enlil, 7n7, 37, 37n223, 90n226

Enūma Eliš, 8, 11, 31n180, 32n185, 111n365
Erra, 33n191, 103n311, 111n365
Ezekiel, 125n457, 144n112, 159n216
Ezra, 62n26

generosity, 68n68, 74n120, 74n121, 91n230, 97, 126, 132n24, 135n48, 142, 152, 152n172, 153, 153n177, 164, 172n46, 197
genre, 1n5, 3, 3n14, 3n16, 6, 24, 25n128, 25n131, 43n268, 54n343, 61, 93, 117n396
Gilgamesh, 24n120, 27n146, 36, 36n219
Goethe, 165n5
Greece, 2, 13n57, 119n412, 129, 130, 135n43, 171n39, 171n40, 186n133
greed, 60n11, 63, 63n36, 73n110, 90, 92, 100n296, 125n454, 148n144, 152, 153n174, 170n34, 187, 197

Hammurabi, 5, 11, 13, 15n67, 29n162, 30n168, 42n261
Ḫattuša, 7, 46, 47n294, 52
heir, 8, 8n15, 19, 21n98, 41, 41n256, 54, 64n42, 85n192, 197n47
Herodotus, 158n214
Hesiod, 171n39, 178n86
Hittite, 5, 19n85, 26n137, 27n146, 34n201, 39n245, 40n252, 42n261, 46, 46n289, 47, 50, 52n327, 52n331, 53, 53n336, 53n337, 54, 79n155, 88n215, 133n31, 181n106, 190
Hurrian, 46n289

inheritance, 9, 12, 21, 21n97, 21n98, 22, 22n102, 41n257, 55n351, 58, 85, 85n192, 93, 95n261, 102n308, 104n322, 122n435, 133n33, 134, 134n41, 135, 140, 157, 157n202, 157n205, 164, 197, 198
interest/usury, 9n22, 15n67, 39n244, 41n258, 42n262, 44n276, 45n281, 46n285, 52n332, 68n72, 69n77, 87, 87n202, 87n204, 158n215, 159n216, 172n49, 192n16
Isaiah, 158n215
Israel(ite), 2n7, 11, 41n260, 53, 55n347, 60n14, 64n38, 68n72, 69n77, 72, 86n200, 94n257, 110, 112n371, 122n438, 138n69, 157, 157n207, 171n39, 184n120

James, Letter of, 5, 37n227, 64n42, 88n212, 91n230, 97n275, 141n89, 144, 151n161, 154n183, 159n217, 160n225, 161n230, 165n3, 166, 172n45, 174, 176, 176n68, 177, 185, 187
Jeremiah, 35n205, 62n24, 111, 117n400
Jerome, 160n223
Job, 5, 10n27, 23, 25n131, 31, 31n175, 31n178, 34, 37, 37n228, 42n266, 55n347, 60, 60n10, 60n12, 62n27, 66n51, 67n61, 98n286, 105n324, 110, 111, 111n365, 112, 113n376, 114, 115n389, 116, 117, 119n413, 120, 121n423, 122, 126, 140n82, 154n188, 163, 165n3, 166, 174n56, 185n128, 186n135
Jonah, 24n125
Josephus, 153n173
Juvenal, 151n159

Katumuwa, 64n37

labor(er)/work(er), 7, 10, 12, 16, 17, 17n75, 22, 27n146, 30, 47, 47n294, 48, 49, 54, 57, 57n369, 58, 67n59, 70, 70n83, 70n88, 70n90, 76, 76n131, 76n133, 79, 79n153, 82, 82n169, 82n170, 83, 83n175, 84, 84n181, 84n184, 85n189, 94n254, 99, 99n295, 101, 103, 103n318, 104, 104n321, 104n322, 105, 105n325, 106, 107, 107n337, 107n342, 108, 108n344, 108n346, 109, 109n352, 118n411, 122n437, 124, 124n447, 139n75, 140n82, 146, 147, 147n130, 148, 148n139, 148n143, 149n151, 152n169, 163, 174n55, 181, 182, 182n109, 182n110, 190, 196

land, 9, 9n23, 12, 13, 13n58, 22, 39n245, 47n293, 50n316, 54, 58, 70n87, 76, 76n128, 76n133, 85, 91, 93, 93n246, 93n247, 94, 94n253, 94n258, 95, 95n260, 100n297, 114, 115n387, 115n388, 118n406, 119, 119n415, 121, 124, 125, 127, 127n471, 127n474, 138n72, 171n42, 195
law(code), 11, 11n32, 12, 15n67, 17, 17n73, 17n77, 18, 19, 20n92, 21, 22, 37n222, 42, 42n261, 42n262, 46n291, 53, 53n337, 54, 62n21, 69n75, 75n122, 82n167, 83n173, 87n202, 87n204, 101n302, 118n411, 120n421, 129n5, 151n159, 152n167, 172n45, 175n65, 179, 182, 183, 183n115, 183n116, 187, 187n138, 195, 196, 197
Lazarus, 166n8, 168n23, 170n34, 174n59
laziness, 70n84, 70n90, 73n108, 76, 78n146, 79n153, 82, 83, 83n175, 83n177, 83n178, 84, 85, 92, 104n321, 196, 104n321, 196
loan, 9, 17n79, 18n79, 26, 26n142, 39n245, 40, 40n253, 41, 41n259, 43, 44, 44n276, 45, 45n281, 45n283, 57, 66n56, 68, 68n71, 69n77, 80, 81, 81n162, 81n163, 81n165, 110n354, 120n421, 132, 135, 135n48, 170n37, 172n48, 173, 180n103, 191, 192n16
Lucian, 151n159
Ludlul bēl nēmeqi, 5, 24, 24n121, 24n123, 25, 25n131, 25n134, 28n158, 29n160, 30, 30n172, 33, 43, 43n269, 103, 111n365, 112, 114, 121n430, 127
Luqmân, 55, 55n345
Luther, 176n68
Lysias, 156n197

Ma'at, 72, 72n103
mammon, 64n40, 71n96, 96n272, 106n334, 107n341, 116n393, 146n126, 175n63, 190, 190n8, 190n9
Marduk, 11, 24, 24n122, 25, 25n132, 25n133, 25n134, 26, 28n150, 28n156, 28n158, 29, 29n162, 30, 30n166, 30n168, 30n172, 31n177, 32n185, 32n188, 33n194, 44n277, 96n268, 118n406
marriage, 12, 18, 18n84, 19, 20n90, 20n93, 22, 58
merchant, 7, 13n56, 14, 17n79, 18, 18n80, 39, 39n248, 40, 40n250, 41n259, 42, 42n264, 46, 53, 54, 58, 63n33, 76, 76n127, 83n168, 87n205, 88n211, 89n216, 156, 156n196, 195, 197
Mesopotamia(n), 6, 7, 7n11, 11n36, 13, 14n63, 17, 23, 26n135, 29n161, 30, 34n199, 41n258, 46, 50, 53, 53n337, 58, 59, 111n365, 115n390, 116, 196

Nebuchadnezzar, 38, 115n386
Nehemiah, 137
Nippur, 7, 7n7

Persia(n), 59, 59n8, 91, 98n287, 101n302, 104n320, 108n344, 109n353, 171n40
pessimistic, 6, 22, 31, 43n269, 53n336, 60, 98, 98n286, 165n3
Philo, 100n297, 132n25, 132n28, 145n119, 148n143, 152n169, 153n173, 155n188, 155n189, 155n192, 160n226, 161n229, 161n230, 162n237, 171n44, 172n48, 172n50, 173n52, 175n62, 175n64, 176n70, 180n103, 181n108, 183n115
Phocylides, 179n94
Plato, 154n186, 161n229, 161n231
pledge, 15, 16n72, 26n137, 68n71, 81, 120, 120n421, 125, 133n34, 134n39, 135, 135n48, 196
Plutarch, 145n118
possess(ions), 10n27, 36, 36n213, 57n368, 67, 67n62, 75n121,

81n161, 84n185, 92, 94, 95, 95n260, 101, 102, 102n308, 108n347, 112n369, 112n371, 114, 119n415, 144, 145n119, 156
poverty/poor, 1, 4n27, 10, 16, 35, 37, 37n222, 37n227, 38, 48, 54, 56, 57n362, 57n363, 64n43, 67n61, 67n64, 68n72, 70n83, 71, 71n91, 71n93, 71n94, 71n96, 73, 73n108, 74n120, 74n121, 76n134, 77, 77n135, 77n136, 77n138, 77n142, 78, 78n144, 78n145, 78n149, 79, 79n149, 79n151, 79n153, 80, 80n156, 81, 81n162, 82n167, 82n169, 83, 84n185, 85n190, 86n195, 87, 87n204, 88, 88n209, 88n212, 88n213, 88n215, 90n224, 91n229, 91n234, 92, 93n246, 94, 94n252, 94n253, 106n332, 109n353, 110, 110n355, 110n358, 112, 118n404, 118n411, 119, 119n414, 120n418, 122, 122n435, 124, 125, 126, 130, 132, 132n26, 133, 133n33, 134, 135, 140, 141, 141n86, 142, 143, 143n106, 144, 144n111, 144n112, 148, 148n141, 148n144, 149, 149n150, 150, 151, 152, 152n167, 152n169, 153n173, 157, 159n216, 160, 160n225, 171n44, 172n48, 175n64, 177, 181n106, 183, 185n128, 187, 194
productivity, 9, 11, 19, 19n89, 29, 29n162, 30, 32n187, 33n192, 47n293, 64, 65n48, 71n97, 73, 75n122, 76, 91, 96n273, 98, 100n297, 101n304, 106n335, 123, 138n71, 175, 1944q
profit(able), 9n22, 28, 28n155, 32n189, 33n192, 34, 34n204, 39, 39n244, 39n246, 40, 41, 45, 45n284, 46, 58, 63n36, 73, 75n123, 76, 84, 84n183, 84n185, 85n187, 99, 99n295, 102, 102n309, 102n310, 103, 103n311, 103n314, 104, 104n319, 104n320, 105n327, 114n383, 118n409, 137n59, 138, 138n70, 145n120, 146, 150, 151n159, 155n192, 157n205, 158n215, 161, 161n228, 183, 184, 184n123, 185, 185n126, 185n130, 192, 192n18, 195
Prometheus, 178n89
property, 12, 14, 15, 19n87, 20n92, 22, 27, 33n193, 39n245, 41, 48n301, 52, 54, 56n354, 58, 67, 67n58, 87n204, 90n224, 100, 100n297, 100n299, 101n302, 106n334, 112, 112n369, 112n371, 118n407, 119n415, 125n461, 138n72, 140n80, 156, 195, 197, 197n47
prosperity, 7, 23n116, 25, 26n135, 27, 27n149, 28, 28n150, 32, 32n189, 34n199, 35, 35n205, 41n260, 52n325, 59n8, 60n16, 72, 74n119, 79n151, 80n159, 86n200, 89n222, 90, 91, 113n376, 123, 123n439, 124, 129n1, 139n73, 157, 162, 170n37, 185n127, 191n13, 194

Qohelet, 1n4, 5, 31, 43, 85n194, 98, 98n284, 98n287, 99, 99n290, 99n294, 100, 100n296, 102n310, 103, 103n315, 104n320, 106, 107, 108n346, 109, 110, 112, 132n27, 136n56, 166, 177, 186n131
Qumran, 67n64, 130, 130n10, 131n13, 133, 137n58, 140, 140n80, 171n39, 190n9
Qur'an, 9n22, 10n25, 10n27, 22n102, 28n158, 42n262, 50n317, 55n345, 56n357, 62n29, 65n47, 67n59, 72n105, 74n120, 77n138, 81n165, 84n180, 84n184, 85n192, 87n203, 87n204, 87n208, 88n215, 90n224, 96n273, 119n416, 124n445, 131n19, 154n181, 157n204, 185n126, 189n2

redemption, 25n134, 26, 26n137, 29, 48, 48n301, 49, 49n311, 54, 96, 96n268, 96n270, 114n377, 121n430, 137n59, 181n106, 195

sage, 2n7, 4, 4n25, 7n8, 9, 10, 17n74, 31n173, 60, 60n12, 61n20, 65, 65n48, 66, 66n57, 68n73, 69n75, 70, 70n83, 75n124, 77n138, 78n149, 80n156, 80n161, 82n170, 85n194, 92, 94n256, 96n273, 97n273, 99, 101, 105n328, 108n346, 110, 132, 136, 141, 145, 146n122, 148n142, 151n160, 160, 164, 174, 195, 196, 198
Saggil-kīnam-ubbib, 31, 31n177
Šamaš Hymn, 5, 14n59, 25n133, 27n143, 38, 38n239, 42, 46, 76n127, 85n192, 102n310, 104n320, 184n123
Seneca, 171n39
Shakespeare, 165n5
Sheba, 162n236
Sirach, 5, 60n12, 66n51, 68, 73n110, 78n144, 80n157, 81n165, 94n256, 100n301, 110, 112, 129, 129n5, 131, 135n48, 136n49, 136n55, 136n56, 141, 141n90, 142n98, 143, 144, 146, 151n160, 151n163, 155n194, 157n205, 161n228, 165, 166, 167n16, 168n25, 169n31, 173n44, 174, 175, 177, 182n110, 187
slave(ry), 7, 10n24, 10n27, 12, 14n63, 17, 17n77, 18, 18n80, 22, 33n198, 35, 42, 42n265, 43, 43n271, 44, 45, 48n301, 49, 50, 50n317, 54, 58, 69n77, 82n167, 85, 85n194, 87n207, 87n208, 94n253, 100, 100n298, 110, 111n365, 112, 112n365, 112n370, 115n390, 116, 132, 136n50, 137, 138n66, 139n75, 140, 146n124, 146n125, 152n167, 155n193, 171n44, 196
Socrates, 154n186
Solomon(ic), 5, 55, 55n347, 60, 60n12, 60, 62n21, 68, 72, 90n225, 92, 99, 99n290, 100n300, 130, 130n7, 160, 160n225, 161, 161n233, 184n123
Sophia, 65, 65n45, 65n46, 65n48, 66, 66n53, 70n84, 71, 72n100, 75n124, 75n125, 83n179, 121n428, 129, 129n4, 161, 162, 162n234, 162n237, 163, 163n241, 165, 165n4
Šubši-mešre-šakkan, 24, 25n132, 26n135, 28n158, 29, 30n172
Sumer(ian), 3n13, 7, 7n7, 10, 25n134, 39n241, 47n293, 62n22
surety, 68n69, 69n79, 81n161, 120n421, 135n48, 136n49
Šuruppak, 5, 9, 10, 34n200, 45n282
Sybilline Oracle, 49n305

tax(ation), 12, 12n52, 13, 15n67, 34n201, 35n208, 39n245, 47n296, 69n77, 91, 109n353, 116n391, 138, 138n71, 139, 139n76, 164, 171n42, 196
Telipinu, 70n82, 74n117
Thomas, 168n20
Thucydides, 179n93
tithe, 77n136, 157, 158, 158n211, 164
Tobit, 33, 63n33, 171n43
Torah, 1, 32n186, 62n21, 65n44, 87n204, 93n247, 94n256, 102n310, 110n354, 129, 129n5, 132n24, 147n130, 158n209, 158n215, 166, 173n50, 176, 178n89, 180n104, 183n115, 187n140
trade(r), 12, 13, 14n60, 22, 39, 39n244, 42, 42n262, 58, 64n40, 65, 65n47, 68n72, 74n120, 76n127, 76n130, 76n133, 82n168, 87n202, 133n34, 141n87, 146, 191, 195
tribute, 12n52, 71n96, 91, 139n76, 196
Tudḫaliya, 49, 49n306

Utnapishtim, 9n18

Vergil, 84n186

wealth(y)/rich, 1, 7, 10, 10n29, 15n67, 21n94, 28, 28n151, 30, 32, 32n186, 33, 34, 34n199, 35, 37, 37n222, 37n230, 38, 39n244, 41, 43n270, 45n282, 48, 49n305, 56, 56n352, 56n354, 59n4, 62n22, 63, 64n43, 65n46, 66, 66n52, 66n56, 67n58, 67n59, 67n60, 67n63, 71, 71n91, 71n94, 71n96, 73, 73n108, 73n109, 73n110, 73n111, 74, 74n116, 74n118, 74n119, 74n120, 75, 75n121, 75n122, 75n123, 75n124, 76, 77n135, 78, 78n144, 78n145, 78n147, 78n148, 78n149, 79, 79n149, 79n150, 79n151, 80, 81, 81n162, 81n163, 82, 82n169, 83n175, 84, 85n194, 86, 87, 87n202, 88, 88n213, 90n229, 91n229, 92, 93, 96, 97, 97n275, 97n276, 99, 100, 100n297, 100n300, 101, 102, 102n310, 103, 103n318, 104n321, 107n341, 108, 108n346, 108n347, 110, 115n388, 119, 119n415, 121n425, 121n428, 122, 122n437, 123, 126, 130, 135, 135n44, 137, 139n73, 142, 144, 145, 145n119, 146, 146n122, 147, 147n135, 148, 148n143, 149, 149n145, 151, 151n164, 152, 152n167, 153, 153n173, 154, 160n227, 161, 162, 162n234, 163, 163n240, 169, 171n42, 174, 174n60, 176, 177, 179, 184, 185, 185n127, 186, 190

widow, 20n91, 49n305, 121, 121n425, 125, 125n456, 126, 126n465, 126n466, 142n101, 160, 194, 121, 121n425, 125, 125n456, 125n459, 126, 126n465, 142n101, 160, 194

W/wisdom, 1, 2, 2n6a, 2n9, 3n13, 4, 5, 6, 7, 11, 11n32, 23, 23n116, 23n118, 24, 25, 25n128, 29n161, 31n175, 42n266, 43, 46, 46n289, 46n291, 53, 53n336, 53n337, 54n343, 55, 55n347, 59, 59n2, 59n8, 60, 60n13, 61, 61n20, 62n21, 64, 64n39, 65n44, 65n49, 66n51, 67n64, 71, 71n91, 72, 72n103, 73n112, 74n119, 75, 75n122, 77n138, 78n148, 88n209, 92, 93, 95n264, 98n287, 99, 105, 106, 108, 109n348, 120n418, 128n479, 129, 129n5, 130, 130n12, 139n77, 142n97, 159n219, 160n223, 163, 163n240, 165, 166, 177, 196

Yeshu`a/Jesus, 165, 166n7, 167, 167n16, 170, 170n37, 171n42, 182 185n127, 187, 187n138, 195, 195n31, 197

Ziusudra, 9, 9n18

Author Index

Achtemeier, 187n138
Adams, R., 172n47
Adams, S., 122n366, 131n12
Adamson, 177n79
Ahearne-Kroll, 191n13
Aiken, 3n18
Aimers, 113n374, 113n376
Alaura, 46n291, 59n7
Albertz, 25n133, 36n216
Albright, 31n183
Alcoff, 152n172
Allen, 103n311
Allison, 176n74, 177n77, 177n82
Al-Maydânî, 89n221
Al-Rawi, 30n168
Alster, 2, 3n13, 7n9, 7n10, 9n20, 25n131, 34n200, 55n347
Alter, 8n13, 60n15, 81n164, 121n427
Andersen, 122n434, 122n438
Anderson, 142n96
Andreau, 172n49
Annus, 4, 4n24, 24, 24n120, 24n125, 25n128, 25n131, 26n142, 27n144, 28n155
Ansberry, 62n22
Aphergis, 39n245
Archi, 47n293, 47n296
Argall, 131n16, 145n116, 159n220
Armitage, 4n27, 132n27, 175n67, 194n27
Asencio, 111n364, 142n97, 151n159, 159n218
Askari, 81n165
Assmann, 23n110, 35n206, 72n103
Atkin, 20n92
Atkinson, K., 141n87
Atkinson, T., 104n322
Audet, 11n34

Baarda, 168n21
Baasland, 177n78
Bailey, 123n442
Balentine, 117n399, 127n477
Bales, 51n324
Balla, 62n22
Bammel, 168n21
Banerjee, 192n15
Barbalet, 30, 30n169
Barclay, 129n2
Barnes, 147n132
Barré, 2n6, 167n19
Bartholomew, 60n13, 72n104, 92, 92n237, 98n287, 165n5, 166n7
Barton, 167n11
Batten, 177n81
Bauckham, 179n97
Beal, 47n293
Beaulieu, 2, 2n11, 7n7, 24, 24n127, 29n161
Beckert, 20n94
Beckman, 46n289, 47n292, 47n295, 53n337, 59n7
Beentjes, 131n16, 142n97
Beinhocker, 177n81

Bellah, 18n83
Ben Zvi, 10n25, 65n49, 70n84, 75n123, 75n124, 76n133
Berges, 60n11
Berjak, 120n416
Berquist, 128n480
Berry, 72n105
Betz, 167n15
Biggs, 10n31
Black, 7n7
Bland, D., 62n22, 79n152, 86n199
Bland, R., 100n297
Bledsoe, 65n46
Blenkinsopp, 4n25, 11n32, 91n235
Blomberg, 145n113
Boadt, 78n148, 90n225
Boccaccini, 55n347
Boda, 59n2
Bodi, 55n350
Boer, 111n2364, 159n218
Böhl, 43n268
Bonhoeffer, 168n26
Borger, 33n199
Boring, 168n20
Boström, 68n73, 80n157
Botha, 60n11, 93n245
Bottéro, 31n180, 42n265, 46n288
Bovon, 166n10, 175n66
Bowler, 28n151
Bradley, 157n206, 197n44
Brainard, 88n213
Brake, 67n58
Bredenhof, 159n219, 166n8
Brichto, 12n49
Brinkman, 13n57
Brodersen, 97n278
Broekhoven, 165n4
Brown, J., 3, 4n20
Brown, W., 61n17, 99n290, 107n337, 108n346
Brueggemann, 4n23
Bryce, 49n310, 53n337
Buccelatti, 25, 25n130
Bulgakov, 65n51
Burkett, 168n26

Cahana-Blum, 165n4
Cammarosano, 52n326, 52n329, 52n331
Camp, 66n53, 92n237, 142n92, 146n122, 150n159, 151n160, 159n220
Carlotti, 169n29
Carter, 166n9
Cartledge, 69n74
Ceresko, 59, 60n9
Charlesworth, 137n58
Charpin, 16n70, 20n94, 38n240
Chavalas, 14n63, 17n73
Cheung, 4n21, 59n2, 60n11, 93, 93n240, 93n242, 93n244, 93n246
Chirichigno, 15n66, 17n79, 18n79, 68n72, 69n77, 136n50, 137n60, 196n36
Christianson, 99n291
Christidès, 146n126
Civil, 10n31, 37n224
Clements, 74n119, 75n123
Clermont-Ganneau, 190n5
Clifford, 2, 2n12, 23n118, 72, 72n100, 72n105, 74n118, 74n120, 77n141, 78n144, 78n145, 78n146, 85n188, 88n210, 90n229, 120n421
Clines, 59n2, 62n24, 110, 111n359, 113n376, 114n382, 126n466, 127, 127n477
Coggins, 195n30
Cohen, 4n26, 6, 6n5, 8n13, 23n104, 24n124, 27n143, 28n158, 71n93
Colberg, 169n27
Cole, 7n7
Coleman, 3n14
Collins, B., 25n133, 29n163
Collins, J., 11, 11n35, 61n20, 129n3, 129n5, 147n135, 157n206, 163n240
Collins, R., 185n127, 196n38, 197n40
Conybeare, 55n350
Cooper, 8n11
Corley, 152n171
Couturier, 11
Cowan, 103n314
Cowley, 56n354, 57n364, 57n366
Crane, 186n136
Creach, 95n259

Crenshaw, 10n30, 23n114, 23n119, 59n2, 59n4, 60n13, 98n286, 99, 99n289, 103n318, 105n328, 122n432, 126n463, 158n210
Cross, 191n12
Crüsemann, 93n241
Curtis, 38n241, 40n250

Dahood, 98n287, 99n295
Dalley, 8n12, 20n91
Dalman, 63n36
D'Amato, 51n324
D'Andrade, 51n323
Dardano, 47n296, 48n302
Davids, 176n72, 178n91
Davis, 142n98
Dawson, 111, 111n361, 111n364, 112n370
Day, 113n374
Deissmann, 177n76
de Jong, 98n287
Delekat, 107n340
Delitzsch, 83n176, 99n288, 105n326
Delkurt, 78n149
Dell, 95n264
Del Olmo Lete, 140n78
de Moor, 23n106
Denning Bolle, 25, 25n129
DeSilva, 153n177
De Soto, 118n411
Dibelius, 176n75
Dick, 28n152, 126n467
Di Lella, 145n114, 147n133, 154n183, 156n198
Dnes, 67n58
Douglas, 134n40
Driver, 17n74
Duflo, 192n15
Duhaime, 195n29
Dumbrell, 62n21
Dunham, 117n401, 117n402, 119n412, 120n419
Dunn, 129n4

Eaton, 99n295, 103n311
Ebeling, 43n267
Ehrlich, 71n93
Eissfeldt, 61n19
Elgvin, 130n10, 133n34, 139n76
Elliott, 153n175
Ellis, 148n138
Emerton, 65n46
Engels, 159n218
Engle, 92n239
Erman, 73n107
Esler, 168n21
Evans, 55n349, 166n9

Farber Flügge, 35n211
Farmer, 88n211, 88n213, 90n225
Fassel, 108n345
Fee, 28n151
Finkelstein, 196n36
Finn, 30n168, 30n169
Fischer, 95n265
Firth, 2n7
Fitzmyer, 169n33
Fontaine, 166n6
Foster, 9n20, 23n112, 23n113, 24n120, 24n121, 25n133, 30n170, 38n239, 39n248, 42n263, 43n268, 44n275, 46n285, 59n6
Fowler, 3, 3n16, 93n242, 93n243
Fox, 1n5, 61n17, 61n20, 68n73, 74n115, 75n122, 77n141, 80n157, 82n167, 82n168, 83n177, 85n194, 87n204, 87n205, 87n207, 90n227, 91n231, 98n287, 99n293, 104n320, 129n5
Foxvog, 10n31
Frahm, 7n7
Franke, 7n6
Fried, 39n245
Friedrich, 47n295, 51n323
Friesen, 178n91
Frey, 129n3, 194n28
Frow, 1n5
Frymer-Kensky, 65n46, 68n72, 75n124, 138n62, 196n36
Fuller, 157n207

Gardner, 167n13
Garelli, 13n56
Garfinkle, 40n253
Garrison, 158n212

Geller, 142n97
Gemser, 79n76
George, 29n160, 29n162, 30n168, 36n217
Gerhards, 24n123
Gerleman, 136n52
Gerstenberger, 11n34, 59n8, 98n287, 107n340
Gese, 165n2
Giambrone, 166n11, 167n15
Gilat-Gilad, 92n240
Gilbert, 130n8, 142n92, 160, 160n222, 164n243
Ginsberg, 56n358
Giovino, 34n199
Glicksman, 163n241
Gnuse, 142, 142n93, 195n34
Goetze, 12n49, 13n56
Goetzmann, 68n69
Goff, 22n103, 112n366, 130n6, 130n10, 130n12, 131n18, 131n20, 131n22, 132, 132n27, 133n34, 134n38, 135n48, 136n53, 136n55, 137n62, 138n66, 139n76, 140n81, 140n82, 141, 141n85, 145n113, 145n116, 151n160, 194n26
Goldingay, 61n19, 81n163, 93n246
Goodchild, 176n71
Goody, 195n35
Gordis, 99n293, 103n315, 104n321, 122n434
Gordon, 7n9
Görg, 93n248
Gottwald, 60n14, 166n6, 195n34
Gowan, 152n170
Grabbe, 98n287
Gray, 147n132, 165n3
Grayson, 13n57
Green, 167, 167n18
Greenfield, 55n344
Gregory, 68n68, 132n28, 135n48, 142, 142n95, 153n173, 154n182, 155n193, 155n194, 159n221
Grelot, 55n350, 56n352, 56n353, 56n354, 57n366
Groneberg, 7n6
Grünewald, 38n238
Guillaume, 36n216
Gunkel, 93, 93n241
Gunn, 62n24
Gurney, 24n123
Güterbock, 51n323
Gutiérrez, 114, 114n381
Gutman, 51n324
Gzella, 49n312

Haag, 98n287
Habel, 113n375, 121n428, 123n443
Halivni, 11n391
Halliday, 67n59
Hallo, 7n6, 7n9, 10n31, 42, 42n264, 60n9
Hamilton, 113n372
Harper, 11n36, 12n50, 12n51, 12n52, 14n60, 18n80, 18n84, 20n90
Harrington, 130n10, 130n11, 131n15, 132n28, 133n34, 134n38, 136n51, 138n65, 138n71, 139n75, 139n76, 139n77
Harris, 20n91
Hatcher, D., 159n216
Hatcher, K., 169n34
Hartley, 23n117, 42n265, 44n275, 44n277, 111, 111n360, 125n454, 125n460 126n463, 126n465, 127n472
Harvey, 111n364
Haspecker, 155n190
Hauck, 190n8
Hausmann, 78n149
Hawley, 7n7, 117n398
Hayes, E., 98n283
Hayes, K., 127n41
Hays, 166n11
Heim, 100n296, 108n344
Helck, 23n105
Hempel, 139n77
Hendon, 52n324
Hengel, 98n284, 98n287, 104n320, 129n2, 129n3, 130n6, 165n2
Hering, 146n124
Hershkowitz, 135n43
Hertzberg, 99n292
Hildebrandt, 61n19
Hilton, 36n219

Hoffman, 111n363, 113n376, 117n401, 127, 127n476
Hoffner, 46, 46n290, 47n292, 47n296, 48n300, 48n301, 48n304, 53n338, 53n339, 73n111, 74n117
Holland, 129n2
Hoppe, 132n27, 133, 133n31, 133n32, 190n10
Hornborg, 28n151
Horsley, 144n109, 148n138
Horwitz, 54n343
Hossein, 189n2
Hossfeld, 93n241, 98n283
House, 13n53
Howard, 20n93
Hron, 168n22
Hundley, 29n163
Hunter, 93n241
Hurowitz, 37, 37n221, 37n223, 41n259, 43n268, 46, 46n286, 46n287
Hutt, 141, 141n88

Irving, 67n58
Isaksson, 105n325
Izre'el, 8n12

Jackson-McCabe, 177n76, 177n83, 187n140
Jacobsen, 115n384
Jameson, 3n18
Janssen, 73n111
Janzen, 104n320, 115n385, 125n459
Jaruzelska, 159n218
Jastrow, 38n241, 99n294
Jauss, 176n70
Jefferies, 130n6
Jensen, 106n336
Jiménez, 24n119, 33n199
Jobes, 165n5
Jodock, 4n20
Johnson, 144n111, 149n148, 166n11, 168n22, 180n101, 195n31
Johnston, 108n343
Jones, R., 114n378
Jones, S., 3n13, 116n393
Joosten, 93n247, 141n90

Kamell, 176, 176n73, 188, 188n146
Karavites, 40n252
Karenga, 72n103
Kassis, 55n345, 55n347, 59n8, 90n225
Kayatz, 61n18, 61n19
Kellermann, 63n36, 109n349
Keenan, 184n121
Keener, 158n211
Kessler, 190, 190n10
Khanjian, 59n6
Kim, 61n19, 98n286, 109n353
Kirk, 178n87
Kloppenberg, 172n45
Knox, 177n79
Koester, 165n2
Köstenberger, 141n87
Kottsieper, 54n343, 55n346
Kramer, 7n7, 7n8
Krämer, 190n8
Krauss, 95n262
Kreeft, 98n286
Kronholm, 112n371
Kruger, 35n206
Krüger, 24n122, 37n221, 60n14
Kugel, 98n287, 99n295, 101n302, 102n309, 109, 109n353
Kuran, 22n102
Kuntz, 93, 93n244, 93n246
Kynes, 1n5, 3n14, 4n24

Laato, 23n106
La Caze, 152n172
Lambert, 2, 10n30, 14n59, 24, 24n120, 24n121, 24n125, 24n126, 25n131, 31n173, 31n175, 32n186, 32n189, 32n190, 33n193, 35n206, 35n211, 35n212, 37n222, 37n227, 39n244, 42, 42n263, 43n268, 43n271, 44n275, 44n277, 46n285, 76n127
Landsberger, 31n173
Langdon, 43n267
Lange, 131, 131n17
Larcher, 125n461
Larrimore, 22n104
Lau, 140n80
Lee, 60n12

Legaspi, 2, 2n10
Leick, 24n122
Lemos, 20n91, 111n362, 111n365, 196n35
Lenski, 24n121
Lenzi, 4, 4n24, 24, 24n120, 24n125, 25n128, 25n131, 25n132, 26n142, 27n144, 28n155, 29, 29n160, 29n163, 45n279
Levin, 160n225, 194n27
Lewis, 113n375
Lichtheim, 6n2, 103n311
Lie, 34n199
Lim, 141n87
Lindblom, 59n2
Lindenberger, 2n9, 55n348, 56n352, 56n353, 56n354, 56n358, 57n366, 57n368, 65n46
Liverani, 65n49
Livingstone, 34n199
Lo, 116n393
Loader, 61n16, 61n17, 72n102, 99n292
Lohfink, 93n247, 93n248, 110, 110n357
Lohmeyer, 146n124, 146n125
Longenecker, 61n20
Longman, 9n18, 61n17, 74n121, 79n151, 79n156, 81n163, 83n179, 98n286, 99n291, 104n319, 105n325, 105n326, 105n330
Loretz, 42n265
Luukko, 24n123
Lyu, 61n20, 71n96, 86n196

MacGinni, 52n333
Maier, 92, 92n236, 125n459
Malchow, 148n142
Maloney, 192n16
Marazzi, 47n296, 49n312
Marcel, 98n286
Markter, 28n153
Marshall, 166n10
Marsman, 19n87, 20n91
Martin, 179n96, 179n99
Marx, 159n218
Mathews, 146n122, 151n160, 162n236
Mathewson, 124n451
Matusova, 130n8
Maynard-Reid, 178n91, 187n141
Mays, 60n11, 97n279
McCarter, 189n3
McCartney, 177, 177n76, 184n121, 187, 187n142, 187n144
McKane, 2n6, 68n73, 80n157
McKnight, 186n132
McLaughlin, 59n8
Meek, 12n50, 12n51, 13n52, 13n54, 14n60, 18n80, 18n84, 20n90
Meier, 82n168
Meinhold, 68n73, 80n157
Méndez-Montoya, 66n51
Mercer, 69n74
Metz, 143n101
Metzger, 166n11
Michel, 13n56
Miles, 17n74, 62n21
Miller, C., 93n242
Miller, J., 3, 3n19, 4n24, 46n291, 47n292, 47n293, 47n295, 47n296, 48n301, 48n304, 49n306, 49n307, 49n312, 50n314, 51n321, 51n323, 51n324, 53n335
Minissale, 150n157, 151n162, 151n163
Moberly, 113, 113n375
Mongstad-Kvammen, 168n21
Montero, 151n161, 172n46
Moo, 179n99
Moore, 1n2, 1n3, 2n6, 3n18, 4n20, 4n26, 8n12, 9n23, 10n28, 12n49, 16n71, 18n81, 21n94, 26n136, 28n152, 28n154, 28n155, 31n175, 31n178, 33n191, 33n197, 35n211, 36n218, 38n236, 59n2, 60n14, 61n20, 62n24, 64n38, 65n45, 65n46, 66n52, 70n82, 74n118, 77n140, 96n272, 105n326, 107n340, 113n374, 114n383, 115n390, 120n417, 121n426, 121n429, 125n457, 125n458, 127n472, 129n3, 130n12, 133n31, 137n60, 142n96, 145n113, 145n116, 145n118, 146n123, 161n232, 166n8, 166n9, 166n11, 169n28, 171n43, 175n63, 176n70,

182n112, 190n5, 190n8, 195n34, 196n35, 197n39
Moran, 25n133, 173n50
Morenz, 103n311
Morley, 4n27
Morris, 169n30
Mouton, 52n325
Mowinckel, 59n2, 93n241, 95n264
Moxnes, 166n11
Mugerauer, 60n14
Müller, 109n348
Murphy, C., 67n64, 130, 130n10, 130n12, 131n13, 131n15, 131n17, 131n22, 133n34, 134n36, 135n48, 136n51, 139n75, 145n113
Murphy, N., 176n68
Murphy, R., 4, 4n25, 31n175, 61n17, 66n51, 80n157, 82n170, 83n179, 87n209, 95n264

Nadel, 112n366
Nakata, 42n263
Nemat-Nejat, 42n265, 43n268
Neville, 111n365
Newsom, 3n17, 31n173, 93n242, 117n396, 119n412, 119n413, 125n462, 126n466
Nickelsburg, 149n148, 166n8, 194n29
Nielsen, 115n384
Nolan, 24n121
Nötscher, 137n58
Nougayrol, 59n6

O'Connor, 69n75
O'Dowd, 60n13, 72n104, 92, 92n237, 165n5, 166n7
Ogden Bellis, 83n175
Oeming, 2, 2n9
Oesterly, 144n109
Olyan, 30n167, 140n80
Oppenheim, 41n258, 42n263
Orlin, 13n56
Ortlund, 70n89
Orwell, 183, 183n118
Osburn, 168n25
Oshima, 7n9, 22n103, 24n120, 25n134, 26n138, 26n140, 26n141, 27n144, 30n172, 31n175, 31n176, 32n189, 32n190, 33n193, 34n200, 35n212, 37, 37n222, 37n230, 55n346, 60n10
Osing, 23n110
Otto, Eberhard, 23, 23n105
Otto, Eckhart, 155n191
Otzen, 105n324, 171n43

Paffenroth, 165n5
Palmer, 177n75
Paper, 59n8
Pardee, 64n37
Parrott, 165n4
Parry, 180n100
Patterson, 111n362
Paul, 114n380, 115n384
Peake, 119n412
Pecchioli Daddi, 27n146
Pemberton, 66n53, 92, 92n238, 100n296
Penchansky, 60n12
Perdue, 54n343, 60n14, 66n53, 66n55, 66n57, 67n64, 73n112, 75n123, 78n149, 80n161, 86n195, 95n262, 95n264
Perry, 98n286, 103n315
Peterson, 98n285, 104n319
Petrany, 158n210
Pfeiffer, 43n267
Pilgrim, 172n47, 194n26
Pioske, 160n224
Pippin, 66n52
Pitt-Rivers, 153n177
Pleins, 42n265, 132n28
Plöger, 68n73, 80n157
Polanyi, 13n57, 39n244
Pope, 8n15, 25n131, 125n461, 126n463, 126n464, 127n473, 127n474
Porten, 56n358, 65n46
Porter, 34n199
Potts, 42n263
Powell, 57n369
Preuss, 73n113
Puech, 56n352

Rabin, 3, 3n15
Rachman, 28n151
Rapson, 13n53

Reiner, 7n6, 38n239
Reines, 100n296, 110n356
Reiterer, 60n14, 109n348, 129n5
Renfrew, 56n355
Resnick, 38n241, 40n250, 111n364
Rey, 130n10, 130n12, 134n41, 135n48, 138n65, 141, 141n86, 141n90, 145n113
Reyes, 182n112
Rhee, 187, 187n145, 192n18, 192n19
Richardson, K., 165n3
Richardson, M., 12n50, 12n51, 12n52, 14n60, 18n84, 20n90, 36n213
Ringe, 167n12
Ristvet, 44n278
Rizzo, 103n314
Ro, 133, 133n30
Roberts, 38n240, 60n14, 192n17
Robertson, 73n111
Roche-Hawley, 7n7
Rogers, 129n5
Rosenzweig, 96n273
Rositani, 17, 17n78
Ross, 94n258, 154n184
Roth, M. 11n36, 11n38, 12n43, 12n50, 12n51, 12n52, 13n54, 14n60, 18n80, 18n84, 20n90, 20n91, 22n101, 42n261
Roth, S., 151n159
Rowe, 54n343
Rowthorn, 67n58
Rudman, 110n355, 110n357

Sachau, 55n348
Sack, 38n237
Sadler, 32n186
Saebø, 71n91
Sallaberger, 11n36, 42n261
Salters, 31n175
Salyer, 103n317
Sandmel, 60n13
Sandoval, 61n20, 62n25, 63n33, 64n41, 64n43, 66n54, 67n60, 68n65, 68n69, 68n72, 69n76, 71n94, 73n108, 76n134, 77n135, 77n138, 78n149, 79n151, 111n351, 132n28, 175n63
Sanmartín, 130n78
Schifferdecker, 37n228, 60n10
Schipper, 6, 6n3, 10n30, 62n21, 65n44
Schmid, 60n14,, 64n39, 177n80
Schmidt, 131n16, 140n78, 148n139, 152n170
Schnabel, 65n45
Schneider, 6n4
Schofttroff, 170n37
Schoors, 102n309
Schroeder, 146n124
Schwartz, 129n2
Schwemer, 53n335
Scott, M., 165n5
Scott, R., 90n223, 90n228, 141, 181n90
Sekki, 137n58
Seow, 60n14, 98, 98n287, 99n288, 104n320, 109n353, 114n377, 115n383, 115n388, 117n401, 118n411, 124n445, 124n446, 186n131
Seri, 32n188
Sheldon, 111n365
Sheppard, 60n11, 166, 166n6
Shipp, 115n386
Shupak, 59n4, 73n107
Shutt, 130n8
Sider, 159n221
Sidursky, 28n155, 32n189
Siegfried, 99n291
Sinding, 3, 3n17
Singer, 46n289
Sinnott, 66n51
Sitzler, 23, 23n106, 23n114, 23n115, 23n119, 30n170, 31n173, 60n10, 112n366, 127n475
Skehan, 61n19, 145n114, 147n133, 154n183, 156n198
Smith, 123n440
Sneed, 1n5, 4, 4n22, 25n128, 31n174, 59n2, 60n12, 61, 61n17, 61n20
Snell, 40n251, 191n11
Sommerfeld, 30n168
Speiser, 43n268, 43n271, 44n276, 44n277
Spieckermann, 25, 25n133, 29n160
Spielvogel, 13, 13n58
Stagg, 148n148
Stassen, 176n68

Stearns, 196n39
Steck, 11n32
Stegemann, 170n37
Steiner, 64n37
Stern, 61n20
Stewart, 93n244
Stokes, 113n374
Stol, 20n93
Stoner, 67n58
Story, 62n21
Strack, 62n21
Strecker, 166n9
Strugnell, 130n10, 133n34, 134n38, 138n65, 138n71, 139n76, 139n77
Stuckenbruck, 130n12
Stulac, 178n91
Sunkara, 110n356
Swartley, 184n125

Taggar-Cohen, 6n5, 7, 7n8, 46n290, 46n291
Talisse, 3n18
Talon, 8n12
Tambiah, 196n35
Tan, 72n101
Taylor, 7n10
Terkel, 107n342
Theissen, 173n54
Thurow, 28n151
Ticciatti, 113n373
Tiemstra, 176n69
Tigchelaar, 130n10, 130n11, 131n18, 135n48, 136n53, 137n62, 138n64, 138n65
Tiller, 144n109
Tov, 189n2, 189n3, 192
Townsend, 182n112
Toy, 62n21, 78n145, 83n173, 83n178, 84n180, 86n200, 86n201
Treier, 67n60
Tsafrir, 50n317
Tsai, 18n79, 18n81
Tur-Sinai, 87n207

Ünal, 69n81
Unger, 43n272
Ungnad, 43n267, 43n271
Uusimäki, 93n244

van de Mieroop, 13, 13n57, 15n67, 17n76
van den Brink, 167, 167n19
van der Toorn, 2n10, 24n124, 26n137, 26n139, 128n479
van Dijk, 2n6
van Leeuwen, 73n108
Vanstiphout, 2n8, 9n20
Vassiliadis, 178n91
Vayntrub, 64n38
Veenhof, 13n56
Veldhuis, 7n9, 7n10, 7n11, 8, 8n14, 9n16
Venter, 132, 133n29
Vesely, 120n418, 123n444
Volgger, 130n8
Volk, 7n7, 7n10
von Klinger, 25n132
von Leibniz, 22, 23n104
von Rad, 28n151, 59n2, 64n39, 142, 142n92, 159n219
von Schuler, 49n312
von Soden, 14n60, 32n188, 37n222, 38n238, 38n241, 42n263

Wachob, 187, 187n138
Wagner, 107n338, 190n7
Walker, 28n152
Waltke, 61n18, 68n73, 70n90, 72, 73n106, 77n142, 80n157, 91n230, 91n231, 113n376
Walton, 9n18, 116, 117n395
Ward, 183n117
Washington, 59n4, 73n107, 81n164, 91n235
Watson, 77n143, 92n236
Wazana, 104n321
Weeks, 1n5, 2n6, 6n2, 7n9, 22n103, 23n116, 59n3, 62n22, 73n106, 108n346
Weigel, 21n94
Weigl, 55n346
Weinfeld, 25n134, 46n291
Wells, 69n74
Welten, 190n5
Welz, 22n104

Westbrook, 11, 11n33, 13n55, 18n82, 19n87, 20n91, 42n261, 49n306, 49n307, 49n312, 50n314, 51n322, 51n323, 196n35
Westermann, 80n157, 93n241, 169n30
Whitley, 99n292, 103n318
Whybray, 60n16, 61n17, 61n20, 63n34, 64n43, 70n83, 73n108, 92, 92n240, 99n293, 169n30
Wilcke, 48n303
Wilson, J., 69n74, 103n311
Wilson, L., 4n26, 69n79, 80n159, 80n160, 82n170
Wink, 171n41, 171n42
Winston, 130, 130n7, 130n9, 160n223
Wischmeyer, 150n157
Witherington, 144n112
Witte, 18n83
Wittgenstein, 3n16
Wold, 130n10, 133, 133n29, 136n51, 139n75
Wolff, 111n264
Woodard, 49n306, 49m307, 49n312, 50n314, 51n322, 51n323
Wright, A., 99n289
Wright, B., 129n3, 129n5, 130n8, 141, 142n91, 142n92, 146n122, 150n159, 151n160, 159n220
Wright, D., 17n77, 64n42
Wright, N., 182, 182n114
Wunsch, 20n93
Wyatt, 64n42

Yardeni, 56n358, 65n46
Yadin, 73n111
Yoder, 66n53, 75n124, 83n174, 88n214, 91n235

Zabán, 63n31, 66n52, 72, 72n102
Zaccagnini, 13n55
Zenger, 93n241, 97n278
Žižek, 111, 111n361, 111n364
Zuckerman, 42n266, 115n389

www.ingramcontent.com/pod-product-compliance
Lightning Source LLC
Chambersburg PA
CBHW050341230426
43663CB00010B/1944
* 9 7 8 1 7 2 5 2 8 9 6 4 2 *